The Best Interests of the Child in Healthcare

When making decisions about children requiring medical care, the child's best interest is a familiar legal standard, and seems uncontroversial. Children, as particularly vulnerable members of society, must surely deserve the highest levels of protection this suggests. However closer examination reveals significant problems with the definition and application of such a standard in practice.

While these problems are common in all areas of decisions concerning children, they are most focused upon in the medical context, where some of the most difficult and sensitive problems arise, concerning as they do the extent to which the child's body can be examined and operated upon, or affected by medicines and other procedures intended to bring about physical or mental change. Important and challenging issues arise, such as the appropriate scope of parental choice and authority, at what stage in their development children should be able to make their own healthcare decisions, whose interests are expected and how to make decisions on behalf of the child. In cases of parental conflict, for example, over the treatment for their child, or over separating organs to brothers and sisters, or in providing treatment for children which children require protection, including protection from their parents and even from themselves.

This book considers how the best interests test has been developed and interpreted in legal cases concerning medical care of children, and seeks to highlight the potential difficulties inherent in its use

Sarah Elliston is a lecturer in medical law at the University of Glasgow where she has taught undergraduate and postgraduate courses in medical law for 13 years. Her particular research interests are in the medical treatment of children and aspects of human reproduction and the law.

Biomedical Law and Ethics Library

Series editor: Sheila A. M. McLean

Professor Sheila McLean is International Bar Association Professor of Law and Ethics in Medicine and Director of the Institute of Law and Ethics in Medicine at the University of Glasgow.

Scientific and clinical advances, social and political developments, and the impact of healthcare on our lives raise profound ethical and legal questions. Medical law and ethics have become central to our understanding of these problems, and are important tools for the analysis and resolution of problems – real or imagined.

In this series, scholars at the forefront of biomedical law and ethics contribute to the debates in this area, with accessible, thought-provoking and sometimes controversial ideas. Each book in the series develops an independent hypothesis and argues cogently for a particular position. One of the major contributions of this series is the extent to which both law and ethics are utilised in the content of the books, and the shape of the series itself.

The books in this series are analytical, with a key target audience of lawyers, doctors, nurses and the intelligent lay public.

Human Fertilisation and Embryology (2006)
Reproducing regulation
Kirsty Horsey and Hazel Biggs

Intention and Causation in Medical Non-Killing (2006)
The impact of criminal law concepts on euthanasia and assisted suicide
Glenys Williams

Impairment and Disability (2007)
Law and ethics at the beginning and end of life
Sheila McLean and Laura Williamson

Bioethics and the Humanities (2007)
Attitudes and perceptions
Robin Downie and Jane Macnaughton

Defending the Genetic Supermarket (2007)
The law and ethics of selecting the next generation
Colin Gavaghan

The Harm Paradox (2007)
Tort law and the unwanted child in an era of choice
Nicolette Priaulx

Assisted Dying (2007)
Reflections on the need for law reform
Sheila McLean

Medicine, Malpractice and Misapprehensions (2007)
Vivienne Harpwood

Euthanasia, Ethics and the Law (2007)
From conflict to compromise
Richard Huxtable

Best Interests of the Child in Healthcare
Sarah Elliston

Forthcoming titles:

Values in Medicine
The realities of clinical practice
Donald Evans

Medicine, Law and the Public Interest
Communitarian perspectives on medical law
J Kenyon Mason and Graeme Laurie

Healthcare Research Ethics and Law
Regulation, review and responsibility
Hazel Biggs

The Body in Bioethics
Alastair Campbell

The Best Interests of the Child in Healthcare

Sarah Elliston

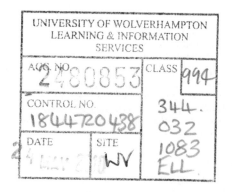

Routledge·Cavendish
Taylor & Francis Group
LONDON AND NEW YORK

First edition published 2007 by Routledge-Cavendish
2 Park Square, Milton Park, Abingdon, Oxon OX14 4RN

Simultaneously published in the USA and Canada
by Routledge-Cavendish
270 Madison Ave, New York, NY 10016

*Routledge-Cavendish is an imprint of the Taylor & Francis Group,
an informa business*

© 2007 Elliston, Sarah

Typeset in Times by
RefineCatch Limited, Bungay, Suffolk
Printed and bound in Great Britain by
T J International Ltd, Padstow, Cornwall

British Library Cataloguing in Publication Data
A catalogue record for this book is available from the British Library

Library of Congress Cataloging-in-Publication Data
A catalog record for this book has been requested

Hardback ISBN 10: 1–84472–043–8
Hardback ISBN 13: 978–1–84472–043–9

Paperback ISBN 10: 1–84472–042–X
Paperback ISBN 13: 978–1–84472–042–2

eISBN10: 0–203–94046–6
eISBN13: 978–0–203–94046–4

Contents

Acknowledgements

I must give heartfelt thanks to the many people who have helped me see this book through to publication. First, to the editor of this series and my colleague, Professor Sheila McLean, without whose constant encouragement and helpful insights, my work would have been much the poorer. Also to my publishers, particularly Fiona Kinnear, Katie Carpenter and Madeleine Langford, for their guidance and patience throughout the process; to Grace McGuire and Alison Clement for their help in getting the manuscript into shape; to Jane-Louis Wood for her proofreading skills above and beyond the calls of even our friendship, and to Euan Averbuch for the loan of a laptop when my own gave up under the strain. Like all academics, I have of course benefited greatly from working with colleagues and students over the years and while I hope they will find at least some of the ideas in this book convincing, where they do not, I expect they will challenge me, just as they should. All of my friends have been more than generous with their support. They have made time for me while understanding I have not always been able to reciprocate as I would have wished, for which I am profoundly grateful. My partner, Cameron Fleming, has seen me through every day and plenty of nights of my work on this and only he can know how important he has been to me. I give him an IOU on this for his PhD, which I fully expect him to collect. Last, but certainly not least, I must thank my family: especially my parents, Reg and Wendy, and sister, Sue, who have provided me with all the love and care I could have wished for through the years of my childhood and beyond, and to my nephews and niece: Stefan, Jake, Ben, Kirren and Jenna, who are taking our family through to a new generation. Throughout the writing of this book, I have been particularly aware of how much we continue to gain from the wisdom and experience of others when childhood is long past, even if in the end we decide to act against it. For any errors or omissions, therefore, I naturally take full responsibility.

Table of cases

Chapter I

Setting the scene

Introduction

Where decisions concerning children are made, the mantra of the decision needing to be made in the child's best interest is familiar and seems unobjectionable. After all, children as potentially vulnerable members of our society surely deserve the highest levels of protection such a standard suggests? Closer inspection, however, reveals significant problems with the definition and application of such a term in practice. While these are common to all areas of decision-making concerning children, this book is focused upon the healthcare context. Here some of the most difficult and sensitive problems arise, concerning as they do the extent to which a child's body can be examined and operated upon or affected by medicines, devices and procedures that are intended to bring about physiological or psychological change. Healthcare decisions made in childhood may have a significant impact upon the experiences and opportunities children will have both now and in the future and, in some cases, it is not only their physical and mental health but also their lives that are at stake.

How decisions should be made where medical interventions on children are involved has become an important area of concern in United Kingdom (UK) law and the number of cases dealing with this issue has grown considerably over the last 30 years or so. In part, this reflects a general trend in healthcare litigation. Here, though, additional reasons, centring on changing attitudes towards children, also play a part. Increased concentration on the need of children to be protected during their immaturity has been reflected in the development of both domestic and international law dealing with this issue.[1] At the same time, the rights of parents to determine their children's upbringing and of children to make their own decisions have also been asserted.[2]

---

1 Children Act 1989, Children (Scotland) Act 1995, The UN Convention on the Rights of the Child.
2 The classic example is of course *Gillick v West Norfolk and Wisbech Area Health Authority* [1985] 3 All ER 402, HL.

Taken together, this has the obvious potential for conflict between concepts of children's welfare, respect for parental authority and for children's autonomy, which may need to be resolved by the law.

One difficulty that arises in this area is the power of assumptions about children and their welfare discussed by Piper (Piper, 2000). While concentrating on other parts of child law, some of her observations are equally relevant to healthcare decisions. She notes that:

> Assumptions are those ideas, events and principles which are taken for granted as being true. They are no longer – or may never have been – subject to critical scrutiny, either because they appear self-evident or because it is assumed they have been proved to be 'true'. Spelling them out, thinking about their provenance and querying their validity is therefore not necessary.

> . . . we may have reached that stage in the family justice system in recent years. In relation to establishing the best interests of children, there have emerged strong general presumptions which constrain the process of working out what is best for individual children in the situation in which they find themselves.

> (Piper, 2000, pp 261–2)

One major assumption that I wish to challenge here is in fact even more fundamental and that is that the best interests test does and should form the basis for making decisions about children's healthcare. While doing so may seem heretical, there have increasingly been doubts raised about the dominance of this test and its application in a variety of contexts (Mnookin and Szwed, 1983; Reece, 1996; Eekelaar, 2002). My contention is that similar concerns may arise in healthcare.

In brief, my argument contains two main strands. The first concerns the position of children who are unable to meet standards for making decisions for themselves. Here, the vast majority of healthcare interventions are decided by parents in conjunction with medical practitioners. Where people are making decisions on behalf of others, this power cannot be unlimited and there may be a need for independent oversight. The courts, using the principle of the welfare or best interests of the child being of paramount importance, provide this. However, the courts will only normally become involved if there is a dispute between parents or where it is judged that significant interests of the child are thought likely to be compromised. Subject to this, parents have a wide discretion to make such decisions and they are not usually bound to meet the best interests test as the courts have interpreted it. My position is that in overriding parental decisions courts should also be concerned only with ensuring that significant interests of the child are not put at risk and that the decisions made by parents meet a reasonableness standard. To go further usurps the legitimate authority and function of parents and creates inconsistency in the expectation of what is within the scope of parental decision-making.

The traditional approach to the best interests test, while having problems in itself, is particularly hard to apply in some healthcare situations and requires some stretching to be made to fit. The most obvious examples are medical procedures that are of no therapeutic benefit to the child. Some of these may include an additional problem: where the interests of more than one child are concerned, such as live organ or tissue donation. A simpler and more coherent approach, and one that is already prevalent in healthcare practice, would be to require significant risk of serious harm as the threshold for judicial intervention and that, subject to this, parents should be free to decide what interests of the child should be promoted. A departure from the best interests principle already has some support, at least in relation to certain types of court intervention (Ross, 1998; Diekema, 2004). I must make it clear from the outset that I am not suggesting that parents should not be expected to promote and safeguard the welfare of their children. Clearly they should. What I am disputing is the substitution of parental decisions on what this requires by a court, simply because it disagrees with what they think best. Public policy allows parents to have the responsibility to determine what they believe is appropriate, subject to the harm limitation, and what I will argue is that courts should be bound by the same criteria. In fact courts already do perform a balancing test of harms and benefits to children when hearing cases concerning them, so to this extent a change in approach may not seem so radical. My contention goes further than this, however, and is that they should not be asked to declare that there is a single answer to what is best for the child where there are a range of reasonable responses that could be made by parents.

The second strand concerns children who are able to meet the required standard for decision-making. If it is accepted, as it generally is, that the purpose of allowing people to make decisions for others is because they are incapable of doing so, then if they have that capacity, the need for proxy decision-makers disappears. This is not the approach that has been taken by the courts, at least in England and Wales, where both parents and courts are apparently permitted to use the best interests principle to defeat even a competent child's refusal of treatment. Courts may do so in the case of a competent child's consent as well. There are some signs that, despite calls for greater attention to be paid to the views of children in recent times, their rights to self-determination are in fact under increasing threat. Rather than undermining the development and exercise of autonomy, I will contend that children should be supported to make decisions to the extent that they have the willingness and capacity to do so. Although there may undoubtedly be difficulty in determining when a child gains sufficient decision-making abilities to make legally binding choices and when the court should be asked to make a ruling on this, nevertheless the protective function that is claimed by the best interests test is not warranted over reasonable parents nor capable children.

One of the other common assumptions in this area is that it is usually beneficial to children to receive medically recommended treatment. The importance of maintaining health to people's welfare is generally uncontested and unsurprisingly it has proved to be a major concern in international and national law, guidance and policy. For example, Article 6 of the UN Convention on the Rights of the Child (the UN Convention) requires that States 'recognize that every child has the inherent right to life' and 'shall ensure to the maximum extent possible the survival and development of the child.'[3] Similarly, Article 24 provides that they must 'recognize the right of the child to the enjoyment of the highest attainable standard of health and to facilities for the treatment of illness and rehabilitation of health. States Parties shall strive to ensure that no child is deprived of his or her right of access to such healthcare services.' This Article goes on to set out specific issues States could take steps to address to meet this requirement, such as ensuring 'the provision of necessary medical assistance and healthcare to all children with emphasis on the development of primary healthcare.' More recently, the World Medical Association has also issued a Declaration on the Rights of the Child to Health Care.[4]

The provision of healthcare to children in the UK is primarily through the National Health Service (NHS) and there is a requirement on the Secretaries of State to ensure the provision of medical services to meet the reasonable needs of the population, again recognising the fundamental importance of health to all members of society.[5] National frameworks and strategies for improving child healthcare as a special area of concern have been produced, along with much supporting documentation (Department of Health, 2004; Scottish Executive, 2005). There must be few who would deny that safeguarding and improving the lives and health of children is an entirely worthy goal and indeed a crucial requirement for any society. Nonetheless, whether in all cases it trumps any additional considerations may be more open to debate, since there may be other legitimate rights and interests that may be affected. Furthermore, seeing an individual child's health as the determining factor through an application of the best interests test may also be problematic. For example, involving children in medical research may be vital to improving

---

3   The United Nations Convention on the Rights of the Child, adopted and opened for signature, ratification and accession by General Assembly resolution 44/25 of 20 November 1989. It came into force in the UK on 16 December 1991.

4   Adopted by the 50th World Medical Assembly Ottawa, Canada, October 1998.

5   National Health Service Act 1977 and National Health Service (Scotland) Act 1978, s 1(2). Both of these acts have been extensively amended since enactment and the English legislation has now been consolidated in the National Health Service Act 2006.

care for future child patients. However, it may be of no benefit to the children participating now and may even subject them to risks. It is difficult to justify this under an approach that makes the best interests of the individual child the critical factor, especially if this prioritises his or her own health interests. While children's health in general may be being promoted, this is not what the best interests test, as the courts use it, seems to permit. In addition, where competent children are concerned, like competent adults, they should be at liberty to decide that other factors are more important to them, even if others disagree.

In considering medical interventions, it is increasingly true that it is not only doctors that provide healthcare, as the role of nurse practitioners and allied health professionals have been substantially expanded. Healthcare now often encompasses other forms of therapies than those traditionally associated with Western medicine, such as acupuncture. There are also procedures that may in some cases have a treatment purpose, but may also have other significance and are not performed exclusively by doctors, male circumcision being one example. Many of the principles I will be exploring would be equally relevant in these situations, such as the need for parental or child consent, but some may not. The deference of the judiciary to the opinions of the medical profession has been noted in many situations (see, for example, Sheldon and Thomson, 1998; Keywood, 2001; Harrington, 2003). There have been signs of some cracks appearing in this approach with a greater willingness of the courts to advocate closer scrutiny of medical opinion and to allow that other factors may override it (Jacob, 1988; Teff, 1998; Brazier and Miola, 2000). The weight and reliance placed on medical evidence may nevertheless still be an issue. With this in mind, and for the sake of simplicity, I will be considering only healthcare interventions provided by or under the direction of registered medical practitioners and I will use the shorthand term 'doctors' when referring to them.

While there are many complex and fascinating ideas involved in the area of decision-making about future children, such as choices surrounding pre-implantation genetic screening and embryo modification, these cannot be covered here (see, for example, Gavaghan, 2007). Instead, I am concerned only with the medical treatment of children after birth. I will also be focusing upon the position in the UK. England and Wales form a single jurisdiction, but in some matters Scotland has a separate legal tradition and deals with children and young people rather differently, providing some interesting points of comparison. By contrast, for the most part Northern Ireland adopts the same or very similar legislation to that of England and Wales and will not be referred to separately. The age of majority in both Scotland and in England and Wales is 18.[6] However, where medical treatment is concerned, in

---

6 Family Law Reform Act 1969 s 1(1), Age of Majority (Scotland) Act 1969 s 1.

Scotland the dividing line between adults and children is 16.[7] References to children or young people therefore will be taken to mean people under these ages in the relevant jurisdiction unless specified otherwise. The law therefore sets ages that create the binary status of childhood and adulthood and makes some legal consequences contingent on which group a person is assigned to. A brief discussion of the kinds of legal consequences of childhood is necessary to place the best interests and the harm principle in context. Here, it will be seen that children can be regarded as having a range of rights that may be broadly categorised as rights to protection and rights to self-assertion (Bevan, 1989, p 11). The question is whether the best interests test is appropriate in deciding any issues concerning these rights.

Children's rights

Societal attitudes towards the status of children, their need for protection and their developing autonomy are not set in stone and various approaches have been suggested for the appropriate role of children, parents and the State in making decisions concerning them. In modern times, much concentration has been placed on the importance of rights and their place in protecting minority groups and individuals. In the Western world, in particular, enforceable rights are seen as having the potential to enhance the quality of peoples' lives and protect them from unjustified interference by others, most particularly the State. This may be seen, for example, in the growth of international instruments setting out agreements between States on rights that are regarded as being fundamental to human interests and welfare, such as the European Convention on Human Rights and Fundamental Freedoms (ECHR).[8] More specific Conventions, such as the European Convention on Human Rights and Biomedicine (ECB)[9] and the UN Convention on the Rights of the Child show that particular significance is placed on health and on the particular requirements of children, and indicate that more detailed consideration of them may be required than is possible in more general instruments.

Do children have rights?

Despite this interest in the development of rights principles, their application may, perhaps surprisingly, be seen as being problematic when discussing

---

7   Age of Legal Capacity (Scotland) Act 1991, ss 1 and 9. Sixteen is also the age at which people lacking capacity come within the Adults with Incapacity (Scotland) Act 2000.

8   Convention for the Protection of Human Rights and Fundamental Freedoms, Rome, 4 November 1950.

9   Convention for the Protection of Human Rights and Dignity of the Human Being with regard to the Application of Biology and Medicine: Convention on Human Rights and Biomedicine, Oviedo, 4 April 1997.

children. At a theoretical level, there have been doubts whether the concept is applicable to them (see Alston *et al.*, 1992, especially chs 1–5; Bainham, 2005, ch 3; Fortin, 2005, ch 1). These centre on what attributes are necessary to be a rights holder. Theories known as 'will', 'power' or 'claim' theories, which concentrate on decision-making capacity, clearly have difficulty accommodating younger children (MacCormick, 1976; Sumner, 1987). This may be avoided by holding that a child may have rights exercised by a proxy, although it would require the proxy to do so in the way that the child would have chosen if capable (Hart, 1973, p 184). How to decide what this would be remains subject to difficulties, such as how values and preferences can be judged when a person has not had the opportunity to develop them (Archard, 2002). 'Interests' theories, on the other hand, suggest that rights are interests that are protected by normative rules or standards. The existence of these interests imposes a corresponding duty on others to protect them. On this model, a person does not have to demonstrate any understanding or exercise any decision-making capacity, though they may do so, in order to be regarded as a bearer of rights. The person with interests therefore has rights to have those duties performed. It may be uncontroversial to suggest that children of whatever age have interests, and hence may have corresponding rights (MacCormick, 1976; Raz, 1986; Campbell, 1992; Kramer, 1998). Both these approaches have their merits and disadvantages (Campbell, 1992). It has been said that their 'respective vices and virtues have been extensively debated without either gaining evident or agreed supremacy' (Archard, 2000). Notwithstanding this, it is clear that children are accorded rights both under domestic and international law. The way these are approached appears to be more in line with an 'interests theory', since there are duties on others towards children irrespective of a child's decision-making capacity (MacCormick, 1976; Eekelaar, 1986; Fortin, 2005, ch 1). In addition, even if Hart's modification of the 'will theory' were proposed as an alternative, the law does not require proxy decisions to necessarily represent what it is thought the child would have chosen. Even so, the difficulty remains in defining the content and function of the rights stemming from the child's interests.

What kind of rights do children have?

Although children are accepted as capable of having legal rights, there has been debate over whether children should have exactly the same ones as adults or whether their rights should be qualified or enlarged to take into account specific aspects of childhood. Fortin notes the influence of so-called children's 'liberationists' writing in the 1970s, who were early advocates of rights for children (Fortin, 2005, pp 4–5). Some argued against drawing any distinctions between adult and child rights, but this has always been a minority view (see, for example, Foster and Freed, 1972; Farson, 1974; Holt, 1974). Most commentators instead contend that there are additional factors to be taken into account when looking at children's rights compared with adults (Eekelaar, 2002; Fortin, 2005, pp 4–5). At the heart of the matter is the recognition that children need support and care while they are developing physically, emotionally and intellectually, until they are able to take responsibility for themselves. At the same time, if children are ever to become capable of exercising autonomy, they also need to develop decision-making abilities and to have the chance to use them without putting themselves at undue risk. Children's rights therefore should take into account a level of protection that is not deemed to be necessary for most adults.

Several ways of framing children's interests that should be translated into rights have been proposed. Eekelaar divides children's interests into categories that include immediate physical, emotional and intellectual care and well-being; claims to be enabled to maximise their potential, within the social and economic limitations of the society in which the child lives and claims to be able to make decisions in accordance with their own preferences and goals (Eekelaar, 1986, pp 170–1). In similar vein, Freeman has also drawn up categories of children's rights that he saw as being subject to an overarching principle of 'liberal paternalism': rights to welfare, rights of protection, rights of children to be treated as adults and rights against parents (Freeman, 1983).

What these frameworks have in common is the tension between protecting children and respecting their emerging autonomy. The simpler classification by Bevan illustrates this concisely. He suggests two categories of children's rights: *protective* and *self-assertive* (Bevan, 1989, p 11). Protective rights are linked with the child's immaturity and need for protection and assistance during development. Self-assertive rights, on the other hand, enable rights applicable to adults to be claimed, including rights of decision-making. Bevan's terms represent a useful shorthand for the types of claims children may be able to assert. They recognise that children do have interests that require protection while they are incapable of taking care of themselves and that others have responsibilities to provide this. Equally, they take account of the fact that the ability to exercise autonomy does not spontaneously arise at whatever the legally set age of adulthood is. Parents are entrusted with the primary responsibility for caring for their children, but in some cases outside intervention to protect children's welfare will be required. In addition, where conflict arises between children's rights to protection and self-assertion, a decision will need to be made as to which takes priority. In other words, if a child can demonstrate abilities commensurate with exercising adult rights, should these still be constrained by the fact that the law deems him or her to have childhood status and to be in need of protection? It must of course be said that children may have interests that are not easily translated into legally enforceable rights. For instance, it might seem reasonable to suggest that children have an interest in receiving love and affection from their parents. However, such an interest would be impossible to enforce.

The rights of children and the responsibilities on others, including parents and the State, have been given specific consideration in the UN Convention. Here, international recognition has been given to the principle of the best interests of the child. Seeking to secure children's welfare during the crucial years of their development has achieved widespread support as a fundamental requirement for States.

The United Nations Convention on the Rights of the Child (UN Convention)

While it was not the first international instrument to specifically formulate children's rights, previous documents were of no binding force on signatories (Fortin, 2005, pp 35–6; Sutherland, 1999, paras 3.6–3.33). The UN Convention is the most widely ratified international convention in existence and although it confers no directly enforceable rights for individuals in UK courts – even the children it was enacted for – it does have significance in placing obligations on State signatories to comply with it and to ensure domestic law reflects its provisions. They must also send reports to the Committee on the Rights of the Child on a regular basis.[10] In addition, the articles of the Convention can be referred to in domestic courts as a means of considering the approach that should be taken under UK law. The European Court of Human Rights (ECtHR) has also taken them into account when interpreting ECHR rights (Norrie 2001: para 8.20). The UN Convention applies to all people under the age of 18, unless the law of majority is earlier in the particular State (Article 1). The UK at its ratification declared that it interpreted the UN Convention as applicable only following a live birth.[11]

The UN Convention may be thought of as concerned with three broad issues: the provision of goods and services to children; the protection of children; and ensuring the participation of children in decisions that concern them. While children are said to have a range of rights, it is arguably the protective function, embodied in the 'best interests' standard that has been emphasised rather than self-assertive rights and the promotion of children's autonomy.

The 'best interests of the child' is the overarching principle contained within it. Article 3(1) of the UN Convention states that:

> In all actions concerning children, whether undertaken by public or private social welfare institutions, courts of law, administrative authorities

---

10 The last report by the UK was in 2002: Committee on the Rights of the Child, Concluding Observations of the Committee on the Rights of the Child: United Kingdom of Great Britain and Northern Ireland. CRC/C/15/Add.188, 9 October 2002. At the time of writing the next report was due to be submitted by the UK in July 2007.
11 The UK Reservation and Declarations. CRC/C/2/Rev 4, at 32, 16 December 1991.

or legislative bodies, *the best interests of the child shall be a primary consideration.*

(Emphasis added)

The meaning to be attached to best interests is, however, left unspecified. It might be thought that this is understandable, since setting all possible considerations and the weight to be attached to them would be a Herculean task and one in which there could have been considerable scope for disagreement (Van Beuren, 1995, ch 1; Breen, 2002, ch 1). This may be even more so since, in fact, the best interests of the child principle is not a creation of international law but one that has its foundation in domestic law and hence has developed in rather different ways in individual States (Breen, 2002). However, it may be safely assumed as a minimum that they include the kinds of issues dealt with in the UN Convention itself.

Children's rights to express themselves are provided in Article 12, where States Parties:

> . . . shall assure to the child who is capable of forming his or her own views the right to express those views freely in all matters affecting the child, the views of the child being given due weight in accordance with the age and maturity of the child.

The voices of children are therefore to be listened to, but it is not stated that they are determinative of issues concerning them. While children are to have the right to freedom of expression – including seeking and imparting information – to freedom of thought, conscience and religion, and to privacy, these are also not absolute and may be subject to limitations, for example, 'such limitations as are prescribed by law and are necessary to protect public safety, order, health or morals, or the fundamental rights and freedoms of others' (Articles 13 and 14). The Convention places great importance on the child's right to life, survival and development, and there is a recognition of the obvious relationship of health to these rights (Articles 6 and 24).

At the same time, it stresses the role of parents and the family. Article 18 includes a statement that 'Parents or, as the case may be, legal guardians, have the primary responsibility for the upbringing and development of the child. The best interests of the child will be their basic concern'. Furthermore, it is also stated in Article 5 that:

> States Parties shall respect the responsibilities, rights and duties of parents . . . or other persons legally responsible for the child, to provide, in a manner consistent with the evolving capacities of the child, appropriate direction and guidance in the exercise by the child of [the Convention rights].

Nevertheless, the State has the duty to protect children from all forms of abuse and neglect by their parents (Article 19). While the majority of the language employed by the UN Convention is in terms of children's rights, the content in many cases empowers people other than children to make decisions that affect them. As Fortin notes:

> The aims of the Convention . . . are difficult to reconcile. In particular it emphasizes the need to promote children's capacity for eventual autonomy, whilst simultaneously supporting the traditional role of the family and society and the authority of parents over their children.
>
> (Fortin, 2005, p 41)

Despite this, as she later goes on to say, the UN Convention has been 'enormously influential – indeed to many it is regarded as the touchstone for children's rights throughout the world' (Fortin, 2005, p 49). UK law is intended to be consistent with these rights, but since they are so widely drafted and contain principles that may come into conflict, they allow considerable scope for interpretation. This may be true even of fundamental concepts, such as the best interests of the child.

The welfare/best interests principle in UK child law

The welfare or best interests of the child is a constant theme in UK child law and has been described as the 'golden thread' running through it (Lord Fawsley, 2007). The central principle endorsed in UK law is that when courts make decisions about children, the welfare of the child is paramount, or the decision must be in accordance with the best interests of the child. While these terms have different origins, and as we shall see, may have different meanings, they are in practice used interchangeably by the courts. The welfare principle is enshrined in the major legislation concerning children: in England and Wales, the Children Act 1989 (CA 1989) and in Scotland, the Children (Scotland) Act 1995 (C(S)A 1995). Although they are not the only statutes affecting the care of children or relevant to medical treatment, they set out the essential framework establishing rights and responsibilities in respect of children and young people and also provide mechanisms for adjudication and enforcement. The Children Acts cover a wide range of issues concerning children, but only those relevant to healthcare will be outlined here. The statutes contain similar provisions but there are some differences worth noting.

For proceedings under the CA 1989, when a court determines any question with respect to the upbringing of a child, *the child's welfare shall be the court's paramount consideration.*[12] The same principle is found in the C(S)A 1995,

---

12 CA 1989 s 1(1).

when a court is making an order in respect of parental responsibilities or rights or guardianship.[13] It also occurs elsewhere in both Acts in connection with specified matters. Decisions about medical interventions on children would fall within these provisions. They are usually dealt with as specific issue orders, giving directions to those concerned where a particular issue has arisen or seems likely to arise in respect of a child, such as whether proposed treatment should be given.[14] It would be relatively unusual to seek a prohibited steps order or, in Scotland, an interdict asking that medical treatment not be given.[15] This is because the default position is that, absent lawful consent from a parent or a competent child, treatment may not proceed, save exceptionally in the case of a medical emergency, under the doctrine of necessity.[16] Such orders perhaps might be sought where the child's parents are in disagreement with each other. In the vast majority of cases, however, the courts are dealing with applications by, or on behalf of, those seeking to undertake medical procedures where either one or both parents or the child have refused consent. Cases may also be brought where practitioners are unwilling or unable to provide treatment without a court's authority.

In addition to the courts' statutory powers under the Children Acts, they also have an inherent jurisdiction which enables them to make orders in respect of children: the *parens patriae* jurisdiction (for more detailed discussion, see Seymour, 1994; Laurie, 1999). It has been described as an ancient prerogative jurisdiction of the Crown, which was delegated to the courts to protect the persons and property of those who were unable to do so for themselves.[17] In Scotland, this jurisdiction was revived specifically in relation to the medical treatment of incompetent adults and its scope for such use in respect of children is uncertain in modern times.[18] However, in principle, the Court of Session can consider cases concerning any incompetent person under this jurisdiction, save that there is no equivalent to making a child a ward of the court (Wilkinson and Norrie, 1999, para 853). An attempt to use the inherent jurisdiction over children in Scotland is unlikely, so discussion will centre on the position in England and Wales.

Here, the inherent jurisdiction now only applies to people under the age of 18.[19] One aspect of the courts' power is making a child a ward of court.

---

13 C(S)A 1995 s 11(1) and (7)(a).
14 CA 1989 s 8(1), C(S)A 1995 s 11(2)(e).
15 CA 1989 s 8(1), C(S)A 1995 s 11(2)(f).
16 The principle of necessity is described in *F v West Berkshire Health Authority and Another* [1989] All ER 545.
17 *F v West Berkshire Health Authority and Another* [1989] All ER 545, 552 per Brandon LJ.
18 See *L, Petitioner*, 1996 SCLR 538, CS and *Law Hospital NHS Trust v Lord Advocate* 1996 SCLR 49, IHCS.
19 *F v West Berkshire Health Authority and Another* [1989] All ER 545, *Airedale NHS Trust v Bland* [1993] 1 All ER 821, Fam D, CA and HL.

The effect of this is that no important decision concerning the child, whether or not this was the original reason for the wardship, can be taken without the leave of the court. Wardship was historically the procedure used to exercise the courts' inherent jurisdiction. Since the passing of the CA 1989, the circumstances in which it can be imposed have been substantially limited. This step is now rarely undertaken in medical treatment cases, since the High Court and those above it can still make decisions using the inherent jurisdiction without doing so.[20] It may be considered appropriate where the child's condition is chronic but changeable.[21] It is quite common to seek to use the inherent jurisdiction in the event of a dispute over a proposed course of treatment or in the absence of any other lawful authority to proceed. Under the inherent jurisdiction it has been said that '. . . it is settled law that *the court's prime and paramount consideration must be the best interests of the child*. That is easily said but not easily applied'.[22] Closer examination of the principle supports this contention.

Although the preferred term when using the inherent jurisdiction is that it is the best interests, rather than the welfare, of the child that are paramount, the courts have held that they are applying the same principles under the inherent jurisdiction, wardship or the provisions of the CA 1989.[23] Despite this, there may be reasons to doubt that these terms are in fact equivalent. The best interests test seems to demand that there is only one solution to the court's enquiry: the one that is best for that person after evaluating the harms and benefits of the alternatives (Beauchamp and Childress, 2001, pp 99–103). This has been confirmed in a case involving the proposed sterilisation of an adult woman with learning disabilities where it was held that where there were a range of possible treatment options that could be recommended: '. . . the best interests test ought, logically, to give only one answer.'[24] Obviously the range of factors that could be taken into account in establishing that best option are infinitely variable and opinions may differ sharply over the evidence needed to establish them and the weight that should be given to competing factors.

If a decision is taken to apply a best interests standard, further considerations arise in respect of what weight should be given to this principle. There are several approaches that could be taken. Archard notes that the specific terms 'paramount' and 'primary' have been used both in legislation and by

20 *Re Z (a minor) (freedom of publication)* [1995] 4 All ER 961, CA, at 986 per Bingham MR.
21 *Re J (A Minor) (Medical Treatment)* [1992] 2 FCR 753, CA and also *R v Portsmouth Hospital NHS Trust ex parte Glass* [1999] 3 FCR 905, CA.
22 *Re J (a minor) (wardship: medical treatment)* [1990] 3 All ER 145, CA, per Taylor LJ.
23 *Re B (a minor) (wardship: medical treatment)* (1981) 3 All ER 927, CA; *Re B (a minor) (wardship: sterilisation)* [1987] 2 All ER 206, HL.
24 *Re SL (adult patient) (medical treatment)* [2000] 2 FCR 452, *sub nom Re S (adult patient: sterilisation)*, CA, per Dame Elizabeth Butler-Sloss P at 464.

courts, along with either the indefinite or definite article, to limit the consideration that should be given to a child's (best) interests. He concludes that at least four possible weightings can be given to the interests of a child in making a decision affecting him or her. These are that the child's interests should be:

(1) the paramount;
(2) a paramount;
(3) the primary;
(4) a primary consideration.

(Archard, 2002)

As he points out, a fifth possibility, that a child's (best) interests should merely be 'a consideration', seems unnecessary since a child's interests surely must be given some place in any proceedings concerning them. The suggested distinction between 'paramount' and 'primary' is simply explained in that a paramount consideration outweighs all others. By contrast, a 'primary' consideration, while in the first order of considerations, remains one of several and hence does not necessarily determine the outcome. The weight that should be given to a standard is therefore an important part in considering its application.

The majority of cases concerning decision-making about children will come before the courts under the Children Acts or, in England and Wales, under the inherent jurisdiction of the courts. Although both Children Acts are intended to be consistent with the UN Convention, the standard to be adopted and the weight to be given to it in making decisions about a child differ. As we have seen, the UN Convention states that 'the best interests of the child shall be a primary consideration' when decisions are taken by outside agencies, including courts.[25] This followed considerable debate over the wording to be used (Breen, 2002, pp 78–84). However, it is not the expression used in the UK legislation, which is that the child's welfare is the paramount consideration. A welfare test may be said to differ from a best interests one in that it does not suggest that a decision need be regarded as the single 'best' option for the child. At first glance, then, the Children Acts appear to apply a less protective standard of decision-making than the UN Convention, but this factor is then given overriding importance. On the other hand, the test under the inherent jurisdiction of the courts is that the child's best interests are the prime and paramount concern. While consistent with the UN Convention on the standard to be used, it gives a higher weighting to it. Although the UK tests are not identical, it is clear that the courts seek to render any difference between them irrelevant in practice. A number of possibilities arise

---

25 UN Convention, Art 3(1).

as to why the courts equate the welfare of the child and the best interests test. One may be that there is no difference between these terms, although this seems untenable. Another may be that the courts do not recognise that the tests are potentially different. However, the most likely is that it is a pragmatic solution to try to ensure that all children coming before the courts are dealt with according to the same principle. Effectively, therefore, the standard adopted is that *the best interests of the child are the paramount concern of the court*. Arguably, the test adopted seems to impose an even stronger level of protection over children than that set out in the UN Convention.

Nevertheless, no matter how simply such a proposition may be stated, applying it in practice is no easy task. In respect of children, it may be argued that this test promotes their wellbeing to the fullest extent and as such protects them by ensuring that the effects of any decision will, so far as possible, be positive ones. It also places the child at the centre of consideration, which may be regarded as a necessary corrective to the dominance of adult-centred concerns (Herring, 2005). As such, any departure from it may be thought as lessening the importance of the child's interests. However, much rests upon what factors a court is permitted and chooses to take into account in its assessment, and how those factors are weighed in the balance. The CA 1989 contains a welfare 'checklist' that a court must have regarded to when considering making, varying or discharging an order. Among the things the court must consider are:

(a) The ascertainable wishes and feelings of the child concerned (considered in light of the child's age and understanding);
(b) The child's physical, emotional and/or educational needs;
(c) The likely effect on the child of any change in his/her circumstances;
(d) The child's age, sex, background and any other characteristics, which the court considers relevant;
(e) Any harm which the child has suffered or is at risk of suffering;
(f) How capable each of the child's parents, and any other person in relation to whom the court considers the question to be relevant, is of meeting his/her needs;
(g) The range of powers available to the court under the Children Act 1989 in the proceedings in question. (S 1(3))

A further consideration mentioned in the CA 1989 is that, in matters concerning the child's upbringing, 'any delay in determining the question is likely to prejudice the welfare of the child' and must be avoided.[26]

In Scotland, there is no general welfare checklist, following the recommendations of the Scottish Law Commission that this was unnecessary, would be incomplete and might lead to a mechanistic approach by judges

26 CA 1989 s 1(2).

(Scottish Law Commission, 1992, para 5.20–23). Nevertheless, Scottish courts would be expected to take into account a similar range of issues to their English and Welsh counterparts. Specific mention is made in the C(S)A 1995 of the need to involve the child. A Scottish court considering whether or not to make an order in respect of parental responsibilities and rights is required to take into account the child's age and maturity and so far as practicable:

(i)   give him an opportunity to indicate whether he wishes to express his views;

(ii) if he does so wish, give him an opportunity to express them; and

(iii) have regard to such views as he may express.[27]

This reflects the same requirement to take into account the child's views placed upon any person making a major decision in the exercise of parental rights and responsibilities.[28] Under this legislation, a child aged 12 years of age or more is presumed to be of sufficient age and maturity to form a view.[29] There is no equivalent under the English legislation, but there is no minimum age restriction for child participation in either statute. Providing that children must be able to express their own views is in accordance with the UN Convention,[30] although it seems that the Scottish statute places more obligations on parents to consult with their children than the English one. It would seem to follow that children must be provided with sufficient information to enable their views to be canvassed. However, this does not mean that the child's own wishes are to be regarded as decisive, which opens the way for potential conflict should these be in opposition to the views of parents or a court.

It may therefore be suggested that it is children's interests in choice rather than the right to choose that is being provided for here, as part of the welfare assessment. It is notable that the language of children's rights is not used at all in connection with these proceedings. It is parental responsibilities and rights that are said to be under consideration, not the rights of the child. However, despite the lack of rights terminology in their respect, undoubtedly children's rights are engaged in terms of the level and type of protection that they must receive and the extent to which their own views should be determinative. The type of protection offered by the best interests test is therefore worthy of closer examination and it can be argued that it may not be as immune to criticism as its wide endorsement might suggest.

27 C(S)A 1995 s 11(7)(b).
28 C(S)A 1995 s 6.
29 C(S)A 1995 s 11(10).
30 UN Convention, Art 12.

Problems with the best interests of the child principle and healthcare

The dominance of the best interests of the child having paramount importance and the way this has been interpreted by the courts has raised some
concerns. As a general principle, it has been attacked, for example in areas such
as child custody, where it has been said of the best interests standard that:

> The phrase is so idealistic, virtuous and high sounding that it defies
> criticism and can delude us into believing that its application is an
> achievement itself. Its mere utterance can trap us into the self-deception
> that we are doing something effective and worthwhile. However the flaw
> is that what is best for any child or even children in general is often
> indeterminate and speculative and requires a highly individualized choice
> between alternatives.
>
> (Mnookin and Szwed, 1983, p 8)

It seems nonetheless reasonable to agree with Herring when he suggests that
the uncertainty in the best interests test lies not in whether it is desirable to
promote a child's welfare, but in determining what that entails, so that 'what
is uncertain is what the good things in life are; or perhaps what a good life is'
(Herring, 2005, p 160). While the UN Convention lists various rights for
children, which can be assumed to be relevant to a consideration of the
child's best interests, and the CA 1989 sets out some specific factors that
courts must take into account in assessing the child's welfare, these are
not exhaustive. Indeed the view may be taken, as in the Scottish legislation,
that directing courts on what issues to consider is unnecessary and unhelpful.
Even where the relevant factors can be agreed, it has been said that:

> . . . in spite of the decision-maker's best efforts, there remains a wide
> variety of circumstances that cannot be accounted for both in the present
> and in the future, which may distort the validity of the decision as being
> in the child's best interests. Consequently, according such ability to a
> decision-maker is to bestow upon him or her shamen-like qualities for
> the prediction of future events.
>
> (Breen, 2002, p 17)

Given the unavoidable lack of precision in this area, the values and preferences of decision-makers are bound to enter into the equation in judging
whether the predicted outcomes are what are best for the child (see, for
example, Mnookin and Szwed, 1983; Elster, 1989). Indeed, as Eekelaar puts it:

> . . . the heavily subjective nature of the power granted to the judge means
> that, so long as he or she does not claim to be applying it as a conclusive

rule of law, a judge can consider almost any factor which could possibly have a bearing on a child's welfare and assign to it any weight he or she chooses.

(Eekelaar, 1991, p 248)

While indeterminacy in the application of the best interests test is a criticism that can be levelled in many areas of child law, it is particularly evident when dealing with the medical treatment of children. There are many matters that may be thought of as necessary to a welfare assessment, most obviously medical evidence concerning the diagnosis and prognosis for the child, the treatments available and the likely effect of any treatment or failure to treat. Although this may be regarded as simply a matter of assembling factual evidence, medicine is an area where it is notoriously difficult to establish facts with any certainty and medical opinion will form a large part of such an enquiry. As well as the potential difficulty in establishing with any precision the outcome of illness or injury with and without treatment, whether such an outcome should be regarded as being in the child's best interests may prove even more problematic. The benefits medical expertise can bring are considerable and great strides have been made to reduce morbidity and mortality during childhood. Despite these welcome advances, medical interventions are not risk-free. They may be ineffective, they may themselves cause further or additional harm and there may be situations where the cure may be judged to be worse than the condition itself. This involves considering the wider impact of illness, injury, disability and treatment upon the child's wellbeing.

However, despite the potential for indeterminacy here, some have argued that in fact while the degree of flexibility inherent in the best interests test can be said to be one of its greatest weaknesses, it may also be one of its greatest strengths, since it allows decisions tailored to the particular circumstances of an individual child to be taken into account (Douglas, 2004, p 173; Herring, 2005, p 169). Instead, problems that may lie with it may be that, in some circumstances, the way that the courts approach medical interventions on children is far from indeterminate. As we shall see, the courts generally follow medical recommendations as to whether treatment should be given. Although the courts must reach their own decision on the best interests of the child and may choose not to rely on medical evidence, it seems clear from the cases that will be discussed that this is regarded as having by far the greatest influence upon them.

As Herring notes, in cases such as this the courts may be more confident in making pronouncements about a child's best interests where there is 'scientific' evidence on which they can rely, despite the potential for doubts whether this evidence is always accurate or objective. As he concludes:

... rather than the judiciary too often relying on their own views, a more valid criticism is that there is too much weight attached to supposedly 'expert' objective evidence and not enough judicial assessment of it.

(Herring, 2005, p 162)

The courts have not seemed overly willing to scrutinise medical evidence and, indeed, given the limitations of the court process, they may not be in a position to even attempt to do so. In addition, a best interests test, of necessity, also seems to require that a judgement be made on what will ensure the 'best' outcome for the child, not merely a good or a reasonable outcome from the range of alternatives.[31] Depending on the circumstances, what is best from a medical point of view may be least acceptable to the child or parents when taking into account other factors such as respect for autonomy, parental choice and the impact upon the child and the family of the decision. When considering medical treatment it has been held that 'best interests encompasses medical, emotional and all other welfare issues.'[32] Best interests are not therefore wholly dependent on medical evidence and the extent to which other considerations should influence decisions about a child's treatment would therefore seem to be crucial.

One is the issue of the availability of legal surrogates to make decisions for the child: the child's parents. For example, it has been said that making decisions about children is not the same as making them about incompetent adults since, in the case of children, parental wishes must be taken into account.[33] While adults, too, may require protection because, for example, of temporary or permanent incompetence, the law does not automatically permit others, regardless of their relationship, to make legally binding decisions on their behalf. Relatives or other carers must be consulted, but their views have no legal effect unless the adult had appointed them as proxy decision-makers or they are so appointed by a court.[34] This right is specific to the parent–child relationship and only where the child is under the age of majority. Nevertheless, the courts are not bound to act in accordance with the parents' wishes. If they were, then any protective function of the court over young children against their parents would be impossible.

The ability to override the parent's decisions is of course dependent on two ideas: first that the parents' role is for the benefit of their children rather than to exercise power over them as an independent right of the parent. This is generally taken to be the stance of the modern law on parents and children as

31 *Re SL (adult patient) (medical treatment)* [2000] 2 FCR 452, *sub nom Re S (adult patient: sterilisation)*, CA, at 464 per Dame Elizabeth Butler-Sloss P.

32 Re *A (Medical Treatment: Male Sterilisation)* [2000] 1 FCR 193, CA, per Dame Butler-Sloss P at 200.

33 *F v West Berkshire Health Authority and Another* [1989] All ER 545, at 567 per Goff LJ.

34 Mental Capacity Act 2005, Adults with Incapacity (Scotland) Act 2000. Even here, their decisions may not determine medical treatment decisions.

we shall see, below. Second, for parent's wishes to be overridden by a court, it must be judged that the court's decision will be a better one. The function of the court when considering parental decisions has been said to be that it must act as the 'judicial reasonable parent'. That is to say:

> the court should exercise its jurisdiction in the interests of the children, 'reflecting and adopting the changing views, as the years go by, of reasonable men and women, the parents of children, on the proper treatment and methods of bringing up children'.[35]

However, what if the court concludes that the parents' views are reasonable? There has been some ambivalence by the courts on this point that will be discussed further when considering parental responsibilities and the harm principle. For the moment, it is sufficient to note that, notwithstanding judicial statements like the one above, the best interests test has been interpreted as allowing courts to override parents' decisions, even if they are regarded as being devoted to the child and acting reasonably.[36] Substituting parental decisions may be legitimate where parents are endangering important interests of the child for reasons that do not meet societal expectations. For example, where treatment is conventional, routine and of low risk to the child, but its refusal may result in serious injury to him or her, then safeguarding the health interests of the child justifies overriding their decision. However, allowing courts to override parental decisions here need not rely on an application of the best interests test. It could equally well be justified by applying a harm-based approach and by holding that the decision of the parents does not meet a reasonableness standard.

When dealing with medical procedures outside the standard treatment of the child situation, there may be greater difficulties in assessing the best interests of the child. Such situations may arise where medical procedures having no clear health benefits to the child are proposed. For example, what is best for one child may be controversial where medical interventions are intended to promote and safeguard the health or even life of another, such as through tissue or organ donation. The hope of improving the health interests of a child's siblings may be a powerful motivation to allow such interventions, but these can only take place if a much broader concept of donor children's best interests than their own health are taken into account. The same would also be true of much medical research. Again, appealing to the best interests of the child might allow such interventions, but it may require some manipulation of the concept to do so. Looking at whether medical interventions pose

---

35 *J v C* [1969] 1 All ER 788, HL, per Upjohn LJ at 831.
36 *Re T (a minor) (wardship: medical treatment)* (1996) [1997] 1 All ER 906, CA. *Re C (a child) HIV test* [1999] 3 FCR 289, Fam D.

significant harm to the child's interests without reasonable countervailing benefits seems likely to provide a more realistic and justifiable interpretation of the calculations being undertaken than claiming it is in a child's best interests.

These situations, too, may bring into focus a further problem that has been identified: that by prioritising the best interests of a child, the interests of others are ignored or underestimated. Reece, for example, has suggested that:

> The paramountcy principle must be abandoned, and replaced by a framework which recognizes that the child is merely one participant in a process in which the interests of all participants count.
>
> (Reece, 1996)

As Herring notes, there are many situations in which the best interests principle does not apply, such as divorce and the ordering of blood tests to determine paternity (Herring, 1999b, ch 5). In such circumstances, it can be said that the law has decided that children's interests 'must take their place in a world full of interests' (Eekelaar, 2002, p 239). The rights of others may therefore play a part, even where decisions may profoundly affect a child and be to his or her detriment.

In those cases, though, the child is not the subject of the court proceedings.[37] They can be distinguished from medical interventions on a child who, in most cases, is before the court and upon whom any decision is likely to have the most personal and serious effects. This might suggest it is only his or her interests that should be considered and that these must come first. The best interests test appears to meet these conditions, as it is inherently individualistic (Herring, 1999a). This, however, ignores the fact that the impact of a child's illness on other family members may be considerable and it can be asked whether this should be taken into account. If the parents have particular views on the child's treatment and the burdens this may impose on them, and perhaps the consequences for their care of other children of the family, should this be able to outweigh this particular child's interests in receiving treatment? Usually the courts' answer is 'no', though in a rare case there might be scope to bring these kinds of considerations into the welfare assessment, by arguing that in fact the child's best interests depends on the parents' commitment to the treatment and aftercare of the child, or that their ability to care for the child will be facilitated by undertaking certain medical procedures.[38] This would however be highly unusual. Moving away from a best interests test to take greater account of parental views might be thought to amount to judicial licence to parents to wholly disregard the welfare of

37 See, e.g. *S v S; W v Official Solicitor* [1970] 3 All ER 107, HL.
38 This sort of approach can be seen in *Re T (a minor) (wardship: medical treatment)* (1996) [1997] 1 All ER 906, CA. See also the discussion of the 'Ashley treatment' in Chapter 2.

their child. However, that is not what I will be proposing. Instead, courts should continue to intervene where the circumstances merit it. Children require protection from parents who do not provide a level of care that is considered appropriate and their decisions should be overridden if they are placing their children at a significant risk of serious harm for reasons that do not meet legitimate societal expectations. However, apart from this, parents should be at liberty to determine their child's upbringing, including his or her medical care, and may take into account the wishes and needs of the family as well as those of the individual child.

To take a purely individualistic approach is also problematic where the treatment of one child involves a medical intervention on another. In the case of tissue or organ donation, for example, it is only a donor child that would be likely to be the subject of a court hearing and thus only his or her best interests that fall to be directly considered by the courts, not those of the child receiving the transplant. It could be argued that this should not mean treating the interests of any other child as having no or lesser importance that those of the particular child attended to (Archard, 2002). The interests of both children should surely be given equal weight, though a decision may have to be made between them. The courts have thus far avoided seeing this kind of situation as a direct conflict between donors and recipients. While they have not specifically considered this point in respect of children, the approach they have adopted to incapable adult donors is instructive. Nevertheless, the way that the best interests test is framed makes it difficult to take into account the interests of more than one child at a time. This also raises problems in the case of conjoined twins, where undoubtedly courts will have to consider them both as equal participants. A decision may have to be taken that recognises that the best interests of both children cannot be satisfied.[39] Again, looking at the harms attendant on medical interventions on children and the justifications for imposing them would seem to be one way to resolve this problem.

By contrast, to some, taking the opposite view to Reece, an objection to the court's approach to best interests is that, despite its clear direction to put the child's needs first, in fact there is an absence of transparency in the application of the best interests test. Its use 'conceals the fact that the interests of others, or, perhaps, untested assumptions about what is good for children, actually drive the decision' (Eekelaar, 1986. See, also, Herring, 1999a). This leads on to a problem identified by Archard, which is what perspective the decision-maker should use in seeking to assess the best interests of the child. Some points about this were raised earlier in the discussion on children's rights, but Archard suggests that two different broad approaches could be used: basing decisions on what a child would choose for him or herself

---

39 See, e.g. *Re T and E (Proceedings: Conflicting Interests)* [1995] 3 FCR 260; *Re A (children)-(conjoined twins: surgical separation)* [2000] 4 All ER 961, CA.

(a hypothetical choice approach) and basing decisions on what is best for the child, as distinct from the child's own actual or hypothetical desires (an objectivist approach).

Neither is free of difficulty. The objectivist approach suffers from the problems of indeterminacy, already discussed: how is one to judge what will turn out to be 'best for the child'? As for the hypothetical choice approach, this suggests that the courts ought to make a decision applying a substituted judgment. This test is appealed to most commonly where a competent person has lost capacity and it requires the decision-maker to try to judge what the person would have wanted in this situation. Evidence of past wishes, values and preferences may be sought in an attempt to determine what the person would have been likely to choose. While it is not an approach that has explicitly found much favour with the UK courts, nevertheless, its influence can be seen both in case law and in statutes dealing with incompetent adults.[40] Nevertheless, there are doubts over the extent to which substituted judgments, even where the individual is well known to the decision-maker, truly represent what he or she would have chosen and this must be more so where the decision is made by a court. As McLean notes:

> this test has been dismissed by some as fundamentally flawed, since the assessment of what would have been chosen is, in the absence of real evidence, equivalent to guesswork.
>
> (McLean, 1997, para 5:17)

It may be even more problematic to apply a substituted judgement test where the person has never been capable of expressing choices or preferences, as will be the case with very young children. Here it might be interpreted as what the child would choose if he were capable of making a rational judgement (Archard, 2002). This kind of approach has been advocated by Eekelaar and Freeman, who contend that a rational adult would want his or her developmental potential maximised (Eekelaar, 1994; Freeman, 1983). Freeman, in particular, bases his approach on Rawls' 'Theory of Justice' (Rawls, 1971). Stated briefly this sets out the principles that individuals would hypothetically choose in a just society to secure fair treatment for everyone. In making their choice, no one would know what their own circumstances or position would be, and hence what would result in benefit or disadvantage to them. Freeman argues that justice requires bringing children to the stage when they can participate in society by making free and rational decisions. In order to do this, two rights for children are required: first, equal opportunity with respect to issues like a good upbringing and education; second, liberal paternalism to

---

40 *Airedale NHS Trust v Bland* [1993] 1 All ER 821, Fam D, CA and HL. Mental Capacity Act 2005, Adults with Incapacity (Scotland) Act 2000.

allow interventions to protect children's developmental potential. He framed the second right as follows:

> What sorts of action or conduct would we wish, as children, to be shielded against on the assumptions that we would want to mature to rationally autonomous adulthood and be capable of deciding our own system of ends as free and rational beings?
>
> (Freeman, 1983, p 57)

While it could not be said that everyone would agree that this should be the guiding principle, he considered that it was most likely to meet the requirements of Rawls' theory (for fuller discussion, see Bainham, 2005, pp 107–11; Worsfold, 1974). Basing an argument on what a child would rationally choose is, however, capable of a number of different interpretations (Archard, 2002).

First, it may imply that the courts should choose what the adult that the child will become would choose. This is difficult to apply because it may be that the decision that is taken will affect the adults that the children will become. They might approve of the choice that was made for them precisely because the choice affected their development into the people they are now. To this extent then, there is no single best choice for the child: there are a range of possibilities that might equally well be chosen. Second, the courts might choose for the child as if he or she were an adult – in other words, what any adult it is assumed would choose in that situation. The problem here is that it may not always be clear what an adult would choose. This may be tempered by their values and beliefs, which may never be shared by the adult that the child becomes. Suggesting that maximising developmental potential is what adults would choose in a specific situation may not avoid this problem. Once they were freed from the veil of ignorance proposed by Rawls, people might make very different decisions for themselves (Rawls, 1971). Some might not choose to live lives in a certain condition or as a result of particular treatments and generalisations may be difficult to make in some treatment contexts. It also presupposes that the child has developmental potential, which may not be the case, for example, for the terminally ill child, or that survival and development is necessarily a good thing, irrespective of the condition in which life may be lived.

A third possibility is that an attempt is made to envisage the child, not as the future adult he or she may become, but as an adult version of the child, without the attributes of childhood such as immaturity. However, once these attributes have been removed, it may be suggested that 'it is not clear what remains of the child . . . For the child just is someone who has these childish beliefs and desires. What is it to be a child if it is not to think and want as a child does?' (Archard, 2002). While this may be a fair point, it could be said to ignore the possibility that there may be some views and beliefs that are present in a child without being childish. An example could be religious beliefs that may be held equally by adults. Of course this may be met by the response that such beliefs may be regarded as childish to the extent that they have not been subjected to the benefits of adult reasoning and experience and hence need not be relied upon. If this view is taken, then indeed there will be little left of the child for the courts to work with.

A further objection to the hypothetical choice approach is that it does not take account of the interests of the child in the present, in being a child, and in the satisfaction of interests relevant at that point in time. Lowy has described this kind of idea as the 'projects of children'. She suggests that there are many aspects of childhood that are specific to it and trying to justify decision-making in terms of future interests fails adequately to take account of this (Lowy, 1992). For her, this may be relevant to terminally ill children, who have no long-term developmental potential nor may have the prospect of reaching the standard of autonomy required for rational decision-making, yet could have 'appropriate projects which are protected by autonomy-respecting rights' (Lowy, 1992, p 73).

Given the difficulties inherent in the 'hypothetical choice' test, Adler suggests that the 'objective' test is more commonly encountered so that adults make decisions based on what they perceive is good for the child, rather than what they think the child would decide for him or herself (Adler, 1985). Others too, think it is likely that her view is 'a more realistic reflection of what happens in practice' (Bainham, 2005, p 112; see, also, Campbell, 1992, p 15). However, elements both of 'objectivist' and 'hypothetical choice' reasoning have been shown by the courts when looking at the best interests of children in respect of healthcare. A degree of uncertainty about the proper perspective for decision-makers to adopt when applying the best interests test is therefore not simply an academic question.

A final problem with the best interests test that will be considered here is whether it may allow decisions to be taken in respect of children that override their right to self-determination. The basic justification for allowing others to make decisions for children is that they are felt to be incapable of doing so for themselves and that they require protection until they are able to take personal responsibility. While deciding precisely when children gain the ability to make decisions to an acceptable standard may be no easy task, if they are judged to be able to do so, then the need for others to intervene would seem to disappear. Overriding their decisions in such circumstances would allow paternalistic interventions that would not be accepted for adults in similar situations. While it is considered appropriate to allow others to make treatment decisions for adults in their best interests, or for their benefit, this is usually only permitted where adults are judged to be incompetent.[41] This

---

41 Special exceptions are permitted under mental health legislation: Mental Health Act 1983, Mental Health Care and Treatment (Scotland) Act 2003.

approach has an ethical foundation in the concept of respect for autonomy, both in terms of respect for the bodily integrity of the individual and his or her choices.

The general importance of autonomy has a long tradition and has been justified in various ways. Respect for autonomy is most closely associated with deontological theories, conceiving moral obligations as being based on duties and obligations that are considered as rights in themselves, regardless of their outcome. It can be seen in Kant's view that persons should not be regarded as merely means to an end but as ends in themselves (Kant, 1785; reprinted, 1994, p 279). Respect for autonomy then is grounded in the idea that failing to accord priority to the individual's own beliefs and values would be to treat her as a means to others' ends rather than as having ends of her own. This principle has the status of a moral imperative. However, the importance of autonomy also finds support from utilitarian philosophers such as Mill:

> . . . the only purpose for which power can be rightfully exercised over any member of a civilised community, against his will, is to prevent harm to others. His own good, either physical or moral, is not a sufficient warrant. He cannot rightfully be compelled to do or forbear because it will be better for him to do so, because it will make him happier, because, in the opinion of others to do so would be wise, or even right.
>
> (Mill, 1859, ch 1, para 9)

Respect for autonomy under this formulation is based on the idea that this generally provides a beneficial result or maximises the good for individuals and society. According to Mill, respect for autonomy has the status only of a liberty interest. Whichever view is adopted, it is clear that important values are at stake: whether individuals have the freedom to make their own decisions and in addition whether they have a justified expectation that their decisions will be respected by others. The merit of these aspects of autonomy was asserted by Loewy:

> Knowing that we are 'the captains of our fate', rather than surmising that we are the pawns of another (no matter how benevolent that other might be), is what most adults, at least in Western Culture, want.
>
> (Loewy, 1991)

It might plausibly be argued, then, that it is in a person's best interests that his or her decisions are respected. However, this may not be the approach that the courts take where competent children are concerned. Particularly in the context of refusal of treatment, respect for autonomy may be outweighed by the desire of courts to ensure children receive recommended medical treatment, even if such treatment is manifestly against the child's wishes and even if based on reasons accepted for competent adults, such as religious beliefs.

This requires holding that protective interests may outweigh the self-assertive interests of a child. Such a simple exposition, however, masks deeper and more complex questions. These include whether the threshold for respecting a person's decisions should be determined by age or by the individual's decision-making capacity. UK law sets both types of threshold and each has its own difficulties. Further issues involve whether the type of decision or its outcome should make a difference to the respect due to a person's choices. These will be explored in further detail in subsequent chapters. However, for the moment some of the potential problems may be illustrated by another quote from Mill, who, despite being a staunch advocate of individual liberty, stated that:

> It is, perhaps, hardly necessary to say that this doctrine is meant to apply only to human beings in the maturity of their faculties. We are not speaking of children, or of the young person below the age which the law may fix as that of manhood or womanhood. Those who are still in a state to require being taken care of by others, must be protected against their own actions as well as against external injury.
>
> (Mill, 1859, ch 1, para 10)

Taken as a whole, Mill's formulation implies that those below a legally set age still require supervision and, indeed, to have even autonomous decisions set aside if this is regarded as being for their benefit. This is an approach that persists strongly today although I will argue that it is unjustified. There are therefore clearly many issues to be considered in the application of the best interests test to healthcare decisions involving children. It must be borne in mind, however, that the vast majority of healthcare interventions are carried out with no court intervention and here is the place to consider the harm principle in further detail.

Parental responsibilities, best interests and the harm principle

The law sets out who is to be regarded as having parental responsibilities. Apart from the simple situation, where the child's father and mother are married to each other at the time of the birth and both will have parental responsibilities, others, such as unmarried fathers, can acquire them (Sutherland, 1999, ch 5; Bainham, 2005, ch 6). Any of them can act independently in meeting responsibilities to safeguard and protect the child.[42] The term 'parents' will be used to refer to those people having parental responsibilities.

Although the parental role is primarily defined in terms of responsibilities,

---

42 CA 1989 s 2(7), C(S)A 1995 s 2(2).

the concept of parental rights is not redundant. According legal rights to parents to make decisions on behalf of children is important to allow others to rely on them, particularly in the context of consent to medical treatment. In England and Wales the meaning of 'parental responsibility' is contained in s 3 of the CA 1989 and is said to be 'all the rights, duties, powers, responsibilities and authority which by law a parent of a child has in relation to the child and his property'. The content of these rights is not defined further and must be sought by looking at the common law. Undoubtedly, this includes the right to give a legally valid consent to treatment. Parental responsibilities subsist until the child reaches the age of 18.[43] This corresponds to the age of majority for most purposes[44] and is the same as that set by the UN Convention and most consistently adopted in Europe.

In Scotland the equivalent provisions are rather more specific and a parent has in relation to the child under s 1 C(S)A 1995 the responsibility:

(a) to safeguard and promote the child's health, development and welfare;

(b) to provide, in a manner appropriate to the stage of development of the child –
   (i)   direction;
   (ii) guidance, to the child;

(c) if the child is not living with the parent, to maintain personal relations and direct contact with the child on a regular basis; and

(d) to act as the child's legal representative

but only in so far as compliance with this section is practicable and in the interests of the child.[45]

In order to carry out their parental responsibilities, the C(S)A 1995 also gives parents corresponding rights, in particular to control, direct or guide, in a manner appropriate to the stage of development of the child, the child's upbringing and to act as the child's legal representative.[46] Here too, parents are empowered with rights to make decisions about their children, including giving consent to medical treatment. In contrast to England and Wales, the Scottish statute provides that all parental rights and most responsibilities end when the young person is 16.[47] However, the parental responsibility to provide direction and guidance lasts until the young person is 18.[48]

People who have the care of a child but do not have parental responsibility

43 CA1989 s 105.
44 Family Law Reform Act 1969 s 1(1).
45 C(S)A 1995 s 1(1).
46 C(S)A 1995 s 2(b) and (d).
47 C(S)A 1995 s 2(7) defines a child as a person under the age of 16.
48 C(S)A 1995 s 1(1).

for him or her may also do what is reasonable to safeguard or promote the child's welfare.[49] In Scotland, this expressly includes the ability for carers to give consent to any surgical, medical or dental treatment or procedure, provided that the child is not able to consent on his own behalf. However, it is subject to the proviso that the carer does not know that the child's parent would refuse to give the consent in question. Under the CA 1989, too, it may not be construed as 'reasonable' to agree to treatment that the carer is aware parents would object to.

Parents and the best interests of the child

Undoubtedly parents have always had legal rights in respect of their children and, although the original social purpose of this has been questioned, it has now become the norm to consider parental rights as being granted only to enable parents to fulfil duties towards their children (Eekelaar, 1986; Breen, 2002, chs 1 and 2). The courts have held that parents do not have independent rights that can give rise to actions for interference with their rights.[50] Interestingly, where parents have claimed that their views about their children's treatment have not been taken into account, this has been seen as a violation of the child's human rights under Article 8 of the ECHR, rather than the parents'.[51] Bainham points out that parents can bring actions against outsiders for interfering with the child's rights. They could also seek to prevent such interferences by making claims in respect of parental rights and responsibilities under the Children Acts, though these would be subject to the court's views on the best interests of the child, rather than on the rights of the parents. He concludes that parents have only a liberty to determine their children's upbringing. Equally, however, in order to override their decisions the onus is on others to satisfy a court that parental views should be displaced under the welfare principle (Bainham, 2005, pp 121–2).

Despite this, the paramountcy of the child's best interests is not the test that is applied to parents in their everyday decision-making about their children and the courts do not see themselves as having a role in supervising this.[52] A fundamental concept is that parents are presumed to be their children's best advocates, being, apart from the children themselves, the most intimately concerned with decisions made on their behalf. They are expected to know more about their own children than anyone else and to be in a position to take care of them on a day-to-day basis. We have seen already that children have a range of interests and it is assumed that most parents will do

49 CA 1989 s 3(5), CS(A) 1995 s 5.
50 *F v Wirral Metropolitan Borough Council* [1991] 2 All ER 648, CA.
51 *Glass v UK* [2004] 1 FCR 553, ECtHR.
52 *Re C (a minor) (leave to seek section 8 orders)* [1994] 1 FLR 26.

their best to meet them. Indeed, under the UN Convention, parents are expected to have their child's best interests as their basic concern.[53] It is also commonplace for guidance to healthcare professionals to state that parents must make decisions for their children in their best interests (Department of Health, 2001b, p 8; General Medical Council, 1998, para 24). However, except in limited circumstances, the standard imposed in practice seems less onerous.[54] A simple example may illustrate this. Immunisation has been described as 'one of the most important weapons for protecting individuals and the community from serious diseases' (Department of Health, 2007). It might therefore be expected that, unless there are specific contraindications for a child, it would be in his or her best interests to be immunised against childhood diseases. Nevertheless, this is not compulsory and parents are permitted to refuse on behalf of their children. Despite the view that this may not be in the best interests of the child or may even be against them, unless a court is asked to intervene it is within the range of decisions that parents can lawfully make.

There is a range of explanations as to why parents do not always have a legal responsibility to act in their children's best interests. One is that family life is largely regarded as falling within the private sphere. Outside interference in every exercise of parental decision-making to ensure that it is in what others consider to be the best interests of the child may be seen as unwarranted and counter-productive. Taking decision-making authority away from parents would undermine their confidence and ability to care for their children and consequently undermine the family itself, which is generally seen as being the best place for the rearing of children. Overseeing parents' daily decision-making would in any event be impossible for the State to effectively monitor and police (see, for example, the seminal work by Goldstein, *et al.*, 1980). In addition, there is the further argument that children do not develop in isolation but, in the main, will be cared for as part of families. Within families, parents must make decisions that will take into account the interests of all of those who will be affected and this may mean choosing between the competing interests of individual children and other family members. Again, parents may be thought best situated to make these kinds of evaluations and that this is necessary for the family to function effectively (Ross, 1998).

There is also the problem of determining what the best interests of the child require. This has been addressed earlier, but another way of looking at it can be from the parents' perspective. Here it can be said that there may be a great difference of opinion on what constitutes 'good parenting'. A range of different outcomes for the child may be viewed as being in the child's best interests, depending on the values and priorities given to particular aspects of

---

53 UN Convention, Article 18.
54 See Chapter 3 for such limitations in respect of children's refusal of consent.

child welfare and development. Seen in this light, parents should have the freedom to bring up their children according to their own values, provided that these do not seem likely to result in what is regarded as serious harm. Indeed it can be considered to be part of a social contract:

> It is a hallmark of a democratic society that while parents have the primary responsibility to look after their children, they are free to bring them up in the manner in which they deem best for the children's welfare.
>
> (Thomson, 2006, p 257)

Seen in this light, it is reasonable to suggest that courts should be slow to intervene unless parents are seeking to make a decision that it is believed may place their children at an unacceptable risk of harm or a dispute between them cannot be resolved. It should not be for the courts to make their own determination of what is in the child's best interests.

Parents and the harm principle

In a major treatise on this issue Dickens argues that 'the function of parenthood may appear to be the protection of children against physical, psychological, social and moral harm' (Dickens, 1981, p 464). It is of course the case that some parents may not be willing or able to provide care that is felt to be necessary and appropriate and the State may intervene, for example, under child protection provisions in the Children Acts. In England and Wales, the court may make orders that place a child under the care or supervision of a local authority.[55] They can only be made if the court is satisfied that the child is suffering, or is likely to suffer, significant harm that is attributable to the care being given not being what it would be reasonable to expect a parent to give to him or where the child is beyond parental control.[56] Such orders cannot be made once a child is 17 or 16, if married.[57] It is stated that:

> Where the question of whether harm suffered by a child is significant turns on the child's health or development, his health or development shall be compared with that which could reasonably be expected of a similar child.[58]

The terms harm, development, health and ill-treatment for the purposes of this section are defined in the Act.[59] If a care order is made, the local authority

---

55 CA 1989 s 31. See generally Part IV of the Act.
56 CA 1989 s 31(2).
57 CA 1989 s 31(3).
58 CA 1989 s 31(10).
59 CA 1989 s 31(9).

acquires parental responsibility for the child in addition to the parents, though it may allow them to continue to exercise parental responsibilities towards the child.[60] Care orders may be considered where, for example, parents refuse or are unable to discharge responsibilities on a long-term basis, such as where a child has a chronic illness requiring repeat medical attendance.[61] Supervision orders are more unlikely in the context of medical care.

Scotland has similar child protection provisions contained within the C(S)A 1995, under Part II, and the welfare of the child throughout childhood must be the court's and the local authority's paramount consideration.[62] However, in both jurisdictions courts are required not to make any order unless satisfied that doing so would be better than making no order at all.[63] Again, these provisions may be seen as representing a non-interventionist approach to parents' discretion to make decisions about their children. In Scotland, there is also the Children' Hearings System, which was developed to respond to children in need of assistance and deals with most criminal offences carried out by children as well as with situations where their health and welfare may be at risk. A Children's Hearing is not conducted by a judge, but a Children's Panel, which is composed of lay members and a legally qualified Chair. It has the power to make orders for compulsory measures of supervision of children where it is considered that they are likely either to suffer unnecessarily, or to suffer serious impairment in their health or development, due to lack of parental care.[64] Interestingly, the test here is not the best interests test, but a reasonableness one, that is to say whether a reasonable person could draw the inference of unnecessary suffering or serious impairment from the nature and extent of the parental lack of care.[65]

Parental failure to provide minimum standards of care can result in criminal liability, either as general or specifically child-centred offences. For example, offences can be committed where a person has the care of a child and:

> . . . wilfully assaults, ill-treats, neglects, abandons, or exposes him, or causes or procures him to be assaulted, ill-treated, neglected, abandoned, or exposed, in a manner likely to cause him unnecessary suffering or injury to health (including injury to or loss of sight hearing, or limb, or organ of the body, and any mental derangement) . . .

> . . . a parent or other person legally liable to maintain a child or young

60 CA 1989 s 33(3).
61 This kind of situation arose in *Finlayson, Applicant* [1989] SCLR 601 Sh Ct, although it was dealt with under the Children's Hearings System.
62 C(S)A 1995, ss 16 and 17.
63 CA 1989 s 1(5), C(S)A 1995 s 11(7)(a).
64 C(S)A 1995, s 52(2)(c).
65 *M v McGregor* 1982 SLT 41.

person . . . shall be deemed to have neglected him in a manner likely to cause injury to his health if he has failed to provide adequate food, clothing, medical aid or lodging for him, or if, having been unable otherwise to provide such food, clothing, medical aid or lodging, he has failed to take steps to procure it to be provided . . .[66]

The House of Lords (by a majority decision) has interpreted wilful neglect by failing to provide adequate medical aid as involving either subjective or reckless neglect.[67] Outside these basic duties, parents have a wide discretion to make decisions about and on behalf of their children. As such, Dickens describes a parental 'right' as being rather 'a parental discretion to act regarding a child in a way that others have a correlative duty to permit, or a duty to forbear from preventing' (Dickens, 1981, p 462). Grounds for interference once basic obligations towards the child have been met are relatively limited:

> Parental duties and related rights appear to be defined by reference not to the positive standard of achieving good for children but by reference to the negative standard of protecting children from harm. . . .

> Parental discretion can therefore be used 'to employ control over children for purposes not violating children's interests but equally not advancing their welfare or best interests.'

> (Dickens, 1981, p 464)

Bainham usefully borrows the 'Dworkinian doughnut' analogy to explain the scope of parental discretion. Dworkin has said of legal discretion, exercised by courts or other public officials, that it can only exist meaningfully 'when someone is in general charged with making decisions subject to standards set by a particular authority' and that 'like the hole in a doughnut' it 'does not exist except as an area left open by a surrounding belt of restriction' (Dworkin, 1977, p 52). Bainham suggests that:

> . . . parents have a large area of discretion to determine all manner of issues related to the upbringing of their children, but they are surrounded by a belt of restriction which requires them to ensure that children are given certain basic protections to meet the necessities of life.

> (Bainham, 2005, p 120)

Seen in this way, parents' decision-making will not be challenged unless it violates minimum standards, practically determined by agencies such as

---

66 Children and Young Persons Act 1933 s 1 and Children and Young Persons (Scotland) Act 1937, s 12.

67 *R v Sheppard* [1980] 3 All ER 899, HL. See also *R v Lowe* [1973] All ER 805, CCA.

social workers, police and the courts. In the case of healthcare, the role of doctors in challenging parental decisions is critical and their reasons for doing so will be explored later.

While parents have a moral, and indeed a statutory, responsibility to safeguard and promote their children's welfare, control over parental decision-making is generally exercised only where it is felt there will be a serious detrimental impact on the child or there is a disagreement between parents, which needs external resolution. It may be argued that Dickens' view is in fact less generous in its ascription of parents' discretionary powers than appears to be the case, since parents can even act against their child's interests, as viewed by others, provided that they do not come within the ring of restrictions based on basic obligations of child welfare. The immunisation example is relevant here. If his view is limited to where parents' decisions do not violate the child's basic interests, this seems more plausible. Although the way parental discretion is framed in the Scottish Children Act might seem to preclude taking decisions that are against the interests of the child, it does not seem that the breadth of decisions that can be made by Scottish parents is in fact any less than those south of the border.

In general, however, parents are free to make decisions and act without outside interference. As Fortin notes,

> Despite an attempt to liberalise the parent child relationship by a change of language [from parental rights to responsibilities] the [Children Act] 1989 . . . adopts a non-interventionist approach to family life.
>
> (Fortin, 2005, pp 8–9)

Similarly, support for the importance of family privacy can be found in the ECHR, Article 8, and as a general principle in the UN Convention. There is therefore widespread recognition of parents' entitlement to make decisions for their children, provided they do not act against their basic interests.

Given this, and taken with the objections to the best interests test raised earlier, my contention is that a preferable approach would be for the courts to apply the same approach in all circumstances where they are asked to consider parental decisions. For the reasons given above, the views of parents on what is right for their children should normally be respected unless they are likely to place them at an unacceptable risk of harm. Ross has advocated this kind of approach as a way of making healthcare decisions about children and adopted a model she describes as 'constrained parental autonomy' (Ross, 1998). She derives it from an approach to Kant's principle of respect for persons, so that while there is a general duty on people to avoid treating children solely as a means to an end and to avoid abusive behaviour towards them, parents have an additional duty to 'provide children with the primary goods necessary to become persons capable of devising and implementing their own plans' (Ross, 1998, p 11). Primary goods are explained as being based on the Rawlsian concept of 'what it is supposed a rational man would want, whatever else he wants', which would include social goods (rights and liberties), natural goods (health and vigour), basic liberties and self-respect (Rawls, 1971, p 92; Ross, 1998, p 16). As such, these are in line with the kinds of children's rights and interests already discussed (Eekelaar, 1986; Freeman, 1983; see, also, Dworkin, 1982). Ross contends that:

> The quantity and type of a particular primary good are mainly defined by parents who will give their children varying amounts of each good depending on their conception of the good life. Different parents will distribute different goods in different quantities and forms depending on their beliefs and values. In liberal communities, the state tolerates a wide range of distributions among families provided that the parents provide their children with a threshold level of each primary good. Parents require wide latitude to balance the health care needs of their child with the child's need for other primary goods and with the needs of other family members.
>
> (Ross, 1998, p 8)

Where parents do not respect the child and fail to provide for the child's basic needs the State should intervene, but to this extent only should parental autonomy be 'constrained'. Outside of this, in a liberal democracy that gives primary responsibility to parents to bring up children, they have the right to act in a way that accords with their own values and to promote interests of the family and all family members as they see fit. It also deals with the problems arising where there is more than one child involved, when applying an individualised best interests test may be impossible in practice (Jansen, 2004).

In many respects I share this view, in particular that a best interests test can fail to adequately take into account the legitimate role of parents in making decisions for their families and that a court should not impose its vision of what is in a child's best interests where this conflicts with the opinions of reasonable parents. In her application of this principle in particular treatment contexts, however, there are areas where I disagree with her conclusions. For example, I take issue with the consequences of Ross's model as she applies it to children's own wishes about medical treatment where she argues that, in most cases, it allows decisions of even competent children to be overridden by parents (Ross, 1998, ch 4). Nonetheless, broadly her framework denies the applicability of a best interests test to override parental decision-making, instead focusing on the basic needs of the child.

Diekema also believes that the best interests approach should be abandoned, at least in certain situations (Diekema, 2004). Building on Feinberg's version of the harm principle, that restricting an individual's freedom must be effective at preventing the harm in question and that there is no equally effective option that would be less intrusive to individual liberty (Feinberg, 1984, p 26), he suggests a number of criteria that should be satisfied before a State should override parents' decisions in the specific situation of refusing treatment of a child:

1. By refusing to consent are the parents placing their child at significant risk of serious harm?
2. Is the harm imminent, requiring immediate action to prevent it?
3. Is the intervention that has been refused necessary to prevent the serious harm?
4. Is the intervention that has been refused of proven efficacy, and therefore, likely to prevent the harm?
5. Does the intervention that has been refused by the parents not also place the child at significant risk of serious harm, and do its projected benefits outweigh its projected burdens significantly more favorably than the option chosen by the parents?
6. Would any other option prevent serious harm to the child in a way that is less intrusive to parental autonomy and more acceptable to the parents?
7. Can the state intervention be generalized to all other similar situations?
8. Would most parents agree that the state intervention was reasonable?
   (Diekema, 2004, p 252)

To the objection that terms like 'significant' and 'serious' face the same problems of indeterminacy as the best interests test, he concedes that there will always be an interpretive element in judging whether a parental decision crosses the threshold for State intervention. However, this is answered by arguing that this is not the biggest problem with the best interests standard. Instead, it is that this is the wrong standard. Since it is indeterminate what will be best for a child, parents should be able to judge this unless the harm threshold is breached.

Imminence of harm is set as a condition so that if it is not urgent to make the decision, alternatives can be explored with the family and health carers to try to meet an acceptable compromise. As far as possible, evidence is required to show that the option rejected by the parent really is likely to be effective in safeguarding the child's interests. No alternative that is less intrusive to parental autonomy must be available to achieve the same result, and interference with the parental decision must offer 'net benefit to the child'. The State intervention must be 'generalizable and impartial in the sense that all similar cases would also result in state intervention'. Finally, State intervention must be 'what other parents would agree is appropriate for all children' (Diekema, 2004, p 254). Diekema's model is directed only towards refusal of treatment by parents and requires some modification to be applicable to all types of healthcare procedures. Nevertheless, it provides useful guidance on the priority that should be given to parental autonomy and the need for clear and convincing evidence that it does not meet acceptable standards for child welfare before it can be overridden.

A proposed framework for parental decisions – the harm principle and reasonableness

Having considered the proposals by Ross and Diekema that support a move away from the best interests test for overriding parental decision-making on healthcare in favour of greater recognition of parental autonomy, elements of both inform my own. What I suggest is first that the threshold for court involvement should be based on a significant risk of serious harm to the child. It is this kind of conception I refer to as the harm principle. When assessing what kinds of harm are relevant to risk assessment, this should be approached by considering the effect of the decision on enforceable children's rights. This is consistent with the increased adoption of rights principles in respect of children and also takes into account the fact that they may have many intangible interests, not all of which can be translated into legal rights. These rights may be found in domestic and international law, such as the right to life and to be protected from unnecessary suffering or injury to health and development.

Where there is a significant risk of serious harm, there is also the question whether running such a risk is justified and this will need to take into account the reasons for doing so and the alternatives. In some cases, the scope of parental discretion will be fairly clear so that, for example, parents do not have the right to refuse routine, conventional treatment that will seriously damage the child's health. In others, the protection of the child's rights may require a court hearing, such as where a procedure is considered particularly controversial.

It is my second contention that the courts' role here should depend on whether the decision of the parents is within the bounds of reasonableness – if it is, then they should be free to reach a decision, even if it is one with which the court disagrees. If it is not, then the court can make its own decision, choosing the option that will provide the necessary protection of the child's interests, but at least cost to parental autonomy. In reaching a judgment, the courts should permit parents to take into account the rights of other family members and their own rights to determine the values that are important to them in raising their children, provided that these do not fall below societal standards for child welfare and compromise important rights of the individual child. In addition, for a final decision to be made now, it should be one that cannot reasonably be postponed. Diekema imposes this condition in the hope of reaching informal agreements but clearly, where this seems unlikely, court resolution may be required to provide certainty for all parties. I would also add here that it is necessary to consider whether a child could develop capacity to make a decision for him or herself. The courts should require convincing evidence of harms and benefits so far as this can be provided and, in particular, be prepared to regard medical evidence as being as open to challenge as any other. Decisions to override parental discretion should be based on principles that can be applied to other children in similar situations and that can be justified as setting appropriate boundaries for parental decision-making. Reasonableness of parental choices is the key, not the best interests of the child.

Arguably, it might not be necessary to abandon the best interests principle, if the courts were to hold that it could encompass upholding reasonable parents' views. There has been some support for this; so in an early case on withholding treatment from children, it was said that:

> In deciding in any given case what is in the best interests of the ward, the court adopts the same attitude as a responsible parent would do in the case of his or her own child; the court, exercising the duties of the Sovereign as parens patriae is not expected to adopt any higher or different standard than that which, viewed objectively, a reasonable and responsible parent would do.[68]

Despite this, in later cases courts have been keen to stress that it is not the reasonableness of the parent's decision, but the best interests of the child that are critical. So, for example, in a non-medical case, the question arose whether the courts should intervene if a mother were exercising her parental responsibilities bona fide and reasonably. Bingham MR said:

> I would for my part accept without reservation that the decision of a devoted and responsible parent should be treated with respect. It should certainly not be disregarded or lightly set aside. But the role of the court is to exercise an independent and objective judgment. If that judgment is in accord with that of the devoted and responsible parent, well and good. If it is not, then it is the duty of the court, after giving due weight to the view of the devoted and responsible parent, to give effect to its own judgment. That is what it is there for. Its judgment may of course be wrong. So may that of the parent. But once the jurisdiction of the court is invoked its clear duty is to reach and express the best judgment it can.[69]

This has also been endorsed in the medical context, where the reasonableness of the parents' decision has been said not to be the decisive factor, but what

---

68 *Re J (a minor) (wardship: medical treatment)* [1990] 3 All ER 930, CA. Balcombe J at 941.
69 *Re Z (a minor) (freedom of publication)* [1995] 4 All ER 961, CA, at 986.

the court considers to be in the best interests of the child.[70] I disagree with the courts' approach and propose instead that it should be made clear that it is significant risk of serious harm that the courts will protect children from, not decisions that fall within the range of a reasonable exercise of parental discretion. As noted previously, in some situations the law already accepts this. For example, in the case of blood tests to determine paternity it has been held that a reasonable parent, rather than a best interests, test applies. In interpreting this here, it was said that reasonable parents would not withhold consent to testing, even if this would not benefit the child, unless 'satisfied that it was against the child's interests'.[71] However, this situation is not one where the court is required to have the best interests of the child as its paramount consideration. My argument is that this approach should be extended to all healthcare decisions about a child.

In many cases, adopting these two principles, significant risk of harm and reasonableness of the decision, would not provide a different answer to that which would be reached by a best interests assessment, such as the earlier example of parents' refusal of conventional treatment. It must be remembered that these principles, too, are welfare-based tests and it should not be thought that they represent an abandonment of the interests of the child to the whim of cruel or inadequate parents. It is not a call to return to the kinds of contention notoriously expressed in *Re Agar Ellis* (1883) that the court had no right to interfere with the 'sacred right' of a father over his children.[72] Where decisions may prejudice important interests of the child it is right and proper that they are submitted to careful scrutiny to assess the validity of justifications for doing so, where such justifications may be in doubt. The harm principle permits this and indeed it provides a more consistent means of doing so. It recognises the general rule that parents are entitled to make decisions that they think are appropriate for their children, limited only where they may be placing them at an unacceptable risk. Having significant risk of serious harm as the threshold for scrutiny followed by an assessment of the reasonableness of the decision does not substitute an additional, different standard that allows the potential overruling of a choice that a reasonable parent could make. It prevents polarisation between all of those claiming to know what is best for the child by focusing on situations where serious risk to children outweighs benefits.

In doing so, it may be argued that it may in fact provide greater protection for children against potentially damaging parental choices, since it requires independent scrutiny where significant rights may be prejudiced, rather than

---

70 See, e.g. *Re T (a minor) (wardship: medical treatment)* (1996) [1997] 1 All ER 906, CA. *Re C (a child) HIV test* [1999] 3 FCR 289, Fam D. *Re A (children)(conjoined twins: surgical separation)* [2000] 4 All ER 961, CA.

71 *S v S; W v Official Solicitor* [1970] 3 All ER 107, HL, Per Lord Reid, 44. A similar Scottish authority is *Docherty and McGlynn* 1983 SLT 645.

72 *Re Agar Ellis* (1883) 24 Ch D 317, CA.

leaving this within the scope of medical practitioners and parents to agree what they think is in the child's best interests. A body of case law may be developed that makes it clear that the view of the courts will be that some rights of the child will always prevail over others, for example, that parents' religious beliefs will not be able to override a child's right to receive life-saving treatment. Accordingly, not all cases may need to come before a court once this area has been examined or is otherwise clear. However, where the legal position is less certain, it would require testing of the position in court and it would still allow cases to be brought, based on the particular circumstances of the child, even where there exist previous authorities on the rights engaged in the case. It is of course true that what rights are legally recognised and how they should be weighed may not be immune from criticism. It may also be suggested that requiring cases to be judicially considered places additional strain on families at what may be extremely distressing times, diverts doctors from their primary role of providing care and adds delays and expenses in pursuing legal review. There is force in these contentions. Nonetheless, it allows debate on the principles that are applicable, both in court and by the public, and where significant harms to the child are envisaged and there is doubt as to countervailing benefits, this must be regarded as a necessary part of the protection of young children. As Huxtable puts it, 'Recourse to an impartial arbiter certainly has its place, although even their answers will not and should not evade critical scrutiny'. (Huxtable, 2004).

Parents and competent children

While parents act as proxies to the extent that they can make legally binding decisions on behalf of the child, it seems they are not bound to make ones that they believe that the child would make for him or herself. Here it has been said that children need not only to be supported and cared for, but also subject to discipline and supervision, to enable them to grow into adults able to lead fulfilling lives and to contribute to society in a positive way (Purdy, 1992). Some restrictions on the choices of children are necessary and parents are usually considered best placed to make these decisions. For example, it has been suggested that:

> Children are not always or even usually the best judges of what is good for them, so much so that even the rights that are most important to their long-term well-being, such as the right to discipline or to a safe environment, they regularly perceive as being the reverse of rights or advantages. It does not follow that adults act well if they permit their children to waive those rights or if they enforce them only at their children's insistence.
>
> (MacCormick, 1982, p 166)

It could be contended, therefore, that parents are entitled to exercise a protective function over children, which persists up to the age at which the child is legally recognised as an adult. Ross takes this view and suggests that parents, under the principle of constrained parental autonomy, retain the right to make decisions for their children, even where they are competent (Ross, 1998, ch 4). She bases her approach on a number of grounds. First, she states that if competence were the only criterion, then distinguishing between adults and children would not be justified. She is however concerned that there is no easy test to distinguish between those who are competent and incompetent, and that to require individual tests of competency for all people undergoing medical procedures would be inefficient and in fact undermine privacy and respect for autonomy. She considers that respecting children's wishes would respect their short-term autonomy at the expense of lifetime autonomy and that children should have a protected period in which to develop that will advance their future opportunities. In any event, she doubts children's capacity to make decisions because of their limited life-experience, which makes it difficult for their choices to be part of a 'well-conceived life plan'. While it may be contended that children should at least have the right to make decisions if these accord with other people's ideas of what is best for them, she argues that this is not to respect autonomy, but to make a farce of it. She also sees problems in the extent to which children may be swayed by others and thus not meet the requirement for decisions to be arrived at freely and independently. In addition, she maintains that parents' rights to promote family interests and their own views of what is appropriate for their children persist until emancipation. Although parents may, therefore, see allowing competent children to make their own decisions as what is best for the child, this should be voluntary and parents should be able to override their decisions. Accordingly, she advocates that in almost all cases, children should be regarded as incompetent and that parents be the source of legal decision-making for them. Courts should only be able to intervene, subject to the same conditions as before, that parents are not providing for the basic needs of the child and it is this level of protection that is required.

As noted earlier, while there are points with which I agree with Ross, her conclusion here is not one that I share. My position is that parents are entitled to make decisions for children only because children cannot do so for themselves. Accordingly, competent children's views about medical procedures should take precedence over their parents'. This is based on the belief that one of the most important aspects of the parental role is to foster the skills and abilities in children that will enable them to become autonomous decision-makers. Once this has been achieved, parents may continue to advise, but should not be able to dictate. I concede that it may be appropriate to set a dividing line for where competence can be presumed for the reasons given by Ross. However, this threshold should be set only to distinguish between where competence is presumed and where it requires to be demonstrated. I also acknowledge that what the standard for competence is and how this should be established in an individual case is by no means free from difficulty, but that should not permit blanket denial of what is generally considered to be a crucial right: to determine what is done to one's body. Parents may have a legitimate role in continuing to set parameters for children even where they are able to make decisions for themselves, for example, that may constrain rights such as liberty and freedom of association by requiring children to be home by a certain time. Nonetheless, this should not extend to making decisions about whether medical interventions can be permitted or prevented. Such decisions concern people's rights to be self-governing over the most intimate of all matters and once children are competent, it is not for others to override them, save in circumstances that would be allowed for adults.

There has been some legal endorsement of limitation of parental rights over competent children who can consent to treatment, provided the treatment is said to be in their best interests. Parents do not have a right even to be informed that medical advice has been sought in these circumstances.[73] However, it has been held that parents can override a refusal of consent by a competent child.[74] I agree with Ross that this misunderstands the purpose of allowing others to consent on behalf of children, since it makes what the others see as being in the best interests of the child the criterion rather than respect for autonomy. Unlike her, however, I consider that parents' autonomy should be constrained where it seeks to intervene in competent children's decisions too. These different approaches to the functions and limits of parental decision-making in the healthcare context will be explored further in subsequent chapters.

The role of doctors

The discussion thus far has concentrated on the role of parents, the courts and competent children in making decisions about medical treatment. One last group of utmost importance is of course doctors themselves. Doctors have a central part to play, not only in providing care, but also in determining what medical procedures they are willing and able to provide. They will also be, in the first instance at least, the ones who are expected to question decisions made by parents or children, where they feel these raise issues of concern. Doctors are of course expected to promote and protect health and to offer the care they believe is most appropriate. The courts have thus far refused to compel doctors to provide treatment they feel is against their professional judgement and this provides a major practical limitation on the scope of choices that parents and children may make.[75] On the other hand,

---

73 *Gillick v West Norfolk and Wisbech Area Health Authority* [1985] 3 All ER 402, HL.
74 *Re W (a minor) (medical treatment)* [1992] 4 All ER 627, CA.
75 *Re J (a minor) (wardship: medical treatment)* [1990] 3 All ER 930, CA; *Wyatt v Portsmouth Hospital NHS Trust* [2005] EWCA Civ 1181, CA.

doctors are not free to treat in any way they choose. They must work within the framework of the law, which generally requires a legally valid consent and may restrict the type of interventions that can be undertaken with or without court scrutiny.

However, since doctors will be at the coalface when treatment decisions arise, some separate consideration of the way they may approach them is appropriate. Rhodes and Holzman provide a useful discussion of this issue (Rhodes and Holzman, 2004). Where adults are concerned, the principle of respect for autonomy means that a competent refusal of consent must be respected. A competent consent may or may not be complied with, depending on the doctor's view of the procedure. However, Rhodes and Holzman explain that their professional responsibility to protect patients means that in some cases there is a need to enquire whether the choice of the patient is sufficiently autonomous. If the choice is impaired and does not truly represent the values, beliefs and preferences of the individual, then their decisions need not be acted on if they will lead to serious harm. This necessitates some enquiry into people's reasons for their choice. Building on Scanlon's work they suggest there are three concentric domains of reasons that autonomous agents can use to explain their decisions:

Central core – reasons people everywhere could not reasonably reject.
Second domain – particular core reasons reasonable people could prioritise differently.
Third domain – reasons others could reject without being unreasonable.
(Rhodes and Holzman, 2004, p 372. See, also, Scanlon, 1998, pp 358–9)

As illustrations of these principles in practice they suggest that accepting treatment that is likely to preserve life would fall within the first domain, since this can be taken to be a decision that all reasonable people would approve. However, more than one core value may operate, so that treatment to prolong life might carry with it significant pain and disability. Here, a decision would fall into the second domain and reasonable people could differ on the priority to be given to these factors. The third domain would concern, for example, decisions to refuse life-saving treatment for aesthetic or religious views. These rest on individual values that other reasonable people may not share and have no reason to accept.

Where competent adults are concerned, reasons from any three of the domains should be respected. However, where serious harm may result from the decision, doctors are justified in seeking firm evidence that the person is in fact making a choice based on their own values and beliefs and is not being affected by factors such as illness, undue influence or misunderstanding. Where surrogates, such as parents, are making decisions, only reasons from the first two domains should be accepted. Reasons from the third domain should not, because they do not depend on universal values and hence should not allow an individual who has not endorsed those values to be put at serious risk.

They further illustrate this approach by putting treatment decisions into three categories as follows:

1. Likely poor outcomes – regardless of interventions
2. Uncertain or not dramatically different outcomes – including lack of significant consequences
3. Likely good outcomes – significant treatment benefit while refusal likely to cause significant harm

(Rhodes and Holzman, 2004, pp 376–7)

Category three treatments can be refused by a competent patient, but not a surrogate, as they are paradigmatically unreasonable. Category two can be refused by surrogates since reasonable people could make different decisions here. They are less clear about category one, only suggesting that doctors should encourage palliative care as this would be regarded by most people as the humane response (Rhodes and Holzman, 2004, p 375). Whether they can reject a surrogate's decision to seek treatment is not spelled out, but is probably implied. In addition, they also suggest that in judging surrogates' decisions, their motives may also be relevant. So, for example, if parents do not seem to be concerned with the child's wellbeing, then their appropriateness to act on behalf of their children can be challenged.

In adopting a 'not unreasonable' standard for surrogates, this analysis seems to broadly follow the approach I have suggested. The idea that reasonable parents may differ in their weighing of competing values and have the right to make decisions for their children is maintained. If competent children are included within the scope of respect for autonomy, it is also consistent. Here it may be argued that given the fact that children need to develop autonomy and will do so at different ages, where they are under a legally set threshold, their decisions may justifiably be scrutinised more carefully than those of adults to ensure they can properly be relied on. However, the important point to note here is that Rhodes and Holzman are not attempting to define what the courts should do when faced with medical treatment decisions, only the way that doctors should consider these issues. In practice, the courts have in almost all cases supported doctors' views, considering them to represent the best interests of the child. My contention is that the courts should instead adopt a reasonableness standard, but that in addition they have an important function in delineating what, in our society, are deemed to be within the scope of clinical and parental discretion. Similarly, I consider that if children are deemed to have sufficient autonomy, the courts should accept that the principle of respect for autonomy should apply equally to them.

Conclusion

Having set out the broad framework in which decisions about children are made, I return to my contention that the rationale for the use of the best interests standard as a means of protecting children is in truth more limited than it might seem. Where people are making decisions for those who lack capacity there are legitimate reasons for placing limits on their choices. However, as we have seen, a largely non-interventionist approach predominates and parents are allowed a wide discretion to make decisions for children who are incapable of doing so. This is likely to be restricted only where it is believed that they are placing their children at a significant risk of serious harm.

Where cases concerning parental decisions do come before the courts, they may take a view that differs from parents. The question remains whether, even so, that is sufficient for them to substitute it. After all, many parents who disagree with medical practitioners, or with each other, will claim that they know what is best for the child. I suggest that the harm and reasonableness principles provide a more appropriate standard to decide when courts should overrule healthcare decisions by parents. In some cases it will be clear that parents are entitled to make the choice, but in others the scope of parental discretion may require judicial consideration. Where there is a range of decisions that a reasonable parent could make, the court should not substitute its own view of what is in the child's best interests.

Second, I propose that approaches of the law that seek to prevent competent children from exercising autonomy in healthcare situations are problematic and require reconsideration. If the reason authority is given to make decisions on behalf of children is because of their incapacity, then once capacity is achieved the need for that authority ceases to exist. Respect for autonomy should extend to all those capable of exercising it and should not be subject to age-based constraints that have no sound basis and are unjustifiably discriminatory. While no doubt stemming from entirely worthy intentions, responsible parents and competent children do not require supervision by the use of the best interests test.

That is not to suggest that the protection of children is unnecessary or that there are easy solutions. Children, parents, healthcare professionals and the judiciary are often faced with difficult tasks in making decisions that those of us looking from the outside should not underestimate. In such circumstances, balancing competing rights and attempting to find a solution that will satisfy everyone is likely to be asking the impossible. Nevertheless, their decisions and the legal framework in which they are made deserve examination where such important matters are concerned and I seek to do this here. The following chapters will explore these issues in more detail in specific situations: consent and refusal of treatment; withholding or withdrawing treatment from infants and young children; medical research and where medical procedures involve more than one child.

Chapter 2

Best interests and consent

The requirement of consent to treatment

Prior consent to medical treatment is now regarded as essential to healthcare practice. Indeed it has been said that since the 1970s, promoting and protecting autonomy within healthcare has become one of the major concerns of bioethics (see, for example, Flamm and Forster, 2000, p 142). It includes protection of the right to bodily integrity and freedom of choice. It is also an important legal issue and the position on this has been clearly stated:

> It is trite law that, in general, a doctor is not entitled to treat a patient without the consent of someone who is authorised to give that consent. If he does so, he will be liable in damages for trespass to the person and may be guilty of a criminal assault.[1]

It must be remembered, though, that consent may be necessary, but not sufficient to make actions lawful.[2] While consent is an essential element in surgeons' immunity from criminal or civil actions, it has been observed that:

> ... it cannot be a direct explanation for it, since much of the bodily invasion involved in surgery lies well above any point at which consent could even arguably be regarded as furnishing a defence. Why is this so? The answer must in my opinion be that proper medical treatment, for which actual or deemed consent is a prerequisite, is in a category of its own.[3]

---

1 *Re R (a minor) (wardship: medical treatment)* [1991] 4 All ER 177, CA, 183 per Lord Donaldson MR. In Scotland, the equivalent would be a civil assault, *Smart v HMA* 1975 SLT 65.
2 *Smart v HMA* 1975 SLT 65, *R v Brown* [1993] 2 All ER 75, HL. *Laskey, Jaggard and Brown v UK* (1997) 24 EHHR 29, ECtHR.
3 *R v Brown* [1993] 2 All ER 75, HL, per Mustill LJ at 109.

It is thus the purpose of the procedure that renders it within the category of conduct that can be consented to. In addition, even if procedures can be lawfully provided, this does not mean that they must in all cases be undertaken. Within these limitations, however, the principle of adult self-determination over treatment had been described as a basic human right long before the Human Rights Act 1998 (HRA 1998).[4] It is now supported in the UK by provisions such as Article 8 of the European Convention on Human Rights (ECHR); the right to respect for private and family life.[5] This right exists, even where decisions may be thought unwise by others and even though they may involve risk to the adult's health or even result in death, provided that they fall within the parameters outlined above. However, for those undoubtedly incapable of exercising personal autonomy, respect for their present choices cannot be the guiding principle and parents usually have the legal responsibility and right to give consent for their young children. In what circumstances, then, should the courts decide that children need protection from parental decisions? While presently this rests on the best interests test, it will be argued here that the two principles I propose provide a better justification.

Where older children are concerned, not only may there be practical difficulties in determining what standard should be set for recognising the autonomy of a child or young person, but there may be objections that in fact, even if they meet it, they should still be subject to protection from decisions that others regard as being unwise. Nonetheless, where children are able to demonstrate competence, my contention is that their decisions should be respected and that the best interests principle is inapplicable. Respect for autonomy should be given priority and prevent parents and courts from substituting their decisions for those of the child. The position where children lack capacity will be considered first, followed by children who may be regarded as capable of giving their own consent. The majority of cases in this chapter have arisen in England and Wales, but where there may be important differences in principle in Scotland, these will be raised.[6]

Consent for children who lack capacity

Clearly, babies and very young children cannot meet standards of decision-making involving matters such as an understanding of treatment options, the ability to weigh them and to express a choice, which is what is usually expected of adults.[7] Consent may be given on children's behalf by their

---

4   *Sidaway v Bethlem Royal Hospital Governors* [1985] 1 All ER 643, HL, per Lord Scarman at 649.
5   See, e.g. *YF v Turkey* [2004] 39 EHHR 34, ECtHR. See also *X and Y v the Netherlands* (1985) EHRR 235, ECtHR.
6   Some parts in this chapter are adapted from Elliston, 1996.
7   *Re C (adult: refusal of medical treatment)* [1994] 1 All ER 819, Fam D.

parents, acting as their legally authorised representatives, under the Children Act 1989 (CA 1989) or the Children (Scotland) Act 1995 (C(S)A 1995). Their right to act in this capacity has been endorsed under Article 8 of the ECHR, where it is seen as an aspect of protection of the rights to private life of the child.[8] It is also the approach taken in Article 6 of the European Convention on Biomedicine (ECB), although the UK is not a signatory. Where parents consent to medical treatment of their young children, cases seldom reach the courts. External scrutiny is not felt necessary because ordinarily parents are agreeing to a course of treatment proposed by medical practitioners who are willing to provide it and where the child's opinion, even if capable of being given, has no legal effect. Parental consent to treatment is seen as simply part of the normal care of the child, securing important rights to health and welfare, and to be within the scope of parental discretion. Exactly how far this discretion extends, however, requires some consideration.

Basic requirements for parental decision-making

Of course, one preliminary issue must be dealt with and that is the capacity of parents to make treatment decisions on their children's behalf. It would seem necessary that parents, like anyone asked to give consent to treatment, should be competent, have adequate information and make their decision voluntarily. While these conditions will be explored in more detail in the context of children's decision-making capacity, below, a few points are worth mentioning here. There may be circumstances in which there are doubts about whether parents meet the requisite conditions. In the first place, this may be questioned where a parent is him/herself, a child. In law, no matter the age of parents, they have parental responsibilities and rights.[9] However, the Department of Health (DoH) advises that:

> If the mother is herself under 16, she will only be able to give valid consent for her child's treatment if she herself is 'Gillick competent' to take the decision in question . . . Whether or not she is able to give valid consent on behalf of her child may therefore vary, depending on the complexity of the decision to be taken.
>
> (DoH, 2001b, p 7)

The same would presumably be true for a similarly young father if he has acquired parental responsibilities. Second, the circumstances in which the parents' consent may be sought may be thought to preclude competence. An example given by the DoH would be where parents of a seriously ill child are

---

8   *Glass v UK* [2004] 1 FCR 553, (2004) 39 EHRR 15, ECtHR at para 70.
9   See, for example, *Birmingham City Council v H (a minor)* [1994] 1 All ER 12, HL.

not able properly to consider the information they are given because of extreme distress (Department of Health, 2001b, p 17). Other factors may affect competence, such as mental illness or disorder, or the influence of drugs, but where parents are 16 or older, their competence would normally be presumed.

Next, it is a legitimate expectation that for parents to carry out their responsibilities they need 'the fullest possible account of what is proposed, the alternatives, the risks and the possible outcomes' (Bristol Royal Infirmary Inquiry, 2001, ch 29, para 18). This is supported by guidance to professionals (Department of Health, 2001b, p 8). Some concerns have surfaced about the quality of information given to parents, both in terms of what is disclosed and how it is presented, and recommendations have been made to try to improve this (Bristol Royal Infirmary Inquiry, 2001, ch 23). Part of the reason for failures in communication may be a wish by professionals to avoid upsetting parents, and the lack of training in providing information to parents in an appropriate way has also been highlighted (Simons, 2000). Unless adequate information is provided, any consent given may be either wholly invalid or may give rise to an action in negligence. In this event, parents could pursue civil actions on their children's behalf.

Parents' decisions must also be sufficiently voluntary. The General Medical Council (GMC) recognises the potential for doctors to influence decisions and states:

> It is for the patient, not the doctor, to determine what is in the patient's own best interests. Nonetheless, you may wish to recommend a treatment or a course of action to patients, but you must not put pressure on patients to accept your advice. In discussions with patients, you should:
>
> – give a balanced view of the options;
> – explain the need for informed consent.
>
> (General Medical Council, 1998, para 15)

When advising parents, it is not the patient's own view of what is best that is at issue and it might be suggested that a higher level of persuasion might be called for where doctors believe a child should have treatment. However, any consent obtained from parents as a result of improper pressure would be invalid and where rational persuasion has not worked, doctors must simply accept, however reluctantly, that this is the parents' view. Disagreements may then need to be resolved through the courts. The consequences where parents are unable or refuse to consent will be discussed in Chapter 3.

One other point that may be reiterated here is where there may be doubt about the motives of parents and whether they are sufficiently concerned with the child's welfare, for example because of their apparent lack of interest and involvement (Rhodes and Holzman, 2004, pp 380–1). Ross shares this concern and her 'constrained parental autonomy' model presupposes what she describes as an 'intimate family' where the wellbeing of the child is a central concern of the parents (Ross, 1998, ch 2). Where this condition is not made out, there may be a need to take steps to appoint other legally author-ised people to make decisions for the child, such as through care proceedings (for further discussion on medical negligence and consent see, for example, Mason and Laurie, 2006; Jackson, 2006).

The parameters for parental consent

Once these basic requirements for parental decision-making have been met, the next question is precisely how wide parental discretion is. Of course, it would be quite impossible and highly undesirable to require court involve-ment every time a child needs medical treatment. Quite apart from the fact that this would be impracticable and in most cases would result in a mere rubber-stamping of the parents' decision, it is contrary to the general prin-ciple that ordinarily parents are believed to be best placed to make decisions for their children, in part, based on assumptions that they will want what is best for their child, but in part because of the non-interventionist policy that has been described. If doctors and parents are in agreement over a proposed course of action then generally treatment will proceed without any judicial oversight. Even where parents are not united over treatment, the onus is upon the parent who objects to bring the matter before the courts, since all those with parental responsibilities share them and can act independently.[10] So it has been said that:

> If the parents disagree, one consenting and the other refusing, the doctor will be presented with a professional and ethical but not with a legal problem because, if he has the consent of one authorised person, the treatment will not without more constitute a trespass or criminal assault.[11]

This appears to endorse the default position being that recommended medical treatment should be given. It safeguards the legal position of the doctor wishing to provide it if s/he can proceed with the agreement of only one parent, rather than needing both to consent. It might be suggested that if a doctor is prepared to undertake treatment, that should be treated as conclusive grounds for believing that it will not be harmful to the child. After all, it has been said to be a basic precept of medical ethics in the Hippocratic tradition

10 CA 1989 s 2(5) and (7), C(S)A 1995 s 2(2).
11 *Re R (a minor) (wardship: medical treatment)* [1991] 4 All ER 177, CA, per Lord Donaldson MR at 184.

that a practitioner should 'to the best of his ability do [patients] good and he must do nothing which he knows will cause harm' (Mason and Laurie, 2006, para 1.24). If it may not be possible to improve the patient's condition, at least nothing should be done that is likely to be considered harmful. Doctors are bound by rules of professional practice and can be subject to sanctions if they breach them (General Medical Council, 2006). However, medical practice may not always be in accordance with societal expectations, as was seen in the case of the retained organs inquiry (Retained Organs Commission, 2002) and in any event must be subject to the law. Simply because treatment is in accordance with professional practice cannot be the sole determinant for allowing parents to consent to it.

It has been said that where a child is unable to make a reasoned decision about the desirability of treatment, there are two broad common-law propositions:

> The first of these propositions is that parental authority exists to authorise [treatment] for the purpose, and only for the purpose, of advancing the welfare of the child. It does not extend to authorising surgery because of a perception that it is in the interests of those responsible for the care of the child or in the interests of society in general (e.g. for eugenic reasons). That which constitutes the welfare of a child in a particular case falls to be determined by reference to general community standards, but making due allowance for the entitlement of parents, within the limits of what is permissible in accordance with those standards, to entertain divergent views about the moral and secular objectives to be pursued for their children.

> The second broad proposition is that, at least in relation to a serious matter such as a major medical procedure, parental authority can be validly exercised only after due inquiry about, and adequate consideration of, what truly represents the welfare of the child in all the circumstances of the case.[12]

In the ordinary case, the assumption is that by consenting to recommended treatment, parents are thereby safeguarding or promoting the welfare of their children, or at least not acting sufficiently against community standards to require independent scrutiny. At this end of the spectrum of parental decision-making, routine diagnosis and treatment for childhood ailments, such as consenting to X-rays to check for fractures or the prescription of antibiotics, are unlikely to be challenged, even though they may expose a child to risks. For example, anyone may have idiosyncratic reactions to medicines, no

---

12 *Secretary, Dept of Health and Community Services v JWB and SMB* (1992) 175 CLR 218, at 295.

matter how commonly they are prescribed. Even where major surgery is concerned, therapeutic intent and conventional treatment are usually taken to provide sufficient justification to leave decisions in the hands of parents acting on medical advice. Indeed, it is where parents refuse consent or fail to seek treatment that this is much more likely to be disputed. Applying the concentric domains approach set out in the previous chapter, accepting routine medically recommended treatment is generally taken to be within the central core of reasons for decisions that all reasonable people would approve (Rhodes and Holzman, 2004; Scanlon, 1998). At the other end of the spectrum, certain medical procedures are unlawful, even with parental consent and even if a doctor was willing to perform it, such as female circumcision, unless on medical grounds.[13] Some other statutory and common-law prohibitions, for example, concerning live organ donation, raise specific issues and will be considered in later chapters. However, the law has determined that certain procedures cannot fall within the scope of personal choice for oneself, let alone that of proxy decision-makers. The difficulty lies in-between, in determining in what circumstances court involvement is required and when a court should override parental consent. I suggest that the two principles I propose provide a stronger basis for approaching these questions than the best interests test.

The application of the harm and reasonableness principles

Here we are concerned with assessing the potential harms of a proposed medical intervention, compared with not performing it. I have suggested that in some cases, clinical willingness to perform a procedure and parental consent may not be sufficient. Some factors may take it outside the norms of routine medical treatment. These would include where proposed treatment is unusual in children, untested, may be premature, or where therapeutic intent is not the primary justification for performing it, and any of them may be sufficient alone or in combination. The harm principle would suggest that where the nature and consequences of the intervention are sufficiently serious, external review is required to ensure that significant interests of the child are protected. These need not be confined to health consequences, but could encompass any factors thought to impact upon the welfare of the child. As a result of its review, a court may decide that a reasonable parent could properly give consent. For example, the child's right to bodily integrity and to protection from distress and pain, will need to be balanced against other rights, such as the protection of health and development of the child, and the right of parents to make decisions affecting not just the child, but the family. However, having these as thresholds for court intervention leaves

---

13 Female Genital Mutilation Act 2003, Prohibition of Female Genital Mutilation (Scotland) Act 2005.

intact parental discretion to make decisions that are widely accepted as being within societal boundaries but recognises that clear, objectively agreed justifications may be needed where decisions may fall outside them.

While there has been little case law where parents' consent to medical intervention on a child by a willing doctor has been challenged, *Re D (a minor)* (1976) provides a useful example. It involved an 11-year-old girl with a condition causing some physical and mental impairment. Her mother was concerned that D might be seduced and become pregnant. She felt D would be unable to care for a child, which might also have abnormalities, and wished her daughter to be sterilised. The paediatrician responsible for D's medical care agreed and a gynaecologist was prepared to undertake the operation. Others having a role in D's wider care successfully applied to make D a ward of court. D's paediatrician had contended that this operation was one that fell within the scope of his sole clinical discretion, provided he had the parent's consent. Heilbron J did not agree:

> I cannot believe, and the evidence does not warrant the view, that a decision to carry out an operation of this nature performed for non-therapeutic purposes on a minor can be held to be within the doctor's sole clinical judgment.[14]

The court reviewed evidence on D's condition and prognosis and concluded that her understanding and capacity might improve to the extent that she would be able to marry and be capable of considering whether to be sterilised for herself. Given the uncertainty of her future and the major step that permanently removing her reproductive capacity would involve, it was held that sterilisation would not be in her best interests.

Despite the concerns raised by this case, however, it must be emphasised that had other people involved with the child not applied to the courts, the operation would almost certainly have been performed as clearly both the doctors responsible for the child's care and her mother were firmly of the opinion that it was within their power to proceed and represented what they felt was best for her. Subsequent case law recommended that, as a matter of good practice, virtually all proposed sterilisations of minors should have the prior authorisation of the High Court in England and Wales.[15] Indeed it was said that a doctor failing to do so and performing a sterilisation operation simply with the consent of the parents might be liable in criminal, civil or professional proceedings.[16] This was reinforced by the Official Solicitor's Practice Note: Sterilisation 1996. It stated that:

---

14 *Re D (a minor) (wardship: sterilisation)* (1976) 1 All ER 326, Fam D, at 335.
15 *Re B (a minor) (wardship: sterilisation)* [1987] 2 All ER 206, HL. *Re F v West Berkshire Health Authority* [1989] All ER 545, HL.
16 *Re B (a minor: wardship sterilisation)* [1987] 2 All ER 206, HL, per Templeman LJ at 214.

The purpose of the proceedings is to establish whether or not the proposed sterilisation is in the best interests of the patient. The judge will require to be satisfied that those proposing the sterilisation are seeking it in good faith and that their paramount concern is for the best interests of the patient rather than their own or the public's convenience. The proceedings will normally involve a thorough adversarial investigation of all possible viewpoints and any possible alternatives to sterilisation.

[para 8]

The involvement of the courts here has been supported as follows:

If the question whether the operation is in the best interests of the . . . minor is left to be decided without the involvement of the court there may be a greater risk of it being decided wrongly or at least of it being thought to have been decided wrongly. If there is no involvement of the court, there is a risk of the operation being carried out for improper reasons or with improper motives. The involvement of the court in the decision to operate, if that is the decision reached, will serve to protect the doctor or doctors who performed the operation and any others who may be concerned in it from subsequent adverse criticism or claims.

(Harper, 1999, p 107)

Whether the judiciary is capable of deciding what is in a child's best interests any more than parents, is of course a matter on which opinions may differ considerably. Kennedy, for example, has argued that it is not in fact a 'test', but a 'crude conclusion of social policy' which allows the courts to believe that they are applying a principled approach while avoiding any detailed analysis of what the best interests are and what weight should be given to them (Kennedy, 1991, p 90). While there may still be some truth in this, over the last 15 years, subsequent case law and practice directions have sought to clarify what courts should consider when sterilisation of incompetent people is proposed and to provide some means of evaluating the competing interests involved.

The courts have stated that decisions about treatment for incompetent patients should take a two-stage approach. First, that the treatment proposed must as a minimum meet the standards laid out in the *Bolam v Friern Hospital Management Committee* (1957),[17] so that it is in accordance with responsible medical practice. Second, it must still be considered as a separate issue whether treatment is in the patient's best interests.[18] It had been previously

17 *Bolam v Friern Hospital Management Committee* [1957] 2 All ER 118, QB D.
18 *Re SL (adult patient) (medical treatment)* [2000] 2 FCR 452, sub nom *Re S (adult patient: sterilisation)*, CA, per Dame Butler-Sloss P at 464.

asserted that when dealing with incompetent adults, that sterilisation would be in the best interests of the patient provided that it met the *Bolam* standard.[19] While this proposition has never been applied to any cases concerning children, using purely a negligence standard to assess whether treatment should be provided is clearly unsatisfactory and this position has been retreated from as a general principle. In assessing the patient's best interests, a passage from the case of *Re A* (2000) has been influential and is worth quoting in full:

> There can be no doubt in my mind that the evaluation of best interests is akin to a welfare appraisal. . . . Pending the enactment of a checklist or other statutory direction it seems to me that the first instance judge with the responsibility to make an evaluation of the best interests of a claimant lacking capacity should draw up a balance sheet. The first entry should be of any factor or factors of actual benefit. In the present case the instance would be the acquisition of foolproof contraception. Then on the other sheet the judge should write any counterbalancing disbenefits to the applicant. An obvious instance in this case would be the apprehension, the risk and the discomfort inherent in the operation. Then the judge should enter on each sheet the potential gains and losses in each instance making some estimate of the extent of the possibility that the gain or loss might accrue. At the end of that exercise the judge should be better placed to strike a balance between the sum of the certain and possible gains against the sum of the certain and possible losses. Obviously, only if the account is in relatively significant credit will the judge conclude that the application is likely to advance the best interests of the claimant.[20]

While this statement was also made in a case concerning an adult's sterilisation, it has been supported as being applicable to children with necessary modifications 'not least of which being the weight to be given to parents' wishes.'[21] This may seem to be rather a mechanistic approach to the evaluation of the child's interests and still gives room for differences of opinion on the factors brought into the assessment, their probability and the weight given to them. Despite this, it does go some way towards greater transparency and appears more in line with the requirements of the HRA 1998. This will be returned to, particularly in the context of withholding and withdrawing

---

19 *Re F v West Berkshire Health Authority* [1989] All ER 545, HL.
20 *Re A (medical treatment: male sterilisation)* [2000] 1 FCR 193, CA, per Thorpe LJ at 206.
21 *Wyatt v Portsmouth Hospitals NHS Trust* [2004] EWHC 2247 Fam D, per Hedley J. See, also, *Re L (a minor)* [2004] EWHC 2713, Fam D and *A NHS Trust v MB* [2006] EWHC 50, Fam D.

treatment, but where sterilisation is proposed there has also been greater clarification of the factors that a court ought to consider.

So, where a child's life or health are at immediate risk by delaying surgery, such as where there is cancer of the reproductive organs, it has been said that court involvement is unlikely to be necessary, since there is a strong therapeutic justification for proceeding.[22] Preserving reproductive capacity is not unreasonably seen as being a lower priority in such cases. While it has been held that the courts will not make a distinction between therapeutic and non-therapeutic reasons for permitting sterilisation to be undertaken, it does provide a ground for distinguishing between whether it requires court involvement or not.[23] If the reasons for sterilisation are anywhere near the boundary line, however, they should be referred to the courts.[24] Where therapeutic intent does not provide the primary justification for sterilisation, the courts must assess the risk of pregnancy, the potential psychological damage of pregnancy and birth compared with sterilisation, and alternative methods of contraception.[25] The trend in relation to sterilisations appears to be increasingly to avoid them unless there is a real likelihood of pregnancy occurring and even if there is, to seek less intrusive and permanent alternatives.[26] There has also been an attempt to provide a more evidence-based approach for the courts' judgments.[27] In addition, clearly mindful of *Re D* (1976), it has been cautioned that 'In the case of a minor her youth and potential for development may make it difficult or impossible to make the relevant finding of incapacity.'[28] The present views of the child must not be forgotten either. The importance of encouraging a child's participation in decision-making to the extent appropriate to his or her age and understanding is a right expressed in the UN Convention. The Children Acts state that the courts must consider children's views when making decisions about them and this requirement also extends to parents in Scotland. In the medical context the same position is widely recognised in professional guidance (Department of Health, 2001a and b; British Medical Association, 2001; GMC, 1998). While there may be additional difficulties in ascertaining a child's views where s/he has learning disabilities, and they will have no direct

---

22 See *Re GF (Medical Treatment)* [1992] 1 FLR 293, Fam D.
23 *Re B (a minor) (wardship: sterilisation)* [1987] 2 All ER 206, HL. *Re E (a minor)* [1991] FCR 771, Fam D. This distinction is also drawn when considering sterilisation of adults with incapacity in Scotland in accordance with the Adults with Incapacity (Scotland) Act 2000.
24 *Re SL (adult patient) (medical treatment)* [2000] 2 FCR 452, sub nom *Re S (adult patient: sterilisation)*, CA, per Thorpe LJ at 469.
25 Official Solicitor's Practice Note: Sterilisation 1996.
26 *Re SL (adult patient) (medical treatment)* [2000] 2 FCR 452, sub nom *Re S (adult patient: sterilisation)*, CA.
27 In relation to adults, see Official Solicitor (2006) Practice note: declaratory proceedings: medical and welfare decisions for adults who lack capacity, annex: sterilisation cases.
28 Official Solicitor's Practice Note: Sterilisation 1996.

legal effect, it should not be assumed that they are of no importance and they may have a part to play when considering the psychological effects of sterilisation compared with other options.

Nevertheless, there may be circumstances in which a real risk of pregnancy is identified and no other alternatives are suitable. In such circumstances, the need to protect other interests may suggest that these outweigh any interest in retaining reproductive capacity, though in truth they may be rather easier to justify with adults than children. For adults, minimising unnecessary restrictions upon them, preserving their rights to freedom of association and to participate in sexual relationships, without incurring the risks associated with pregnancy and childbirth or abortion, can be more readily brought into the equation. In all likelihood, where the effects of pregnancy were felt to be so significant, a pregnancy would not be allowed to continue and it would be terminated. Accordingly, in these situations, sterilisation can be seen as not removing a reproductive capacity that the person would ever be able to practically exercise.

However, protecting a person from pregnancy does not protect them from other risks, such as abuse or sexually transmitted diseases. In addition, if a person is incapable of understanding the link between sex and pregnancy, then s/he may be considered incapable of giving consent to sexual intercourse. Such concerns may be compounded where the person is a child and indeed judicial disquiet about sexual activity by minors is evident, even where they do not have learning disabilities.[29] Sexual intercourse with children under the age of 16 is a criminal offence, so it may be thought that what the child needs protecting from here is sexual intercourse, not the possible consequences of it.[30] Nevertheless, in England and Wales, *Gillick* (1985) made it clear that medical treatment to prevent pregnancy may be given to those under the age of legal consent if this is in the child's best interests, without those doing so being found to have facilitated unlawful sexual intercourse. This is now covered by statute.[31] The position has not been tested in Scottish courts but it is believed to be the same. These conclusions of course concern children who are able to consent to sex and, in *Gillick*, at least, involved reversible methods of contraception. However, it must be borne in mind that an inability to give a valid consent to sterilisation does not automatically preclude giving a valid consent to sexual intercourse. Nevertheless, with all this in mind, it would be expected to be a very rare case where a court would authorise sterilisation of a child for contraceptive reasons alone, but it may not be impossible.

29 *Gillick v West Norfolk and Wisbech Area Health Authority and another* [1985] 3 All ER 402, HL.
30 Sexual Offences Act 2003, s 9. Criminal Law (Consolidation) (Scotland) Act 1995, s 5. There are also specific offences dealing with sexual intercourse with children under the age of 13.
31 Sexual Offences Act 2003, s 73.

Having outlined the approach of the courts' judgments and practice directions, it appears that the issues raised in terms of the best interests assessment
could be dealt with at least as well by the principles I propose, since they, too,
represent a welfare evaluation. The removal of a natural function such as
reproductive capacity must surely be regarded as involving significant harm
to the child, even if it is not accepted that this amounts to an interference with
a right to reproduce, which is itself a matter of contention.[32] In addition,
sterilisation is not a minor medical procedure; it is intended to make a permanent change to the child and be irreversible. It may also be considered
premature to make a decision where the child might gain capacity to make the
decision for herself or be at no imminent risk of pregnancy. If there were a
definite risk of pregnancy or childbirth, then the need for sterilisation as
opposed to alternative options would need to be considered. Jeopardising
such significant interests of a child should require clear, objectively agreed
justification rather than simply being within parental and clinical discretion,
and review by a court would seem, in most cases, to be appropriate. If the
courts allowed the procedure to be performed, this would be justified because
it was deemed to be reasonable in the circumstances for parents to give
consent, rather than because the judges took the view that it satisfied their
idea of what was in the child's best interests.

Nevertheless, if the same conclusions are likely to be reached here, then it
may be asked what benefit there would be in replacing the best interests test?
To some, this may seem like a difference only of semantics; to others it may be
felt to be potentially dangerous, since it would not seek to arrive at an answer
that is 'best' for the child. There will be other reasons put forward to support
my approach in respect of specific issues such as medical research. For the
moment, though, there are two points to note. The first is that it requires
involvement of the courts based on the significance of the child's interests
that may be compromised and the need to make out sufficient justification for
doing so to the court's satisfaction, where the usual considerations of therapeutic benefit and conventional treatment are absent. The best interests test
may be thought to take this into account already; so, for example, it has
been said that as a general principle for making decisions for people lacking
capacity:

> . . . in cases of controversy and cases involving momentous and irrevoc-
> able decisions, the courts have treated as justiciable any genuine question
> as to what the best interests of a patient require or justify. In making
> these decisions the courts have recognised the desirability of informing

---

32 Compare the views of Heilbron J in *Re D (a minor) (wardship: sterilisation)* [1976] 1 All
ER 326, Fam D with Hailsham LJ in *Re B (a minor) (wardship: sterilisation)* [1987] 2 All ER
206, HL.

those involved whether a proposed course of conduct will render them criminally or civilly liable; they have acknowledged their duty to act as a safeguard against malpractice, abuse and unjustified action; and they have recognised the desirability, in the last resort, of decisions being made by an impartial, independent tribunal.[33]

It has also been said that such an enquiry is merited in particular 'where there is any doubt as to either capacity or best interests' and that court authorisation is required 'where there is a lack of unanimity amongst the medical professionals as to the best interests of the patient' or 'where the patient [or] members of her immediate family . . . have opposed, or expressed views inconsistent with [what is proposed]'.[34] The danger of this is that, despite the alleged generality of the proposition, it may direct the focus of attention to where there is disagreement, either between professionals or between professionals and parents, over what is in the child's best interests. As the previous discussion of Rhodes and Holzman's model illustrates, doctors might well categorise sterilisation as being a category three decision – one where it has a likely good outcome and failing to perform it might cause serious harm (Rhodes and Holzman, 2004). As such, they could feel justified in proceeding on the basis of parental consent. Relying simply upon the views of doctors on accepted practice would leave them as sole arbiters of what is lawful. However, as the example of sterilisation shows, the courts have been prepared to put certain types of procedures in a 'special category' that requires court intervention even where, as in *Re D* (1976), doctors and parents are in agreement over what is in the child's best interests. It is already recognised, therefore, that some novel or controversial medical procedures with potentially far-reaching effects do not lie solely within clinical and parental discretion, and the protection of children mandates a publicly held review of the rights and interests of the child. This is enhanced by the need to ensure that the child's rights under the HRA 1998 are sufficiently considered.[35] However, it can be argued that concentrating on the concept of significant harms to children seems more likely to bring such matters before a court in such cases. Second, having said this, the court must only overrule the decision of the parents where, after a thorough review of the evidence, it considers that the option they have chosen does not meet societal standards for the welfare of children. It recognises that parents, doctors and the courts may reasonably differ in their conclusions on what is in the child's best interests, but that, irrespective of this, some procedures

---

33 *Re S (Hospital Patient: Court's Jurisdiction)* [1996] Fam 1, per Bingham MR at 18.
34 *Re S (Hospital Patient: Court's Jurisdiction)* [1996] Fam 1, per Coleridge J at 32–5. See, also, *Re J (child's religious upbringing and circumcision)* [2000] 1 FCR 307, CA.
35 This point is made in relation to adults in *D v A NHS Trust* [2004] 1 FLR 1110, per Coleridge J at para 31.

should be considered so unusual for children that their justification needs independent review.

For those who contend that this would amount to the courts dictating medical practice, it can be observed that doctors have shown a far greater willingness to approach the courts for their views on the appropriateness of proceeding by looking at the number of cases that have been instituted by doctors or their employers over the last 30 years. In part this may be driven by fears of litigation where the legal position is uncertain, but it may also be due to the acceptance of the view that medical interventions do not simply involve medical expertise and that there are a far wider range of considerations to be taken into account when evaluating predicted risks and benefits. For example, doctors' professional organisations clearly advise their members that they must give specific consideration to human rights in making their decisions (British Medical Association, 2000). They also recommend seeking legal advice in a variety of circumstances, including 'where the proposed care is beyond the scope of parental consent because it is controversial or non-therapeutic' (British Medical Association, 2001). Emphasising that there may be a need for judicial endorsement in such cases should not be seen as a revolutionary concept.

It must also be remembered that the courts do place a high value on medical opinion – indeed, some would say too high a value. Even where a court is prepared to say that treatment can be authorised by parents, this does not mean that they will compel doctors to provide it.[36] At the end of the day, clinical discretion not to provide treatment would remain, though it may cause doctors to review their decisions in the light of court judgments. The courts merely set the limits of professional practice. Of course, objection may be made to the judiciary, rather than the Parliaments, setting societal standards and it may be that legislation in some cases would be more appropriate. Arguably, though, matters that prove to be of public concern are more likely to reach the attention of legislators if they have been addressed in the forum of a court rather than dealt with as a matter of professional practice and parental discretion. Reviewing cases through the courts may thus perform a useful function in encouraging public debate on the appropriate response to certain kinds of medical intervention and promote law reform where this is felt necessary.

The application of the harm and reasonableness principles in areas of uncertainty

While it has now been made clear that sterilisation of a child does not come within the sole discretion of parents and doctors, it is not the only potentially

---

36 *Simms v Simms, A v Another* [2003] 1 All ER 669, Fam D; *Re J (a minor) (medical treatment)* [1992] 2 FCR 753, CA; *R v GMC ex parte Burke* [2005] 3 FCR 169, CA.

controversial procedure that may be proposed for children. A few examples may give further illustrations of the potential for these principles to be applied in medical situations. One area that has yet to be considered by the UK courts is cosmetic surgery, such as on children with Down's syndrome. Leshin reports that from the 1970s, surgery to alter the appearance of these children's faces and reduce tongue size began to be advocated. Although some suggestion has been made that operations to reduce tongue size might lead to improvement in function by making speech more intelligible, evidence that it does so is at best debatable (see studies cited by Leshin, 2000). The major reason given for performing such procedures is that the facial features of the child may lead to social stigma and assumptions being made about the child's abilities that will make it more difficult to integrate him or her into society. In addition, it may be thought to improve the appearance of the child as an independent goal, with Down's syndrome features being perceived as being unattractive (see, also, Jones, 2000).

It has been said that this is a matter for parents to make an informed choice about (Leshin, 2000). This is also the view taken by some organisations supporting families with Down's syndrome (Down's Syndrome Scotland, 1998; see also the views of the American organisation: National Down Syndrome Society). It is understandable that some parents may feel that the best way to protect their children is as far as possible to reduce any differences between them and others. In doing so, an attempt may be made to compare this with 'removing birthmarks, pinning ears and other surgical corrections of minor defects in children' (Leshin, 2000). Such procedures are normally taken to be within the scope of parental discretion. Nevertheless, it has been argued that even here:

> Surgery of this type is often claimed as being 'in the best interests of the child' because, allegedly, a child with protruding ears will be prone to teasing at school. This argument however, is specious and represents a projection onto the child of parental anxieties over conformity. Teasing is not a medical problem. Likewise, such surgery has no medical value and if performed necessarily violates the human rights of the child.
>
> (Hodges *et al.* 2002, p 1213)

They point out that ears come in a variety of shapes and sizes and that it cannot be predicted in advance how a child would feel about them. Changing their shape through surgery is also likely to leave a scar that may be viewed more negatively than the angle of the ears would have been. Furthermore, if children wish to tease others they will find a reason to do so and '(i)n any event, teasing is more appropriately handled by discipline and psychological counselling for the teaser rather than by ill-conceived attempts at pre-emptive surgery for the potential victim of teasing' (Hodges *et al.*, 2002, p 13).

A similar analysis can be adopted in relation to altering the appearance of a Down's syndrome child, where it may be argued that it is society that needs changing, not the child. Applying the harm principle as a threshold for court scrutiny, I would contend that significant interests of the child are engaged when subjecting him or her to major surgery for what are largely cosmetic reasons. In order to justify these interventions, the court would have to consider whether the risks and burdens associated with surgery could be regarded as being outweighed by countervailing benefits. The evidence for improved social functioning of children after such operations is limited and the idea that Down's syndrome children are in fact treated badly because of their appearance has been challenged, although parents generally seem to be pleased with the effects of the surgery (see studies cited by Leshin, 2000; Jones, 2000). On the other hand, it has been suggested that having characteristic facial features may actually encourage others to be more protective of Down's syndrome children (Suziedelis, 2006). Interestingly, research into the opinions of parents with Down's syndrome children showed that the majority felt that their children's facial features did provide social cues for others and that these were in the main, beneficial (Goeke et al., 2003). Overwhelmingly, most parents in this survey felt that surgery on their children for cosmetic reasons was not something they would wish to pursue, so it is unlikely to be an issue that commonly arises. Parents were also very aware of the need to involve the children themselves in the decision, if this was possible. It is worth noting that just under half felt that a child should make a final decision, although slightly more believed it should be made by the parents. This may indicate a parental wish to veto surgery or doubts about their children's ability to consider such issues, rather than a belief that it would be appropriate to impose surgery on an unwilling child. For courts asked to hear a case, there seems no strong evidence of benefit to children to set against the risks and burdens imposed by major reconstructive surgery. Indeed, there have even been calls for these kinds of operations to be outlawed, as is female circumcision, since it is 'major, painful and always therapeutically unnecessary' (Jones, 2000, p 102). In order to allow such operations to proceed, the court would need to be convinced that this type of operation should fall within parental discretion in conjunction with medical advice, having undertaken a welfare assessment. They need not consider surgery to be in the child's best interests, but I would suggest that the balance here, as in sterilisation, would mean it would be a rare case where it would be justified and it should require the court to consider whether it could be reasonable for parents to consent.

Whether this should extend to all forms of cosmetic surgery may be more debatable. Where it is being performed to attempt to restore appearance and possibly, also function, for example after burns injuries, I would suggest that it falls within the parameters of parental consent, although careful consideration of the effects of surgery and its predicted results would be needed. As such it can be seen to be fulfilling one or more of the expected purposes of treatment and to be covered by the usual approach to this. Where, however, the operation is aimed at changing the child's appearance to 'normalise' it from the way that the child was born, a more wide-ranging and critical examination may be required (see the contributions in Parens, 2006). The use of surgery to repair conditions such as cleft lip or palate could be regarded as acceptable, even if part of the justification concerns social considerations, since it may be said that 'although major social advantages result from the cosmetic improvement, equally great benefits result from the functional improvement obtained' (Jones, 2000), although evidence on this is not unequivocal (Mouradian, 2006). This conclusion has been reached by a number of commentators in an academic review of surgically shaping children:

> Our working group unanimously supported waiting for children to be old enough to participate in decisions about risky and painful surgeries that might fail to reliably retain function and produce more normal appearance (for example, surgery for intersex and achondroplasia). With one exception, however, our group did not argue that parents should wait to involve children in decisions about primary cleft lip surgery, which carries relatively small risks and achieves its stated purpose.
>
> (Parens, 2006, p xxix)

On the other hand, surgery to pin ears, for example, has no functional improvement in mind and is subject to the kinds of criticism raised earlier. In these cases, the views of the child assume particular significance and performing such procedures before the child has developed a view on the matter might be considered premature. Whether these kinds of interventions require court scrutiny, however, depends on the level of risk posed by the procedure, taking into account physical and psychological effects on the child. Where these are likely to be low, they may not meet the threshold of significant harm to the child's interests and be permissible with parental consent. Although children undoubtedly have a right to bodily integrity and to be protected from unnecessary and intrusive medical interventions, it may be considered that if the risks are minor and parents believe it will benefit a child, minor cosmetic surgery is not something that will have such a detrimental effect on the child's interests that it needs to be judicially considered. This would take this kind of intervention into the second category of decisions suggested by Rhodes and Holzman (2004). I have some doubts about this, as I am unconvinced that permanent body alterations to an incompetent child are justifiable where these are proposed for social or cultural reasons. One's view may depend on the evidence of significant risk of serious harm involved and the benefits to be obtained and, where these are in doubt, a court hearing would be appropriate. In addition, even if automatic court involvement is not necessary, such procedures might fall within the category of decisions that require joint parental consent. This will be returned to in the next chapter.

Another example raising different kinds of issues where court intervention may be called for is provided by a young American girl named Ashley (Gunther and Diekama, 2006). Here, by contrast to the situations just considered, this was not an attempt to 'normalise' the child, but rather to restrict her growth and development. Ashley had been diagnosed as having a permanent brain injury whose cause could not be identified. Her parents describe the effects of this as follows:

> Ashley cannot keep her head up, roll or change her sleeping position, hold a toy, or sit up by herself, let alone walk or talk. She is tube fed and depends on her caregivers in every way. . . . The chance of Ashley having significant improvement, such as being able to change her position in bed, let alone walk, is non-existent. She has been at the same level of cognitive and mental developmental ability since about three months of age.
>
> (Ashley blog, 2007)

Ashley was expected to have a normal physical development and life expectancy. However, when she was six and a half she began to develop signs of puberty and her parents consulted doctors to see if this could be accelerated further to minimize her adult height and weight, through high-dose oestrogen treatment. The aim of this was to keep Ashley smaller and lighter as this would make it:

> . . . more possible to include her in the typical family life and activities that provide her with needed comfort, closeness, security and love: meal time, car trips, touch, snuggle etc.
>
> (Ashley blog, 2007)

In other words, as she grew, her parents foresaw greater difficulty in providing the kind of practical and loving support for her that they wished to do. They were adamant that this was not as a matter of convenience to them, but was rather intended to improve her quality of life. In addition, they were concerned about her having the pain of menstrual cramps and that given her family history she was likely to be at risk from cancer and fibrocystic disease. She was also more likely to develop large breasts, which given her difficulty in supporting herself, might cause her additional discomfort. Accordingly, they wished Ashley to have a hysterectomy and surgical removal of her breast buds.

Since the case was unusual, to say the least, the doctor who was willing to perform these treatments referred it to the hospital's ethics committee. It decided that the parents could make these decisions on behalf of Ashley, subject only to confirmation that this would not contravene the legal position on sterilisation. Since sterilising her was regarded as being therapeutic in nature, the legal advice given was that this would not be unlawful and all these procedures were performed. When the case was reported, it caused strong opinions both in favour and against the strategy adopted.

For some disability rights organisations, advocating the need for support of those with disabilities and their families, the major difficulty encountered by Ashley and her family was insufficient resources to enable her to be provided with proper care (Scope, 2007; Disability Rights Commission, 2007). Gibbs has commented that the potential adverse effects of growth on her care were in any event exaggerated. Other concerns surrounded her right to bodily integrity and to the body that she would naturally have developed, echoing similar points made earlier about cosmetic surgery (Gibbs, 2007). More intangible concepts, such as dignity have also been raised (Verhovek, 2007; Ashley blog), though opposing views have been taken on this with the argument even being made that a full-grown and fertile woman endowed with the mind of a baby is undignified and 'grotesque' (Dvorsky, 2006).

Despite these various arguments, the hospital ethics committee deciding Ashley's case was clearly most comfortable with taking the position that there were in fact medical benefits to be obtained from the procedures, with low perceived risks. Oestrogen treatment to suppress height had been given to teenage girls in the 1970s, since it was considered less desirable for women to be tall (Lee and Howell, 2006). The risks, such as thrombosis, were seen as minimal and given that hysterectomy and breast bud removal were also being undertaken, this would reduce the risk to Ashley of the major cancers associated with hormone treatment. In addition, it was said that a smaller more 'portable' child would have better circulation, digestion and muscle condition, and fewer sores and infections, quite apart from the physical and emotional benefits put forward by the parents (Gunther and Diekema, 2006).

Nevertheless, the fact that teenage girls were given hormone treatment without evidence of substantial physical risk is not necessarily a strong argument in favour of it here. After all, it can plausibly be suggested that there may be doubts whether such 'treatment' based on gender stereotypes is acceptable, no matter how low the risk. Such doubts are even more likely where it is being used to suppress a normal growth pattern in a child, even for the types of benefits contended. Another worrying factor, however, is that it seems clear that this form of treatment is experimental on children of this age. It has been pointed out that the outcome, in terms of its effects on the growth patterns of young children with disabilities, its improvement on the child's quality of life and any possible side effects, is at present speculative (Brosco, 2006). While this does not mean that experimental treatment can never be given to children, as will be discussed in a later chapter, it gives grounds for caution in placing too much credence in assertions that predicted benefits will materialise where significant interests of the child may be put at risk.

Once again however, the question arises whether in the UK context, the decision should properly fall within the discretion of parents and doctors willing to undertake the 'Ashley treatment'. Should it be open to them to decide that such novel treatments are in the child's best interests without further scrutiny? I would argue that a thorough investigation of the child and the family's circumstances should be undertaken where such radical treatment is concerned before it could proceed, for the type of reasons given earlier. It is major, irreversible, experimental and, here, impacts on a child's normal development. It is also undoubtedly controversial. Evidence of potential health benefits and the likelihood of maintaining or improving the family's ability to care for a child would need to be compared with alternative, less drastic options. In considering the reasonableness of the parents' decision, I agree with Ross that the needs of the family are a matter to be properly taken into account as well as the effect of treatment on the child. She suggests, for example, that if a decision is only based on the individual interests of the child, this would require optimisation of the child's wellbeing and the possible sacrifice of the interests of parents and other family members and that this would be too much to demand (Ross, 1998, p 50).

The effect that Ashley's normal development would have upon the family is therefore a legitimate ground for court enquiry, even apart from whether it would affect the care that they can give her. A court might decide that the only way of allowing the family to function effectively and to continue to provide proper care would be to permit treatment to proceed, but this is a matter that requires them to evaluate the rights of all concerned. If it seemed the family would be incapable of providing for Ashley's needs with adequate assistance, then a decision would have to be taken whether her interest in being cared for by them, rather than her care being transferred to others, outweighed undertaking the measures proposed. The court would then have to consider whether the parents' planned course of action could be deemed reasonable. Given the inclusion of sterilisation in Ashley's case, it would be expected that it would require judicial consideration in any event, but even if growth retardation by hormone treatment were the only proposed intervention, the implications are so far-reaching for the child that an independent evaluation of the proposed interventions is indicated.

These examples – and many more could be given – provide illustrations of using the harm and reasonableness principles to protect children and ensure that parental consent to medical interventions is within acceptable limits. These principles are appropriate where children lack capacity to make autonomous decisions, not where they have it.

Children with capacity to consent

Normally, children's ability to consider treatment decisions for themselves would be expected to develop as they do and the need to involve children as far as possible in decisions that concern them has already been addressed. However, participation in decision-making is not the same as an entitlement to have the final say. The benchmark for legally valid medical decision-making is that of the 'adult of sound mind' and an outline of the approach taken here will be given before turning to children.[37]

Medical decision-making by adults

On attaining the legal status of adulthood, people are presumed to have the abilities necessary to exercise autonomy. Precisely what these abilities are is not generally explicitly articulated by either the courts or in legislation, save in relatively limited respects. However, three main requirements are generally regarded as necessary for a person's decision to be legally valid: competence, the provision of adequate information and that the decision is sufficiently voluntary (Beauchamp and Childress, 2001, p 145).

Competence

Adults are presumed to be competent and others can usually only make decisions for them if this presumption is rebutted. In England and Wales, a three-part test for competence was adopted at common law: whether the person could understand the nature, purpose and effects of the treatment, believe the information and use it to arrive at a choice.[38] In Scotland, the principal cases concerning the powers of the courts and tutors' dative to make decisions on behalf of adults lacking capacity did not directly address the issue of a determination of competence.[39] However, the same kind of approach is likely to have been applicable here, too. The Mental Capacity Act 2005 now sets out the regime for treatment of incompetent adults in England and Wales. It defines competence in negative terms: that is, it sets out requirements for lack of decision-making capacity, but it follows fairly closely the common-law test. It is further stated that even if a person is only able to retain the information for a short time, this does not prevent him from being capable of making the decision. Relevant information includes information about the reasonably foreseeable consequences of deciding one way or another or failing to make the decision.[40] A similar approach is taken in Scotland.[41] In neither jurisdiction is there any mention of the decision made

37 *Schloendorff v Society of New York Hospital* (1914) 211 NY 125, 105 NE 92 NY, Ct of Apps, per Cardozo J at 93.
38 *Re C (adult: refusal of medical treatment)* [1994] 1 All ER 819, Fam D. See, also, *Re MB (an adult: medical treatment)* [1997] 2 FCR 541, CA.
39 *Law Hospital NHS Trust v Lord Advocate* 1996 SCLR 49, IHCS. *L, Petitioner* 1996 SCLR 538, CS.
40 Mental Capacity Act 2005, s 3.
41 Adults with Incapacity (Scotland) Act 2000, s 1(6).

by the adult having to be mature, wise or rational. Indeed, as we shall see, the right to make an irrational decision has been strongly advocated by the courts and there appears to be no intention to depart from this principle under the statutory schemes.

Although it has been explicitly stated that competence is a legal matter,[42] it will in practice, in most cases, be determined by medical evidence. However, as has been pointed out, 'The search for a single, operational standard of competency has been described as "a search for the holy grail" ' (Roth *et al.*, 1977). One of the main problems seems to lie in formulating a practical test for competence, which is sufficiently specific to be useful, while being sufficiently flexible to be applied to the wide variety of situations in which such determinations must be made. Widespread support has been voiced for what is referred to as a 'functional approach'. This has been described as focusing on 'the decision itself and the capability of the person concerned to understand at the time it is made the nature of the decision required and its implications' (Lord Chancellor's Department, 1997, para 3.7). It stresses that a finding of competence is specific to the particular decision that is to be made, so that incompetence to make one type of decision does not mean the patient is incompetent for all purposes. Methods of reliably and satisfactorily assessing competence in adults are disputed, but some of the professional bodies have identified a number of factors that should be considered in any attempt to make such a determination. They recommend that the patient must be able to understand in simple language what the medical treatment is, its purpose and nature, and why it is being proposed; its principal benefits, risks and alternatives and, in broad terms, what will be the consequences of not receiving the proposed treatment (British Medical Association and Law Society, 2004). It has been suggested that the level of understanding needed is therefore greater than mere understanding of the 'broad nature and purpose' of the proposed procedure, that is, the level of information that need be given to avoid an assault action (Kennedy and Grubb, 2004, para 3.75).

Where an adult's competence is challenged, investigation focuses on the rationality of the decision-making process rather than of the decision itself. It has been said, for example, that 'In the ideal of autonomy day-to-day decisions should be rational, i.e. consistent with the person's life plans (Hope *et al.*, 2003, p 34). However, what is being referred to here is rationality from the perspective of the patient, rather than other people. It has been held that the right to make a decision:

> . . . exists notwithstanding that the reasons for making the choice are rational, irrational, unknown or even non-existent . . . An adult patient

who ... suffers from no mental incapacity has an absolute right to choose whether to consent to medical treatment, to refuse it or to choose one rather than another of the treatments being offered.[43]

As discussed in Chapter 1, there are strong grounds to question this formulation. Unless the reasons are given for a person's decision, it may be difficult or impossible to determine how it has been reached and whether the patient is able to arrive at a choice consistent with his or her own beliefs. A decision may, for example, be based on a misunderstanding. In practice, such inquiries are only likely to be made where a patient makes a decision that appears misguided, such as a refusal of treatment, or where mental illness or disorder may be a factor. While the latter do not preclude competence, it is more likely for practitioners to be cautious here. Some studies suggest that many patients are in fact incompetent to make decisions but, unless they refuse treatment, this issue is not identified or explored (see, for example, Raymont et al., 2004). It is usually only where the decision is seen as being unreasonable that doctors will feel obliged to pursue the matter. As has been said, however, consenting to treatment does not carry with it the corollary that a doctor must provide treatment that s/he does not feel is appropriate. Although there have been some challenges to this which will be discussed further in Chapter 4, so far, the position remains that courts are as a rule disinclined to even countenance ordering doctors to perform treatment that is against their professional judgment.[44] A competent adult's consent therefore allows medical procedures to be undertaken but does not mandate it.

Adequate information

For adults' consent to be legally valid, they must have been given adequate information on which to make their decision. While in theory patients would need full information on all matters that might possibly affect their decision, this standard would be hard to meet in practice and the law does not require it. If patients are informed in broad terms of the nature and purpose of the treatment and give consent, this will be regarded as legally valid and prevent a civil action for battery/trespass to the person or assault. A failure to provide adequate information about material risks associated with a procedure, while it will not invalidate consent, may lead to an action in negligence.[45] There has been considerable debate over how much and what kind of information is adequate. Suffice it to say here that, in treatment situations, the UK has by

---

43   *Re T (adult: refusal of medical treatment)* [1992] 4 All ER 649, CA, at 652–3.
44   *R v GMC ex parte Burke* [2005] 3 FCR 169, CA.
45   *Chatterton v Gerson* [1981] 1 All ER 257, QB D.

and large endorsed the 'professional standard', taken from *Bolam* (1957).[46] In essence, whether sufficient information has been provided is based on a standard set by a 'responsible body of medical opinion'.[47] This approach has been criticised as a sign that the courts pay excessive deference to the medical profession on matters not requiring medical expertise (see, for example, McLean, 1989). There are some indications that this may be changing and that the focus may be shifting more towards reasonable patient expectation and enhancing patient autonomy than supporting professional practice.[48] However, academic opinion is divided on the extent that judicial statements reflecting this will result in a significant change in the judgments reached (see, for example, Teff, 1998; Brazier and Miola, 2000; Maclean, 2002).

Once the necessary information has been given, it is for the adult patient to decide what decision to make on that basis and accordingly, treatment can be accepted or rejected, no matter the predicted result.

Voluntariness

It has been said that:

> Virtually all theories of autonomy agree that two conditions are essential
>
> (1) Liberty (independence from controlling influences) and
> (2) Agency (capacity for intentional action)
>
> (Beauchamp and Childress, 2001, p 58)

Agency is dealt with as a matter of competence and we are here concerned with the idea of liberty. It must be acknowledged that the ability of an individual to be free of controlling influences can never be absolute. We are all products of our make-up (genetic and biological) and our environment (physical, social and cultural). Rather, autonomy is a continuum, within which a person is more or less free to make decisions, depending on the extent of internal and external influences upon their thought processes, behaviour and actions. It is only possible to say that a person can be regarded as being autonomous if they have a substantial degree of liberty, so that they are for practical purposes able to behave in a self-governing fashion (Beauchamp and Childress, 2001, pp 59–60).

The view that doctors take will usually be a highly significant factor affecting peoples' choices about treatment. So it has been said that:

---

46 *Bolam v Friern Hospital Management Committee* [1957] 2 All ER 118, QB D.
47 *Sidaway v Bethlem Royal Hospital Governors* [1985] 1 All ER 643, HL. *Moyes v Lothian Health Board* 1990 SLT 444, CS.
48 *Pearce v United Bristol Healthcare NHS Trust* (1998) 48 BMLR 118, CA. See also *Bolitho v City and Hackney Health Authority* [1997] 4 All ER 771, HL.

... every decision is made as a result of some influence: a patient's decision to consent will normally be influenced by the surgeon's advice as to what will happen if the operation does not take place.[49]

However, they may have a broader role than the simple provision of information. Some degree of persuasion can be considered professionally appropriate, provided that it is limited to reasoned argument rather than force or coercion. As such, doctors are clearly in a position to influence the decisions that people make. Nonetheless, when considering whether a person's decision has been made sufficiently freely, the courts have been rather more interested in the scope for the influence of other people in a close relationship with the patient, such as relatives and religious advisers.[50] As with competence, however, it is where objection is taken to the outcome of the patient's decision, most notably where medically recommended treatment has been refused, that the voluntariness of the person's decision is most likely to be investigated.

Children's development of decision-making capacity

Where children are concerned, the question must be whether the same standards that are used for adults can and should be applied to them. The law sets a basic dividing line between adulthood and childhood, based on age. This has the benefits of clarity, consistency and ease of application. It may also be thought an appropriate way to register the very real differences between adults and developing children (Archard, 2002). As Fortin notes, the views of some children's 'liberationists', equating all adults and children, have been subjected to criticism in that they fail to properly take this into account and hence place expectations on children that are unrealistic and may be dangerous for them (Fortin, 2005).

However, as Archard explains, there are two major criticisms of age-based criteria. One is to say that that any such criterion is faulty, since it is bound to create errors at the margins. So, it could be expected that there will be a big difference between the decision-making capacity of a 40-year-old and a four-year old. By comparison, no such great distinction is likely between a person aged 18 years and one who is 17 and 11 months. Setting an age threshold to acquire rights may therefore 'risk unfairly penalizing some who are in fact competent just as it may unfairly risk rewarding some who are in fact incompetent' (Archard, 2000). The second line of criticism is the difficulty in determining where any age-based divide should be drawn. Research on child development suggests that there are stages at which children develop

---

49 *Re T (adult: refusal of medical treatment)* [1992] 4 All ER 649, CA, per Staughton LJ at 669.
50 Ibid.

cognitive and evaluative skills and this must be relevant to whether children are capable of making choices that others are entitled, and even required, to rely on.

There is much that has been written on this subject and only an outline can be provided here (for reviews of the literature, see New South Wales Law Reform Commission, 2004, ch 1; Fortin, 2005, ch 3; Alderson, 2006). It may be thought self-evident that the younger children are, the less likely it is that they will be able to understand information about proposed treatments, perform the kind of abstract analysis required to evaluate them, or have the kind of life experiences to contextualise treatment and its effects. For example, for a young child, weeks or months of treatment may be conceived of and experienced differently than they would be for an adult. It is commonplace to say that time passes more quickly as we age, in part because adults have experienced life for so much longer than a young child that a few weeks or months can seem a short time in comparison with the years that have been lived. It does seem to be generally agreed by researchers, and may be observed by anyone dealing with children, that young children are more concerned with immediate problems and the satisfaction of desires than older ones and adults. Long-term planning, to the extent that it occurs at all, is unlikely to be thought through or considered objectively. The ability to understand other viewpoints and to deal with more abstract concepts is one that takes time to develop. Children in their early years tend to see things in black and white rather than shades of grey, and more sophisticated reasoning skills, including the possibility of there being more than one answer to a question are acquired as they develop greater intellectual and emotional range and have improved ways of understanding and expressing ideas (see, for example, Piaget and Inhelder, 1969; Rutter and Rutter, 1993; Coleman and Hendry, 1999). However, some studies have suggested that by at least the time children are 14, they are likely to have achieved the same level of intellectual skills as adults to make decisions about medical interventions. Even younger children, though they may show less sophisticated reasoning abilities, may not necessarily differ substantially in the decisions they make, compared with older children and adults (Piaget and Inhelder, 1969; Weithorn and Campbell, 1983).

Despite this, in addition to intellectual and conceptual skills, notions of autonomy, as we have seen, focus on rights to self-determination. As they develop, children are in the process of working out their own view of themselves: what kind of people are they, what values do they hold and what are their goals in life? This may pose some problems if it is thought that children's opinions and preferences will change over time and are not as fixed as those of adults. Relying on their views at an early stage in their lives may be thought to preclude opportunities for them to change their minds and close off options they might later wish to pursue, or indeed result in a premature death that will close off any options for them. In addition, it may be argued that their ideas are too uninformed and too easy to influence by those close to them to be treated as autonomous choices that should be relied on (Grisso and Vierling, 1978). These are all issues that have surfaced in some of the case law. On the other hand, it may be claimed that children finding their place in society as individuals, far from being influenced by those close to them, may instead seek actively to rebel against them as a means of asserting independence and challenging societal mores. In either case, choices made by children may be felt to be less deserving of being taken seriously than those of older people.

Despite these observations about childhood development, some have argued that children's abilities have been underestimated and that even very young children may be capable of properly assessing proposed medical treatment. Leading proponents of this view are Alderson and Montgomery who, through research with sick children, conclude that children as young as five could be deemed competent to make a legally valid decision about their treatment, though it must be said that they would limit the binding nature of this to where the decision does not seriously impact on the child's wellbeing. They also remind readers that studies of children who are not ill may produce different results to those who have experience of illness and treatment. Such children may even be considered to be in a better position to judge the effects of treatment than adults concerned with their care (Alderson and Montgomery, 1996b, ch 5). Others, such as Harris, also suggest that many children can be more intelligent and capable of sophisticated reasoning than many adults. It must be noted that in order to be regarded as being sufficiently autonomous he sets out a number of conditions that must be satisfied. The person must be free from: defects in the ability to control their desires or actions; defects in reasoning; defects in the information available to them; and defects in the stability of their desires (Harris, 1982). While he is considering children's political enfranchisement, the same points could be made in the context of medical decision-making. Indeed, Cauffman and Steinberg contend that intellectual comparisons with adults are not enough and that children's maturity of judgement must also be considered. There may be differences between children and adults in their sense of personal responsibility, their ability to consider the context of decisions, including wider issues, such as morality, and in their ability to control impulsive behaviour (Cauffman and Steinberg, 1995, p 1788). However, it has been noted that 'the way in which these differences affect the young person's maturity of judgement has not been sufficiently subjected to empirical research to make any considered assessment of their decision-making capacity in respect of medical treatment' (New South Wales Law Reform Commission, 2004, ch 1).

Research into child development allows a more scientific and structured assessment to be made about the appropriateness of according rights at a certain age, rather than simply basing it on assumptions about children's abilities that may be very wide of the mark. Nonetheless, even the best-conducted studies can only provide generalisations about children. If the possession of rights to self-determination is considered valuable, then it can be argued that an individualised test of capacities should be used instead. This is not to deny that there are also difficulties with subject-specific tests of capacity, such as agreeing the standard to be adopted before a person can exercise rights and the practical problems in carrying out such an assessment. There is the potential for bias in the testing procedure, which may result in unfair discrimination, and the possibility of misapplication and self-interest by those administering it. These are charges that cannot be levelled against age-based tests (Archard, 2000). Notwithstanding this, if respect for autonomy has the central value generally accorded to it in law and healthcare, my contention is that those who are capable of exercising it should not be denied the freedom to do so simply because they have not met whatever age it is that is set for adulthood. While the latter would have the benefit of certainty, it fails to protect the rights of individuals to self-determination on a basis that is arbitrary and discriminatory. It should be remembered that the age of majority has varied over time and was until comparatively recently 21. While having a set age for matters such as the ability to vote is acceptable, since the administrative difficulties involved in questioning every citizen in order to establish their competence for enfranchisement would be practically insurmountable, the same is not true where decisions about the management of health of an individual are concerned. Here his or her ability to make a decision can be examined at the point of treatment.

The appropriateness of age or capacity-based criteria to make medical decisions is therefore a matter of contention. However, this does not mean that these are mutually exclusive alternatives and, in fact, UK law sets both: a presumptive test for capacity, which is age-based, and an evidential test of individual capacity for those below this age. It thus provides both an element of recognition that children do develop capacity individually over time, not on reaching a particular birthday, and that some threshold for presuming that individuals have the requisite capacity is appropriate.

Children's decision-making under UK law

The question when children and young people should be deemed capable of making decisions about medical treatment for themselves is a matter that has brought several cases before the courts in England and Wales and has attracted considerable controversy. There has been less activity before the Scottish courts and a number of issues remain more open to speculation. However, it seems that there is a different approach that is more supportive of competent children's autonomy in Scotland, and my belief is that that is the most appropriate response. Although there are some difficulties in connection with the standard that is set for competence, in England and Wales the primary difficulty is the use of the best interests test. Here, the purpose of obtaining consent from children has been interpreted not as being to respect the autonomy of children, but rather as simply to provide an alternative to consent from parents that allows doctors to provide medically recommended treatment. Accordingly, I propose that this approach should be reconsidered. I will first consider how the law establishes the legal validity of children's consent. The consequences of this can then be examined.

Presumptive competence

In England and Wales, the age of majority is 18.[51] However, there is a statutory presumption that children of 16 years of age are competent to consent to medical treatment. The relevant provision is s 8(1) of the Family Law Reform Act 1969 (FLRA 1969):

> (1) The consent of a minor who has attained the age of sixteen years to any surgical, medical or dental treatment which, in the absence of consent, would constitute a trespass to his person, shall be as effective as it would be if he were of full age; and where a minor has by virtue of this section given an effective consent to any treatment it shall not be necessary to obtain any consent for it from his parent or guardian.
>
> (2) In this section 'surgical, medical or dental treatment' includes any procedure undertaken for the purposes of diagnosis, and this section applies to any procedure (including, in particular, the administration of an anaesthetic) which is ancillary to any treatment as it applies to that treatment.

Thus the statute appears to intend that the consent of 16-year-olds should be as valid in law as if they were legally adults and that they are to be regarded as self-determining for this purpose. No stipulation is made as to the assessment of their competence and the *Gillick* competence test has been said to be inappropriate for young people between the ages of 16 and 18.[52]

The position in Scotland at first sight appears to mirror that of England and Wales in that the age of majority remains 18, but young people can make many legally binding decisions before that age.[53] The Age of Legal Capacity (Scotland) Act 1991 (ALC(S)A 1991) provides a statutory presumption that a person can make a majority of legal decisions at 16. It provides as follows:

---

51 Family Law Reform Act 1969 s 1(1).
52 See, e.g. *Re W (a minor medical treatment)* [1992] 4 All ER 627, CA. *A Metropolitan Borough Council v AB* (1997) 1 FLR 677 and *Re C (detention: medical treatment)* [1997] 2 FLR 180, Fam D.
53 Age of Majority (Scotland) Act 1969 s 1.

a person of or over the age of sixteen years shall have legal capacity to enter into any transaction.[54]

'transaction' means a transaction having legal effect and includes . . . the giving by a person of any consent having legal effect.[55]

Since consent to medical treatment can have the legal effect of preventing an action for assault, medical treatment is covered by these sections. The statute contains provisions designed to protect children from having made unwise choices by allowing them to set aside prejudicial transactions, under certain conditions. However, consent to medical, dental or surgical treatment is not included within them.[56] Again, there is no statutory definition of competence in relation to these sections and once a person has reached the age of 16, they must be presumed to be competent to give consent to treatment on the same basis as any adult. In Scotland, however, parental responsibilities and rights in this regard end at the age of 16, although the responsibility to provide guidance ends only at the child's 18th birthday.[57] The courts also have no power to make treatment decisions on behalf of those aged 16 and over, unless the person is incompetent.[58] There is thus no equivalent in Scotland to the position of children aged 16 to 18 in England and Wales.

Evidential competence

The legal presumption is reversed for children under 16 and they must prove their competence in order for their consent to treatment to be legally valid. In England and Wales the position is covered by common law, where the leading case is of course *Gillick v West Norfolk and Wisbech Area Health Authority* (1985).[59] Although it was concerned specifically with contraception, the term '*Gillick* competence' has become shorthand for the abilities that need to be demonstrated in all areas of medical treatment. Its status as authority in this area is such that detailed consideration of it may seem superfluous. However, despite its ubiquity, the reasoning of the judges in *Gillick* was rather different and it is important to look at this closely, along with how the case has been interpreted subsequently, to see whether its status is justified.

54 ALC(S)A 1991 s 1(1)(b).
55 ALC(S) Act 1991 s 9.
56 ALC(S)A 1991 s 3(3)(e).
57 C(S)A 1995 ss 1(2) and 2(7).
58 *Law Hospital NHS Trust v Lord Advocate* 1996 SLT 848, (1998) 39 BMLR 166 (IHCS) and see, also, now the Adults with Incapacity (Scotland) Act 2000. Treatment for mental illness or disorder remains largely governed by the Mental Health (Care and Treatment) Scotland Act 2003.
59 *Gillick v West Norfolk and Wisbech Area Health Authority* [1985] 3 All ER 402, HL.

Mrs Gillick was challenging advice issued to doctors that in exceptional cases, they could provide contraceptive advice or treatment to girls under 16 without the knowledge of their parents. Part of her argument concerned whether doctors would be committing criminal offences by facilitating unlawful sexual intercourse, but this is not of primary relevance here.[60] At first instance, Woolf J held that the provisions of the FLRA 1969 did not imply that people under 16 were barred from giving a legally valid consent. Although expressing reservations about a child's ability to consent to procedures with long-term consequences, he concluded that whether a child was able to consent without parental involvement depended 'upon the child's maturity and understanding and the nature of the consent which is required.'[61] By contrast, the majority in the Court of Appeal did not concentrate on a child's competence, but upon the rights of parents in respect of children in their custody, and reversed the decision.[62] The case finally reached the House of Lords, where the decision was reversed yet again by a bare majority. Lords Fraser and Scarman gave the leading judgments. Lord Bridge purported to agree with both of their opinions on this issue but their approaches were not in fact identical.

Lord Fraser first dealt with the impact of the FLRA 1969 and considered that there was:

> no statutory provision which compels me to hold that a girl under the age of 16 lacks the legal capacity to consent to contraceptive advice examination and treatment *provided that she has sufficient understanding and intelligence* to know what they involve.[63]

(Emphasis added)

He set out a checklist, sometimes referred to as the Fraser Guidelines, of the circumstances where a doctor could lawfully provide contraceptive advice or treatment. This could be done if:

i.   the girl (although under 16 years of age) will understand his advice;
ii.   he cannot persuade her to inform her parents or to allow him to inform the parents that she is seeking contraceptive advice;
iii. she is very likely to begin or to continue having sexual intercourse with or without contraceptive treatment;
iv.   unless she receives contraceptive advice or treatment her physical or mental health or both are likely to suffer;

60 Sexual Offences Act 1956, ss 6 and 28.
61 *Gillick v West Norfolk and Wisbech Area Health Authority* [1984] 1 All ER 365, QB D, Per Woolf J at 373.
62 *Gillick v West Norfolk and Wisbech Area Health Authority* [1985] 1 All ER 533, CA.
63 *Gillick v West Norfolk and Wisbech Area Health Authority* [1985] 3 All ER 402, HL, at 423.

v.   her best interests require him to give her contraceptive advice, treatment or both without the parental consent.[64]

Lord Scarman, however, while seeming to approve of Lord Fraser's opinion, opted to deliver his opinion in his own words.[65] Like Lord Fraser, he concluded that the power of parents to consent on their children's behalf was one that ended 'if and when the child achieves a sufficient understanding and intelligence to enable him or her to understand fully what is proposed'.[66] He went on to say that:

> When applying these conclusions to contraceptive advice and treatment it has to be borne in mind that there is much that has to be understood by a girl under the age of 16 if she is to have legal capacity to consent to such treatment. It is not enough that she should understand the nature of the advice which is being given: *she must also have a sufficient maturity to understand what is involved*. There are moral and family questions, especially her relationship with her parents; long-term problems associated with the emotional impact of pregnancy and its termination; and there are the risks to health of sexual intercourse at her age, risks which contraception may diminish but cannot eliminate. It follows that a doctor will have to satisfy himself that she is able to appraise these factors before he can safely proceed upon the basis that she has at law capacity to consent to contraceptive treatment.[67]
>
> (Emphasis added)

The need for an element of emotional and social judgement was also echoed by Lord Templeman. However, the conclusion he drew was that although some medical matters could be consented to by a young person, not all could. He stated that while 'a doctor with the consent of an intelligent boy or girl of 15 could in my opinion safely remove tonsils or a troublesome appendix', contraceptive advice and treatment involved broader factors.

> ... any decision on the part of a girl to practise sex and contraception requires not only knowledge of the facts of life and of the dangers of pregnancy and disease but also an understanding of the emotional and other consequences to her family, her male partner and to herself. I doubt whether a girl under the age of 16 is capable of a balanced judgment to embark on frequent, regular or casual sexual intercourse fortified by the

64 Ibid at 413.
65 Ibid at 414.
66 Ibid at 423.
67 Ibid at 424.

illusion that medical science can protect her in mind and body and ignoring the danger of leaping from childhood to adulthood without the difficult formative transitional experiences of adolescence. There are many things which a girl under 16 needs to practise but sex is not one of them.'[68]

For these two judges, the crucial issue was establishing not only understanding of medical matters, but also the ability to place this treatment in a wider social context, although they reached opposing judgments about whether children could meet this standard. This has led commentators to conclude that there are fundamental differences between the approaches of Lords Fraser and Scarman (Parkinson, 1986; Norrie, 1994). Lord Fraser, while basing the threshold for competence at the relatively low level of understanding medical advice, limits the decisions that can be made by a young person to those that are in his or her best interests. By contrast, Lord Scarman does not refer to this principle at all. His method for restricting children's decision-making is by setting a higher threshold for competence. Taking Lord Scarman's opinion at face value, Norrie argues that it supports the concept of the autonomous minor since 'once the child has satisfied the maturity condition, there is nothing more that can be demanded of the child' (Norrie, 1994, p 110).

It has also been held that the capacity to consent will vary with the gravity of the treatment proposed.[69] This position is hard to justify, since it is surely the complexity of the decision, rather than the gravity of the treatment or its outcome, which demands greater intellectual capacity and discrimination. For example, deciding whether to accept life-saving treatment, such as antibiotics for infection, is arguably much less conceptually difficult than assessing a number of different types of non-life-saving treatment, all of which have differing probabilities of a range of risks and likely success. Discriminating between these takes far more skill, even if the outcome is not likely to represent a life or death decision. What seems to be at issue in demanding greater evidence of competence, if there are more serious consequences for the patient, does not appear to be concern over ensuring the decision of the young person is sufficiently autonomous. Instead, it focuses on the outcome of the decision and the desire to protect the child from consequences that others see as being against his or her interests.

In addition it has been held that *Gillick* competence must be understood as a developmental concept and for this reason it is not a matter that can fluctuate over time.[70] There has been some uncertainty in the application of this

68 Ibid at 432.
69 *Re W (a minor) (medical treatment)* [1992] 4 All ER 627, CA and *Re R (a minor) (wardship: medical treatment)* [1991] 4 All ER 177, CA.
70 *Re R (a minor) (wardship: medical treatment)* [1991] 4 All ER 177, CA.

principle however. The case of *Re R* (1991) involved a young woman suffering from a mental condition in which she had periods of lucidity. In considering *Gillick* competence, Lord Donaldson MR stated that:

> . . . there is no suggestion that the extent of this competence can fluctuate upon a day to day or week to week basis. What is really being looked at is an assessment of mental and emotional age, as contrasted with chronological age . . .[71]

He went on to say that 'even this test needs to be modified in the case of fluctuating mental disability to take account of that misfortune'. In the circumstances of this case he held that even if on a good day R did have a sufficient degree of understanding to meet the *Gillick* criteria, R's mental disability was such that on other occasions she was not only *Gillick* incompetent, but sectionable. Therefore he concluded that 'no child in that situation can be regarded as *Gillick* competent'. This approach appears contradictory: if she had developed *Gillick* competence, then she would remain *Gillick* competent and should instead be regarded as having her capacity temporarily reduced by mental illness, as would be the case for an adult in similar circumstances. In addition, it allows competence to be judged not on the present, but on the past and the predicted mental condition of the person – quite a different approach to the expected assessment (a similar point is made by Brazier and Bridge, 1996, p 95). Indeed, in later cases where the mental health of a young person has been at issue, it has been suggested that the *Re C* three-stage test of competence is in fact the appropriate one.[72] Presumably, with the coming into force of the Mental Capacity Act 2005, the criteria for understanding would now follow its formulation.

While it is commonplace to use the phrase *Gillick* competence, therefore, the question remains what this actually means. If it incorporates both the leading judgments, this may result in a stricter threshold than either contemplated, needing both a high level of decision-making skill and that the decision is in the child's best interests. If it does not, then there is no such test as *Gillick* competence: there are individual judgments that do not form an easily reconcilable standard. The British Medical Association (BMA) is among those who have observed the difficulty in extracting a clear ratio from the case (British Medical Association, 1995, p 73). In this guidance, the British Medical Association seems to have taken more of the Lord Fraser approach to competence than the Lord Scarman line. While noting that one view put forward was that 'the young patient should also understand the wider issues,

---

71 Ibid at 187.
72 See *Re C (detention: medical treatment)* (1997) 2 FLR 180, Fam D and *Re B (a minor) (treatment and secure accommodation)* [1997] 1 FCR 618, Fam D.

such as the moral implications and the impact the decision may have on the family', their specific advice to doctors did not refer to this again and focused on understanding of the procedures, risks and consequences. More recent guidance from the British Medical Association does seem to pay greater attention to the child's social and emotional understanding of treatment decisions, but it remains unclear how significant these factors should be in assessing competence (British Medical Association, 2001, ch 5). Concentration on intellectual, rather than social and emotional, skills is also shown in the guidance of both the DoH and the GMC (Department of Health, 2001b, p 9; General Medical Council, 1998, para 23). Ironically, without the qualification of best interests, arguably Lord Fraser's approach becomes more like the way that the law treats adults than Lord Scarman's. As we have seen, where adults are concerned, attention is fixed on the ability to understand information about the nature and purpose of treatment and reasonably foreseeable consequences. No explicit requirement is placed for them to demonstrate an understanding of the broader context of the decision, even where there are doubts about their capacity. This approach may be justifiable when dealing with a person temporarily affected by conditions such as mental illness or disorder. It is rather less so when an adult has learning disabilities and their capacity to exercise mature decision-making skills may be in as much doubt as children. Indeed, it is not uncommon for judges to describe such adults by comparing them with children of particular ages.[73] Although the comparison might not be entirely accurate, there may be a case for extending the concept of mature decision-making skills here, too.

The precise meaning of *Gillick* competence was reconsidered in the case of *Axon* (2006), where a Mrs Axon sought to challenge DoH advice on the provision of contraceptive and abortion services and information about sexually transmitted infections to girls under 16 without their parents' knowledge. She had argued that this was an interference with her parental rights under Article 8 of the ECHR, but this contention was dismissed.[74] As Fortin notes, in doing so the court squarely rested its decision on the lack of parental rights to be informed once the child attains competence, rather than a preferable approach, with the implementation of the HRA 1998, which concentrates on the child as a bearer of rights of his or her own (Fortin, 2006). The court took the approach that it was bound by *Gillick* (1985) and that this had not been affected by the coming into force of the HRA 1998. The court concluded that the Fraser Guidelines applied, but also held that Lord Scarman's statements in relation to assessing the understanding of the child

---

73 See, e.g. *F v West Berkshire Health Authority and Another* [1989] All ER 545.
74 *R v Secretary of State for Health and the Family Planning Association, ex parte Axon* [2006] 1 FCR 175, QB D.

should be read into them.[75] Accordingly, in the context of advice on sexual health at least, the position appears indeed to be that not only must children demonstrate broader decision-making skills than the law requires adults to show, but that the medical services must be regarded as being in the child's best interests.

In Scotland, too, there is an evidentiary standard of competence for those under 16, but here it is provided by statute. Section 2(4) of the ALC(S)A 1991 states that:

A person under the age of sixteen years shall have legal capacity to consent on his own behalf to any surgical, medical or dental procedure or treatment where, in the opinion of a qualified medical practitioner attending him, he is capable of understanding the nature and possible consequences of the procedure or treatment.

Precisely what kind of understanding the child should have is not further defined. However, it is useful to look at the report by the Scottish Law Commission, which provided the basis for this statute and which, in this area, was enacted without change. Here, they refer to children being deemed by the medical practitioner to have the 'maturity' to consent and cite Lord Scarman's judgment in *Gillick* (1985) with approval (Scottish Law Commission, 1987, paras 3.72–3, 3.77). What was contemplated, then, seems to be the ability to make a mature judgment, taking into account broader considerations than mere understanding of the medical procedure.

It is important to note that under s 2(4) there is no restriction on children consenting to treatment regarded as being in their best interests. In addition, since the section applies to procedures as well as treatments, it can be interpreted as including measures that are not considered to be therapeutic for the child (Scottish Law Commission, 1987, paras. 3.76–3.78). Some have suggested that the matter may not be quite so straightforward and that the ALC(S)A 1991 must be read in conjunction with the Children (Scotland) Act 1995 (C(S)A 1995), where of course the paramount consideration of the court must be the welfare of the child. If this takes priority, then it might be possible for a court to contend that it has the power to override a decision by a person under 16 if that is in accordance with the welfare principle, by making an order under s 11 of the C(S)A 1995 (Blackie and Patrick, 2001, paras 11.18–20; Edwards and Griffiths, 2006, paras 2.33, 4.36). Their contention is specifically addressed to the situation where a child refuses consent, and will be returned to in the next chapter, but my own view is that this approach cannot be supported. Any requirement of best interests was rejected by the Scottish Law Commission and its proposals were enacted without change in the legislation. While it preceded the C(S)A 1995, the

75 Ibid at para 154.

ALC(S)A 1991 contains the more specific provisions and it was introduced following consultations on this particular area. There does not appear to have been any intention to alter the legal position on this point. More dubiously, there is also the Court of Session's *parens patriae* jurisdiction, which possibly could be appealed to as a means of overriding a competent child's decision, but again this would seem to defeat the clear intention behind enacting s 2(4) ALC(S)A 1991.

Respecting children's autonomy

My position is that once a child achieves the ability to be regarded as sufficiently autonomous, his or her consent should be legally binding. Nonetheless, given what has been said about children's developmental differences from adults, it is reasonable to require a child to demonstrate evidence of decision-making capacity. Looking at Lord Scarman's judgment, this appears to be what he has in mind. It could be said that requiring such evidence, when it is not similarly required of adults whose capacity is in doubt, in fact introduces a higher threshold of evidential competence for young people. This may be true but it can be justified if what is expected is mature decision-making ability and, as I have suggested, this concept could legitimately be extended to adults with learning disabilities. As we have seen, the capacity for intellectual understanding and development of conceptual tools for decision-making take time and experience to develop. Studies of children suggest that this may be expected of children by the time they are at least 14, so it might be said that the current age for presumptive consent at 16 is somewhat on the high side and the threshold for presuming capacity can be questioned. Nevertheless, intellectual capacity alone may not be sufficient if it is also considered that other factors, such as the ability to take into account long-term consequences, exercise personal responsibility and consider matters other than medical ones, are important to mature decision-making skills. As was pointed out earlier, empirical research on this is harder to assess, so erring on the side of caution in setting a presumptive standard may perhaps be defensible, provided that individuals who can show such skills are allowed to exercise them.

Nonetheless, there should be a clear distinction drawn between the ability to make a mature judgement and making a decision in what is considered to be one's best interests. In other words, it should not be permitted to draw the conclusion that children who make decisions that are not in their best interests are thereby demonstrating that they are not mature enough to make them. There are signs that the judiciary in England and Wales has taken the opposite view, at least in the context of refusal of consent.[76] Some commenta-

---

76 *Re R (a minor) (wardship: medical treatment)* [1991] 4 All ER 177, CA.

tors have taken a similar view on the position in Scotland, at least in certain situations so that:

> If the treatment is not unequivocally in the child's best interests – e.g. cosmetic surgery or tissue donation – then part of the doctor's task in assessing maturity will be to consider why the child wishes to undergo this treatment and whether they have thought through the risks and the advantages. It is unlikely, for example, that a 14-year-old seeking cosmetic surgery in order to attain a more gracious nose is displaying a high level of maturity.
>
> (Edwards and Griffiths, 2006, para 2.34)

While they may be correct to draw attention to the need for a child to be able to properly consider what is proposed and explain her reasoning, to conclude from her decision that she is immature is unwarranted. To take this stance denies the importance of autonomy in that its purpose is to allow people to make decisions that others disagree with, since it equates an approved outcome of the decision with rational decision-making. While Lord Scarman's general approach, endorsed in Scotland, is therefore a preferable one to assessment of understanding, it is only so if it is interpreted as requiring the child to show a level of maturity that indicates s/he is a sufficiently autonomous agent. Being below a legally set age can legitimately trigger such an enquiry. Although Lord Templeman reached the conclusion that girls under 16 could not demonstrate such skills in relation to contraceptive advice and treatment, this is based on making assumptions about 16-year-olds and clearly also on very negative views about underage sex. While many might share them, they ignore the individual capacity of a particular child who, if she is capable of assessing the kinds of considerations set out by Lord Scarman, should be deemed capable of making treatment decisions that she considers right in her circumstances, even if others think them unwise. Of course, this does not mean that every child seeking such treatment should automatically be provided with it. For example, if she is not deemed mature enough or is thought to be at risk of abuse, steps may be taken to involve parents or other agencies. The same would be true in Scotland.

Since the level of understanding of the child is crucial to my argument that his or her decisions should be respected, some further points about the role of doctors in assessing this is necessary. In Scotland, s 2(4) ALC(S)A 1991 states that the assessment of the child's understanding is to be made by 'a qualified medical practitioner attending the child'. It has been suggested that the decision to refer to 'qualified' medical practitioners rather than 'registered' medical practitioners, which is the term generally used in statutes such as the Abortion Act 1967, means that any health professional qualified to perform the treatment or procedure can make the assessment of the child's understanding. Qualified would then seem to refer to qualification to perform the procedure or treatment rather than qualified to assess understanding (Wilkinson and Norrie, 1999, para 15.09). The statute certainly does not have an express requirement that the medical practitioner has any specific training or experience in the assessment of understanding of children, although clearly this would be desirable.

The decision of the qualified medical practitioner on this matter was intended to be final. In drafting s 2(4) the Scottish Law Commission (SLC) considered a number of options, one of which was for doctors to provide treatment to those under 16 where the child 'was capable' of understanding the nature and consequences of proposed treatment. The SLC rejected this approach, as it would require the doctor to determine *as a matter of fact* whether the child was capable, where another doctor or a court might come to a different conclusion. It was thought to 'give little protection to doctors and might make them reluctant to give treatment on the basis of a young person's consent except in the most obvious and uncontroversial cases'. Instead, they chose to draft this provision so that a child has legal capacity 'where *in the opinion* of the qualified medical practitioner' the child was capable of understanding the nature and possible consequences of the proposed treatment (Scottish Law Commission, 1987, paras 3.73–4).

A single doctor's opinion is enough to give the child legal capacity and it seems this decision cannot be challenged. It was not contemplated that a second opinion should be sought, since this would be unduly burdensome and raise practical difficulties (Scottish Law Commission, 1987, para 3.75). Although this prevents second-guessing of the doctor's opinion, it may not deal with the situation where there are a number of medical practitioners 'attending' the child who disagree on the extent of the child's understanding. It may well be that the opinion of any one of them would be sufficient to afford the child legal capacity, since there is no stated mechanism for dealing with professional disagreement. By contrast, the Adults with Incapacity (Scotland) Act 2000 provides that it is the medical practitioner with *primary responsibility* for the care of the adult who is to certify incompetence and who has authority to either provide treatment himself or instruct others to do so.[77] Even this may cause some difficulties in interpretation, but it does provide a hierarchical structure for resolving differences of opinion, which is absent in respect of children.

In England and Wales, the position is rather different. Although the law sets the standard of competence, the assessment of competence largely remains a matter for the doctors treating the young person and it is their evidence that holds most sway in the cases that have come to court.[78] It is,

77 Adults with Incapacity (Scotland) Act 2000, s 47.
78 *Re E (a minor) (wardship: medical treatment)* [1992] 2 FCR 219, Fam D. *Re R (a minor) (wardship: medical treatment)* [1991] 4 All ER 177, CA. *Re W (a minor) (medical treatment)* [1992] 4 All ER 627, CA.

however, increasingly common for judges to interview patients themselves, including children, where possible. This approach was undertaken, for example, in *Re E* (1992).[79] It seems, therefore, that a court could come to a different view of the competence of a child than the child's doctors, since the test laid down by Lord Scarman is that the child understands, rather than is believed by the doctor to be capable of understanding. The courts have not so far taken a different view on competence from doctors in any reported judgment. This may indicate that doctors are carrying out assessments in line with judicial expectations, although it might equally be argued that this is yet another instance of judicial deference to medical opinion. For example, Scarman LJ said that:

> I accept that great responsibilities will lie on the medical profession. It is, however, a learned and highly trained profession regulated by statute and governed by a strict ethical code which is vigorously enforced . . .

> The truth may well be that the rights of parents and children in this sensitive area are better protected by professional standards of the medical profession than by 'a priori' legal lines of division between capacity and lack of capacity to consent since any such dividing line is sure to produce in some cases hardship and injury to health.[80]

There are advantages and disadvantages to both approaches. Allowing courts to have the final say could have the effect that the Scottish Law Commission anticipated – that doctors may be more cautious about finding that a child has capacity. This may especially be the case since, if they are subsequently held to have been wrong, it creates the potential for a civil suit, although criminal liability is unlikely. If doctors are less willing to hold children competent, this may also lead to problems where broader policy considerations suggest that children should not be deterred from seeking medical advice and treatment.[81] However, if the doctor cannot be challenged, as noted earlier, it is possible that maturity of judgement may be equated with the values and views of the person making the assessment. It has been suggested that in failing to provide further specific criteria for the medical practitioner in his or her assessment of the child's understanding, the ALC(S)A 1991 may be in breach of Article 6(1) of the ECHR, in the light of *Osman v UK*[82] (Blackie and Patrick, 2001, para 11.17). Article 6 provides that 'in the determination of his civil rights and obligations or of any criminal charge against him,

---

79 *Re E (a minor) (wardship: medical treatment)* [1992] 2 FCR 219, Fam D.
80 *Gillick v West Norfolk and Wisbech Area Health Authority* [1985] 3 All ER 402, HL at 425.
81 *Gillick v West Norfolk and Wisbech Area Health Authority* [1985] 3 All ER 402, HL. *R v Secretary of State for Health and the Family Planning Association, ex parte Axon* [2006] 1 FCR 175, QB D.
82 *Osman v UK* (1998) (1999) 1 FLR 193, ECt HR.

everyone is entitled to a fair and public hearing within a reasonable time by an independent and impartial tribunal established by law'. As it stands, there is the danger that a child could be deprived of legal capacity and have no recourse to the courts, simply because s/he disagrees with the opinion or advice of the doctor. One way round this would be to hold that the doctor's assessment that a child was capable of understanding would be final as respects anyone other than the child. Children would be restricted to contesting a decision that they lack capacity, so that their consent would prevent actions based on assault or trespass to the person. Like adults, they would retain the right to bring actions for failures in adequate information disclosure. This would be my suggested position. Given what has been said already, it may perhaps be doubtful whether a court would go against the doctor's assessment, but the legal right to have this tested should be recognised. Of course, one way of avoiding legal action would be for the child simply to seek another doctor's opinion and a similar approach might be advocated to that taken in connection with the conscientious objection clause under the Abortion Act 1967 (British Medical Association, 1999). If a doctor has particular views, for example, on underage sex, which make him or her unwilling to provide contraceptive advice or treatment, this would need to be explained to give the child fair notice and the option to seek care elsewhere. This relies on doctors being aware of and honest about the extent to which their personal beliefs are influencing their judgement, both with themselves and with children. It also will not solve all problems here, but it is my belief that a clear explanation of why the doctor finds the child to lack capacity should be given in any event and this might provide more of an incentive to do so. The point made by the SLC should also be borne in mind: 'the fact that legally effective consent is given does not oblige a doctor to proceed with that treatment' (SLC, 1987, para 3.81). However, this is not a matter of denying the competence of the individual child; it merely asserts that even competent patients, of whatever age, do not have the right to demand treatment that the medical practitioner believes is inappropriate.

Care must of course be taken to ensure that the child is able to weigh up the risks and benefits of treatment and of any alternatives, including non-treatment, and to understand their implications. This necessarily introduces an element of imprecision into the assessment and since there are the concerns already raised about compliance with the ECHR, some further guidance to doctors on the way that this should be approached might be welcome. There is still a limit to how specific guidance can be, given the range of circumstances in which advice and treatment may be sought, and whether it will be properly adhered to in practice. It might be of more value if it concentrated on the kinds of issues discussed earlier: that it is maturity of decision-making skills, such as being able to assess long-term consequences, intellectual capacity and reasoning abilities, as well as an appreciation of the wider consequences of treatment, that should be stressed, not the maturity of the decision.

My proposal is therefore set in terms of the level of understanding that is necessary, focusing on the child's right to respect for autonomy, where they are either able to demonstrate they have achieved this or are presumed competent. I suggest that this is in line with the approach that is adopted in Scotland. However, at present, in England and Wales, competence is not enough. While later cases have mainly concerned refusal of treatment and hence will be discussed in greater detail in the next chapter, it has been stated that, although parents cannot override consent given by a competent child, the application of the best interests test means a court can.[83] This prioritises a protective approach to young people, but what it seeks to protect is the views of others, in particular, the medical profession, on what is in the child's best interests. It must be noted, though, that judicial statements on this point are strictly *obiter* since they have involved overruling refusal rather than consent of competent children. Nevertheless, it has been clearly stated that:

> Section 8 of the Family Law Reform Act 1969 gives minors who have attained the age of 16 a right to consent to surgical, medical or dental treatment. Such a consent cannot be overridden by those with parental responsibility for the minor. It can, however, be overridden by the court.
>
> . . . A minor of any age who is '*Gillick* competent' in the context of particular treatment has a right to consent to that treatment which again cannot be overridden by those with parental responsibility, but can be overridden by the court.[84]

There is some support for this approach from the United Nations Committee on the Rights of the Child, which has produced additional guidance on adolescents' health and development. Indeed, it may be seen as taking an even more conservative view. In interpreting Article 3 of the UN Convention, it is stated that:

> Before consent is given by parents, adolescents need to be given a chance to express freely their views and they should be given due weight, in accordance with article 12 of the Convention. However, if the adolescent is of sufficient maturity, informed consent shall be obtained from the

---

83 *Re W (a minor) (medical treatment)* [1992] 4 All ER 627, CA. *Re L (medical treatment: Gillick competence)* (1998) [1999] 2 FCR 524, Fam D.

84 *Re W (a minor) (medical treatment)* [1992] 4 All ER 627, CA, per Lord Donaldson at 637. See, also, Lord Balcombe.

adolescent her/himself, while informing the parents, if this is in the 'best interest of the child'.[85]

While endorsing greater recognition of the possibility that adolescents, at least, may be able to give their own consent to medical treatment and the consequent need to maintain confidentiality, parents' involvement and the best interests of the child are endorsed.[86] This also raises the question whether courts overriding a competent child's consent could be a breach of his or her Article 8 rights under the ECHR. This is a matter which has provoked rather more discussion in the context of refusal of consent and will be dealt with there.

Emphasising a best interests rather than an autonomy-based approach has been criticised (see, for example, Lee, 1987). The Scottish Law Commission put the argument succinctly and it is a view that I share:

> The best interests test seems too restrictive and would, in our view, be unnecessary. If it is accepted that a child may consent if he is of sufficient maturity to understand the treatment proposed then that test should apply whether the treatment is for his benefit or not. In that respect the young person should be treated no differently from anyone else capable of consenting. . . . In our view this is the logically coherent approach.
>
> (Scottish Law Commission, 1987, para 3.77)

Others disagree. Laurie, for instance, has objected that the proposition that a mature minor test should replace that of best interests is just as crude a threshold as that of the age of majority, so that 'the presumption shifts and you are free to take all the bad decisions that you want irrespective of their consequences'. He goes on to say that:

> In the context of the child . . . where there is a presumption of incapacity and where there is a continuing obligation to protect his or her welfare, such an all-or-nothing attitude to autonomous decision-making can be seen as tantamount to an abandonment of the patient. While we may find this acceptable in the case of the competent adult, there are too many doubts and unresolved issues to justify the bringing forward of the 'clear line approach' to maturity and autonomy. There is no such clear line.
>
> (Laurie, 2006, p 142)

---

85 United Nations Committee on the Rights of the Child, General Comment No. 4: Adolescent health and development in the context of the Convention on the Rights of the Child (CRC/GC/2003/4, 2003), para 32.

86 Confidentiality is dealt with Ibid, para 33.

In such circumstances, where autonomy and welfare are in opposition, he believes that it is welfare rather than autonomy that should triumph (see, also, Mason and Laurie, 2006, para 10.52). I freely acknowledge that assessment of maturity has the problems inherent in any form of individualised test for capacity, so that drawing a 'clear line' may be impossible and there may be mistakes either side of it. However, this is equally the case for age-based criteria, where presumptions about capacity are as apt to allow people's decisions to be respected or not on what I would argue is an even more arbitrary basis. At the heart of the matter is why a welfare test should be applied and I return to my contention that it is justified only where the person is unable to make a sufficiently autonomous choice. Where a person reasonably appears to meet that standard, as the SLC concluded, their protection is no longer warranted. There are legitimate reasons for requiring sufficient autonomy to be demonstrated rather than presumed for younger people, but not for taking a different approach in principle.

The role of parents

The judges in *Gillick* took opposing views on whether parents should decide on treatment for their children until the age of majority. The strongest opinions in favour of this were expressed in the Court of Appeal. In particular, it was emphasised that there could be no interference with parental rights, other than by a court or other lawful authority, and that a doctor's reliance solely on the consent of a child would be such an interference. So, for example, it was said by Parker J that:

> as a matter of law a girl under 16 can give no valid consent to anything in the areas under consideration which apart from consent would constitute an assault, whether civil or criminal, and can impose no valid prohibition on a doctor against seeking parental consent.[87]

Unless the situation is an emergency, in which case consent was said to be unnecessary, a doctor would require either parental consent or an application to a court. This conclusion was greeted with surprise and some dismay by commentators such as Kennedy:

> The Court of Appeal introduces into the law the notion of a child as a chattel, an object of possession and control. This is hardly the posture that a court, a legal system, or a society committed to the welfare of children would ordinarily adopt. That it gives serious consideration to a

---

87 *Gillick v West Norfolk and Wisbech Area Health Authority* [1985] 1 All ER 533, CA at 551.

parent who refuses consent to treatment which a competent young girl wants and a doctor thinks appropriate is, frankly, alarming.

(Kennedy, 1991, pp 85–6)

Other commentators do not interpret support for parental autonomy in this way. Ross contends that it is wholly appropriate for parents to continue to make decisions for their children unless they are not sufficiently promoting their basic interests (Ross, 1998). She considers that this forms part of a liberal community's respect for parents and favours laws that, for example, 'allow parents to decide upon the nature of their children's sex education and laws which require parental involvement in the procurement of medical care pertaining to sexual activity' (Ross, 1998, p 164). However, this is dependent on her view that children under the age of majority should be considered globally legally incapacitated.

As it turned out, the majority in the House of Lords was not prepared to uphold the supremacy of parental authority. Lord Fraser disputed the approach of the Court of Appeal that parental rights were virtually absolute over children:

> It is, in my view, contrary to the ordinary experience of mankind, at least in Western Europe in the present century, to say that a child or a young person remains in fact under the complete control of his parents until he attains the definite age of majority, now 18 in the United Kingdom, and that on attaining that age he suddenly acquires independence. In practice most wise parents relax their control gradually as the child develops and encourage him or her to become increasingly independent. Moreover, the degree of parental control actually exercised over a particular child does in practice vary considerably according to his understanding and intelligence and it would, in my opinion, be unrealistic for the courts not to recognise these facts.[88]

Accordingly, he quoted with approval Lord Denning's observation in *Hewer v Bryant* that:

> . . . the legal right of a parent to the custody of a child ends at the 18th birthday: and even up till then, it is a dwindling right which the courts will hesitate to enforce against the wishes of the child, and the more so the older he is. It starts with a right of control and ends with little more than advice.[89]

---

88 *Gillick v West Norfolk and Wisbech Area Health Authority* [1985] 3 All ER 402, HL at 410–11.
89 *Hewer v Bryant* [1970] 1 QB D 357 at 369.

Where a doctor finds the child competent, then parental rights to consent or even to be informed, disappear. This has been upheld in *Axon* (2006), where as we have seen, the introduction of the HRA 1998 has been held not to have changed the position.[90] The court noted that despite earlier rulings giving priority to parental rights to determine their children's treatment, the ECtHR has more recently held that in 'judicial decisions where the rights under Article 8 of parents and of a child are at stake, the child's rights must be the paramount consideration'.[91] Nevertheless, the court concentrated on the termination of parental rights rather than the separate Article 8 rights of children, which is disappointing.

In Scotland, only one reported case has dealt with the interpretation of s 2(4) ALC(S)A 1991 – *Houston, applicant* (1996).[92] The case concerned a 15-year-old boy who refused consent to treatment for mental illness. Since it deals with refusal of consent it will be examined in more detail in the following chapter, but a few observations were made about consent that are relevant here. Evidence was led by the boy's doctors that despite his condition, he was 'capable of understanding the nature and possible consequences of the procedures and treatment' in accordance with s 2(4) of the ALC(S)A 1991. While there was some uncertainty over whether his mother would be willing to override his refusal of consent, it was suggested to the court that as a matter of law she had the power to do so, because s 5(1) ALC(S)A 1991 expressly preserves the powers of guardians that existed before the act came into force. The judge, Sheriff McGowan, held that:

> . . . it seems to me illogical that, on the one hand, a person under the age of 16 should be granted the power to decide upon medical treatment for himself while, on the other hand, his parents have the right to override his decision. I am inclined to the view that the minor's decision is paramount and cannot be overridden. The 1991 Act itself does not provide any mechanism for resolving a dispute between a minor and guardian but it seems to me that logic demands that the minor's decision is paramount.[93]

This is partly due to the effect of the ALC(S)A 1991, defining parental rights in terms of 'guardianship, custody and access'. According to the SLC, while the decision to take a child to a doctor was an exercise of the power of custody, consent to medical treatment on the child's behalf was an exercise of the right to act as the child's legal representative. Since the purpose of

---

90 *R v Secretary of State for Health and the Family Planning Association, ex parte Axon* [2006] 1 FCR 175, QB D.

91 *Yousef v Netherlands* (2003) 36 EHRR 345, ECtHR at para 73,

92 *Houston, Applicant* 1996 SCLR 943, Sh Ct.

93 Ibid at 945.

allowing parents to represent their children was to enable legally binding decisions to be made on their behalf, once a child gains the ability to act for him or herself, such a parental right ceases to be necessary and is extinguished (Scottish Law Commission, 1987. See, also, Sutherland, 1999, para 3.69). *Houston* (1996) was heard before the Children (Scotland) Act 1995 came into force. In fact, it appears to reinforce this position. Section 15(5) states that a person may act as a child's legal representative only if the child is not capable of acting on his or her own behalf, which points to the same conclusion as that reached by the sheriff. This is the interpretation I favour, although it has been suggested that since parents retain the responsibility and right to give direction until the child is 16 and guidance until the child is 18, parents need at least to be informed where children seek medical treatment to be able to provide advice (Thomson, 2006, para 11.9). It must be remembered, though, that the C(S)A 1995 also states that these responsibilities only exist 'in so far as compliance with this section is practicable and in the interests of the child'.[94] A finding of competence carries with it an obligation to respect confidentiality, which would necessarily be breached by informing parents, even if they had no legal power to override the decision. I would argue that in these circumstances disclosure is not permitted and compliance with this section is impracticable. Higher courts have not examined the position, so any conclusions drawn from *Houston* (1996) remain speculative, but it provides some support for the conclusion that, as in England and Wales, parents cannot displace a competent child's consent. This seems to me to be the right approach.

Conclusion

Protecting the welfare of children requires that they should be provided with appropriate medical care and where they are unable to give a legally valid consent, it makes sense for this to be given by their parents. Exercising this power in conjunction with medical advice is, in most cases, the most suitable approach. However, in some situations parental and clinical discretion may not be sufficient to safeguard properly children's rights. The harm and reasonableness principles should be applied here to determine in what circumstances court involvement is necessary and whether the courts should overrule parental choices. Where children have capacity to make their own decisions, respect for their autonomy should mean that their consent is legally valid and exclude parents and the courts from overriding it. This already seems to be the position in Scotland, although it cannot be said to be certain. In the next chapter I will go on to consider the more vexed situation where parents or competent children refuse consent.

94 C(S)A 1995 s 1.

Chapter 3

Refusal of consent

Allowing recommended medical treatment to be undertaken is generally seen as promoting the welfare of the child, or at least not being sufficiently against it to warrant judicial intervention, and either parents or competent children can give consent. However, where treatment is refused, it may more clearly bring a range of other factors into play, such as personal values and social and cultural concerns, that challenge the priority that it is often assumed should be given to medical benefit (Bridge, 1999a).[1] As in the previous chapter, I will deal with children who lack capacity first, followed by those who may have it.

Refusal of consent for children who lack capacity

Procedures requiring parental unanimity

Where medical procedures are regarded as being within parental discretion, usually one parent's consent is sufficient.[2] Despite this, it has been held that there is 'a small group of important decisions' that should only be carried out where both parents agree. If they do not and cannot resolve this informally, performing the procedure would require a court to decide this was in the child's best interests.[3] Essentially this gives the parent who refuses a right of veto, unless a court overturns this. The case in which this apparently new category of situations was coined concerned the circumcision of a male infant, which the Muslim father wanted performed, against the wishes of the non-Muslim mother, who was the child's primary carer. Ritual male circumcision had been held in an *obiter dictum* to be acceptable under the common law.[4]

---

1 Some parts in this chapter are adapted from Elliston, 1996.
2 *Re R (a minor) (wardship: medical treatment)* [1991] 4 All ER 177, CA, per Lord Donaldson MR at 184.
3 *Re J (child's religious upbringing and circumcision)* [2000] 1 FCR 307, CA.
4 *R v Brown* [1993] 2 All ER 75, HL, per Templeman LJ at 79.

Clarification of the legal position has been recommended, but no legislation has so far been enacted (Law Commission, 1995a, pp 119, 128). In its absence, the *obiter dictum* was relied on in *Re J* (2000). The court held that circumcision was being sought for social and cultural reasons, rather than medical necessity, but accepted that nonetheless this was normally a matter for parents to decide.

Given the arguments that were made about cosmetic surgery in the previous chapter, it is questionable whether this should be the case as there is considerable disagreement over the risks and benefits of male circumcision (British Medical Association 2006b, General Medical Council, 1997). The British Medical Association (BMA), for example, notes the practical argument that 'if there is a risk that a child will be circumcised in unhygienic or otherwise unsafe conditions, doctors may consider it better that they carry out the procedure, or refer to another practitioner, rather than allow the child to be put at risk' (British Medical Association, 2006b). As it recognises, this could also be said of female circumcision, save that the latter has been prohibited by statute. As a matter of rights, it observes that Art 24.3 of the UN Convention on the Rights of the Child requires States to 'take all effective and appropriate measures with a view to abolishing traditional practices prejudicial to the health of children'. However, this must be balanced against Art 9.2 of the European Convention on Human Rights (ECHR), which protects the rights of individuals to practise their religion (British Medical Association, 2006b). The HRA 1998 may also be used either to support or reject non-therapeutic circumcision on other grounds.

> One reason why it is not clear where the balance of rights lies is that the medical evidence is equivocal. Some argue that circumcision is a relatively neutral procedure that, competently performed, carries little risk but can confer important psychosocial benefits. Others argue that circumcision has, or can have, profound and long-lasting adverse effects on the person who has been circumcised. If it was shown that circumcision where there is no clinical need is prejudicial to a child's health and well-being, it is likely that a legal challenge on human rights grounds would be successful. Indeed, if damage to health were proven, there may be obligations on the state to proscribe it.
>
> (British Medical Association, 2006b)

Some, such as Feldman, suggest that such practices contravene Arts 3 and 8 of the ECHR (Feldman, 2002, pp 270–2). Permitting such procedures on the basis of parental choice has been criticised as being an area where both professional guidance and law are uncharacteristically tolerant of risks inflicted on young children, given the absence of clear medical benefits (Fox and Thomson, 2005). Whether parental rights to practise their own religion should extend to permitting ritual circumcision upon children who are too young to consider the issue for themselves is therefore a subject where opposing opinions are manifest. Nevertheless, although it amounts to an invasion of the child's bodily integrity for reasons that are either not primarily or not at all therapeutic, it can be justified under a welfare assessment as follows:

> ... the welfare of a child demands his conformity to the standards and practices of his family and his religious group. He may be disadvantaged by a failure to conform. From a religious, cultural, and, indeed, historical perspective, circumcision is a necessary part of family traditions for some people.
>
> (Bridge, 1999b. See, also, British Medical Association, 2006)

It may therefore be justified not only under Art 8 of the ECHR, but under Arts 9 and 14, which could be used to support circumcision as being in accordance with the child's own rights to non-interference with family life, freedom of religion and nondiscrimination (Fortin, 2005, p 332). The courts appear to share the view that the welfare argument can be applied here, but where there is a dispute between parents, clearly this will depend to a large extent on the environment in which the child will be brought up. In the case of *Re J* (2000), it was held that since the primary carer objected, circumcision should not be performed since it was not thought likely to prejudice the child's social integration in the circumstances in which he was being cared for. Nevertheless, this does not give the primary carer permission to have a child circumcised, if the views of the parents were reversed, without court authorisation. Unlike the situation of consent to recommended medical treatment, where the onus is on the objecting parent to bring the case before a court, here the onus will be on the parent seeking the procedure. The same stance was taken in *Re S* (2005).[5]

This could be criticised for failing to take into account the traditions of minorities, by effectively holding that their practices do not conform to societal norms and hence require external supervision. As Viens puts it, there is a need for tolerance and 'to differentiate between rituals and practices that are in fact grievously harmful and those which relate to the enhancement of a child's religious and cultural identity' (Viens, 2004, p 246). On the other hand, it may be regarded as another example of the premise that interventions that will be irreversible and are not being carried out for therapeutic purposes require more in the way of clear, objectively argued justification to ensure that they do not compromise significant interests of the child. Where parents agree, the welfare of the child is felt to be met by allowing them to consent to circumcision. Where they do not, the court must examine whether circumcision is in the child's best interests. The same kinds of argument could

---

5   *Re S (children) (specific issue order: religion: circumcision)* [2005] 1 FLR 236, Fam D.

also be made where even relatively low-risk cosmetic surgery is proposed and, while the courts have not addressed this, the need for joint parental consent can be suggested to be equally appropriate. The BMA has advised that where parents are in dispute over 'controversial and elective procedures', doctors should not proceed without the authority of a court (British Medical Association, 2006a).

Interestingly, though, immunisation has also been said to fall within this small group of decisions requiring joint parental consent, although precisely why this should be the case is more uncertain. In the cases of *C and F* (2003), unmarried fathers with parental responsibility sought court orders for a range of immunisations to be carried out on the only child of the family. The children, girls aged four and 10, were living with their mothers who were strongly opposed to immunisation. It was held that each girl's best interests lay in having most, but not all, of the immunisations and ordered that they should be given, listing appropriate immunisations for each child. This case will be returned to later, but for the moment I am concerned with whether immunisation should require joint parental consent or a court order. Although it is not being performed for directly therapeutic purposes, it is usually intended to safeguard the child's health, is generally regarded as being low risk and would on those grounds surely be expected to be able to be consented to by one parent alone. However, it has been described as a 'hotly contested issue' and, since immunisation is not compulsory, the degree of public debate over it appears to have tipped the balance in this situation.[6]

What I have proposed is that the threshold for court involvement should be based on a significant risk of serious harm to the child and that the courts should not overrule parents' decisions that are within the bounds of reasonableness. In consequence, parents should be permitted to determine the values that are important to them in raising their children, provided that these do not fall below societal standards for child welfare and compromise important rights of the child. However, I share Fortin's view that male circumcision is a matter where serious consideration should be given to postponing decisions until children are of an age to be able to consider them for themselves, and I would say the same for other forms of elective surgery, such as minor cosmetic procedures (Fortin, 2005, pp 329–32). Enabling parents to bring up their children in their own family and cultural traditions is important for a liberal society and it is a policy that I support. Nevertheless, I am unconvinced that permitting permanent body alterations upon an incompetent child for social or cultural reasons is justified. Notwithstanding my reservations, at present the courts consider that, where parents agree, male

---

6   *Re B (a child) (immunisation)* [2003] 3 FCR 156, CA, affg sub nom *Re C (a Child) (Immunisation: Parental rights); Re F (a Child) (Immunisation: Parental rights)* [2003] EWHC 1376, Fam D.

circumcision of children is not a decision they need be concerned in. A joint decision is taken as an indication that the social or cultural goal that is the justification for allowing the non-therapeutic procedure is met. In such cases it must in fact be seen by the courts as not breaching a 'harm to the child threshold' and to be within the scope of reasonable parental decision-making. However, where the social or cultural goals are not shared by the parents, the justification for performing such irreversible procedures on an incompetent child is correspondingly less weighty and a case requires to be made to the court's satisfaction as to why they should be permitted. In such cases, the involvement of the courts presupposes a judgment being taken that will pri-oritise one parent's views over those of the other. This evaluation could equally well be performed under a harm and reasonableness standard. The court must still undertake a welfare assessment and in this case come to a conclusion on where the balance lies between the views of parents who may both be considered to be reasonable. However, it does not allow the court to make the dubious claim that it knows what is 'best' for the child in this situation.

Immunisation, on the other hand, normally has therapeutic intent, although it is prophylactic in nature, and is usually regarded as a routine form of intervention. In my view, despite the approach currently taken by the courts, this seems a case where the decision could reasonably be taken by a parent to consent to immunisation and it should be for a parent disagreeing with this to bring the matter before a court for resolution.

Parental refusal of treatment

From what has already been said, it is clear that, as the legal representatives of their child, parents may refuse medical treatment, choose options that doctors feel are not optimal, or even not seek treatment at all. Their decisions will in many cases not be felt to warrant court involvement since they will not meet the threshold for compromising significant interests of the child. Providing treatment without consent would be unlawful, unless the situation can be regarded as an emergency, when the doctrine of necessity would apply.[7] However, in some cases the consequences may be regarded as so serious that a refusal of consent is believed to be against the best interests of the child.

One of the most litigated areas has been refusal of blood transfusions by parents on behalf of their children.[8] The usual reason given is that the parents

7   *F v West Berkshire Health Authority and Another* [1989] All ER 545.
8   *Re S (A Minor) (Medical Treatment)* [1993] 1 FLR 376, Fam D; *Re O (a minor) (medical treatment)* [1993] 1 FCR 925, Fam D. *Re R (A Minor) (Blood Transfusion)* [1993] 2 FCR 544, Fam D; *Re S (A Minor) (Consent to Medical Treatment)* (1994) [1995] 1 FCR 604, Fam D.

object on religious grounds and indeed, as a result, the Jehovah's Witness Society is probably best-known to those outside it as a faith that forbids acceptance of blood transfusions, although certain procedures such as autologous transfusions may be acceptable. This rests on an interpretation of certain passages from the Bible.[9] Christian Scientists have a wider range of objections to medical treatment, believing that healing is the will of God and as a result, blood products, blood transfusions, organ donation and life support are likely to be objected to. In addition, medication is considered inappropriate (Eddy, 1875). Other groups may also have faith or culturally based objections to certain types of interventions. In all cases brought before the UK courts, blood transfusions have been authorised on the basis that this represents the best interests of the child. The first case dealing with this issue illustrates this position. It concerned a four-year-old with T-cell leukaemia, intensive treatment for which would result in the need for blood transfusions.[10] The parents, both Jehovah's Witnesses, opposed this. The doctor in charge of S's care had sought to provide nonstandard treatment to comply with parental wishes but, through the intervention of the local authority, wanted permission to move to the intensive treatment. Medical evidence was put by the judge thus: 'The choice is between the full treatment with a 50 per cent prospect of cure or mere palliation with no hope of cure'. The father gave evidence to the court of his beliefs and was described by the judge as follows:

> There was no impression of the bigot, of the closed mind, or of unreasonable obstinacy. His acceptance of the inevitability of life and death coupled with his faith seemed to make it easy for him to conclude that faith comes first and is not to be abandoned simply because it leads to awful decisions.[11]

However, his faith was not by itself regarded as being sufficient to countervail considerations of the child's interests in being treated. One other aspect of the parents' beliefs was also raised:

> Finally, [Counsel] invites the court to look ahead to the later years of childhood. If this treatment is applied in the face of parental opposition what would be the difficulties and stresses for S in years to come – parented by parents who believe that his life was prolonged by an ungodly act? Well, that consideration seems to me one that has little foundation in reality. The reality seems to me to be that family reaction will recognise

9   The Bible: Genesis 9:4; Leviticus 17:11–14; Acts 15:20, 29. Jehovah's Witness Society, 1990.
10   *Re S (A Minor) (Medical Treatment)* [1993] 1 FLR 376, Fam D.
11   Ibid at 379.

that the responsibility for consent was taken from them and, as a judicial act, absolves their conscience of responsibility.[12]

Taking all of these factors into account, the court was clearly persuaded of the priority to be given to the medical evidence of benefit to the child and that this outweighed any parental objections. This pattern has been followed in later cases so that it seems now settled beyond doubt that blood and blood products may be provided to young children against parents' wishes, if this is thought to provide a medical benefit.[13] Indeed, given the strong rulings on this by the courts, cases are far less frequent now as parents are likely to be advised that a court order will be sought and litigation may not be pursued if they accept that the transfusion is inevitable. Resort to the courts will be necessary if parental objection is sustained and the situation is not an emergency (Royal College of Surgeons of England, 2002).

A significant underlying theme can be found in the words of Justice Holmes in the American case of *Prince v Massachusetts* that:

> Parents may be free to become martyrs themselves, but it does not follow that they are free in identical circumstances to make martyrs of their children before they have reached the age of full and legal discretion when they can make choices for themselves.[14]

This case has been referred to with approval in English cases and relies on the idea that to reject conventional, life-saving treatment, the individual must accept religious beliefs, freely and voluntarily and as an informed choice.[15]

Under my proposals the same result would be reached, but on a more defensible basis. As Diekema explains, where the best interests test is used, this notion is:

> ... inherently a question of values, and most parents believe they are making a decision in the best interest of their child. Parents who are Jehovah's Witnesses, for example, may truly believe that they are making a decision in the best interest of their child when they refuse to consent to a blood transfusion. Loss of salvation is not, after all, a trivial consequence of acting on the physician's recommendation.
>
> (Diekema, 2004)

---

12 Ibid at 380.
13 *Re S (A Minor) (Medical Treatment)* [1993] 1 FLR 376, Fam D; *Re O (a minor) (medical treatment)* [1993] 1 FCR 925, Fam D. *Re R (A Minor) (Blood Transfusion)* [1993] 2 FCR 544, Fam D; *Re S (A Minor) (Consent to Medical Treatment)* (1994) [1995] 1 FCR 604, Fam D.
14 (1944) 321 US Reports 158.
15 See, e.g. *Re E (a minor) (wardship: medical treatment)* [1992] 2 FCR 219, Fam D and *Re R (a minor) (wardship: medical treatment)* [1991] 4 All ER 177, CA.

Applying the harm principle instead, permitting treatment can be justified. Even for Ross, who supports a wide degree of parental discretion, this does not extend to situations where the treatment refused is of proven efficacy with a high likelihood of success and refusal puts the child at a considerable risk of death, serious injury or illness (Ross, 1998, p 135). Withholding treatment must amount to a significant risk of serious harm, which will undoubtedly be the case where the child's death is likely. The treatment would normally be provided and is well-established. Although there may be risks of harm associated with it, including the parents' feelings about the child following treatment against their wishes, these can reasonably be regarded as being less than the risks of non-treatment. To the charge that this disregards the parents' religious views, the answer can be given that while their opinions must be respected regarding their own treatment, they fall within the range of views that reasonable people do not have to accept and should not be made by proxy decision-makers (Rhodes and Holzman, 2004).

As far as the immediacy of the need for treatment and pursuing options that the parents would agree with are concerned, here there is scope for different responses. It could be argued either that the medically recommended option should always be given, if this gives the greatest likelihood for successful treatment, or that an option with less success should be accepted as reasonable if this better fits in with the parents' wishes. In *Re S* (1993), in addition to religious objections, some mention was made of parental concerns over medical risks of transfusion, but these were dismissed as being enormously outweighed by the benefits. However, it was also suggested on behalf of the parents that there was advice to American judges at the time that read that:

> If there is a choice of procedures, if, for example, a doctor recommends a procedure which has an 80% chance of success but of which the parents disapprove, and the parents have no objection to a procedure which has only a 40% chance of success the doctor must take the medically riskier but parentally unobjectionable course.[16]

The court also rejected this approach, with Thorpe J holding that, under the inherent jurisdiction, the welfare of the child remained the paramount consideration. Choosing a less objectionable, but medically riskier alternative, did not meet that standard.

Clearly much here rests on the comparison of the risks and benefits of the compared options and how strong the evidence is to support them. A 40 per cent higher risk of death posed by less conventional treatment is most

---

16 Counsel of Judges in America, 'Guides to the Judge in Medical Orders Affecting Children', 27. Cited at in *Re S (A Minor) (Medical Treatment)* [1993] 1 FLR 376, Fam D at 380.

unlikely to meet a reasonableness standard. On the other hand, a difference of a few per cent, especially given the likely imprecision of the statistics when they are applied to an individual child, may be rather harder to judge as being so unreasonable that no parent could make such a choice, even if the actual grounds on which the parents rest their opinion are ones which others could reasonably disagree with. Of course, other matters than simply survival, such as the relative pain and suffering likely to result from the different options, would also need to be factored into the equation, but where the predicted treatment outcomes are not thought to be very different from a medical point of view, arguably more weight should be placed on the wishes of the family than *Re S* (1993) would seem to allow. This would involve taking the decision from being a third category decision to a second category one, where there is room for different opinions if there are uncertain or not dramatically different outcomes (Rhodes and Holzman, 2004). At present, it seems likely that the court would not be prepared to allow this conclusion to be drawn. I suggest that they should take this into account. Advice to doctors is that they should seek to try to accommodate the wishes of the parents, provided this does not compromise the child's welfare and I believe that the reasonableness of the parent's views should also be the guiding principle for the courts (Royal College of Surgeons of England, 2002, para 31).

While religious convictions will not meet the reasonableness threshold where there is a serious risk of significant harm to the child, other cases have concerned refusal of conventional medicine based on fears that it may itself lead to harm to health, for example in the case of testing for HIV. In *Re C (a child) (HIV test)* (1999) an HIV positive mother and her partner refused to allow testing of their newborn child.[17] Contrary to medical advice she had given birth to the child by waterbirth and was breast-feeding, both of which were thought to increase the risk of infection to the child. The parents disputed conventional medical evidence on the transmission and treatment of HIV and viewed testing of their baby with deep suspicion because of what they felt would be the scope for further unwanted medical intervention in the event of a positive test result. Despite some support for their position being led by a medical expert on their behalf, the judge stated that the witness 'was the first to accept that his is a dissident view. It is none the worse for that. Orthodoxies are there to be challenged; and I would hope that there is no better place to do so than in a court of law.'[18] However, the weight of scientific evidence and experience of the doctors seeking to test the child and, if necessary, provide treatment, persuaded the judge that the case for testing was 'overwhelming' and it was ordered to take place.

Interestingly however, the practical limitations where parents do not wish

17 *Re C (a child) HIV test* [1999] 3 FCR 289, Fam D.
18 Ibid at 295.

to comply with medical advice were recognised. The Local Authority had made it clear they did not seek an order to prevent the mother from breast-feeding. The judge agreed and said:

> My belief is that the law cannot come between the baby and the breast. Indeed, if she cannot be persuaded by rational argument that she must curb her instinct to feed, I doubt whether the mother would comply with a court order, which would be, in effect, impossible to enforce. The parents will respond better to this judgment if they realise that it has intellectual integrity and makes no idle threats.

Of course, this response ignores the possibility that a child could be removed from its parents under child protection grounds, as discussed in Chapter 1. However, this requires a high threshold of evidence of harm to be met. In looking at this situation then, a degree of risk to the child was thought to be within the scope of the parents' discretion and that any other decision would involve too great a level of outside interference with their choices. Some parental choices were accepted, albeit reluctantly, by the doctors, some were not and the court sided with their views on the benefits of proceeding with testing as opposed to not doing so. While I would contend that the harm principle and reasonableness threshold would equally meet this situation, it does however raise the need to examine the strength of medical evidence and the seriousness of risks posed.

The joined cases of *C and F* (2003) were discussed earlier in the context of intraparental disputes but some of the points raised in them have wider application. The crucial factor in the judgment was the medical evidence about the relative risks and benefits of giving the various immunisations. The medical expert called for the mothers was a general practitioner and homeopath, who had become interested in the subject of vaccinations and formed her views by reading a large number of medical papers. The judge concluded her general position was broadly that the decline in disease rates has been due to factors other than immunisation and that immunisation does more harm than good.[19] The medical experts appointed for the fathers and for CAFCASS (Children and Family Court Advisory and Support Service) Legal, representing the child, were described by the judge as impressive witnesses with considerable expertise in infectious diseases. They were agreed on most points that the benefits of the proposed immunisations to the children far outweighed the possible risks and referred to a wealth of published articles to support their opinion. They concluded that the GP's arguments were not supported by the articles she had cited or any other evidence she presented.

19 *Re C (a child) (immunisation: parental rights); Re F (a child) (immunisation: parental rights)* [2003] EWHC 1376, Fam D, per Sumner J at para 40.

The judge felt it unnecessary to read or even scan most of the medical papers himself, but relied on the analysis and reports the experts had produced and their evidence in court. He was highly critical of the GP's conduct as an expert witness, concluding that she had neither understood nor complied with her duty to the court. As he put it 'Had I heard her evidence alone, I might have been misled and could well have reached a decision not supported by the research upon which she largely relied'.[20]

The duties of expert witnesses are set out in the Civil Procedures Rules Part 35. Although these do not formally apply to family proceedings, the guidance given on the duties of expert witnesses in family cases effectively follows them.[21] Among other matters, they require an expert witness to help the court on matters within his/her own expertise. This duty is paramount and over-rides any obligation to the person from whom the expert has received instructions or by whom s/he is paid. Of particular significance here is the duty to assist the court by providing objective, unbiased opinion on matters within his/her expertise, and that s/he should not assume the role of an advocate. Furthermore, an expert should consider all material facts, including those that might detract from his/her opinion. An expert should make it clear when a question or issue falls outside his/her expertise and when s/he is not able to reach a definite opinion, for example because s/he has insufficient information.[22] Sumner J did not suggest there was any bad faith on the GP's part; rather that she had allowed her deeply held feelings on the subject of immunisation to overrule the duty she owed to the court. He was driven to the conclusion that he lacked 'a reliable opinion which differs from [the other expert witnesses]'.[23] While conceding that this was a disadvantage on such an important subject, nevertheless he felt confident enough to proceed on it.

A key factor is therefore the esteem in which expert witnesses are held and it must be said that those working in approaches to health and wellbeing such as homeopathy start with a disadvantage compared with those in the more established medical profession. Similarly, those taking views that are not well supported by published research may find it an uphill struggle to convince a court that they should be accepted. Of course, in reply it can be argued that if there is no clear evidence to support claims then naturally the court should take some convincing. To this extent the medical/scientific and judicial approach may be seen to be comparable, both requiring persuasion that sufficient reliable evidence exists to support a conclusion. The consequence of reliance on an evidence-based approach in *C and F* (2003) was the conclusion

20 Ibid at para 45.
21 Ibid at paras 55–56. See *Re R (a minor) (expert's evidence)* (1991) 1 FLR 291, Fam D and *Re AB (child abuse: expert witness)* (1995) 1 FLR 192, Fam D.
22 Civil Procedure Rules 35.3 and 35.10.
23 *Re C (a child) (immunisation: parental rights); Re F (a child) (immunisation: parental rights)* [2003] EWHC 1376, Fam D, per Sumner J at para 59.

that not all of the immunisations should be given to both girls. For example, in the case of pertussis (or whooping cough) vaccination, there was no vaccine that was licensed for use in children over seven, so there had been no research or trial in this group. The suggested reason for this was that the vaccine was usually given in infancy, so it was not generally necessary to use it in older children. Nevertheless, while one medical expert witness recommended immunising the 10-year-old, the other, adopting a more cautious approach, did not. The judge chose to adopt the more cautious view since there was no approved vaccine for her. This was confirmed on appeal.[24] Nevertheless, while inquiry into the risks and benefits of proposed medical interventions undoubtedly should be undertaken where there is disagreement, the question remains whether giving the vaccine would have been so outside the scope of a reasonable parent's choice as to not permit a parent to choose it. If the judge's conclusion is correct, then arguably this vaccine should not be given to any children of this age unless there are strong indications for doing so in an individual case.

Further points about using the court's use of the best interests test may be made here. First, the mothers had appealed the case on the basis that the trial judge had adopted a two-stage test: examining the expert evidence first, followed by the wider considerations. This, they argued, meant that it became harder to displace the presumption that the immunisations should be given than by adopting a more holistic approach to the best interests of the child. The Court of Appeal disagreed, holding that it was sensible for the judge to have determined where the weight of expert evidence lay. If this had not supported giving the immunisations then it would have been unnecessary for him to continue considering the case. This seems the correct approach under the harm and reasonableness principles too, since justification for performing a disputed procedure must surely be made out first.

However, the best interests principle is rather harder to justify on other matters. For example, immunisation for rubella is not given primarily to protect that individual. It is a relatively mild condition and indeed children generally recover more quickly from it than adults and can develop antibodies from exposure. Immunisation is given principally in order to protect foetuses that are at risk of developing congenital problems if the mother contracts it during pregnancy. As such it is debatable whether immunisation for rubella is in the best interests of the child being immunised. While it will prevent her/him developing symptoms that may be unpleasant, this is not the primary justification for giving it. As such it can only be described as being in her/his best interests if a very broad definition, encompassing women giving birth to

---

24 *Re B (a child) (immunisation)* [2003] 3 FCR 156, CA, affg sub nom *Re C (a child) (immunisation: parental rights); Re F (a child) (immunisation: parental rights)* [2003] EWHC 1376, Fam D, Per Thorpe J at para 117.

healthy children, is accepted. Even so, it is quite hard to accept this in the case of a 10-year-old girl, where there was no suggestion that she was at risk of becoming pregnant. In addition, there is the question whether this judgment could be viewed as setting the standard for immunising children, since it was decided on the basis of best interests and gave explicit recommendations on which immunisations were required and why. Accordingly, could it be said all parents must allow immunisations, as to do otherwise would be to act against the child's best interests? However, the judge was at pains to say that this was not a case setting a precedent for compulsory vaccination. One reason for this was the fact that other evidence in other cases might reach a different conclusion and it was not appropriate for the courts to set standards of medical practice. The same point could also be made in respect of the immunisations that the judge did not permit.

A harm and reasonableness threshold meets these objections, by not claiming that immunisation is in the child's best interests, but that it is within the scope of reasonable parental decision-making. This allows them to decide whether, weighing up the risks and benefits and including matters such as public policy considerations of immunising school-age children for rubella, they feel it is appropriate. A similar conclusion has been reached in the Irish Supreme Court, where parents refused to allow doctors to perform a test on their baby to screen for phenylketonuria (PKU).[25] The test screens for a number of inherited conditions, both metabolic and endocrine, and is routinely performed on newborns. In PKU, the child has a defective gene, which means the liver is unable to break down protein, resulting in a build-up of a substance called phenylalanine in the blood, which eventually passes into the brain, causing mental retardation and other neurological problems.[26] Testing infants allows treatment to be given at an early age by altering diet to include artificial protein to prevent problems developing and it is undertaken by taking a small blood sample from a heel prick. Despite holding that the decision of the parents was 'manifestly unwise and disturbing', and that the test was of benefit to children, the court held that the parents were at liberty to make it. Any other conclusion would be to render testing compulsory, a position that the law, through the Irish Parliament, had refused to take. Accordingly, requiring the test to be performed would, according to Denham J, 'have a far reaching effect', turning healthcare policy into law, and would set a 'very low threshold' for court intervention in medical decision-making. It was also considered that to allow testing would be in breach of Irish constitutional rights that protected the rights of the family from outside interference. This includes the right of parents to make decisions for their children, unless exceptional circumstances warranted intervention. These circumstances were not held to be exceptional.

---

25 *North Western Hospital Board v W(H)* [2001] IESC 90, Irish SCt.
26 Ibid at para 187.

It remains to be seen whether UK courts would reach the same conclusion (see Laurie, 2003). While the PKU test was diagnostic, unlike immunisation, which is prophylactic in itself, it could be contended that both are preventive in seeking to avoid future ill-health for the children concerned. On a strict application of the best interests test, where the court can substitute its own decision for that of the parents as to what is best for the child, it could authorise immunisation or PKU testing, even where both parents oppose it. Although this may be a matter of the weight of medical evidence, it may also involve a matter of principle on the extent to which intervention in parental choices is appropriate. The significance of using the harm and reasonableness standard instead is that it should allow parents to make a decision, even if it is one with which the court disagrees. It has been my contention that the courts do have a place in setting the boundaries of medical practice. They can do so by determining whether what is contemplated properly falls within parental choice where the Parliaments have not legislated on the issue. This has been the case, for example, in respect of the sterilisation of people lacking capacity. Nevertheless, as I have argued earlier, immunisation is an area where I consider that these thresholds mean that parents should be free to consent to or refuse it. Immunisation and PKU tests are widely recognised as being beneficial, or at least, not to compromise significant interests of the child. Where parents disagree, it is objecting parents who should be required to raise this in court. Of course there are practical problems in implementing such an approach, particularly in the objecting parent being alerted to the possibility that such procedures are being proposed in time to prevent them pending court action. However, this is no different to any other area of recommended medical intervention and indeed it is already true under the existing approach that unless a doctor is told there may be objection, they have no reason not to proceed.

The wishes of parents have not been regarded as an overriding factor in the courts' decisions where medical treatment is concerned. In only one reported case has the court taken a different approach, the case of *Re T* (1996).[27] Here a 4-year-old child had a life-threatening liver defect. Medical opinion was unanimous that a liver transplant would be successful and provide good prospects of prolonging his life to a normal life expectancy, without serious residual disability. The boy's mother refused consent, believing that he should be allowed to enjoy his life without invasive surgery and the continued treatment required in consequence, even if this meant his life would be short. She had effectively sole parental responsibility since her husband was abroad, though he supported her decision. At first instance leave to proceed with treatment was granted, since it was held that the refusal of consent was unreasonable, but this was overturned on appeal. The Court of Appeal

27 *Re T (a minor) (wardship: medical treatment)* (1996) [1997] 1 All ER 906, CA.

criticised the emphasis that had been placed by the trial judge on the reasonableness of the parent's views, re-emphasising the point that the decision taken by the court must be based on the welfare of the child. However, more surprisingly, Butler-Sloss LJ, seemed to place great importance on the fact that the mother would be the child's main carer and that a good outcome for the child would depend on her wholehearted commitment to the treatment.[28] It may have weighed with the court that both she and her husband were themselves healthcare professionals, and so their views may have been regarded as being better informed than those of other parents. Significantly, it was said by Waite LJ that the parental objection here differed from those 'prompted by scruple or dogma of a kind which is patently incompatible with the principles of child health and welfare widely accepted by the generality of mankind' (at 513–14). He also stated that:

> ... the greater the scope for genuine debate between one view and another, the stronger will be the inclination of the court to be influenced by a reflection that in the last analysis the best interests of every child include the expectation that difficult decisions affecting the length and quality of its life will be taken for it by the parent to whom its care has been entrusted by nature.[29]

The approach of the court and, in particular, its acceptance of parental views, has received strong criticism (see, for example, Fox and McHale, 1997) and it seems to have been regarded with little enthusiasm in later cases. It was for example suggested that Re T (1996) was wholly exceptional, turning on its facts, and that it should be seen as being based on a rejection of the trial judge's views on the reasonableness of the parent's decision.[30] It is, however, still not easy to reconcile Re T's conclusions on the best interests of the child with other cases in this area, particularly those involving quality of life decisions. These will be discussed further in a later chapter.

I advocate a harm and reasonableness standard, which is more akin to the test employed by the trial judge. Having said this, I would endorse statements made in the Court of Appeal that medical opinions, even if unanimously in favour of treatment as they were here, 'are not determinative'.[31] Similarly, I have no quarrel with their wish to consider the overall circumstances of the child, including the likely effect on the family, including the aftercare of a child. Where the outcome of treatment, or a failure to treat, is borderline, then I agree that parental wishes should be given priority. While I support

28 Ibid at 915 and 917.
29 Ibid, per Waite LJ at 918.
30 Re B (a child) (immunisation) [2003] 3 FCR 156, CA, per Thorpe LJ at para 21.
31 Re T (a minor) (wardship: medical treatment) (1996) [1997] 1 All ER 906, CA, per Butler-Sloss LJ at 915.

these aspects of the Court of Appeal's judgments, even so, to me this is a prime example of the kind of situation where the parent's decision can be regarded as paradigmatically unreasonable. Like the cases concerning refusal of life-saving blood transfusions, the chance of success here in restoring a normal quality and length of life was thought to be high. Although the liver transplant was major surgery and likely to be painful and distressing, and would result in life-time immunosuppressant treatment, compared with failure to treat, the difference is so significant that it ought to have been authorised, regardless of the parent's views.

Perhaps surprisingly, there are no reported cases in Scotland under the C(S)A 1995 or the inherent jurisdiction dealing with parents' refusal of treatment for their young children. However, it is interesting to consider a case dealing with an alternative procedure for dealing with children in Scotland: the Children's Hearings System. In the case of *Finlayson, applicant*, a child had been found to suffer from severe haemophilia when he was six months old.[32] His parents were informed and asked to bring him in for treatment if any bleeding occurred. The parents were concerned at the possibility that he might contract AIDS through blood transfusions and favoured alternative medicine and homeopathic remedies. By the age of six, after a number of falls, he developed a chronic condition in his knee and doctors wished him to receive Factor VIII. After missed hospital appointments a Reporter to the Children's Hearings System was involved to investigate whether the child was in need of compulsory measures of care, such as a supervision requirement with a condition requiring the child to attend for medical examination or treatment. The Reporter decided that grounds for referral to a children's hearing were satisfied, but the parents disagreed. The matter was therefore taken to the Sheriff Court to determine whether the grounds for referral were indeed satisfied.

The Sheriff held that in spite of the fact that the parents were loving and concerned with the health of the child, their refusal to consent to conventional treatment constituted wilful neglect and lack of parental care likely to cause the child unnecessary suffering or serious impairment to his health or development. The Sheriff reached this conclusion, based on what a 'reasonable person' would consider acceptable conduct. The grounds for referral were established and the case was referred to a Children's Hearing for its decision on how to proceed. The outcome of this referral is not reported, but the court, at least, was swayed by medical evidence about the appropriateness of conventional treatment. It is noteworthy that the court used a reasonableness rather than a best interests standard, a strategy I of course endorse. This was possible because of the test that is used when considering whether there has been wilful neglect and lack of parental care. As outlined in Chapter 1, this is

---

32 *Finlayson, Applicant* [1989] SCLR 601, Sh Ct.

an objective standard; that is to say whether a reasonable person could draw the inference of unnecessary suffering or serious impairment from the nature and extent of the parental lack of care.[33] In other types of court proceedings where they must place the welfare of the child as paramount, it is expected that they would follow the same pattern as those in England and Wales, with all the problems this entails.

Children with capacity to refuse

The statutory framework for determining the competence of children does not directly refer to refusing consent to medical treatment. As a result, this gives potential leeway to the courts to differentiate between consent and refusal of consent. If respect for autonomy is the reason for seeking a competent person's consent to treatment, drawing any such distinction may be felt to be quite illogical. If one is able to weigh up the considerations in order to agree to treatment, surely one is equally capable of weighing up the same considerations, even though arriving at a different conclusion? As has been said, the right to say 'yes' must carry with it the right to say 'no' (Norrie, 1991). Indeed, the reason for seeking consent is precisely because it is anticipated that a person may, for whatever reason, refuse. Proceeding without permission is a violation of the respect due to the person, both in terms of his or her bodily integrity and freedom of choice. It has, however, been suggested that:

> It is reasonable to suppose, paternalistic though it may sound, that a qualified doctor knows more about the treatment of disease than does a child. Thus, while consent involves acceptance of an experienced view, refusal rejects that experience – and does so from a position of limited understanding.
>
> (Mason and Laurie, 2006, para 10.52)

While this may be true, it is no less likely to be true where adults are asked to make the same choice. Most patients will know less about the treatment of illness than a qualified doctor (Huxtable, 2000). The critical point should surely be whether the patient, whatever their age, is able to understand the risks, benefits and possible outcomes of their decision and to properly weigh them to arrive at a choice. Those under the legally set age may legitimately be required to demonstrate that they are capable of mature decision-making, but whether the result is to consent or refuse is not relevant to whether their choice should be respected. To rule that no one under the legally set age for adulthood can be competent to refuse treatment ignores the individuality of

---

33 *M v McGregor* 1982 SLT 41.

the patient by focusing on the status of minority and allows a welfare assessment to predominate in the name of protecting the child until adulthood. A further observation Mason and Laurie make is that:

> . . . a refusal of medical treatment may close down the options – and this may be regretted later in that the chance to consent has now passed. The implications of refusal may, therefore, be more serious and, on these grounds refusal of treatment may require greater understanding than does acceptance. A level of comprehension sufficient to justify refusal of treatment certainly includes one to accept treatment but the reverse does not hold; the two conditions cannot be regarded as being on a par.
>
> (Mason and Laurie, 2006, 10.52)

Again, however, this may be met by the response that embarking on a particular course of treatment may also close down options, necessitating adherence to a particular regime of surgical or pharmacological interventions, with significant physical and emotional consequences for the patient. A distinction between consenting to and refusing treatment is therefore hard to maintain on this ground. It is fair to say, of course, that refusing life-saving treatment will close down entirely any future options, but this is no less so for an 18-year-old than a 15-year-old. There are limited reported cases in Scotland, but it appears that the law there and that in England in Wales is developing differently and this has important implications both in practice and in principle. I consider that the Scottish approach is preferable, since it appears to pay due respect to the autonomy of the competent child, and will consider this first before turning to the way that the law has developed in England and Wales.

Scotland

The general presumption is that competent adults have the right to refuse medical treatment.[34] There are strong arguments to suggest that a Scottish child who is competent under either the evidential or the presumptive standard set out in Chapter 2 should also have his or her decisions respected, whatever their outcome. These hinge on an interpretation of the existing legislation and according respect for autonomy as the guiding principle. The Age of Legal Capacity (Scotland) Act 1991 (ALC(S)A 1991) gives young people full legal capacity to enter into most transactions at the age of 16.[35] Accordingly, they have the ability not only to consent, but also to refuse, treatment and they are thus given the respect for their decisions accorded to adults of any age. There appear to be neither grounds for parents to override

---

34 *Whitehall v Whitehall* 1957 SC 252.
35 ALC(S)A 1991 ss 1(1)(b) and 9.

a refusal of consent nor for the courts to do so (Thomson, 2006, pp 274–5). If a person of or over the age of 16 refuses medical treatment, it can only be given in limited situations. First, if they are deemed to lack capacity, in which case treatment decisions would need to be made under the Adults with Incapacity (Scotland) Act 2000 (AWI(S)A 2000). In an emergency, immediately necessary treatment can be provided outside the procedural requirements of the Act. There may also still be scope to treat incapable adults under the *parens patriae* jurisdiction (Ward, 2003). In addition, if they are suffering from mental illness or disorder, which falls under the Mental Health (Care and Treatment) (Scotland) Act 2003, this also provides authority for treatment – in some circumstances, even if they are competent to refuse it. There are additional protections for people aged between 16 and 18 under this Act, but the grounds for deeming a person to lack capacity are the same for everyone (for further discussion, see Patrick, 2006, ch 41). There is no developmental test of capacity requiring maturity to be demonstrated past the age of 16 and the outcome of the decision, whether to accept or refuse treatment, is not by itself sufficient to overrule a decision. As with any adult there may be grounds for seeking to establish that the choice made is truly an expression of self-determination where it appears unreasonable, but no more (Rhodes and Holzman, 2004).

Those under 16 are governed by s 2(4) of the ALC(S)A 1991. The first point to consider is the parental power of consent, since this is not mentioned here. It was held in the case of *V v F* (1991) that it was unnecessary to resort to mental health legislation to treat a 15-year-old girl refusing treatment since the parents' consent would suffice.[36] However, the Sheriff did not make a ruling on whether the girl was competent. Although he expressed little doubt that she understood the evidence and in general terms the requirements of the proposed order, he also described her as vulnerable and ill. For this reason, *V v F* may be simply an illustration of parental powers in respect of incompetent children and in any event it preceded the ALC(S)A 1991. To date, the sole case discussing medical treatment under this statute is that of *Houston* (1996).[37] It will be remembered that the Sheriff had held that, as the boy was deemed to have met the test of sufficient understanding in this section, his mother no longer had the power to give a legally valid consent to treatment on his behalf. Strictly speaking, this may be regarded as being an *obiter dictum*, since there were doubts over the mother's consent being clear and settled (Grubb, 1997, p 239). However, if it is correct, there is no power for parents to intervene in the treatment decisions of a competent child. The Sheriff stated that logic demanded this conclusion.

Equally importantly, he held that the decision-making capacity conferred

---

36 *V v F* 1991 SCLR 225, Sh Ct.
37 *Houston, Applicant* 1996 SCLR 943, Sh Ct.

by the ALC(S)A 1991 covered refusal of consent. This approach has been endorsed by a number of commentators (Wilkinson and Norrie, 1999, para 8.51; Sutherland, 1999, para 2.16; Thomson, 2006, para 10.2). It is supported by interpretation of other parts of the statute so that:

> It has never been suggested ... that capacity to refuse is not carried by the words granting capacity to consent to adoption. Capacity to consent to medical treatment is conferred by section 2(4) and it would be difficult to argue that refusal is implicit in section 2(3) but not in section 2(4).
>
> (Wilkinson and Norrie, 1999, para 15.09)

Similarly, equating an ability to give consent with one to refuse is in line with the subsequently enacted provisions of the Children (Scotland) Act 1995 (C(S)A 1995), which state that a competent young person must consent to examination or treatment, even if a court or a Children's Hearing directs it.[38] So it has been said that 'If the young person has the power to refuse in these circumstances, consistency requires recognition of a more general power to refuse' (Sutherland, 1999, para 3.70). Against this, as we shall see, the English courts have been able to avoid this result, even in the face of similar statutory provisions, so it may be possible that Scottish courts would also try to do so.[39]

In this regard, there are a number of issues to consider. First, detailed argument was not undertaken in *Houston* on whether any distinction should be drawn between consent to treatment and refusal, and the case was only decided at first instance. It remains possible that a higher court might take a different view though this would seem, for the reasons given, to be illogical. Second, the court did not consider whether it had the power itself to override the boy's decision. There was an alternative way of disposing of the issue, by authorising treatment under the Mental Health (Scotland) Act 1984. The Sheriff was clearly anxious to avoid the possible stigma of compulsory detention and treatment if possible, so resorting to the legislation may imply that he believed he did not have the power to authorise treatment himself. Indeed, even if he had considered the issue, I believe the answer should have been the same. If parents lose their right to override a competent child's refusal of treatment, as it is no longer considered necessary, then this would apply equally to a court. Despite this, some have suggested that courts do have the power to override a refusal of consent by a person under 16 by making an order under s 11 of the C(S)A 1995, since here the welfare of the child is the paramount consideration (Edwards and Griffiths, 2006, para

38 C(S)A 1995, s 90.
39 *South Glamorgan County Council v W and B* [1993] 1 FCR 626, Fam D.

2.33; Blackie and Patrick, 2001, para 11.18–20). In the unlikely case that the *parens patriae* jurisdiction were to be used, the same conclusion could follow. Blackie and Patrick support such an approach, at least in some circumstances:

> It may seem acceptable that the welfare principle embodied in Scottish children's legislation should include provisions where, in a life or death situation, a young person can be protected even against themselves.
> (Blackie and Patrick, 2001, para 11.20)

Against this there is a very strong argument that neither the C(S)A 1995 nor the inherent jurisdiction should take priority here. As discussed in Chapter 2, the omission of a welfare or best interests test in the ALC(S)A 1995 was deliberate.

> The Scottish Law Commission, after extensive consultation, on this point, came to the conclusion that if a child was deemed to have sufficient maturity then it should not matter if the treatment was for his or her benefit or not. The implication is that if the child is found to be competent, then, like an adult, the child has a right to take risks or make wrong choices.
> (Edwards and Griffiths, 1997, para 2.22)

Since this statute specifically deals with children's capacity to make medical treatment decisions, then the C(S)A 1995 should not be allowed to undermine it without explicit provisions to this effect. In fact, as has been said, s 90 of the C(S)A 1995 can be said to support respect for competent children's rights to refuse treatment. The same position should also hold true for the inherent jurisdiction, where the ALC(S)A 1991 would be thought to take precedence. While the position may most accurately be described as uncertain, guidance given to professionals suggests that a refusal of consent by a competent child is binding on doctors (NHS Management Executive in Scotland, October 1992, para 14). Although it was issued before the enactment of the C(S)A 1995, there has been no subsequent revision on this point. However, since there is a lack of clear authority on the matter, the BMA advises its members to apply to the courts if they are faced with such a situation (British Medical Association, 2001, ch 3).

The legal validity of a refusal of consent, then, apparently rests solely on doctors deeming the child to have capacity. There may be doubts whether they would be prepared to make such a finding and that this could provide a way of avoiding complying with a minor's wishes. Thomson for example suggests that:

> In practice, if a child is refusing consent to a proposed procedure or

treatment, the medical practitioner is unlikely to take the view that the child is capable of understanding the consequences of the procedure or treatment and consequently the child will not have s2(4) capacity.

(Thomson, 2006, para 11.9)

There may indeed be a temptation to subvert the concept of competence in order to provide treatment that the doctor thinks is best for the child. How this might be done will be considered when looking at the way the courts have approached this issue in England and Wales. Since the test of capacity in Scotland rests on the basis of the opinion of the qualified medical practitioner, who will in almost all cases be the person responsible for providing treatment, the dangers of this will be obvious. However, as discussed in the previous chapter, an attempt to challenge the doctor's opinion may prove a double-edged sword, since allowing courts to have the final say on the matter has its own pitfalls. Protection of the child's autonomy necessitates placing this as the priority, rather than the health interests of the child, and whether doctors or courts may be more willing to do so remains to be seen. My own preferred solution is to allow children, but no one else, to challenge a finding of incapacity. Despite some uncertainty, therefore, where the doctor is prepared to hold that the child is competent, there seems to be a widespread view that a refusal of consent in Scotland is conclusive.

England and Wales

The Family Law Reform Act 1969 (FLRA 1969) and *Gillick* (1985) share the same defect as the ALC(S)A 1991 by failing to deal explicitly with the issue of refusal of consent. However, the English courts have developed an approach that allows them and parents to veto a refusal of consent by a child. In part this has been achieved by distinguishing between the requirements for competence where children consent or refuse treatment, but it also rests on the courts not according exclusive decision-making power to the competent child. The best interests test is then used to override respect for autonomy in these situations, an approach I consider unjustified.

Competence, information disclosure and voluntariness

The first case to consider a young person's refusal of consent was *Re E* (1993).[40] It concerned a boy with leukaemia who refused to consent to a blood transfusion. His parents fully supported his decision, as they were all practising Jehovah's Witnesses. An application was made to make E a ward of court and for treatment to be authorised. Although he was within three

---

40 *Re E (a minor) (wardship medical treatment)* [1993] 1 FCR 219, Fam D.

months of his sixteenth birthday, the evidential standard applied and assessing his competence became crucial to the judgment. Ward J chose to quote from Lord Scarman's speech as representing the 'nub' of *Gillick*.[41] However, the level of understanding and intelligence required to be shown by E appeared to introduce still further nuances into this test, as it was applied to refusal of consent. The main strand of the judgment was that although the boy was intelligent enough to make most decisions regarding his own wellbeing, he did not understand what the effect of his refusal would be. The test for competence that was described was a particularly stringent one to meet, since it required E to be able to turn his mind to the manner in which he might die and to the extent of his and his family's suffering. There are a number of problems with this, not least that it is quite clear from the judgment that E had not been asked to turn his mind to such matters, nor indeed given the information necessary to do so. Ward J said that:

> I did not judge it right to probe with him whether or not he knew how frightening [the dying process] would be. Dr T did not consider it necessary to spell it out for him and I did not feel it was appropriate to do so.[42]

Ward J therefore provided a novel way of denying competence, by endorsing the withholding of information thought necessary to the decision-making process. It has been held that doctors have a therapeutic privilege to withhold information that may be harmful to their patients.[43] Nonetheless, its use needs caution precisely because it denies the patient the opportunity to exercise autonomy. If information is thought relevant to a person's decision-making, then for this reason alone it ought to be given. There was clearly a wish to avoid causing distress, particularly to a young patient, but using this as a mechanism to deny a person competence seems to stretch the doctrine of therapeutic privilege beyond its limits. Second, even if the information had been given, the requirements set for competence here are not ones that have been applied to any adults in a similar situation, although why is unclear. If it is because adults do not need to take such issues into account, there is no good reason to expect children to do so either. Alternatively, it may be being assumed that adults will naturally be able to consider their own and their families' suffering as part of their reasoning. While I have argued that mature decision-making requires the ability to consider wider aspects of treatment than what is involved in the procedure itself, whether what is being sought here really represents a way of distinguishing between the intellectual and

41 *Gillick v West Norfolk and Wisbech Area Health Authority and another* [1985] 3 All ER 402, HL.

42 *Re E (a minor) (wardship: medical treatment)* [1993] 1 FCR 219, Fam D at 224.

43 See, e.g. *Sidaway v Bethlem Royal Hospital Governors* [1985] 1 All ER 643, HL, per Scarman LJ at 633–5.

developmental skills of adults and children is highly doubtful. As has been said, 'was E . . . any less capable of understanding such grave matters than say a sick and frightened 20 or 60 year old?' (Brazier and Bridge, 1996, p 104). In any event, since these questions were not raised with E, it seems difficult to conclude that he would have been incapable of considering them if he had been given the opportunity, since there was no evidence on this matter either way.

A further issue raised by the case was that even if E did have the ability to make a judgement on these matters, it seems to have been assumed that children's views should not be respected because their views may change as they get older. Ward J put this strikingly:

> When making this decision, which is a decision of life or death, I have to take account of the fact that teenagers often express views with vehe- mence and conviction – all the vehemence and conviction of youth! Those of us who have passed beyond callow youth can all remember the convictions we have loudly proclaimed which now we find somewhat embarrassing. I respect this boy's profession of faith, but I cannot dis- count at least the possibility that he may in later years suffer some dimin- ution in his convictions. There is no settled certainty about matters of this kind.[44]

Again, this is a specific requirement being placed into the test for competence to refuse consent for children that it is either presumed adults meet by virtue of being adults, or that they do not need to. However, decision-making abil- ities, including evaluating long-term rather than short-term implications, develop over time in childhood, and adolescence in particular may be a period of experimentation with attitudes and ideas. If this is accepted, it may be argued that the court is taking a perfectly reasonable position. However, what is being focused on is the patient as a member of a class – children – and this fails to take into account the individual capacities of the particular child. If competence is to be judged based on the abilities of the patient, as the law usually suggests it should be, this approach appears mistaken. Some adult patients with learning disabilities or mental illness may not be competent to make a particular decision, but it cannot be assumed that this is the case.[45] Where they are concerned, assumptions based on membership of a group are not permitted to dictate their decision-making ability, which is to be judged by an evaluation of their own circumstances. This does not appear to hold true for children.

A similar concern was expressed that the undoubted sincerity of E's present

---

44 *Re E (a minor) (wardship: medical treatment)* [1992] 2 FCR 219, Fam D at 226.
45 *Re C (adult: refusal of medical treatment)* [1994] 1 All ER 819, Fam D.

beliefs had been formed within the context of the strong influence of his family and hence might not be freely chosen. While Ward J was careful not to say that this had amounted to undue influence, nevertheless in his view this also recommended caution in reliance on E's wishes.

> I have also to ask myself to what extent is that assertion of decision, 'I will not have a blood transfusion', the product of his full but his free informed thought?... I find that the influence of the teachings of the Jehovah's Witnesses is strong and powerful. The very fact that this family can contemplate the death of one of its members is the most eloquent testimony of the power of that faith. He is a boy who seeks and needs the love and respect of his parents whom he would wish to honour as the Bible exhorts him to honour them. I am far from satisfied that at the age of 15 his will is fully free. He may assert it, but his volition has been conditioned by the very powerful expressions of faith to which all members of the creed adhere.[46]

Although it may be contended that young people's views are still being formed, the judge here again appeared to generalise about the effects of children's upbringing and to reject the clear evidence that E did believe the precepts of his family's faith. Indeed, elsewhere the judge referred to E's convictions as being 'deeply held and genuine'. Similar concerns about the voluntariness and free will of teenage Jehovah's Witnesses have surfaced in later cases *Re S* (1994)[47] and *Re L* (1998).[48]

In order to be regarded as autonomous, a person's decision must be an expression of his or her own will. Being influenced by others is not in itself a reason for denying that a decision is sufficiently one's own, but there may be circumstances where closer scrutiny is needed to ensure this is the case. The effects of illness or injury may also pose risks to decision-making capacity. Both issues were discussed in the case of *Re T* (1992).[49] Here, a pregnant woman had been involved in a car accident. She had an emergency Caesarean section leading to the need for a blood transfusion. This she refused, after discussing it with her mother, who was a Jehovah's Witness. It was said that:

> When considering the effect of outside influences, two aspects can be of crucial importance. First, the strength of the will of the patient. One who is very tired, in pain or depressed will be much less able to resist having his will overborne than one who is rested, free from pain and cheerful.

---

46 *Re E (a minor) (wardship: medical treatment)* [1992] 2 FCR 219, Fam D at 226.
47 *Re S (a minor) (refusal of medical treatment)* (1994) [1995] 1 FCR 604, Fam D.
48 *Re L (medical treatment: Gillick competence)* (1998) [1999] 2 FCR 524, Fam D.
49 *Re T (adult: refusal of medical treatment)* [1992] 4 All ER 649, CA.

Secondly, the relationship of the 'persuader' to the patient may be of crucial importance. The influence of parents on their children or of one spouse on the other can be, but is by no means necessarily, much stronger than would be the case in other relationships. Persuasion based upon religious belief can also be much more compelling and the fact that arguments based upon religious beliefs are being deployed by someone in a very close relationship with the patient will give them added force and should alert the doctors to the possibility – no more – that the patient's capacity or will to decide has been overborne. In other words the patient may not mean what he says.[50]

While there is evidently a need for people's choices to reflect their beliefs and values, *Re T* (1992) gives considerable scope for courts to override even the clearly expressed wishes of the individual. There may be doubts about children's opportunities to make a sufficiently free decision if they are living a relatively sheltered upbringing and under the strong influence of family members, committed to beliefs that do not accept certain forms of treatment. Indeed, the greater the love and respect shown by children to their parents, the more readily may the courts judge that the child has been conditioned to accept their beliefs and may be refusing treatment simply to please them, no matter what the child says. Nevertheless, once more this adopts a blanket approach rather than examining the individual child's intelligence, understanding and personal commitment to beliefs. It is also worth noting here that the same approach has been taken even to presumptively competent young people, so that in *Re P* (2003), a boy who was nearly 17 was required to be given blood against his religious beliefs.[51] It will be remembered that given the different age of presumptive capacity in Scotland, anyone over 16 cannot be forced to accept even life-saving treatment, unless they are proved to be incompetent, but the test that must be applied then would be under the AWI(S)A 2000. While the scope for overruling decisions due to lack of voluntariness remains, as for any adult, it does point up the problems of arbitrariness if too much reliance is placed on an age-based threshold, rather than looking at the capacities of the individual. The coda to *Re E* (1993) is that E's treatment continued to necessitate blood transfusions. When he reached his 18th birthday, his right to refuse treatment had to be legally recognised.[52] Further transfusions ceased and he succumbed to his illness. While caution must be used when assessing cases with the benefit of hindsight, it is still worth noting that neither E's views on the merits of treatment nor his beliefs had altered. Acting on a presumption that children's views will change as

50 Ibid, per Lord Donaldson MR at 662.
51 *Re P (Medical Treatment: Best Interests)* [2003] EWHC 2327, Fam D.
52 See, also, *Re AK (medical treatment: consent)* [2001] 2 FCR 35, Fam D.

they get older must therefore be open to challenge. They may change, they may not and indeed the same can be said of adults. At best, what may be contended is that children's views may be less free and settled than adults, but this relies on assumptions that should be tested in respect of each individual child.

The effect of illness and injury will also need to be considered. This was considered in the case of *Re R* (1991), which involved a 15-year-old girl with fluctuating mental health.[53] The adolescent psychiatric unit in which she had been placed wished to treat her with antipsychotic drugs, which they considered she needed to receive, even in her periods of remission from mental illness. However, in her lucid intervals she refused to take the medication. The local authority therefore commenced wardship proceedings and sought leave from the courts to administer the medication, even without her consent. The court held that the *Gillick* competence test was a developmental one and that it could not fluctuate on a day-to-day basis.[54] Doubts have already been expressed about the Court's interpretation of this point in Chapter 2. Nonetheless, it might be thought justifiable to attempt to prevent a person from lapsing back into a mentally disordered state. However, administering treatment to competent people against their will for this reason would normally be expected to have to take place under the stricter safeguards of mental health legislation, rather than being authorised by the common law. This conclusion was avoided here, by finding R incompetent even in lucid periods and treatment was authorised in her best interests. There seems no justification for interpreting competence in this way.

Concerns about the effects of illness on rational decision-making have also arisen with presumptively competent children. *Re W* (1992) involved a girl with anorexia nervosa, under local authority care.[55] W was 16 years old when her physical condition deteriorated to the extent that the authority wished to place her in a specialist eating disorder clinic for treatment. She objected, saying that she would cure herself when she felt ready to do so. The local authority sought directions from the court under the inherent jurisdiction of the courts, since the Children Act 1989 (CA 1989) did not allow them to seek wardship. The principles to be applied by the court were the same. At first instance, although it was held that she did have sufficient understanding and intelligence to make an informed decision, nevertheless the court had the power to make the orders sought and in the light of the medical evidence, it did so. The orders were upheld on appeal. However, the Court of Appeal based its decision on the finding that the nature of W's condition involved a desire not to be treated. While stressing that anorexia

---

53 *Re R (a minor) (wardship: medical treatment)* [1991] 4 All ER 177, CA.
54 Ibid, per Lord Donaldson MR at 187.
55 *Re W (a minor) (medical treatment)* [1992] 4 All ER 627, CA.

nervosa was no more the fault of the sufferer than pneumonia or appendicitis, it was said that:

> It is, however, much more difficult to treat and cure, not least because one of its clinical manifestations, which is part and parcel of the disease, is a firm wish not to be cured, or at least not to be cured unless and until the sufferer wishes to cure herself . . . it is a feature of anorexia nervosa that it is capable of destroying the ability to make an informed choice. It creates a compulsion to refuse treatment or only to accept treatment which is likely to be ineffective. This attitude is part and parcel of the disease and the more advanced the illness, the more compelling it may become.[56]

In these circumstances the girl's refusal of consent could be overruled, despite the fact that she appeared quite capable of understanding the information she had been given and that, being 16, she fell within s 8 of the FLRA 1969 and so was of an age to be presumed competent. A finding of incompetence, based on her condition, allowed a decision to be made in her best interests and this was held to require treatment being imposed. This approach was followed in the case of *Re C (Detention: Medical Treatment)* (1997), where another 16-year-old girl with anorexia nervosa was held to be incompetent and her detention and the use of reasonable force to provide treatment against her wishes were authorised by the court as being in her best interests, without the need to be dealt with under mental health legislation.[57]

It may not be a condition from which a child suffers, but the situation in which s/he finds herself that may be thought to threaten competence. In *Re M*, a 15 and a half-year-old girl with sudden onset congestive heart failure refused a life-saving heart transplant, without which she was expected to die within a week.[58] M's mother was prepared to given her consent to the operation, in the face of her daughter's refusal. Owing to M's age, and the gravity of the treatment, the consultant sought court approval. M gave her reasons as follows: 'I don't want to die but I would rather die than have somebody else's heart. I would rather die with 15 years of my own heart.' In addition, she did not want to be put in the situation of taking tablets for the rest of her life.[59] Bearing in mind what was said in *Re E* to be necessary for competence, it is interesting to note that M said that she knew her family would be sad if she died and if she had children she would want what was best and not let them die. In these circumstances, even if *Re E*'s rather questionable criteria for

---

56 *Re C (Detention: Medical Treatment* [1997] 2 FLR 180, Fam D.
57 Ibid.
58 *Re M (child: refusal of medical treatment)* [1999] 2 FCR 577, Fam D.
59 Ibid at 581.

competence are accepted, M would seem to have satisfied them. Despite this, it was decided that the operation should proceed in accordance with her doctor's clinical judgement. The view of the Official Solicitor was that '. . . M felt overwhelmed by her circumstances and the decision she was being asked to make'.[60] While quoting this evidence, it is noteworthy, and rather extraordinary, that the judge, Mr Justice Johnson, made no explicit finding on M's competence, but ruled that surgery should proceed in her best interests. After further counselling and on being told the court's decision, M gave her consent. Since the court order had already been made, her consent in practical terms really amounted to no more than assent to the procedure. By contrast, if M had consented to the procedure straightaway, there seems little doubt that her ability to make this decision would not have been examined so rigorously.

Although the extent of her competence was not directly addressed, the terms of her refusal were in fact remarkably similar to those given by the patient in *Re C* (1994).[61] Here, a 68-year-old man with chronic paranoid schizophrenia developed gangrene in a foot. Medical opinion was that he would die imminently if the leg was not amputated below the knee. C refused consent, saying that he would 'rather die with two feet than live with one'. In addition, C held the delusional beliefs that he had medical experience and disagreed with the prognosis offered by the consultant. He put his faith in God.[62] Despite obvious concerns about his capacity, he was judged to be competent and treatment against his wishes was not authorised. The outcome of his decision, that his death was considered likely, was not regarded as being the critical factor. While his beliefs were regarded as irrational and even though his mental capacity was impaired, it was held that the proper question was 'whether it has been established that C's capacity is so reduced by his chronic mental illness that he does not sufficiently understand the nature, purpose and effects of the proffered amputation'.[63] M was not affected by mental illness and arguably her reasons for refusing treatment, though many might regard them as irrational, should have been relevant only to initiating an inquiry to ensure that this was an expression of self-determination, as with C. Of course it is true to say that M's life-threatening condition had a more sudden onset than C's. Accordingly, this situation may be regarded as more akin to those that have arisen where women in labour have refused treatment.

Here, much attention has been paid to the stresses of the situation in considering whether the individual is capable of making a voluntary decision. In *Norfolk and Norwich HealthCare (NHS) Trust v W* (1997) a woman with a

60 Ibid at 582.
61 *Re C (adult: refusal of medical treatment)* [1994] 1 All ER 819, Fam D.
62 Ibid, at 821–22.
63 Ibid, per Thorpe J at 824.

history of mental disorder arrived in hospital in labour, but denying she was pregnant.[64] She refused forceps delivery or a Caesarean section, but a judge found her incompetent and authorised treatment, saying that:

> She was called upon to make that decision at a time of acute emotional stress and physical pain in the ordinary course of labour made even more difficult for her because of her own particular mental history.[65]

A similar approach was taken in *Re MB (an adult: medical treatment)* (1997).[66] MB, having been advised that normal delivery posed significant risks to the life of the foetus, initially agreed to a Caesarean section. However, when attempts were made to give her an anaesthetic, it became evident that she had a needle phobia and she would not allow it to be administered. At first instance, the judge formed the opinion that MB was 'not really capable of considering matters lucidly'.[67] The Court of Appeal began its examination of the case by restating the principle that a mentally competent adult has an absolute right to refuse to consent to medical treatment for any reason, rational or otherwise:

> Although it might be thought that irrationality sits uneasily with competence to decide, panic, indecisiveness and irrationality in themselves do not as such amount to incompetence.[68]

However, MB's fear of needles was held to be more than irrationality and to have led to actual incompetence. The Court attached significant weight to the fact that MB had earlier consented to the operation, but when faced with its imminent prospect:

> She could not bring herself to undergo the caesarean section she desired because, as the evidence established, 'a fear of needles . . . has got in the way of proceeding with the operation.'[69]

How to properly distinguish between a phobic reaction that may override competence, and mere panic, indecisiveness and irrationality, which will not, may be hard to determine in practice. Nevertheless, questions are raised whether doctors and courts may be too willing to infer incompetence even with adults. In situations where death or serious injury may be the result of

---

64 *Norfolk and Norwich Healthcare (NHS) Trust v W* [1997] 1 FCR 269, Fam D.
65 Ibid, at 272.
66 *Re MB (an adult: medical treatment)* [1997] 2 FCR 541, CA.
67 Ibid, quoted at 548.
68 Ibid, per Butler-Sloss LJ at 553.
69 Ibid, at 554.

relying on a refusal of consent, the temptation to allow treatment to be given may be very strong. This temptation may be even greater where a child is concerned and there is a strong suspicion that panic, indecisiveness and irrationality will be held to render a child incompetent, even if they do not an adult. Even Mason and Laurie, who generally promote the view that children need protecting from unwise decisions, conclude that the *Re M* case must 'surely represent the outermost reaches of paternalistic practices' (Mason and Laurie, 2006, para 10.54).

It could be argued that it would be wrong to base general propositions on the court's attitude to determining competence of children based on these cases, because of their particular circumstances. After all, *Re E* (1993) and *Re R* (1991) involved children who were required to establish their competence as they were under 16. However, this loses some of its force when it is remembered that the tests for competence appear to include elements that are of dubious merit in distinguishing between children and adults, and that a finding of incompetence can be made even during periods of lucidity. A further factor in *Re R* (1991) and also in the case of the presumptively competent *Re W* (1992) and *Re C* (1997) was that the very condition for which treatment was proposed involved mental and emotional disturbance. This, it might be thought, would make it impossible for them to undertake a rational decision-making process. Indeed, similar arguments have been made that adults with anorexia nervosa are incompetent to decide on treatment for the condition.[70] If a desire not to be treated is part of an illness, it is difficult to conclude that a refusal of consent is a true expression of the patient's own will, since the decision is affected by the disorder. Nevertheless, adults in such circumstances have usually been treated under mental health legislation rather than under the common law, with the additional safeguards that this entails. In addition, when making a finding of incompetence due to the effects of a condition, this needs to be done with great care, since it may be all too easy to undermine the concept of competence in order to hold that a patient's desire not to be treated is a symptom of illness rather than an expression of autonomy (for a detailed review of the legal approach to anorexia nervosa, see Lewis, 1999).

Running through these cases, though, is the thread that refusal of consent requires greater levels of decision-making ability than consent. As we have seen, this judicial attitude is not confined to children. In *Re T* (1992) it was suggested that, where an adult refused consent, he must show an understanding 'commensurate with the gravity of the decision which he purports to make. The more serious the decision, the greater the capacity required'.[71]

---

70 *R v Riverside Mental Health Trust* [1994] 2 FCR 577, CA; *Re KB (adult) (mental patient: medical treatment)* 19 BMLR 144, Fam D; *B v Croydon Health Authority* (1995) 1 All ER 683, CA. See, also, Lewis, 1999.

71 *Re T (adult: refusal of medical treatment)* [1992] 4 All ER 649, CA, per Lord Donaldson MR at 661.

However, I have already argued that it is doubtful this is correct, since it focuses on outcome rather than upon the complexity of decision-making. Even some judges have been driven to concede that distinguishing between the abilities needed to consent and refuse is hard to defend.[72] Logic suggests that there should be no such distinction, but as Davies says, 'medical law does not appear to follow logic here' (Davies, 1996, p 135). He contends that even where adults are concerned:

> It may be that the test of competence is being manipulated to facilitate treatment, thus being based on a paternalistic notion of patient's welfare, rather than being a true test of the ability of the particular patient to act in an autonomous manner.
>
> (Davies, 1996, p 121)

Reliance on the expressed wishes of the person may not be perceived as being in their best interests and attempts to avoid complying with them have been made. This may most easily be done by making a finding of incompetence. The dangers of this have been recognised even by the courts:

> When a human life is at stake the pressure to provide an affirmative answer authorising unwanted medical intervention is very powerful. Nevertheless, the autonomy of each individual requires continuing protections even, perhaps particularly, when the motive for interfering with it is readily understandable, and indeed to many would appear commendable.[73]

Notwithstanding this clear statement, it appears that in some circumstances the English courts are prepared to shift the determination of competence from being a test of the person's ability to undertake a rational decision-making process to one of the ability to make what is, in their view, a rational decision. Although this is not solely a matter that affects children, the desire to intervene where they are concerned may prove overwhelming. 'In other words, the clear and consistent policy of the law is to protect the child against wrong-headed parents and against itself [sic]' (Lowe and Juss, 1993, p 872).

However, judgments about treating children in the face of their refusal do not rest solely on their competence. Lord Donaldson MR did not confine his ruling in *Re W* (1992) to competent children, stating that 'No minor of whatever age has power by refusing consent to treatment by someone who has parental responsibility for the minor and *a fortiori* a consent by the

72 *Re W (a minor) (medical treatment)* [1992] 4 All ER 627, CA, per Balcombe LJ at 641.
73 *St George's Healthcare NHS Trust v S, R v Collins, ex p S* [1998] 3 All ER 673, CA, per Judge LJ at 688.

court'.[74] While it must be said that his comments were strictly *obiter*, since he had found W to lack capacity, his words have been regarded as being authoritative. If this approach is correct, then it would seem that the competence of the child need not be explored in detail as it is not the determining factor. The overriding principle governing provision of treatment is to be found, not in the child's ability to meet even a modified test of competence, but in finding a legal mechanism to enable treatment to be lawfully provided and this is done through the application of the best interests test. This is one way of understanding the judgment in *Re M* (1999), where the court made no explicit finding of competence at all. Simply avoiding the issue by moving straight to the conclusion that the transplant was in her best interests does not seem a sufficiently rigorous approach, as it does not recognise the significance of failing to respect autonomy. Given the serious nature of overriding a competent person's wishes, it should surely be necessary for there to be some specific consideration and explanation for a finding of incompetence to be made first.

The application of the best interests test to refusal of consent

In *Re R* (1991) Lord Donaldson MR concluded that the law provided for there to be 'concurrent consent' by parents and competent children.[75] The effect of this is that while only a court can override a competent child's consent to treatment, both courts and parents can override a refusal of consent if this is felt to be in the child's best interests. At first sight this may seem difficult to reconcile with the approach strongly taken in the House of Lords in *Gillick* by all of the leading judges. In particular, it will be remembered that Scarman LJ had said that a 'parental right yields to the child's right to make his own decisions when he reaches a sufficient understanding and intelligence to be capable of making up his own mind on the matter requiring decision'.[76] Lord Donaldson MR in *Re R* (1991) chose to interpret this as meaning only that the parental right of overall determination terminates when the child attains '*Gillick* competence'. While the parental right to veto the child's consent expires at that time, the parental right to consent does not. He tried to explain his conclusion by the use of a 'keyholder' analogy.

> . . . consent by itself creates no obligation to treat. It is merely a key which unlocks a door. Furthermore, whilst in the case of an adult of full capacity there will usually only be one keyholder, namely the patient, in

74 *Re W (a minor)(medical treatment)* [1992] 4 All ER 627, CA at 637.
75 *Re R (a minor) (wardship: medical treatment)* [1991] 4 All ER 177, CA, at 187 per Lord Donaldson MR.
76 *Gillick v West Norfolk and Wisbech Area Health Authority and another* [1985] 3 All ER 402, HL.

the ordinary family unit where a young child is the patient there will be two keyholders, namely the parents, with a several as well as a joint right to turn the key and unlock the door.[77]

Although Lord Donaldson MR attempted to harmonise the two decisions in this way, he recognised the possibility that Scarman LJ did in fact mean to say that the parental right to consent terminates, regardless whether the competent child consents or refuses consent. He was quick to point out, though, that if this were the case, Lord Scarman's comments were *obiter*, and furthermore, that they were wrong.[78] His conclusion on this point was not explicitly endorsed by the other judges and was roundly condemned by commentators at the time (see, for example, Bainham, 1992; Kennedy, 1992; Thornton, 1992). It was certainly viewed with some surprise, since it had previously been thought that the *Gillick* judgment applied to all decisions of a competent child, regardless of the outcome (Eekelaar and Dingwall, 1990, p 24; Murphy, 1992).

In addition to being a questionable interpretation of the dicta in *Gillick*, it has already been argued that distinguishing between consent and refusing consent is hard to justify. No such distinction appears to have been drawn by Scarman LJ, who concentrated on the conditions for autonomous decision-making rather than its outcome (Garwood-Gowers, 2001, p 206). Admittedly, *Gillick* was not directly concerned with children's refusal of consent, though I would argue this should make no difference. Nevertheless, further support for the principle that a competent child has the right to refuse treatment can be found in the provisions of the CA 1989. Where courts are making supervision orders, they may include a term requiring a child to undergo psychiatric or medical examination or treatment. However, this cannot be done unless the court is satisfied that, where a child has sufficient understanding to make an informed choice, he or she consents to its inclusion.[79] It might be thought that, where either a child is under a supervision order or the court is contemplating making one, a greater degree of control might be accorded over the child, since such orders will be made only where s/he already appears to be at some degree of risk. However, the statute specifically provides that not even a court may require competent children to submit to examination or treatment where they object. These provisions were inserted in the CA 1989 after a Commons' amendment in response to fears that a competent minor's wishes might be disregarded. It was also suggested that doctors would object in any case to complying with a court order to this effect.[80] The provisions were felt

77 *Re R (a minor) (wardship: medical treatment)* [1991] 4 All ER 177, CA, at 184.
78 Ibid at 185.
79 CA 1989 s 38(6), Schedule 3, Part I, paras 4–7.
80 Baroness David, House of Lords, Official Report, 19 January 1989, col 405.

to be uncontroversial since they were taken to be in accordance with the existing law on the matter, as it was widely believed that the *Gillick* judgment encompassed both consent and refusal of consent. If the courts could not authorise treatment against a competent minor's wishes, despite their powers being greater than those of parents, there should have been absolutely no scope for a parent to do so. These views and the arguments by analogy with the CA 1989 proved to have no influence on subsequent legal developments in relation to the general approach of the law to refusal of consent by children, nor were even the specific statutory provisions to prove a barrier to the courts' intervening in what they deemed to be children's best interests.[81]

Lord Donaldson MR was given the opportunity to reconsider the matter in *Re W*. In the wake of critical academic commentary, he conceded that he might have been mistaken in his interpretation of Lord Scarman's intentions in *Gillick*.[82] He also retracted from the 'keyholder' metaphor he had adopted in *Re R* (1991). Despite this, he went even further towards defining the purpose of consent to treatment of children as being primarily a method of achieving the desired medical outcome. He moved away from the 'keyholder' description because he recognised that 'keys can lock as well as unlock'. Accordingly, a 'keyholder' would be permitted to refuse treatment as well as being allowed to give consent.[83] Instead, he sought to use the image of consent as a legal 'flak jacket', which would protect a doctor:

> . . . from claims by the litigious, whether he acquires it from his patient, who may be a minor over the age of 16 or a *'Gillick* competent' child, under that age, or from another person having parental responsibilities which include a right to consent to treatment of the minor. Anyone who gives him a flak jacket (i.e. consent) may take it back, but the doctor only needs one and so long as he continues to have one he has the right to proceed.[84]

The power to authorise treatment could of course also be exercised by a court.[85] Lord Donaldson MR maintained his view that holding children to be *Gillick* competent did not involve the disappearance of parental rights to consent. For children who were presumptively competent, he noted that s 8 of the FLRA 1969 was silent on refusal of consent and he found himself 'quite

---

81 See *South Glamorgan County Council v W and B* [1993] 1 FCR 626, Fam D, discussed later in this chapter.

82 *Re W (a minor) (medical treatment)* [1992] 4 All ER 627, CA at 634.

83 Ibid at 635.

84 Ibid at 634.

85 Ibid at 637.

unable to see how, on any normal reading of the words of the section, it can be construed to confer such a right'.[86] Instead, the section was, in his opinion, intended only to enable children to consent and for this purpose alone were children to be treated as adults. Since s 8(3) of the FLRA 1969 preserved existing common-law rights, this was taken to include the right of parents to consent, leading to concurrent powers of consent of 16–18-year-olds and their parents. If there was any ambiguity, Lord Donaldson MR suggested this could be clarified by referring to the Latey Report 1967, paras 474–89, which preceded the statute. In fact, all professional bodies providing evidence to the Latey Committee, with the exception of the Medical Protection Society, had recommended that legislation should provide for refusal of consent. The BMA, for example, had made a submission that was quoted by the Committee as follows:

> Consent by a person of 16 years of age or upwards, who appears to the medical practitioner to be capable of understanding what is involved and of expressing his own views, should be considered to be a valid consent to medical or surgical treatment without the necessity of confirmation by his parent or legal guardian. *Of course* the refusal of a person over 16 to undergo treatment should also be respected providing that it appears to the medical practitioner that the person clearly understands the implications of his decision.
>
> (Latey Report, 1967, para 480)(Original emphasis)

This position on refusal of consent was not specifically endorsed in the Report, but neither was it rejected. The fact that the Committee had emphasised the words 'of course' may be taken to indicate that they took this approach in making their recommendations and felt that explicit reference to this in legislation was unnecessary. However, Lord Donaldson MR took the opposite view and concluded that:

> The point with which we are concerned was therefore well in the mind of the committee. It did not so recommend. It recommended that: '*without prejudice to any consent that may otherwise be lawful,* the consent of young persons aged 16 and over to medical or dental treatment shall be as valid as the consent of a person of full age . . . I am quite unable to accept that Parliament in adopting somewhat more prolix language was intending to achieve a result which differed from that recommended by the committee.[87]
>
> (Emphasis added)

---

86 Ibid at 639.
87 Ibid at 634.

It might seem strange to deduce that the Committee intended to support what was clearly a minority view, in evidence submitted to it, without giving an explanation for this and accordingly, this interpretation appears mistaken. Instead a better explanation might be that the Committee's approach, reflected in the legislation, was simply to provide for the validity of a presumptively competent person's decision, but to retain parental consent where this was unable to be given.

While not going into the detail of the background to the legislation, the other Court of Appeal judges also held that s 8 FLRA 1969 did not prevent parents and, *a fortiori*, courts from giving consent. In addition, they shared the view that as children became older, their wishes should be given more weight. Balcombe LJ, for example, saw this as being integral to the assessment of the child's best interests:

> In a sense this is merely one aspect of the application of the test that the welfare of the child is the paramount consideration. It will normally be in the best interests of a child of sufficient age and understanding to make an informed decision that the court should respect its integrity as a human being and not lightly override its decision on such a personal matter as medical treatment, all the more so if that treatment is invasive. In my judgment, therefore, the court exercising the inherent jurisdiction in relation to a 16- or 17-year-old child who is not mentally incompetent will, as a matter of course, ascertain the wishes of the child and will approach its decision with a strong predilection to give effect to the child's wishes.[88]

His approach was based squarely on the application of s 1(3)(a) of the CA 1989, which states that a court 'shall have particular regard to the ascertainable wishes and feelings of the child concerned (considered in the light of his age and understanding)'. Nevertheless, respect for the child's wishes was not to be determinative of the issue. It is clear that the role of the court was seen as being protective of the child in the sense of maintaining health and life. Lord Donaldson MR acknowledged that children should be given greater scope to make decisions for themselves as part of the transition into adulthood, as it is 'only by making decisions and experiencing the consequences that decision-making skills will be acquired'. However, he went on to say that 'As I put it in the course of the argument, and as I sincerely believe, "good parenting involves giving minors as much rope as they can handle without an unacceptable risk that they will hang themselves".'[89] The court ultimately must make its decision based on the paramount consideration of the

88 Ibid at 641.
89 Ibid at 636.

welfare of the child.[90] It is therefore the best interests test that determines whether medical treatment can be given, not the wishes of even a competent child.

Fears had been raised after *Re R* (1991) that abortions might be carried out on protesting 16- and 17-year-olds in reliance on their parents' wishes (Brazier and Bridge, 1996). Lord Donaldson's response in *Re W* was that:

> While this may be possible as a matter of law, I do not see any likelihood taking account of medical ethics [sic], unless the abortion was truly in the best interests of the child.[91]

Despite his optimism concerning medical ethics, he foresaw the possibility that such a flagrant disrespect for a competent adolescent's autonomy might occur, in concluding ominously, 'that is not to say that it could not happen', citing the case of *Re D* (1976)[92] as an example of medical ethics failing to provide an obstacle to medical treatment against the child's best interests. In such a situation, the fallback position appears to be relying on the judiciary to intervene, as he believed that they would prevent any such abuse by requiring the treatment to be in her best interests. This is of course ironic, since resort of the child to the protection of the judiciary in this scenario is only necessary because the courts have declared that her parents can over-rule her decision. If a competent child's refusal of consent was regarded as determinative, there would be no need to bring in the judiciary to consider whether her decision was better calculated to be in her best interests than that of her parents. In addition to subjecting an adolescent to additional pressure of a court hearing on what are deeply personal matters, as we have seen, having resort to the courts may prove less of a protection for the competent minor's decision than Lord Donaldson MR suggests.

This was taken a stage further in *South Glamorgan County Council v W and B*, where the court found that its inherent jurisdiction remained unlimited, even in the face of statutory provisions appearing to restrict them.[93] Here, a local authority started care proceedings in respect of a 15-year-old girl with behavioural problems. It obtained an interim care order with a direction under s 38(6) of the CA 1989 for psychiatric examination and treatment. However, s 38(6) gives children a statutory right to refuse to submit to medical or psychiatric examination or other assessment that has been directed by the court for the purpose of an interim care, supervision, child protection or emergency protection order, if they are of sufficient understanding to

---

90   CA 1989, s 1(1).
91   *Re W (a minor medical treatment)* [1992] 4 All ER 627, CA at 634.
92   *Re D (a minor) (wardship: sterilisation)* [1976] 1 All ER 326, Fam D.
93   *South Glamorgan County Council v W and B* [1993] 1 FCR 626, Fam D.

make an informed decision. It is thus not a general statutory right to refuse treatment, but it might appear, as has been suggested earlier, to support the general principle of child autonomy in such matters. In any event, it certainly seemed to apply here, where the girl refused consent.

Leave was granted for the local authority to seek an order under the court's inherent jurisdiction to allow them to take the steps they wished. It was argued on her behalf that the effect of s 38(6) and s 100 (2)(d) of the CA 1989 was to circumscribe the power of the courts to authorise examination and treatment against the wishes of a competent child in these circumstances. Section 100(2)d provided that:

> No court shall exercise the High Court's inherent jurisdiction with respect to children ... for the purpose of conferring on any local authority power to determine any question which has arisen or which may arise in connection with any aspect of parental responsibility for a child.

Notwithstanding this, while holding that the CA 1989 did suggest some limitations on using the inherent jurisdiction of the courts, it was said that:

> The court can in ... rare cases ... when other remedies within the Children Act have been used and exhausted ... resort to other remedies, and the particular remedy here is the remedy of providing authority for doctors to treat this child and authority ... for the local authority to take all necessary steps to bring the child to the doctors so that she can be assessed and treated.[94]

In other words, despite the seemingly explicit nature of the statutory provisions, and what appeared to be the clear intention of Parliament in enacting them, the inherent jurisdiction of the courts still enabled them to override the wishes of a competent minor about medical examination and treatment, in her best interests. Not only was there no support for child autonomy at common law or via the FLRA 1969 after *Re W* (1992), but argument by analogy was taken to mean that even specific statutory protection of a child's right to refuse was no longer available. In respect of the girl's competence the judge held that:

> I am not prepared to find on that evidence that she is 'Gillick incompetent' or that, to paraphrase the words of s 38(6), she is not of sufficient understanding to make an informed decision about medical examination or psychiatric examination or other assessment.[95]

94 Ibid, per Douglas Brown J at 634.
95 Ibid at 635.

In spite of this, the court duly authorised the local authority to proceed with the arrangements for the girl's assessment and treatment, if necessary.

Since it has been said that irrespective of the competence of a child, his or her refusal of consent to treatment can be overridden by parents or courts if the child's best interest requires it, further examination of what the courts understand by this concept is necessary here. The first idea of what might be included can be dismissed relatively swiftly. This is that it is in the person's best interests to have their autonomy respected. Respect for autonomy may be restricted to prevent harm to others, but in other cases it is generally seen as being beneficial, both to the individuals and in the wider societal interest, to regard their wishes as determinative. This is not the case for children. Although the courts are anxious to say that children's wishes should carry more weight with increasing age and maturity, whether this amounts to paying anything more than lip service to the principle of autonomy is to be doubted, since in no reported English case has a child's refusal of consent been respected. In almost all of them, the child does not even get past the hurdle of establishing competence. Of course, this may be due to the precise circumstances of the cases and if a person lacks decision-making capacity then there is no clash between promoting their welfare and respecting their autonomy. However, given the concerns about the approach taken to determining children's competence, whether respect for autonomy is being shown here is doubtful. In any event, the approach of the courts suggests strongly that respect for autonomy is not the deciding factor.

In all the cases considered where medical evidence was accepted that treatment would save or prolong life, the courts have unanimously regarded the fact that the treatment proposed was said to offer at least some chance of survival as being the crucial factor. For example, Ward J in *Re E* held that:

> When, therefore, I have to balance the wishes of a father and son against the need for a chance to save a precious life, then I have to conclude that their decision is inimical to [E's] well-being.[96]

However, this ignores the fact that in other circumstances it has increasingly been recognised that life, no matter the circumstances, is not always considered better than death for that individual. The courts' clear support for upholding the principle of the sanctity of life, or the right to life under Art 2 of the ECHR, does not extend to requiring treatment to be given in all cases. This is implicit in the case of competent adults by virtue of giving priority to respect for their autonomy in this situation. As we shall go on to see in the next chapter, it is also implicit, even in some situations where the individual lacks the capacity to decide for him or herself, as with severely handicapped babies.

---

96 *Re E (a minor) (wardship: medical treatment)* [1992] 2 FCR 219, Fam D at 227.

In the latter instance, the argument for not providing treatment, resulting in death, is in fact rather more problematic, since the children here are incapable of forming or expressing any view on the matter. However, in the case of the competent adult, the law refuses to intervene in a patient's assessment of what would be acceptable for them, allowing them to reject a particular form of treatment, even if this will result in severe permanent injury or even death.[97]

A striking example of judicial unwillingness to pass judgments on the reasonableness of an adult's set of values was provided in the criminal case of *R v Blaue* where the defendant to a manslaughter charge raised the argument that the refusal of the victim to consent to a blood transfusion was a supervening cause of death because it was unreasonable. Lawton J responded:

> At once the question arises – reasonable by whose standards? Those of Jehovah's Witnesses? Humanists? Roman Catholics? Protestants of Anglo-Saxon descent? The man on the Clapham Omnibus? But he might well be an admirer of Eleazer who suffered death rather than eat the flesh of swine ... or of Sir Thomas Moore who unlike nearly all his contemporaries was unwilling to accept Henry VIII as Head of the Church of England. Those brought up in the Hebraic or the Christian traditions would probably be reluctant to accept that those martyrs had caused their own death.[98]

It is interesting to note that this kind of thinking also seems at least in part to be endorsed in relation to children:

> I personally consider that religious or other beliefs which bar any medical treatment or treatment of particular kinds are irrational, but that does not make minors who hold those beliefs any the less '*Gillick* competent.' They may well have sufficient intelligence and understanding fully to appreciate the treatment proposed and the consequences of their refusal to accept that treatment.[99]

Therefore, holding such religious beliefs in itself does not operate to make a child incompetent any more than it would an adult. However, when we look at cases such as *Re E*, it seems that in practice the religious values of children will not be given the same weight as adults. Other factors, such as lack of free choice or doubts about the settled nature of the child's faith will

---

97 See, e.g. *Re T (adult: refusal of medical treatment)* [1992] 4 All ER 649, CA and *Re B (adult: refusal of medical treatment)* [2002] 2 All ER 449, Fam D.

98 *R v Blaue* [1975] 3 All ER 446, CCA, per Lawton at 450.

99 *Re W (a minor) (medical treatment)* [1992] 4 All ER 627, CA, per Donaldson MR at 635.

be raised. Furthermore, these beliefs will not be allowed to displace the courts' assessment of the child's interests in having treatment. In effect they substitute their own views on the benefits and burdens of treatment for those of the child and will in almost all cases place health considerations above any others. Although it was open to the adult C to say that he would rather die with two feet than live with one, it is very much to be doubted that a court faced with a 16-year-old in similar circumstances would respect such statements. It is possible that the courts in *Re C* (1994) were influenced in accepting his wishes by a number of factors, including his age: he was 68. Considerations of the life expectancy of a child with an amputation might well tempt a court to say that survival with a disability is preferable, thereby perhaps forcing a child to live for many years with a disability that an adult, like Mr C, could judge intolerable for a much shorter period and be allowed to reject. While others might see choosing death rather than a life with disability as being irrational, this would not suffice to overrule an adult. This kind of approach towards children seems to have been taken in *Re M*, though here of course the court was able to sidestep the issue by holding her to be incompetent to refuse the heart transplant. While emotional and psychological effects of treatment against her wishes were recognised, it was said that:

> If the operation is successful, then M will live with the consequence of my decision, in a very striking sense. There are risks attached to the operation itself and there are risks continuing thereafter, both in terms of rejection in the medical sense and rejection by M of the continuing medical treatment. There is the risk too that she will carry with her for the rest of her life resentment about what has been done to her. Whatever that risk may be, and it is impossible to assess, it has to be matched against not simply the risk but the certainty of death.[100]

The need to take into account the effects of a court intervention has been considered in advice to doctors and the Department of Health (DoH) has cautioned that:

> As with the concept of best interests, 'welfare' does not just mean physical health. The psychological effect of having the decision over ruled must also be considered.
>
> (Department of Health, 2001a, para 8.1)

Despite this, while acknowledging it as a factor, the courts have not so far been prepared to let it sway them. This question of emotional trauma was also discussed briefly in *Re E*, where the judge had been referred to the

---

100 *Re M (child: refusal of medical treatment)* [1999] 2 FCR 577, Fam D, per Johnson J at 582.

Canadian case of *Re LDK*.[101] Here, the court had found that the emotional trauma of administering a blood transfusion to an unwilling child would have a negative effect on the treatment. Evidence had been led that if an attempt had been made to transfuse her, the girl would 'fight that transfusion with all the strength she could muster. She would scream and struggle, pull the injecting device out of her arm and attempt to destroy the blood in the bag over her head.'[102] The thought of such scenes taking place is surely not an edifying one. While reasonable force has been permitted by courts when dealing with adults, similar concerns about the effects of strenuous resistance have been found to justify not providing it and the same may be true for children.[103]

However, in *Re E*, Ward J was able to hold that there was no evidence to suggest that the boy would make such efforts to resist treatment and accordingly any impact on him of being forced to have treatment was judged to be less than the alternative:

> . . . any emotional trauma in the immediate or in the long term will not outweigh, in my judgment, the emotional trauma of the pain and the fear of dying in the hideous way he could die.[104]

This was from a judge who admitted that he had no real conception of the strength of the boy's belief: 'One has to admire – indeed one is almost baffled by – the courage of the convictions that he expresses.'[105] It also raises the issue that a child having the strength to physically resist treatment might have a better chance of avoiding unwanted treatment than one who chooses or is only able to put their objections in reasoned argument. Such an approach does nothing to encourage intelligent and thoughtful participation of children in the management of their own healthcare.

Several questions then arise: how much physical and emotional distress must a child be forced to endure because others feel it is on balance better for that child to remain alive? Would there ever be a point when this balance would be tipped against treatment and why should others make this judgment, even where a child is deemed competent to make decisions? Much may hinge here on an assessment of the quality of life of the child to be achieved by treatment. Where the child's condition is such that s/he is terminally ill, it might be that the child's views will be given greater weight. Professional guidance from the Royal College of Paediatrics and Child Health (RCPCH) has,

---

101 *Re LDK, Children's Aid Society of Metropolitan Toronto v K and K* (1985) 48 RFL (2d) 164, 23 CRR337.
102 Cited without reference in *Re E (a minor) (wardship: medical treatment)* [1992] 2 FCR 219, Fam D at 227.
103 *An Hospital NHS Trust v S* [2003] EWHC, Fam D.
104 *Re E (a minor) (wardship: medical treatment)* [1992] 2 FCR 219, Fam D at 227
105 Ibid.

for example, suggested that in a situation described as being 'unbearable', children should be able to refuse treatment. It states that:

> The child and/or family feel that in the face of progressive and irreversible illness further treatment is more than can be borne. They wish to have a particular treatment withdrawn or to refuse further treatment irrespective of the medical opinion on its potential benefit.
> (Royal College of Paediatrics and Child Health, 2004, pp 10–11)

This appears to allow for children to assess the benefits and burdens of treatment for themselves, but only in these limited circumstances. Other parts of the RCPCH guidelines have been cited with approval by the courts, but there has been no case so far where this particular issue has arisen.[106] It must remain doubtful, in the light of the courts' judgments to date, whether they would allow a child to make such a decision if they disagreed with it.

While it has been said that an assessment of best interests is not one that is to be measured solely in terms of medical benefit, therefore, it is clearly regarded as being the decisive factor. This may in part stem from the idea that the best interests of children are served by enabling them to 'come to an enjoyment of autonomy' (Kennedy, 1991, ch 5). This would be a view I share, but in practice, the time when such autonomy may be 'enjoyed' in respect of refusing treatment is set at the age of 18 in England and Wales. It will be remembered that once E reached this age, his refusal of treatment had to be honoured, even though it led to his death. For a Scottish child, this age would be 16, highlighting again the arbitrary nature of age-based divisions. For those below the legally set thresholds for adulthood, an individualised assessment of capacity ought to be undertaken. While it must be conceded that there are difficulties in establishing what decision-making skills are required in principle and in their application, some suggestions on this have already been made. Where there are doubts about the reasonableness of the person's choice or the capacity of the individual, enquiry into the reasoning process is justifiable. Nevertheless, if the idea is to protect a child to 'come to an enjoyment of autonomy' if a child is judged to be competent, then surely this has been achieved? No further intervention in his or her choices ought to be contemplated, no matter how strong the desire to do so.

In *Re W* (1992), counsel suggested that in cases involving normal surgical, medical or dental treatment, the child's decision should determine what is in his or her best interests. Only extraordinary cases should fall into a special category. These would include sterilisation, abortion, organ donation and some other non-therapeutic procedures, or where the child refused to submit to life-saving procedures, or those that would lead to the risk of serious and

---

106 *Re C (a minor) (medical treatment)* (1997) [1998] 1 FCR 1, Fam D.

irreparable harm. In these cases, only the court could override the child's views if the child's best interests required it, though even here it should be slow to do so. The Court of Appeal, who refused to draw a distinction between special or extraordinary cases as distinct from normal cases, rejected this approach. In one sense, the Court was correct to do so. If it is the decision-making ability of the person that is at issue, as it has been argued it should be, then the type of treatment under consideration should be irrelevant. However, this masks the distinction that the courts do draw between the outcome of a decision being to accept or reject treatment. The situation we are left with in England and Wales is that the best that a competent child can expect is that their consent to medical intervention will, in many cases, be respected. However, the best interests test allows intervention, whatever the decision, giving even greater scope for doing so if treatment is refused with the notion of concurrent parental consent. Therefore, it may seriously be questioned whether any real question of autonomous decision-making by competent children arises. Their consent may amount to little more than a mere acceptance or endorsement of a procedure that a practitioner is willing to provide and that may be authorised to be carried out on them anyway. In addition, the courts appear to be setting a precedent by which doctors have a disincentive to providing information to children, safe in the knowledge that they can obtain consent from parents or a court anyway. It may therefore lead to a breakdown in the relationship of trust between doctors and competent children since, if the doctor is unable to obtain consent from them, but the law sanctions consent being given by others, doctors may be under a duty to breach confidentiality to obtain it.

In addition to the factors already discussed, it appears that a child cannot seek an alternative form of treatment that would be more acceptable to them, if the form of treatment rejected is believed to be the most effective. The boy in *Re E* was already being treated with a combination of drugs to combat his condition. However, the drugs that were considered to be most effective had side-effects that would almost certainly require a blood transfusion. The current treatment held some prospect of success – some might say a reasonable prospect. On starting the original treatment, it was estimated that E would have a 60 per cent chance of remission as opposed to 80–90 per cent with the proposed treatment. By the time the case was heard, the ratio was said to be 40–50 per cent, compared to 70 per cent. However, that was not held to be sufficient and he should be given the different medication requiring the objected to transfusion. Such decisions again negate the autonomy of the child in that they do not allow for the pros and cons of alternative treatments to be considered by the individual, in accordance with their own values. It is, however, a consequence of using the best interests test, where there is only one answer that can be given as to what is 'best' for the child, in conjunction with prioritising the health interests of the child above any other considerations and places a high value on doctors' opinions. This contrasts with the position where competent adults are concerned, where the medical opinion of health carers as to the merits of the decision in terms of the health of the individual is not a relevant factor, save in exceptional circumstances where it is strictly governed by statute, for example under mental health legislation. In cases concerning children, the opinion of the child's doctors will almost invariably be the decisive factor and they will be permitted to carry out such medical procedures as they deem necessary. It does not compel them to provide treatment they do not believe to be appropriate in the exercise of their professional judgement, but allowing children, parents or a court to consent maximises the scope for enabling treatment to be given. The paramount concern of the medical profession may be expected to be safeguarding the life and health of the child. However, this same professional concern would be expected to apply for any patient, but where adults are competent this will not be allowed to override respect for autonomy. It is worth remembering the views of medical organisations submitting evidence to the Latey Committee, who supported a right for competent children to refuse treatment. Nevertheless, professional guidance now, of course, seeks to follow the approach of the courts (General Medical Council, 1998, para 23; British Medical Association, 2001, chs 2–3; Department of Health, 2001a, paras 8–8.1).

In addition to the concerns about the interpretation of domestic law, there remains the extent to which the English courts' approach complies with the Human Rights Act (HRA) 1998. A failure to respect the refusal of consent of a competent minor could be regarded as a breach of a number of ECHR rights, in particular those under Arts 3, 5 and 8 and by application of Art 14. Article 6 has already been mentioned. In no reported case in the UK have such arguments been attempted on behalf of competent children, but some commentators consider there might be prospects for success. In respect of Art 3, the right to freedom from degrading and inhuman treatment, the European Court on Human Rights (ECtHR) has determined that treatment which is regarded as being therapeutically necessary will not be regarded as breaching this provision, which would seem to make this hard to rely on (Michaelowski, 2001). Article 5 might, however, prove more useful. It concerns the right to liberty and security of the person and has been addressed by the ECtHR in a number of cases concerning the treatment of young people. One of the most significant is *Nielson and Denmark*,[107] where it was argued that this Article had been breached by placing a 12-year-old boy in hospital for psychiatric treatment on the basis of his parent's consent. This claim was dismissed on the basis that 'the exercise of parental powers constitutes a fundamental element of family life' and that the boy 'was still of an age which it would be normal for a decision to be made by the parent even against the wishes of the

---

107 *Glass v UK* [2004] 1 FCR 553, (2004) 39 EHRR 15, ECtHR.

child.'[108] As Garwood-Gowers points out, restrictions on the liberty of the child on this basis may not be unlimited but there could be some scope for its application in other cases. In line with my own views, he does however have concerns that the ECtHR seemed to be focusing on age as a determining factor, rather than competence, although he suggests that it might be inferred that the child in *Neilson* was not regarded as being competent. The decision might be different where an older and demonstrably competent child was concerned, though this has the caveat of course of what abilities a child might need to have to be deemed competent. Whether the ECtHR would be prepared to allow arguments based on the best interests of the child to permit parents to override a competent refusal remains speculative. *Neilson* may be regarded as rather an elderly case, given the growth of interest in children as being holders of rights on their own behalf over the last 20 years, and some optimism has been shown that a court faced with a similar situation today might be less inclined to allow such wide-ranging powers of parents to restrict the liberty of their children (Fortin, 1999b; Garwood-Gowers, 2001, p 237).

An alternative would be to attempt to rely on Art 8 of the ECHR. It has been held by the European Commission that an obligation to submit to an intervention as comparatively minor as a blood test can amount to an interference with the rights under this Article.[109] Being forced to undergo unwanted treatments must surely be included within the scope of this Article. This being the case, the question would then arise whether any justification can exist for this under Art 8(2), which allows interference with the right to respect for private life on a number of grounds, the most significant here being that it will protect health. In addition, it must be shown that the particular interference is necessary to meet a pressing social need and is proportionate to the objectives that it seeks to achieve. This has been found to be met where an adult is incompetent and treatment is in the person's best interests.[110] The same would no doubt be true for incompetent children. However, it has been suggested that:

> It must at least be doubted whether a general denial of the right of self-determination of competent minors fulfils any notion of proportionality. . . . it must, at best be the case that only a more limited power of intervention against the will of the competent minor in cases of prospective health detriment can be justified as proportionate given the importance of the principle of self-determination and its recognition in competent adults.
>
> (Garwood-Gowers, 2001, p 239)

---

108 *Nielson and Denmark* (1988) 11 EHRR 175, para 72.
109 *X v Austria* App No 8278/78; (1979) 18 D & R 154, Europ. Comm.
110 *Herczegfalvy v Austria* (1992) 18 BMLR 48, (1992) 15 EHRR 437, ECtHR.

Furthermore, the argument has been made that 'forcing interventions on the competent minor, but not generally on the competent adult, amounts to age discrimination affecting the right to privacy or liberty and security' (Garwood-Gowers, 2001, p 231). This might then result in a breach of Art 14. A reasonable and objective justification for discrimination would have to be established to avoid such a breach. It may be doubted whether one can be found if the true basis for requiring consent from a competent person is the protection of their autonomy. This must surely be as applicable to all competent persons, whatever their age.

It might be argued that Art 8 also enables parents to assert that their right to private and family life would be infringed if they were not permitted to make decisions about their minor children. It has been held that parents have a right to act as their children's representatives where treatment decisions are concerned. However, this has been where the child in question was incompetent and no clash between a child's and a parent's Art 8 rights was involved.[111] Where they are in conflict, in line with my general approach, I would argue that priority should be given to the child's rights, since the parent's rights to make decisions on such inescapably personal matters as medical treatment only persist until the child is able to take them for him or herself. Whether the ECtHR would agree remains to be seen.

Nevertheless, all commentators do not share such views on the potential impact of the HRA 1998. Mason and Laurie are among those who have their doubts that the application of human rights principles would change the outcome of cases concerning refusal of medical treatment by children in the UK:

> [we] would point to the both the doctrine of proportionality – requiring a balance of community and individual interests – and the margin of appreciation that countries enjoy under the European Convention on Human Rights. The English courts have made a concerted effort to demonstrate their desire to find a balance in [the refusal of consent] cases and there is little in ECtHR jurisprudence that would lead them to upset that delicate equilibrium.
>
> (Mason and Laurie, 2006, 10.53)

In making this assertion, the idea appears to be that countries have the right to set their own standards for determining the age above which people gain the right to make decisions that may be regarded as being against their own interests. Whether this would indeed be the approach of the ECtHR is unclear. There is similar uncertainty about whether the English or the Scottish approach is in line with international obligations under the UN Convention

---

111 *Glass v UK* [2004] 1 FCR 553, (2004) 39 EHRR 15, ECtHR.

on the Rights of the Child. As discussed in Chapter 1, much is left to the discretion of State parties in resolving the tension between supporting the emerging autonomy of the child and his or her protection. Little help can be drawn from it in determining where these boundaries should lie.

Conclusion

Where decisions are taken by either parents or children to refuse conventional medical treatment, the courts may prove extremely willing to intervene. There is greater justification for doing so where the decision to refuse treatment is being made on behalf of an incompetent child. Nevertheless, the extent to which the courts' approach currently prioritises medical expertise and evidence of what is best for the child above any other consideration is worth noting. My own view is that the protection of the child rightly requires court involvement where there is a serious risk of significant harm to the child and the courts have a role in limiting parents' powers to refuse treatment if the parents' decision is unreasonable. There may still be controversy over where they might set these boundaries, but their responsibility to do so provides a public forum where acceptable standards of child welfare and the rights of the child can be considered. Even more controversial, however, is where refusal of consent is by a competent child. I have argued that respect for autonomy should mean their decisions should be upheld, whatever the outcome. However, the way that the law is framed gives courts the opportunity to depart from this principle, both by interpreting the requirements for competence differently in respect of refusal of consent and by allowing what they consider to be in the best interests of the child to take priority. The need to protect health over any other interests has been put forward in support of this, but it remains less than convincing. While the approach of the law in Scotland appears to raise fewer problems in this regard than in England and Wales, the situation there remains uncertain in the absence of more authoritative decisions. Despite this, I consider that so far it appears, with some modifications, to offer a preferable approach by according due respect to the autonomy of the child. I will now go on to consider the position concerning withholding or withdrawing of treatment from children where debate centres over whether their condition means that providing treatment is of no benefit for them.

Chapter 4

Withholding and withdrawing treatment from infants and young children

Having outlined the principles I propose should govern consent and refusal of consent to treatment, this chapter concerns both. At the heart of the issue here is whether treatment that could give a prospect of the continued survival of young children with severe disabilities should be provided. For some, this question will be answered by appeal to the principle of the sanctity of life or, as it is put in Art 2 of the European Convention on Human Rights (ECHR), the requirement to respect everyone's right to life. This might be thought to require all steps possible to be undertaken to save or prolong life, since it has an inherent, overwhelming value, whatever the circumstances. For others, mere existence is not itself a benefit without consideration of the quality of that life. There are situations in which being alive is not only not beneficial, but is positively harmful to a child, to the extent that it requires steps to be taken to bring that life to an end. For yet others, a middle ground may be taken, which suggests that the sanctity of life is not an absolute principle, but that the crucial factors are the benefits and burdens of treatment and its predicted outcome. Clearly, complex and difficult questions are raised and these will be considered here.[1] I will be discussing only children who are unable to consent or to refuse treatment. For competent children, my response has been given in the previous chapter and is that they should be able to refuse treatment on the same basis as those over the legal threshold for adulthood.

Although the issue of withholding or withdrawing treatment can arise with incompetent children of any age, many of the cases that have reached the courts involve premature infants or those who for other reasons are born with severe physical and mental disabilities. Improvements in antenatal care and in the provision of intensive care treatment for infants have meant that many who would otherwise have died at, or shortly after, birth, can be maintained in a very poor condition for weeks, months, or even longer. The question then

---

1 Some of the discussion presented here was first published as Elliston, 2004. Copyright: Cambridge University Press. Reprinted with permission.

becomes whether what *can* be done to prolong the lives of these children *should* be done. When making such decisions, there is an inevitable tension between the desire to do everything possible to save the life of a sick child and the equally strong desire to avoid causing pain and distress, or allow suffering to continue without prospect of improvement.

Naturally the test that is applied by the courts is the child's best interests and they have found various means of justifying decisions to withhold or withdraw treatment, many of which may be thought unsatisfactory. The way in which they have sought to resolve the sometimes opposing convictions about whether to provide treatment is through attempting to weigh up the relative burdens and benefits of treatment to the child. Doing so will often involve an assessment of the utility, or put another way, the futility, of treatment. It will also involve an assessment of the child's condition and likely prognosis with or without treatment, often termed a quality of life judgement. All of these terms, and the meanings that they bear, have been the subject of much debate and disagreement and there is an unavoidable degree of imprecision in their application, since one person's view on the expected benefit or harm from treatment may differ markedly from another's.

The fact that there is scope for a genuine difference of opinion based upon the weight given to predicted benefits and harms of treatment, and indeed in deciding what is a benefit or a harm in the circumstances, makes it essential to consider who has the authority to make this assessment. It is my contention that, while the courts should have the right, and indeed the duty, to decide whether it is reasonable for parents to consent to or refuse medical interventions on their children, there should be scope for parental views to be given more weight than the courts' approach to best interests allows. There has been even less judicial scrutiny of the position in Scotland than in other areas of medical treatment of children but, while there may be some procedural differences, it seems likely Scottish courts would follow the same approach as in England and Wales. This has been the pattern when looking at withholding and withdrawing of treatment from adults and there is little difference between the powers of parents in respect of their incompetent children in the two jurisdictions. An initial issue that must be addressed is that the courts have consistently repeated their commitment to the principle of the sanctity of life. This might be thought to prohibit making a treatment decision that will fail to save or prolong a child's life. As we have seen already, that is not necessarily the case, but the reasons for this need particularly careful examination where withholding and withdrawing treatment from an incompetent child is concerned.

The sanctity of life principle

In the UK, this principle can be seen as stemming from the Christian religious view that treats life as sacred, because it is a gift from God and only

God can take it away. This view is shared by many world religions, but a sanctity of life principle may also be defended by secular approaches that treat life as having intrinsic value (see, for example, Dworkin, 1993). It is now, of course, reinforced by Art 2 of the ECHR, which requires respect for human life. However, even taking a Christian religious perspective, the sanctity of life principle may more properly be described as a prohibition on 'wrongful killing' rather than an absolute prohibition on ending life (Battin, 1994). According to one interpretation, taking steps to assist another in dying is not permitted:

> It is certainly morally unacceptable to aim or intend to bring about someone's death for a reason or reasons incompatible with recognising the basic worth and dignity of that person as a human being, and incompatible, therefore, with justice. One's intent to bring about someone's death will be equally unacceptable whether it is achieved by
>
> (a) a positive act, such as a lethal injection;
> (b) the omission of treatment decided upon precisely to hasten death;
> (c) the omission of care decided upon precisely to hasten death.
> (Linacre Centre, 1994, para 3.1)

On the other hand, a distinction can be drawn between choosing to bring about death and choosing not to provide treatment.

> It can be morally acceptable to withhold or withdraw treatment precisely because it is reasonably judged inefficacious (futile) or excessively burdensome (2.2.3), even if one foresees that in consequence death will occur earlier than it might otherwise have done. One's reason for withholding treatment is not a judgement about the desirability of putting an end to the patient's life but a judgement about the desirability of putting an end to treatment, either because it is inefficacious or because it is imposing excessive burdens on the patient.
> (Linacre Centre, 1994, para 3.2)

Accordingly, a sanctity of life doctrine can be interpreted as not always prohibiting decisions that result in death (see, also, Boyd, 1995). This would also seem to be in accordance with a medical ethos that does not require all possible treatments to be given, but rather emphasises the need to avoid causing harm to the patient (Mason and Laurie, 2006, 16.15). United Kingdom law seems to take a view that fairly closely equates to this position in most respects. It does so by a number of means. First, it distinguishes between acts and omissions. Second, it may allow intention and type of conduct to be taken into account by categorising decisions as 'medical', thereby bringing them within the scope of professional discretion. Finally, where patients are incompetent, the best interests principle is used to justify withholding and withdrawing treatment.

The criminal law evidently sets boundaries on what can lawfully be consented to.[2] It also restricts choices to seek assistance in dying, through prohibitions on assisting suicide.[3] The courts have been unequivocal that doctors have no right to commit acts to accelerate the death of patients, even with their consent, and this position has been found not to breach human rights principles.[4] Whether this should be the case is of course highly contentious, since it denies respect to a competent person's wishes (see, for example, McLean and Elliston, 2004). Various attempts have been made to change the law, but so far with no real prospect of success.[5] Positive interventions to bring about death, such as giving a lethal injection, are deemed to be acts and hence unlawful. However, while they cannot consent to this, we are familiar with the position that competent adults can refuse treatment even if it leads to death.[6] The attitude of the law is clearly set out by Goff LJ:

> To this extent, the principle of the sanctity of human life must yield to the principle of self-determination (. . .), and for present purposes perhaps most important, the doctor's duty to act in the best interests of his patient must likewise be qualified. On this basis, it has been held that a patient of sound mind may, if properly informed, require that life support should be discontinued . . . I wish to add that, in cases of this kind, there is no question of the patient having committed suicide, nor therefore of the doctor having aided or abetted him in doing so. It is simply that the patient has, as he is entitled to do, declined to consent to treatment which might or would have the effect of prolonging his life, and the doctor has, in accordance with his duty, complied with his patient's wishes.[7]

2   *R v Brown* [1993] 2 All ER 75, HL and *Laskey, Jaggard and Brown v UK* (1997) 24 EHHR 29, ECtHR. *Smart v HMA* 1975 SLT 65.

3   Suicide Act 1961 s 2(1), applicable in England and Wales. In Scotland, the position is less clear but assisting suicide is usually charged as culpable homicide.

4   *Pretty v UK* [2002] 2 FCR 97, [2002] ECHR 2346/02, ECtHR.

5   Most recently at the time of writing by the Assisted Dying for the Terminally Ill Bill 2004, HL 17 Session 2003–2004. This was defeated on its second reading in the House of Lords on 12 May 2006 by a margin of 148 votes to 100.

6   *Re T (adult: refusal of medical treatment)* [1992] 4 All ER 649, CA; *Re AK (medical treatment: consent)* [2001] 2 FCR 35, Fam D; *Re B (Adult: Refusal of Medical Treatment)* (2002) 2 All ER 449, Fam D.

7   *Airedale NHS Trust v Bland* [1993] 1 All ER 821, Fam D, CA and HL, per Keith LJ at 866.

In these circumstances, failing to treat is regarded as a lawful omission.[8] Doctors have no duty and indeed no right to provide treatment contrary to a competent person's wishes and I have argued that the same should be true for competent children.

The second distinction that the courts have drawn is between medical treatment that is intended to kill and that where, although death is foreseen, it is unintended. This concept is commonly referred to as the doctrine of double effect. Derived from Catholic theology, it asserts that foreseen but unintended 'bad' consequences will not be culpable, when the intention is 'to do good'.[9] This has also been explained by Lord Goff who said:

> [It is] the established rule that a doctor may, when caring for a patient who is, for example, dying of cancer, lawfully administer painkilling drugs despite the fact that he knows that an incidental effect of that application will be to abbreviate the patient's life . . . Such a decision may properly be made as part of the care of the living patient, in his best interests and, on this basis, the treatment will be lawful.[10]

This kind of approach is curious since generally we are taken in law to intend consequences that we foresee and may be held liable for them, even if the consequences are themselves unwanted or unintended. In the usual case, if we realise that the result of our actions will be the death of another, this would suffice for a murder charge or at the least one of manslaughter or culpable homicide. For example, it has been said that:

> Where the charge is murder . . . the jury should be directed that they are not entitled to find the necessary intention, unless they feel sure that death or serious bodily harm was a virtual certainty (barring some unforeseen intervention) as a result of the defendant's actions and that the defendant appreciated that such was the case. Where a man realises that it is for all practical purposes inevitable that his actions will result in death or serious harm, the inference may be irresistible that he intended that result, however little he may have desired or wished it to happen.[11]

---

8 *R v Blaue* [1975] 3 All ER 446, CCA; *Re T (adult: refusal of medical treatment)* [1992] 4 All ER 649, CA; *Re AK (medical treatment: consent)* [2001] 2 FCR 35, Fam D; *Re B (Adult: Refusal of Medical Treatment)* (2002) 2 All ER 449, Fam D.

9 See Devlin J's summation to the jury in *R v Adams (Bodkin)* [1957] Crim LR 365, CCA. *R v Cox* (1992) 12 BMLR 38.

10 *Airedale NHS Trust v Bland* [1993] 1 All ER 821, Fam D, CA and HL, per Keith LJ at 868. See, also, *Re J (a minor) (wardship: medical treatment)* [1990] 3 All ER 930, CA, per Lord Donaldson MR at 938.

11 *R v Nedrick* [1986] 3 All ER 1, CCA, per Lane CJ at 3–4, upheld in *R v Woollin* [1998] 4 All ER 103, HL.

Here, however, ordinary legal principles are ignored or at least departed from in the context of medical treatment. Interestingly, there has been an attempt to combine the doctrine of double effect with the right to refuse treatment. A woman with an extremely painful and debilitating condition sought to have a coma induced by medication, followed by the withdrawal of nutrition and hydration. It had proved impossible to provide her with adequate pain relief, as she was intolerant to many forms of medication, but she was not receiving life-prolonging medical treatment. Doctors refused her request as they believed this would render them liable to prosecution for assisting suicide. She intended to base her claim that this form of treatment should be available to her by an application of human rights principles, particularly Arts 3 and 8 of the ECHR (Dyer, 2007). However, her legal action was subsequently dropped (BBC News, 18 April 2007). In the absence of a positive court ruling the position seems to be that providing treatment that may incidentally shorten life and refusal of treatment are lawful independently, but together they are not.

Where incompetent patients are concerned, of course they are protected under the criminal laws that prohibit murder and manslaughter or culpable homicide in Scotland. However, the doctrine of double effect may be applied to them as to competent patients.[12] Furthermore, if conduct can be described as an omission, decisions to withhold or withdraw treatment may be permitted to be made on their behalf, even though death will be the consequence. This has been said by the courts to depend on whether providing the treatment is considered to be in their best interests.[13] In addition, the courts have described artificial nutrition, hydration and ventilation as being medical treatment and hence subject to the same considerations.[14] It is worth noting here that there are those who doubt the justification for drawing such a distinction between withholding and withdrawing treatment and ending life through means such as the administration of an overdose because the end result – the death of the patient – is the same in each case (see, for example, Freeman, 2001; Harris, 2001). Distinguishing between acts and omissions assumes that dying as a result of lack of treatment is preferable to having a life ended by other means and is not uncontroversial for this, among other reasons. Despite these doubts, which I share and have explored further elsewhere, the distinction now appears well established in the courts and would be likely to require legislation to change the position (McLean and Elliston, 2004).

The current legal reality is that although the sanctity of life argument is frequently appealed to, it is selectively applied. It prevents active steps being

12 *Re J (a minor) (wardship: medical treatment)* [1990] 3 All ER 930, CA, per Lord Donaldson MR at 938.
13 *Airedale NHS Trust v Bland* [1993] 1 All ER 821, Fam D, CA and HL.
14 Ibid.

taken with the primary intention of ending life, but allows doctors to fail to save or prolong life. Competent adults are permitted to decide that the benefit obtained by saving or prolonging their lives is outweighed by the burdens of treatment. In this situation, their own perception of their quality of life, judged by their values, beliefs and priorities, is paramount. In order to accept this, it must be agreed that simply being alive is not an absolute value and can be outweighed by other considerations, in this case by an appeal to the principle of respect for autonomy. Where incompetent patients are concerned, a quality of life judgement is undertaken here too, but people other than the patient make it and it cannot be judged by respect for the present wishes of the individual. It is this that makes such decisions so controversial, particularly where the patient is a child. Naturally, the test that is used by the courts is that of the best interests of the child being the paramount consideration. While I support the view that treatment need not be given in all circumstances, my concern here is whether courts place too much reliance on medical evidence in reaching their decisions. Doctors' opinions on the likely outcome for the child with or without treatment are unquestionably of great importance, but judging what is best for a child is not solely within the scope of medical expertise and undue weight should not be placed upon this to the exclusion of other important factors. Overemphasis on clinical judgment can, in some cases, lead the courts to fail to exercise appropriate control over clinical practice and in others, result in overriding decisions taken by reasonable parents who disagree with doctors on what is appropriate for their children. The courts have a responsibility to set the parameters for parental decisions, but where reasonable people could come to different conclusions on what is best for the child, decisions about treatment should remain with the parents.

Withholding and withdrawing treatment from children

A series of cases, beginning in the 1980s, involving the treatment of severely ill or disabled infants were among the first in the UK to address whether withholding or withdrawing treatment could be legally acceptable. In accordance with the sanctity of life principle, the courts declared themselves committed to the perspective that, once born alive, an infant has the same rights and is entitled to the same protection of the law as older children and adults, irrespective of its medical or other condition.[15] It must be said that there is a lack of clarity in the legal requirements for determining whether a child should be deemed as being born alive and there have been calls for this area

---

15 See, for example, Farquharson J's summing up to the jury in *R v Arthur* (1981) 12 BMLR 1, at 5.

of the law to be revisited[16] (see, also, Nuffield Council on Bioethics, 2006, paras 8.13–8.16, 9.11). This will be discussed further in Chapter 6. However, once judged to be liveborn, infants are protected by the criminal law like anyone else and their right to life must be respected under Art 2 of the ECHR. Indeed, children are protected further by the law's recognition that parents must provide necessary care, including medical treatment, or must seek assistance to do so.[17] The statutory offences of child neglect and child cruelty are aimed at providing sanctions against parents, but Davies has suggested that they might also be applicable to healthcare professionals who fail to provide appropriate treatment for children in their care. No such cases have been brought and this proposition is considered doubtful by other commentators (Davies, 1996, pp 292–3; Kennedy and Grubb, 2000, p 2165). However, in any event doctors have an independent duty to provide appropriate treatment for their patients. Inadequate care would normally be dealt with as a civil matter, but where patients have died it is possible for doctors to be convicted of manslaughter by gross negligence.[18] Similar prosecutions for culpable homicide would be possible in Scotland.

Given this, it would not be surprising to find the law insisting that life-sustaining treatment must be given to infants, regardless of their condition or prognosis. This, however, is not the approach that the courts have taken. They have concluded that there are circumstances where, despite it being known that conduct by health carers will cause or contribute to a child's death, it will be lawful. The courts have approached the issue as a question about the doctor's duty towards the child, rather than as simply about the sanctity of the child's life. The guiding principle is that treatment should promote patients' health and wellbeing and it is this that determines the child's best interests. Where it is not believed that treatment will achieve this, it need not be provided and no criminal liability will result.

An initial question is therefore the relationship between lawfulness and best interests. One approach would be to regard them as separable, in which case one will need to be considered first. It could be suggested that if a procedure is unlawful, it cannot be in a person's best interests to perform it and vice versa. An alternative view is to consider that it is the person's best interests that make a decision lawful, so that the two issues are indivisibly linked. In cases concerning withholding and withdrawing treatment, the

---

16 *Re A (children)(conjoined twins: surgical separation)* [2000] 4 All ER 961, CA, Counsel's submission to the court, quoted by Walker LJ at para 27.

17 *R v Gibbins and Proctor* (1918) 13 Cr App Rep 134, CCA, *R v Instan* [1893] 1 QB 450, CCR. There are also statutory offences of child neglect in England and Wales under s,1 of the Children and Young Persons Act 1933 and child cruelty in Scotland, under s,12 of the Children and Young Persons (Scotland) Act 1937. See, for example, *R v Lowe* [1973] 1 All ER 805, CCA.

18 *R v Adomako* [1994] 3 All ER 79, HL.

analysis that has been adopted is the latter. In fact, most cases come before the civil courts as applications for authority to proceed in a certain way, generally where there has been a dispute between health carers and parents over whether treatment should be given. It is not possible to apply to the courts for an advance ruling that behaviour will not be prosecuted.[19] Nonetheless, if doctors and parents act in accordance with a civil courts' judgment, public prosecutions are unlikely and private prosecutions will be prevented.[20] It is worth noting that a rather different analysis was adopted in *Re A (conjoined twins)* (2000). Here, the majority in the Court of Appeal concluded that the best interests of the child and the lawfulness of the procedure were independent. They held that the first stage of enquiry was to consider the children's best interests and only if the proposed intervention met that test would it be necessary to move on to stage two, a consideration of the lawfulness of the procedure.[21] However, the circumstances of that case were unusual, in that separation surgery would kill one child but save the life of the other. The analysis adopted by the judges that surgical separation involved a positive act rather than an omission, seems to have been highly influential in the court's approach.

The lawfulness of withholding or withdrawing treatment has rarely been reviewed independently by criminal courts. That this is appropriate is open to question and in the context of incompetent adults in a persistent vegetative state it is notable that the Scottish civil courts have been much more uneasy about making pronouncements having potential criminal law implications than their English counterparts.[22] With this in mind, it is still useful to consider what the criminal law has had to say about doctors withholding care from children.

The criminal law

The single reported criminal prosecution of a doctor for withholding care from a child is that of *R v Arthur*.[23] This case arose because of the parents' wishes that their newborn baby, a boy born with Down's syndrome, should not survive. The consultant paediatrician, Dr Arthur, instructed that the child

---

19 *R v Director of Public Prosecutions ex parte Pretty* [2002] 1 All ER 1, HL and *Pretty v UK* [2002] 2 FCR 97, [2002] ECHR 2346/02, ECtHR.
20 *Airedale NHS Trust v Bland* [1993] 1 All ER 821, Fam D, CA and HL. An attempt to bring a private prosecution was prevented in *R v Bingley Magistrates Court Ex p Morrow* Times, April 28 1994.
21 *Re A (children)(conjoined twins: surgical separation)* [2000] 4 All ER 961, CA, per Ward LJ at 994.
22 Compare *Law Hospital NHS Trust v Lord Advocate* 1996 SCLR 49 (IHCS) with *Airedale NHS Trust v Bland* [1993] 1 All ER 821, Fam D, CA and HL.
23 *R v Arthur* (1981) 12 BMLR 1.

be given 'nursing care only' and prescribed a sedative analgesic. The child was removed to a separate ward where he was given water, but not fed. He died three days later. Dr Arthur was subsequently arrested and charged with murder. The charge was later reduced to attempted murder when the postmortem examination showed that the baby had a number of congenital defects that had not been known about, but which could have caused the child's death. It is in many ways a troubling case and illustrates neatly the dangers of placing too much reliance on professional practice.

In summing up to the jury, the judge, Farquharson J, stated that:

> However serious a case may be; however much the disadvantage of a mongol, or indeed, any other handicapped child, no doctor has the right to kill it. There is no special law in this country that places doctors in a separate category and gives them extra protection over the rest of us. It is undoubtedly the case that doctors are, of course, the only profession who have to deal with these terrible problems. But notwithstanding that they are given no special power ... to commit an act which causes death, which is another way of saying killing. Neither in law is there any special power, facility or licence to kill children who are handicapped or seriously disadvantaged in an irreversible way.[24]

Despite the apparent invisibility of other professionals' involvement in the eyes of the judge in *R v Arthur* (1981), it would have been possible to charge the nursing staff who carried out Dr Arthur's instructions as parties to the crime, although this did not happen. The same should also have been true for the parents, whose request set this chain of events in progress, and there were additional criminal offences in the form of child neglect that could have been brought against them. Nevertheless, attention focused on the doctor in this case.

The judge's statement that there is no basis to deliberately take steps to end an infant's life, no matter how poor the prognosis, might be seen as clearly upholding the sanctity of life principle. In acting on the parents' wishes, Dr Arthur appeared to have intended that the child should die, so in order to avoid successful prosecution, it was necessary to categorise his actions as an omission. This interpretation seems to have been made by a number of the medical witnesses, who described the circumstances as amounting to allowing 'nature to take its course', rather than taking active steps to kill the child.[25] Even so, as has been said, it is perfectly possible to found a prosecution on the basis of an omission where the person is under a legal duty to act. However, it will be important to establish what the nature

24 Ibid at 5.
25 *R v Arthur* (1981) 12 BMLR 1.

and extent of that duty is. Farquharson J put it to the jury in this way, saying that the *Arthur* case:

> ... really revolves round the question of what is the duty of the doctor when prescribing treatment for a severely handicapped child suffering from a handicap of an irrevocable nature where parents do not wish the child to survive.[26]

There are significant doubts about this formulation, bearing in mind that courts are not bound to see either parents' or doctors' views as determinative, not least where what is at issue is the potential commission of a criminal offence. Despite this, Dr Arthur was able to provide evidence from a number of distinguished expert witnesses in his field that the practice of treating babies as he did, in accordance with parental wishes, was within the bounds of accepted professional practice. Although it cannot be said with certainty why the jury acquitted him, it seems likely that the statements of the judge in summing up to them were influential, such as this passage:

> I imagine you will think long and hard before concluding that doctors, of the eminence we have heard ... have evolved standards that amount to committing a crime.[27]

There are several very uncomfortable ideas here. The first is that failing to provide nourishment to a child that it seems would have been perfectly capable of taking it, and where it would in the ordinary case be provided, could be regarded as allowing nature to take its course. Feeding an infant would surely be expected to form part of normal care and not to be optional. The courts were subsequently to decide that artificial nutrition and hydration could be described as medical treatment and that its withdrawal would be lawful if it was providing no benefit to the patient.[28] However, there is no suggestion that this kind of analysis could operate here. The second is that it could ever have been accepted medical practice not to feed babies with Down's syndrome simply because their parents did not want them to survive. If the conduct towards this child is felt to be untenable, as I think most people now would find it to be, this may seem to pose a problem for my proposition that parents should have a wide range of discretion to make treatment decisions about their children. However, I have based this contention on there being restrictions on parental powers where this causes significant risk of serious harm to the child. The decision that was made here would seem to fall

26 Ibid at 1.
27 Ibid at 22.
28 *Airedale NHS Trust v Bland* [1993] 1 All ER 821, Fam D, CA and HL.

very clearly into this category. The third problem is that, even if it was accepted medical practice not to feed a child in these circumstances, it would be upheld by the law. This suggests that it is professional practice that sets the standard of what is lawful rather than the courts. It would normally be imagined that, whatever the views of the medical profession, they are subject to the law and not determinative of it, especially where the situation involves the life of a child. Reliance on a normative standard of professional practice may be seen as being totally inappropriate when what is at issue is a parent's choice that a child, with no apparent physical problems causing it distress, should not be fed. Concerns about leaving decisions entirely in the hands of parents and doctors were evident even at this time. Robertson suggested that:

> If selection or non-treatment is to be morally and socially acceptable, two conditions must be met. The first is that the decision be made according to criteria that are authoritatively articulated and publicly announced. The criteria cannot be whatever doctors and families decide, for the question is which of their decisions are morally and socially defensible. Rather they should be developed by an authoritative body that is representative of the community as a whole, such as legislature, a national commission or some other publicly constituted body that reflects a wide range of societal views.
>
> (Robertson, 1981, p 223)

The difficulty in allowing wholly unsupervised decisions to be made between parents and doctors has been raised before but it becomes particularly acute in situations like this. My view of this case is that the judge failed to ask the jury the right question: whether professional standards properly met societal expectations. In other words, even if doctors did rely on parental wishes in such situations, were they right to do so? Of course it is only fair to say that it is possible that if this approach had been taken, even with a strong direction from the judge, the jury might still have reached the same verdict if it took the same negative view on the quality of life of a Down's syndrome child as the parents. Views of society at the time have been said to have been more tolerant of parents' rejection of mentally handicapped infants, based on the perception that such children had a very poor quality of life expectation and indeed might be seen as having inferior rights to legal protection. Accordingly, decisions about their care were seen as a private matter and the medical profession was content to act in accordance with parental wishes (Fortin, 2005, p 322). There are therefore dangers in reliance on the views of society on acceptable practices at any given time and it may be that where individuals' rights may not be sufficiently protected by this criterion, legislation may be required, although even this will be likely to be determined by existing social norms. However, posing the question in this way takes attention away from sole reliance on professional and parental discretion and allows a level of objective scrutiny of the proposed course of conduct. As far as withholding nourishment from uncomplicated Down's syndrome children is concerned, even if it was considered customary practice then, it has been said that 'it is unlikely that Dr Arthur's regime would be acceptable today and the case has lost any credibility as precedent' (Mason and Laurie, 2006, para 16.24). Nevertheless, the distinction between actively killing and omitting to provide life-sustaining treatment as part of lawful medical practice is one that persists.

The doctrine of double effect also renders it lawful to give palliative care that may shorten the child's life. It appears that this is not uncommon in practice, with a study of physicians working in neonatal intensive care units finding that 70 per cent of those surveyed in the UK reported having made a decision to administer sedatives or analgesics to suppress pain, despite the risk of respiratory depression and death (Cuttini et al., 2000). Even so, the position at present is that the primary intention behind providing medication must be as part of treatment or the relief of pain and distress, not to deliberately set up conditions to end the life of the patient, although in practice separating these motivations may be rather more difficult than this formula implies.

I have proposed that parents in conjunction with doctors should generally make decisions about treatment of incompetent children, but there must be limits on the exercise of their discretion. The law determines boundaries for behaviour towards children considered so serious that criminal penalties should be imposed. While it sets the outermost parameters for acceptable conduct and would be expected to have a deterrent effect, criminal prosecutions will only be available in the event of conduct that has already taken place. As noted earlier, in most situations, cases will come before the civil courts seeking directions and it is their judgments that determine the lawfulness of a proposed course of action, rather than the criminal courts.

The civil law – benefits, burdens and best interests

Within the limits set by the criminal law, there is still scope for disagreement over whether treatment for seriously ill children should be given. These are usually resolved without the need for legal action and parents are permitted to decide between options presented to them by doctors. As the Royal College of Paediatrics and Child Health puts it, 'Parents are almost always their children's first, best and fiercest advocates', but there may be circumstances where the healthcare team responsible for the care of the child find themselves unable to agree with the parents' decision (Royal College of Paediatrics and Child Health Ethics Advisory Committee, 2000, p 9). It may be inevitable that disagreements will arise in some circumstances, since doctors and parents will be assessing the interests of the child from different perspectives.

Doctors' professional role in decision-making is based on their expertise in assessing the child's medical interests, taking into consideration the chances of success of treatment, the relative suffering likely to be experienced by the child and the prognosis. While parents would be expected to take this into account, they are likely to view the child's best interests, not only in medical terms, but also in their social context (Dworkin, 1982).

The scope of disagreements between parents and clinicians over the provision of life-sustaining treatment was described by Hedley J in *Wyatt* (2004) as involving four stages. At one end, there was:

> . . . the position where a course of treatment was advised but rejected by the parents where the clinician concluded that it was an affront to professional conscience to withhold that treatment. The second stage was where the same circumstances existed but where the clinician although disagreeing with the parents could see that there was something to be said for their view. The third is the reverse of the second where the clinician advises against treatment which the parent wants but is able in conscience nevertheless to give it. The last stage is where to do what the parents want is not possible in good conscience.[29]

Either ends of the extreme may be seen as equating with Rhodes and Holzman's 3rd and 1st categories, respectively, where decisions are so unreasonable that doctors should not rely on a surrogate's decision. The middle two options both fall within their 2nd category, where there is room for reasonable people to disagree (Rhodes and Holzman, 2004). Cases are only likely to come before the courts at the two extremes where parents are seeking either more or less treatment for their children than doctors feel is appropriate. In such circumstances, the courts must resolve the issue one way or another and here we come to some of the principal difficulties in this area: how the courts decide what the best interests of the child require and whether they are better able to determine what is right for a child than his or her parents. At present their approach seems very firmly weighted in favour of supporting medical opinion, despite statements supporting parental decision-making and claiming to take into account a broad range of factors in their assessment. My view is that it may be legitimate to decide that treatment is not justified in terms of the benefit it will produce for the child. Part of this assessment will involve looking at the condition of and prognosis for the child; in other words, making a quality of life judgement. However, in many of these very difficult cases there will be scope for a different opinion to be taken by reasonable people. Unless the parents' decision is manifestly unreasonable it is their view of what is best for the child that should be given

29 *Portsmouth Hospital NHS Trust v Wyatt* [2004] EWHC 2247 Fam D, at para 18.

the greatest weight. In order to make my argument it is necessary to set out in some detail how the courts have determined that decisions to withhold or withdraw treatment from children can be lawful, beginning with how they have dealt with the sanctity of life principle.

The development of the law – the interpretation of the sanctity of life principle

Shortly after the *Arthur* case, the civil courts were given the chance to consider the issue of withholding treatment in *Re B* (1981). Like the child in *Arthur* the baby girl here had Down's syndrome. However, it was known that she had an intestinal blockage that could be corrected with surgery. This surgery would normally be undertaken, but the parents refused to agree to it, believing that God had found 'a way out' for their daughter. The local authority was involved and the child was made a ward of court. Permission was sought for doctors to operate without parental consent. The case was eventually decided in the Court of Appeal where the decision was made to allow the operation to proceed. Looked at it in terms of *Arthur*, the question might seem to have been whether nature should be allowed to take its course with the result that the child would die. This is indeed the view that was taken at first instance. While the reason for this was not spelled out, it seems likely to be based on the same kind of presumption as in *Arthur* – that simply having Down's syndrome meant that steps to prolong the child's life need not be taken. Whether this would amount to a criminal failure to provide care for a child was not canvassed at any stage of the proceedings and indeed no mention at all of the criminal law was made, nor the distinction between acts and omissions, which may appear rather surprising. However, on appeal Templeman LJ set out the principles to be applied as follows:

> It is a decision which of course must be made in the light of the evidence and views expressed by the parents and the doctors, but at the end of the day *it devolves on this court in this particular instance to decide whether the life of this child is demonstrably going to be so awful that in effect the child must be condemned to die*, or whether the life of this child is still so imponderable that it would be wrong for her to be condemned to die.

> There may be cases, I know not, of severe proved damage where the future is so certain and where the life of the child is so bound to be full of pain and suffering that the court might be driven to a different conclusion, but in the present case the choice which lies before the court is this: whether to allow an operation to take place which may result in the child living for 20 or 30 years as a mongoloid or whether (and I think this brutally must be the result) to terminate the life of a mongoloid child

because she also has an intestinal complaint. Faced with that choice I have no doubt that it is the duty of this court to decide that the child must live.[30]

(Emphasis added)

Similarly, Dunn LJ in a brief concurring judgment referred to the fact that there was no evidence that 'this child's short life is likely to be an intolerable one'.[31] In looking at these statements, the judges appeared to be considering whether the circumstances of the child were so unfortunate that death would be a preferable outcome. If taken to its logical conclusion, where the child's condition and prognosis are extremely poor, this might imply that it is in the child's best interest to have his or her life ended not just where there is the option of omitting to provide treatment, but by some positive intervention, such as a lethal injection. Interestingly the language used above, in terms of terminating the child's life, could in fact be taken to imply that failing to undertake treatment could be seen as an active step rather than an omission. However, this is not the approach that has been endorsed, as later cases have sought to make clear. The phraseology used in *Re B* (1981) has been criticised as being 'more emotive than accurate' and what the court in these cases has to decide is 'not whether to end life, but whether to prolong it by treatment without which death would ensue from natural causes'.[32]

In reaching this conclusion the courts have accepted that simply being alive is not of itself an overriding benefit. If it were, then no matter how burdensome treatment might be, or how pain-filled and short a child's life, any treatment that might prolong that life would have to be given. This argument was perhaps most decisively rejected in the case of *Re J* (1990).[33] The child in this case was described by one of the judges as having suffered 'every conceivable misfortune'.[34] He had been born prematurely and was severely brain damaged, but despite this it seemed he was able to experience pain. Among other serious difficulties, he was likely to be blind and deaf and to have spastic quadriplegia. It was thought improbable that he would survive until his teenage years. The consultant neonatologist's view was that the child should not be ventilated if he stopped breathing again, and the parents did not disagree. However, for reasons unconnected with his medical care, the child had been made a ward of court, so directions had to be sought. At first instance, permission was granted to withhold artificial ventilation. The Official Solicitor, appointed to represent the child's interests, appealed against this decision.

30 *Re B (a minor) (wardship: medical treatment)* (1981) [1990] 3 All ER 927, CA, at 929.
31 Ibid at 930.
32 *Re J (a minor) (wardship: medical treatment)* [1990] 3 All ER 930, CA, per Taylor LJ at 944.
33 *Re J (a minor) (wardship: medical treatment)* [1990] 3 All ER 930, CA.
34 Ibid per Lord Donaldson MR at 932.

His first claim was that the court should uphold the principle of the sanctity of life and should never grant permission for the withholding of life-saving or life-prolonging medical treatment. The Court of Appeal rejected this approach. Lord Donaldson put it this way:

> There is without doubt a very strong presumption in favour of a course of action which will prolong life, but . . . it is not irrebuttable. As the court recognised in *Re B*, account has to be taken of the pain and suffering and quality of life which the child will experience if life is prolonged. Account has also to be taken of the pain and suffering involved in the proposed treatment itself.[35]

The Official Solicitor's alternative argument was that, following *Re B* (1981), it would have to be demonstrated that this baby's life would be so awful that he should be condemned to die. He suggested that this boy's existence could not be regarded as being so burdensome that it would be better not to treat him. Again, the Court of Appeal upheld the view of the court of first instance, which had applied a balancing test of the relative burdens and benefits of treatment in the light of the child's prognosis. Of particular note was the distress that mechanical ventilation itself might cause the child. This seems to be the reason why, by contrast, it was recommended that other treatment, such as the administration of antibiotics, should continue. The court concluded that the burdens of treatment, the poor prognosis and the likely further deterioration that would accompany future respiratory failure outweighed any benefit to the child in prolonging his life by ventilation if the situation arose. While this child was 'neither on the point of death nor dying' the court took the view that failing to resuscitate amounted to a lawful omission.

> The court never sanctions steps to terminate life. That would be unlawful. There is no question of approving, even in a case of the most horrendous disability, a course aimed at terminating life or accelerating death. The court is concerned only with the circumstances in which steps should not be taken to prolong life.[36]

Accordingly, the death would be deemed to be from natural causes, precluding criminal liability. Subsequent cases also followed this approach so, in the case of a terminally ill child, it was explained that the duty of health carers is not to provide all treatment that may be available, but to provide care and comfort in the dying process.[37] This may of course raise additional questions,

---

35 Ibid at 939.
36 Ibid per Taylor LJ at 943.
37 *Re C (a minor) (wardship: medical treatment)* [1989] 2 All ER 782, CA.

such as when a child with a short life expectancy should be described as being terminally ill. However, the critical issue is not simply the imminence of dying. This is but one factor to be taken into account when deciding whether the possible invasiveness and distress of treatment is justified by the benefit it will provide to the child in the short and the longer term.

Some have objected to quality of life judgements in principle, because of their implications. Keown explains this as follows:

> The question is always whether the treatment would be worthwhile, not whether the patient's life would be worthwhile. Were one to engage in judgments of the latter sort, and to conclude that certain lives were not worth living, one would forfeit any principled basis for objecting to intentional killing.
>
> (Keown, 1997, p 485)

In judging the worthwhileness of treatment he considers that:

> A treatment may not be worthwhile either because it offers no reasonable hope of benefit or because, even though it does, the expected benefit would be outweighed by burdens which the treatment would impose, such as excessive pain.
>
> (Keown, 1997, p 485)

This approach to best interests has been criticised as being a distinction without a difference. Harris and Freeman, for example, argue that treatment is worthwhile only if the life is worthwhile (Freeman, 2001; Harris, 2001). The risks and burdens of treatment, they say, will be a factor, but whether it is worth running those risks and suffering those burdens can only be determined by looking at the predicted outcome in terms of the expected quality of life of the patient with or without treatment. It is simply not the case that the benefits of a treatment can be evaluated in isolation and a quality of life judgement must form part of the assessment. Nevertheless, Keown's line appears to be taken by the judiciary too. It was said by Lord Goff in *Bland* that:

> [T]he question is not whether it is in the best interests of the patient that he should die. The question is whether it is in the best interests of the patient that his life should be prolonged by the continuance of this form of medical treatment or care.[38]

---

38 *Airedale NHS Trust v Bland* [1993] 1 All ER 821, Fam D, CA and HL, per Keith LJ at 869.

Indeed, Keown's analysis was specifically quoted with approval in the case of *Re A (Conjoined Twins)* (2000). Ward LJ, representing the majority of the court, considered Mary's profound disabilities and incapacity to survive independently in this way:

> Given the international Conventions protecting the 'right to life' . . . I conclude that it is impermissible to deny that every life has an equal inherent value. Life is worthwhile in itself whatever the diminution in one's capacity to enjoy it . . . Mary's life, desperate as it is, still has its own ineliminable value and dignity.[39]

This raised the question whether the courts would be required not to undertake any quality of life assessment at all (Fortin, 2003, pp 317–19). Having said this however, the majority in the Court of Appeal went on to agree with Keown's analysis and held that the 'worthwhileness' of the treatment could be considered. In doing so, the treatment's likely effects upon the child, including his or her condition and prognosis, could be taken into account.[40] It is difficult not to conclude that whatever the Court of Appeal said about not judging the relative quality of the twin's lives, that is exactly what they did (Clucas and O'Donnell, 2002, para 3.3c). As such, a quality of life assessment is not a freestanding test, but it remains critical as part of the courts' approach to determining whether treatment would be in the child's best interests. This confines the lawfulness of conduct to situations where some intervention deemed to fall within medical care could be withheld. This argument is more difficult to apply to situations where there is either no or minimal burden to the child from treatment. Here the only reason for withholding it must be that the quality of life of the child is judged to be so poor that it is not in his or her best interests to survive. As with competent adults, however, the current position of the law is that generally the distinction between acts and omissions serves to allow decisions that will end life to be taken only where there is treatment that can be withheld or withdrawn. The situation involving conjoined twins raises additional problems, as we shall see in the following chapter.

This was reiterated more recently in *Wyatt* (2004), where it was interestingly also held that the ECHR 'adds nothing to domestic law' on this point.[41] The case created considerable media interest, as it was the first to deal with withholding treatment from a child to be held in open court with named parties. This was at the request of the parents and with the agreement of the

39 *Re A (children)(conjoined twins: surgical separation)* [2000] 4 All ER 961, CA at 1002.
40 Ibid at 1010, accepted by Brooke LJ.
41 *Portsmouth Hospital NHS Trust v Wyatt* [2004] EWCA 2247, Fam D, per Hedley J at para 25.

court that it would enable the public to have a greater understanding of the way in which such issues were decided. Some parents may see this as a means of generating public support for their position in the hope of influencing the courts, though this at present appears unlikely to be effective. The emotional atmosphere generated by greater publicity in such cases is viewed with concern by some commentators, although to some extent it is accepted as inevitable (Brazier, 2005).[42] *Wyatt* concerned a child who had been born prematurely with a number of serious disabilities, which meant that she was unable to leave hospital. While relations between medical staff caring for Charlotte and her parents were generally good, a number of disagreements about her care arose and the family came before the courts on several occasions for directions on how her treatment should be managed (for a more detailed review, see Brazier, 2005). The main subject of dispute was whether artificial ventilation should be given to her in the event of respiratory failure. The parents wished for this to be given, but her doctors felt it would not be appropriate. In a hearing before Hedley J in October 2004, it was said that:

> Charlotte has chronic respiratory and kidney problems coupled with the most profound brain damage that has left her blind, deaf and incapable of voluntary movement or response. It is very highly probable that she will during this winter succumb to a respiratory infection that will prove fatal.[43]

Furthermore, '[A]ccording to the medical evidence, Charlotte demonstrably experiences pain; whether she can experience pleasure, no doctor knows though most doubt it.'[44] Accepting this, the judge ordered that while most treatments should be given to her as the need arose, 'further invasive and aggressive treatment would be intolerable to Charlotte' and artificial ventilation should not be given.[45] It would require a tracheotomy to be performed, even before it could be undertaken and it was felt the effects of all this would be distressing to her, would not improve her condition and might even make it worse. The judge's declarations were to stand for six months. By that time, the parents contended that she was no longer a terminally ill child and had improved to the extent that the declarations should be lifted. Notwithstanding this, Hedley J again relied upon the medical evidence that there had been no change in her underlying condition and continued the orders. His

---

42 See, also, the case of Luke Winston Jones, reported as *Re L (Medical Treatment: Benefit)* [2004] EWHC 2713 Fam D.
43 *Portsmouth Hospital NHS Trust v Wyatt* [2004] EWCA 2247 Fam D, per Hedley J at para 1.
44 Ibid at para 2.
45 Ibid at para 38.

decision was upheld on appeal.[46] Although the case may be viewed as follow-ing the usual judicial line in these situations, some interesting comments were made in the course of these judgments.

First, the courts appeared to wish to distance themselves from the use of 'intolerability' as a test for whether treatment should be given. First expressed in *Re B* (1981) and *Re J* (1990), it had been referred to in subsequent cases.[47] In *Wyatt*, however, Hedley J held that 'intolerability' should not be seen 'either as a gloss on or a supplementary guide to best interests'.[48] The Court of Appeal agreed, considering that its use had been initiated under pressure of time and that the 'intolerability' threshold had not been accepted by all of the judges.[49] Accordingly, it was held that:

> Inevitably, whilst cases involving the treatment of children will fall into recognised categories, no two cases are the same, and the individual cases will, inevitably, be highly fact specific. In this context, any criteria which seek to circumscribe the best interests tests are, we think, to be avoided. As Thorpe LJ said in *Re S* 'it would be undesirable and probably impossible to set bounds to what is relevant to a welfare determination'.[50]

This approach was consistent with the reasoning that had been taken by the House of Lords in *GMC v Burke* (2005), which had similarly rejected the contention made by Munby J at first instance that when considering incom-petent patients 'the touchstone of best interests in this context is intoler-ability'.[51] Nevertheless, 'intolerability' is not a criterion that is to be utterly dismissed. Although it was not to be elevated above all other factors, the Court of Appeal in *Wyatt* also held that it remains 'a valuable guide in the search for best interests in this kind of case' alongside the broad approach advocated to taking into account 'medical, emotional and all other welfare issues'.[52]

Second, *Wyatt* paid more attention to the need for transparency where these kinds of decisions are concerned. The Court of Appeal strongly recom-mended that when undertaking the balancing exercise required to determine the best interests of the child it would be helpful to draw up a 'balance

46 *Wyatt v Portsmouth Hospital NHS Trust* [2005] EWCA Civ 1181, CA.
47 *Re A (children)(conjoined twins: surgical separation)* [2000] 4 All ER 961, CA. *W Healthcare NHS Trust v KH* [2004] EWCH Civ 1324, CA.
48 *Portsmouth Hospital NHS Trust v Wyatt* [2004] EWCA 2247 Fam D, per Hedley J at para 24.
49 See, for example, Balcombe LJ in *Re J (a minor) (wardship: medical treatment)* [1990] 3 All ER 930, CA.
50 *Wyatt v Portsmouth Hospital NHS Trust* [2005] EWCA Civ 1181, CA, at para 88.
51 *R v GMC ex parte Burke* [2005] 3 FCR 169, CA, at para 63. See also *A NHS Trust v B* [2006] EWHC 507, Fam D at para 17.
52 *Re A (medical treatment: male sterilisation)* [2000] 1 FCR 193, CA, per Butler-Sloss LJ.

sheet'.[53] This approach, discussed in Chapter 2, has been adopted from a case concerning the sterilisation of incompetent adults and now seems to form part of good practice for courts.[54] While, as has been said, it may import a mechanistic rather than a holistic evaluation of best interests, it does provide a clearer and more accountable method of presenting the evidence that the court has found persuasive. In addition, it is in line with the need to clearly articulate the basis for courts' judgments, in accordance with the ECHR, particularly Art 6. Nevertheless, while apparently a more objective way of dealing with the evidence, it must still be remembered that the weight and value to be attached to the benefits and harms of treatment may be viewed very differently, depending on the decision-maker's perspective, and it remains the case that determining the likely effects of treatment may not be straightforward. This may particularly be so when dealing with babies, since there can often be a lack of certainty in the prognosis for the child. Some infants of low birth weight seem to thrive better than others who may be in a better condition at delivery; some complications may not be apparent or develop until later, while others may be completely unexpected. Furthermore, there may also be a lack of consensus about the relative efficacy of treatments, especially since it can be difficult to gain agreement from parents to involve their babies in clinical trials. The problems associated with medical research with children will be addressed in the next chapter. For the moment, however, as well as balancing the benefits and burdens of treatment, there may be situations where the courts have concluded that treatment, although not burdensome, may still be withdrawn lawfully.

Futile treatment

This brings us to the separate, but closely related, issue of the concept of futile treatment. If treatment is described as futile, this may be used as a justification for not starting or continuing it. However, there are various ways in which a treatment may be regarded as futile and the UK courts have taken a particular approach to this. One way in which a treatment may be thought of as futile is where it could not achieve its intended purpose in a narrow physiological sense. An example would be where an infection is resistant to antibiotics. Administering them would be ineffective and hence, futile. A second sense would be where, although the treatment may be physiologically effective, it would achieve no overall benefit to the welfare of the patient. An example here might be where patients could be resuscitated, but their condition is so poor that they are likely to suffer repeated respiratory failure and there is no hope of improving their condition. In such cases, while

---

53 *Wyatt v Portsmouth Hospital NHS Trust* [2005] EWCA Civ 1181, CA, at paras 87 and 90.
54 *Re A (medical treatment: male sterilisation)* [2000] 1 FCR 193, CA, per Thorpe LJ at 206.

resuscitation can achieve its intended aim in a limited sense, when it is considered in terms of the overall benefit it will provide, it may be thought of as futile and even positively harmful. A distinction may therefore be drawn between physiological or normative futility (Veatch and Spicer, 1996, p 32). It has been pointed out that this leads to the argument that 'the former is to be decided on purely medical grounds while the latter involves a quality or value judgment which is the prerogative of the patient or his surrogates' (Mason and Laurie, 2006, para 16.9–10). Put in this way, then, it may be vital to determine what meaning is being attached to futility when it is being used to describe possible treatment. Mason and Laurie consider that it would be preferable to use what they suggest is less ambiguous terminology, such as 'non-productive' treatment where physiological futility is concerned. They believe that this would firmly place the issue in the medical field and clarify intention. It must be recognised that changing the terminology in this way does not resolve the issues that decision-makers would face. After all, if it is clear that treatment will not achieve an intended physiological effect, then there is no point in giving it and it really needs no further consideration. If, as is more likely to be the case, treatment can achieve an effect on the medical condition of the child, then the question whether it should be given in terms of the child's overall welfare still remains to be considered. However, since I suggest that medical opinions are too highly prioritised by the courts in these kinds of cases, deciding whether a decision properly falls within medical expertise has clear merits.

This is evident when looking at the judgments of the UK courts, since it is in fact usually the broader, normative meaning of futility that they have employed.[55] The courts have used this kind of concept when burdens are believed to outweigh any overall benefit to be achieved by treatment.[56] However, it is important to recognise that treatment may be regarded as futile in the wider sense, irrespective of any burdens imposed on the patient. For example, in the case of Re J (1990), withdrawal of ventilation was authorised, since it was held that the distress that might be caused to the child outweighed any benefit that the child might obtain. Despite this, other forms of treatment were not believed to be burdensome and were expected to be continued. Nevertheless, it might have been possible to argue that, for example, the provision of antibiotics would be futile, since it would not result in any overall benefit for the child.

Even though the term 'futility' was not used in it, a case that illustrates this kind of approach is that of Re C (1989).[57] It concerned a baby with severe

55 A NHS Trust v D [2005] EWHC 2439, Fam D.
56 Re C (a minor) (medical treatment) (1997) [1998] 1 FCR 1, Fam D; Re K a minor [2006] EWCA 1007, Fam D.
57 Re C (a minor) (wardship: medical treatment) [1989] 2 All ER 782, CA.

hydrocephalus, who was believed to be dying. The paediatrician caring for her gave evidence that in his opinion the objective of treatment should be to ease suffering rather than attempt to prolong life. At first instance the judge made an order stating that the hospital should be at liberty to treat the baby to die; to give treatment to relieve her from pain, suffering and distress, but that it should not be necessary to prescribe and administer antibiotics for serious infection nor to set up means of artificial feeding. Although the Court of Appeal changed the wording of the order so that the words to treat her 'to die' were replaced with 'to allow her life to come to an end peacefully and with dignity', the rest of this part of the order stood.

Once treatment is judged to be futile in these terms there have even been some judicial statements that suggest that giving it might be regarded as being an assault. This is because the justification for giving treatment to people who cannot consent to it themselves is that it will benefit them.[58] If there is no benefit to be gained from treatment, the explanation for giving it is absent. A possible concern with this is that it seems to shift the responsibility of justification from those who wish to withhold or withdraw treatment to those who wish to provide it, which would strike many as being contrary to the normal expectation that the first duty of health carers is to seek to treat. However, the important point is whether there is likely to be what is viewed as a positive outcome for the individual, since, as has been discussed, the duty to treat is not an absolute one, but is to treat in a manner that is beneficial to the patient. Even so, the difficulties that arise will be obvious. We are once more faced with the problem of the certainty of diagnosis and prognosis and with the judgement of the extent to which providing treatment will result in a benefit or harm to the child.

Making this judgement in the case of so-called futile treatment is likely to be particularly controversial, given that if the treatment may not in itself be considered harmful, the main issue will be whether the child's continued survival is believed to be a benefit or a harm to it. There are those, such as Davis, who suggest that unless the child is in the process of dying, continued survival is always on balance a benefit to the child so that if treatment is not burdensome it should always be given (see, for example, Davis, 1994). Others, including Harris, disagree and suggest that quality of life considerations can permit life-saving or life-prolonging treatment to be withheld, even if the treatment would not itself be unduly burdensome (Harris, 1994). With the acceptance of the withholding of ventilation and other forms of treatment from patients in a permanent vegetative state, who by definition cannot be aware of any burden of treatment, and who might survive for many years if such treatment was continued, the courts appear to have accepted the latter

---

58 *Airedale NHS Trust v Bland* [1993] 1 All ER 821, Fam D, CA and HL.

approach.[59] This has also been endorsed in professional guidance issued by the Royal College of Paediatrics and Child Health that will be discussed later.

Nevertheless, judging certain forms of treatment to be futile in its broad sense continues to raise difficult issues and this may particularly be the case where what is being withheld is nourishment. While the courts have held that artificial nutrition and hydration is medical treatment and subject to the same considerations as any other, there remains some controversy over this. Evidence provided to a House of Lords Select Committee following *Bland* showed that many firmly believe that this should be deemed to be basic care and always provided, the method of administration being of no consequence (House of Lords Select Committee on Medical Ethics, 1994). There is also still occasional unease about bringing about death by this means expressed by the courts, for example in *W Healthcare NHS Trust v KH* (2005). This case concerned whether a displaced feeding tube should be replaced for an adult woman who lacked capacity, had severe multiple sclerosis and was considered to have a poor quality of life. Her family sought declarations not to reinsert the tube because they believed she would have wished to die with dignity. However, it was said that this would lead to KH dying slowly of thirst and starvation, although drugs would have alleviated her suffering. The judge concluded that despite KH's condition, he could not say that life-prolonging treatment would provide no benefit and he found that death by starvation would be even less dignified than the death that she would face in due course if kept artificially alive for more weeks, months or possibly years.[60] In *Re K a minor* (2006), by contrast, a declaration was made to enable doctors to remove a feeding tube from the abdomen of a severely compromised baby in their care. In this case, moving to a regime of palliative care was felt to be appropriate in order to allow K 'to die peacefully over a short period of time'.[61] Although a difference in outcome can be justified by looking at the benefits and burdens associated with the regime for each patient, why it would be a dignified means of death in one case and not in another is less easy to explain. Nevertheless, in certain circumstances withholding or withdrawing artificial nutrition and hydration may be lawful.

Withholding and withdrawing treatment and human rights

Although it has been said in *Wyatt* that ECHR principles have not affected this area, there have been questions about whether withdrawal of life-prolonging treatment would breach Convention Rights, in particular Art 2,

---

59 *Airedale NHS Trust v Bland* [1993] 1 All ER 821, Fam D, CA and HL.
60 *W Healthcare NHS Trust v KH* [2005] 1 WLR 834, CA, para 27 per Brooke LJ.
61 *Re K a minor* [2006] EWCA 1007, Fam D, Sir Potter, P at 1.

the right to life, and Art 3, the prohibition on torture, inhuman and degrading treatment. The first UK case to specifically consider human rights principles in this context concerned a baby boy who had been born prematurely.[62] He developed ventilator-induced injuries and also had a number of congenital defects, leading to serious disabilities and a very short life expectancy. The child's condition continued to deteriorate over the following year and the paediatricians treating him felt it would not be in his best interests to subject him to resuscitation and artificial ventilation in the event of respiratory failure. The boy's parents opposed this, believing such a decision to be premature. In the light of the medical evidence, the judge authorised medical staff not to resuscitate. Despite the fact that the case was heard before the coming into force of the Human Rights Act 1998 (HRA 1998), the judge considered ECHR rights and stated that there was a strong obligation in favour of taking all steps capable of preserving life, save in the most exceptional circumstances. Nevertheless, he concluded that failing to commence life-prolonging treatment would not be in breach of Art 2 if giving that treatment would not be in the patient's best interests.

Subsequent case law has expanded on this approach. Although acknowledging that Art 2 requires States to take positive steps to save life, as explained in *Osman v UK*, this obligation must be interpreted in a way that 'does not impose an impossible or disproportionate burden on the authorities.'[63] In *NHS Trust A v M: NHS Trust B v H*, Dame Butler-Sloss P held that:

> The standard adopted by the European Court bears a close resemblance to the standard adopted in the domestic laws on negligence and approximates to the obligation adopted in the *Bolam* test. Article 2 therefore imposes a positive obligation to give life-sustaining treatment in circumstances where, according to responsible medical opinion, such treatment is in the best interests of the patient but does not impose an obligation to treat if such treatment would be futile.[64]

The effect of the HRA 1998 has been explained by the British Medical Association (BMA) as follows:

> To the extent that best interests remain central to the decision-making process, this reflects an extension, rather than a change, of existing good practice. Since the introduction of the Human Rights Act, however, the

---

62 *A NHS Trust v D* [2000] 2 FCR 577, Fam D.
63 *Osman v UK* (1998) (1999) 1 FLR 193, ECt HR, at para 116.
64 *A NHS Trust v D* [2000] 2 FCR 577, Fam D; *A NHS Trust A v M: NHS Trust B v H* [2001] 1 FCR 406, Fam D.

way in which best interests are assessed and the factors taken into account in reaching those decisions are likely to be open to far greater scrutiny. Doctors must be able to show that the patient's right to life was specifically considered and, where treatment is not provided, to demonstrate legitimate grounds for not taking steps to enforce that right.

(British Medical Association, 2000)

Article 3 has also been used to assert a right to die with dignity.[65] The case of *D v UK* (1997) illustrates this principle and the obligation to ensure that proper medical care is provided, although the circumstances are far removed from those that have been considered so far. It concerned a man who had lived most of his life in St Kitts. He came to the UK and after being convicted of drug offences, was imprisoned, where he developed HIV. On his release he challenged plans to deport him on the basis that he would not be able to receive adequate medical care there. The European Court on Human Rights (ECtHR) held that deportation would be in breach of Art 3, as it would expose him to a real risk of dying under most distressing circumstances, which would amount to inhuman treatment.[66] A failure to provide appropriate care may therefore fall foul of this provision. It has been held that Art 3 requires the victim to be aware of the torture or inhuman and degrading treatment. It cannot be breached where the patient is unaware that treatment is being provided and would be equally unaware of its withdrawal.[67] This was called into question at first instance in *R v GMC and others, ex parte Burke* (2005), but the Court of Appeal appears to have endorsed previous case law on this point.[68] As we have seen, the removal of treatment, such as nutrition and hydration, may in some circumstances be said to lead to a more undignified death than succumbing to consequences of the patient's condition, although how such distinctions are to be drawn remains unclear. All that can be said with certainty is that the ability of a child to experience pain or suffering must always be taken into account when considering the treatment to be given, the consequences of withholding or withdrawing treatment, and the appropriate care to be given. As a corollary to this, it may also be possible for the inappropriate provision of medical treatment to be in breach of Art 3. The ECtHR has said that:

> . . . as a general rule, a measure which is a therapeutic necessity cannot be regarded as inhuman or degrading. The court must nevertheless satisfy itself that the medical necessity has been convincingly shown to exist.[69]

65 Ibid.
66 *D v UK* (1997) 42 BMLR 149, (1997) 24 EHRR 423, ECt HR.
67 *A NHS Trust A v M: NHS Trust B v H* [2001] 1 FCR 406, Fam D.
68 *R v GMC ex parte Burke* [2005] 3 FCR 169, CA at paras 35–7.
69 *Herczegfalvy v Austria* (1992) 18 BMLR 48, (1992) 15 EHRR 437, ECtHR, at para 82.

The right to respect for private and family life, under Art 8, has already been briefly mentioned, but it is worth reiterating that, among other things, it requires family integrity to be protected. The ECtHR has held that parents have the right to be involved in significant decisions about their children and there can probably be no more significant decision than whether to allow a child to die without further treatment.[70] This was considered more recently in the case of *Glass v UK*.[71] It arose as a result of a series of major and sustained disagreements between a family and doctors over the treatment of a severely disabled teenage boy. His doctors finally believed the boy was in a terminal condition and sedated him with diamorphine, despite his mother's objections. At some stage, it also appears that a 'Do Not Resuscitate' order was placed in his medical notes, without his mother's knowledge. Despite the regime adopted by the hospital, the boy survived and notwithstanding the mother's complaints about medical staffs' behaviour, the General Medical Council took no disciplinary action nor was any prosecution instituted. The mother claimed that her son's and her own right to respect for private and family life had been breached by these events and the case eventually reached the ECtHR. A claim that the child's Art 2 right to life had been breached was rejected at an early stage of the proceedings, as were arguments based on a variety of other Convention rights. However, it was eventually held that his Art 8 rights were engaged and had been breached by the doctors failing to institute legal proceedings to resolve the disagreement between them and the child's parents. The case supports the child's right to have its family involved in such supremely significant decisions. However, this in no way means that parental views will be determinative. To this extent *Glass v UK* merely reinforces the UK courts' role as final arbiter in such matters. The ECtHR was keen to stress that it was not its function to question the doctors' clinical judgement nor the appropriateness or otherwise of the treatment. The case turned on the fact that the doctors in this case had ample time to seek a ruling from the domestic courts where there was disagreement between them and the child's parents over proposed treatment.[72]

Other Convention rights that may also be relevant in individual cases have already been raised in previous chapters, such as the right to a fair trial (Art 6), freedom of thought, conscience and religion (Art 9), freedom of expression (Art 10) and the prohibition of discrimination (Art 14). So far, though, there has been no significant change in the courts' approach after the coming into force of the HRA 1998. The way they have addressed human rights has been criticised for effectively attempting to shoehorn domestic judicial statements to make them fit. Maclean suggests that while the outcome of the

---

70 *W v UK* (1987) 10 EHRR 313, ECtHR.
71 *Glass v UK* [2004] 1 FCR 553, (2004) 39 EHRR 15, ECtHR.
72 See also *R v GMC ex parte Burke* [2005] 3 FCR 169, CA at paras 73–80.

judgments may be justifiable under the HRA 1998, the courts have sought 'to ensure that [human rights principles] were compatible with the common law rather than by adapting the common law to concord with those rights' (Maclean, 2001).

Quality of life judgments, best interests and the harm principle

The conclusion that has been reached is that it is lawful to withhold or with-draw treatment from severely ill children if either the burdens outweigh its benefits or it is futile in the sense of providing no overall benefit. I support the view that mere existence is not necessarily beneficial and that the sanctity of life principle should not be regarded as being absolute. In consequence, there will be times when a quality of life judgment is justified in deciding whether treatment should be provided. Nevertheless, although I believe the courts are correct to allow such judgments to be made, in my view the problem lies with the use of the best interests test and, in particular, in the way that it can be used to prioritise medical views at the expense of those of parents.

The role of parents in determining quality of life

From what has gone before it must be acknowledged that parents already do have a significant role to play in making decisions about the treatment of their seriously ill children. Few cases come before the courts and most decisions are made by parents acting on medical advice. Professional organ-isations have stressed the importance of parent's wishes and sought to give practical guidance on seeking and obtaining consent from parents, how to attempt to resolve disagreement and how the issues raised by ceasing further treatment should be addressed.[73] In order to be able to make a proper deci-sion on behalf of their child, it is expected that parents will be enabled to give or withhold their consent freely and should be given sufficient information to enable them to consider the issues. This includes: the benefits and risks of the proposed treatment; what it will involve for the child; what alternatives may be available and the practical effects on the child and the family of having, or not having, the treatment (see Department of Health, 2001b, p 14, and for general issues on consent, Department of Health, 2001a). Apart from the need to satisfy legal requirements for information disclosure to parents, recent research also emphasises the broader point that parents have a need for truthful and accurate information on a poor prognosis. Even well-meaning

73 This guidance includes the British Medical Association 2001 and 2007; Department of Health 2001b; General Medical Council 2002b.

attempts to avoid distressing parents by withholding painful information can have entirely the opposite effect. The way that such information is presented obviously requires care and sensitivity, but failure to give parents sufficient information on the likely prospects for the child, and particularly the effects of the child's treatment or condition, can be perceived as cruel and disempowering rather than kind (McHaffie, 2001; McHaffie et al., 2001).

Professional guidance has also sought to clarify the basis on which doctors should approach these issues. Particularly interesting is the guidance issued by the Royal College of Paediatrics and Child Health (RCPCH) in 2004. It describes five situations in which it believes it may be appropriate not to provide life-prolonging treatment (Royal College of Paediatrics and Child Health, 2004, pp 10–11). The first is the brain-dead child. Here, any treatment would be nonproductive and hence there is no question of it being provided. The second situation concerns children in a permanent vegetative state. Providing further treatment to them, as with adults, may be regarded as futile since there is presently no accepted means of restoring experiential capacity to the patient. The courts have even raised doubts about whether such patients can be said to have any interests at all, but have concluded that extending life in this situation is incapable of producing any benefit to the patient.[74] Recent developments, such as the use of new drugs to try to restore consciousness, may be thought to cast some doubt on this, but for the moment they are best dealt with as innovative treatment or research that will be considered in the following chapter. Apart from this possibility, while not all would agree that life in a permanent vegetative state has no benefit, it would be expected that treatment would be withdrawn in such cases. Since treatment could potentially be continued indefinitely, if parents were unusually to seek this, the question of compelling doctors to provide treatment would arise and this will be returned to later. The remaining three categories open up much more likelihood of debate and disagreement between parents and doctors:

The 'No Chance' situation. The child has such severe disease that life-sustaining treatment simply delays death without significant alleviation of suffering.

The 'No Purpose' situation. Although the patient may be able to survive with treatment, the degree of physical or mental impairment will be so great that it is unreasonable to expect them [sic] to bear it. The child in this situation will never be capable of taking part in decisions regarding treatment or its withdrawal.

The 'Unbearable' situation. The child and/or family feel that in the face of progressive and irreversible illness further treatment is more than can

74 *Airedale NHS Trust v Bland* [1993] 1 All ER 821, Fam D, CA and HL.

be borne. They wish to have a particular treatment withdrawn or to refuse further treatment irrespective of the medical opinion on its potential benefit.

(Royal College of Paediatrics and Child Health, 2004, pp 10–11)

The 'no chance' and 'no purpose' situations may be seen as broadly equating with the notion of futility and best interests accepted by the courts. The 'unbearable' situation is rather more controversial. As discussed in the previous chapter, I would regard it as wholly appropriate to allow a child who is properly able to do so to make a judgement for him or herself on what is unbearable. This statement also makes it professionally permissible to rely on parental views where children are unable to express themselves. However, it does not attempt to place any limits on the nature or effects of illness that would justify acting in accordance with the wishes of the parents, when doctors feel treatment may be appropriate. Given the potential problems in determining the prognosis for severely ill children, particularly premature infants, some practitioners may be more willing to attempt treatment than others and there is likely to be variation in practice. The Royal College of Obstetricians and Gynaecologists (Nuffield Council on Bioethics, 2006, para 8.24) has noted concerns about the potential for a 'postcode lottery'. While there may be professional practice guidelines, these will of course require to be interpreted in practice and they cannot cover every individual situation. The RCPCH guidance advocates a consensus approach, both within the healthcare team and also between them and the parents. It does, however, clearly place priority on the relative experience of the individual team members and puts the final responsibility on the medical side with the consultant in charge of the child's care (Royal College of Paediatrics and Child Health, 2004, para 3.3.1). Where there is scope for professional differences of opinion, there may be even more scope for disagreement between professionals and parents who may believe that their child should be given more or less treatment, depending on the circumstances. The RCPCH guidance advises that it may be helpful for doctors to ask for independent second opinions, but where disagreements cannot be resolved informally, as the last resort, the opinion of a court may need to be sought.

In *Re B* (1981) it was made perfectly clear that the court, rather than doctors or parents, had the ultimate responsibility for making the decision and to this extent it may be seen as doing no more than confirming the position that we are familiar with. In so far as the risks and burdens of the treatment were concerned, the operation appeared to be one that would be carried out as a matter of course on a child unaffected by Down's syndrome. Interestingly, though, there was evidence that the risks of heart disease after surgery were doubled in Down's syndrome children and this led Ewbank J at first instance to conclude that the parents' decision to refuse surgery was not unreasonable. However, it was not the reasonableness of the decision that was the concern of the court, but the child's best interests. Although reaching a different conclusion on whether treatment should be provided, this approach was followed on appeal.

Nevertheless, there has been some support for the idea that parental reasonableness should play a part in the courts' judgments. It was said in *Re J* (1990) that:

> I do not know of any demand by the judges who have to deal with these cases at first instance for this court to assist them by laying down any test beyond that which is already the law: that the interests of the ward are the first and paramount consideration, subject to the gloss on that test which I suggest, that in determining where those interests lie the court adopts the standpoint of the reasonable and responsible parent who has his or her child's best interest at heart.[75]

While the judge is speaking here of the court's role in making the assessment, it might seem to follow that if the parents' own views were found to be reasonable, there would be no need for the court to substitute its decision for theirs. However, that is not the line that has been taken in subsequent cases, most particularly in *Re T* (1996), where a number of statements were made to the effect that the reasonableness of the parents' views was not the decisive factor:

> An appraisal of parental reasonableness may be appropriate in other areas of family law (in adoption, for example where it is enjoined by statute) but when it comes to an assessment of the demands of the child patient's welfare, the starting point – and the finishing point too – must always be the judge's own independent assessment of the balance of advantage or disadvantage of the particular medical step under consideration. In striking that balance, the court will of course take into account as a relevant, often highly relevant, factor the attitude taken by the natural parent, and that may require examination of his or her motives. But the result of such an enquiry must never be allowed to prove determinative. It is a mistake to view the issue as one in which the clinical advice of doctors is placed in one scale and the reasonableness of the parent's view in the other.[76]

---

75 *Re J (a minor) (wardship: medical treatment)* [1990] 3 All ER 930, CA, per Balcombe LJ at 942.
76 *Re T (a minor) (wardship: medical treatment)* (1996) [1997] 1 All ER 906, CA, per Waite LJ at 917. See, also, Butler-Sloss LJ and Roche LJ.

From the cases, it seems clear that, no matter what claims to the contrary, it is the weight given to medical evidence of benefit or harm that has proved to be decisive. As Maclean suggests:

> Historically the courts have relied on a medicalised view of 'best interests'. . . . It is submitted that, for minors, while the court has retained the right to determine the patient's best interests and claims to consider the full spectrum of ethical, personal and medical factors, the reality is that the decision almost always accords with the doctor's rather than the relative's view of the patient's best interests.
>
> (Maclean, 2001, p 784)

Indeed, this has led one commentator to suggest that what the courts are doing is in fact looking at the defensibility of doctors' actions rather than reviewing parental treatment preferences (Pedain, 2005). This may be illustrated by the case of *Re C* (1997) where nonresuscitation of a 16-month infant with spinal muscular atrophy type 1 was authorised as being in the child's best interests.[77] The parents were Orthodox Jews and believed that life should be preserved if it was possible to do so. The court quoted with approval from the RCPCH guidelines and agreed with the evidence given by paediatric neurologists that the child was in a 'no chance' situation.[78] The doctors' views were that further ventilation in the event of respiratory collapse would be futile, as it would only delay inevitable collapse. Mason and Laurie comment that:

> The decision was presented as involving an objective assessment of best interests, and indeed, what counts as futility yet . . . these notions are, in reality, highly subjective. Whichever way one looks at a case such as *Re C*, one cannot avoid the conclusion that it involved a value judgment. That the values of the parents in consenting on behalf of their child were completely ignored was at best paternalistic and, at worst, culturally imperialistic.
>
> (Mason and Laurie, 2006, para 10.22)

Part of the parents' refusal to agree to withhold treatment was based on their religious beliefs. As we have seen already, such beliefs may be ones that reasonable people could reject without being unreasonable and hence need not be determinative when considering decisions being made by surrogates on behalf of incompetent patients (Rhodes and Holzman, 2004). Accordingly, failing to act in accordance with the parents' religious beliefs may not be such

---

77 *Re C (a minor) (medical treatment)* (1997) [1998] 1 FCR 1, Fam D.
78 Ibid per Stephen-Brown LJ at 3.

a strong ground for criticism. However, the parents were described as being 'highly responsible persons' and as Pedain points out:

> ... it was not immediately obvious that their refusal to agree to a proposed course of treatment – withdrawal of artificial ventilation for their child – was irresponsible in the light of the doctors' unwillingness to re-institute artificial ventilation should the child suffer another respiratory arrest. Nevertheless, the court preferred to authorise the hospital to proceed with an attempt to wean the child off the ventilator, ducking the question whether the parental choice to withhold their consent to such a course of action unless the doctors promised to re-institute artificial ventilation, if necessary to prolong the child's life, was reasonable or not.
>
> (Pedain, 2005)

In addition, much of the discussion in the case centred on the unwillingness of the courts to require doctors to treat patients against their clinical judgment, a point which will be returned to later.

Despite acknowledging that the assessment of the benefits and burdens of treatment involves more than the medical view on the child's condition and effects of treatment, there is only one reported case in which the courts have upheld parents' wishes against strong medical opinion.[79] This case has already been referred to, namely *Re T* (1996). It will be remembered that the court determined it was not in a child's best interests to receive a liver transplant where his parents objected. This case has been widely criticised by commentators as being wrongly decided and has even been tacitly disapproved of in a later case where it was described as being exceptional, based on the Court of Appeal's rejection of the trial judge's approach that prioritised the consideration of the mother's reasonableness in rejecting medical opinion to the exclusion of other factors.[80] I have argued the reverse: that it was reasonableness that should have provided the basis for the court's decision. I agree with the Court of Appeal's conclusion, but on the basis that the parent's refusal of consent here does not seem to meet the reasonableness test.

The harm and reasonableness standard

In order to establish whether parental views meet a reasonableness standard however, it is necessary to consider what the appropriate perspective is that

---

79 *Re T (a minor) (wardship: medical treatment)* (1996) [1997] 1 All ER 906, CA.
80 *Re B (a child) (immunisation)* [2003] 3 FCR 156, CA, affg sub nom *Re C (a child) (immunisation: parental rights); Re F (a child) (immunisation: parental rights)* [2003] EWHC 1376, Fam D.

decision-makers should adopt. Fears may rightly be aroused when any assessment of the quality of a person's life is being made by others. It may risk placing a lower value upon the lives of those who may be in most need of protection: the young, the sick and those who cannot speak up for themselves (Gunn and Smith, 1985). The potential problems may be illustrated by the following comments in another case involving a child with severe disabilities:

> . . . a social worker expressed the view that in such a situation the court would expect the doctors to embark on '*treatment appropriate to a non-handicapped child*.' The legal department of the local authority, on the other hand, expressed the view that C should '*receive such treatment as is appropriate to her condition*.'
>
> For my part, I have no doubt that the legal department was right and the social worker was wrong. You do not treat a blind child as if she was sighted, or one with a diseased heart as if she was wholly fit.[81]
>
> (Emphasis added)

To some, this statement may appear to allow unjust discrimination in the provision of treatment to the disabled, permitting doctors not to provide treatment they would normally provide to a non-disabled child. Indeed, this kind of discriminatory approach may be thought to have been precisely what was involved in *R v Arthur* (1981). The treatment of Down's syndrome children has continued to provoke controversy with accusations that operations that could have benefited them have been improperly withheld (Down's Syndrome Association, 1999). Nevertheless, in all discussions on discrimination it must be remembered that it may be entirely proper to treat people differently, depending on their particular circumstances, and indeed inappropriate not to. It seems that this is the approach that the court had in mind here. That being said, much depends on judging what is 'appropriate' for a child in a certain condition and this may be most contentious where what is at stake is potentially life-saving treatment.

The perspective that a proxy decision-maker should take is therefore critical, as discussed in Chapter 1. It was noted that there are two broad approaches that could be adopted: basing decisions on what a child would choose for him or herself (a hypothetical choice approach) or what is best for the child (an objectivist approach) (Archard, 2002). The hypothetical choice approach involves an attempt to make what is more commonly referred to as a substituted judgement, where the decision-maker attempts to don the mantle of the incompetent person. It is perhaps most applicable in the case of previously competent adults who have lost capacity, for example, through

---

81 Ibid at 784.

being in a permanent vegetative state. This line was taken in the USA in *Cruzan v Director, Missouri Department of Health* (1990). Evidence will be required of people's previous wishes, values and preferences in order to try to decide what they would choose if they were able to do so. As such it is generally speculative, since one cannot know that the decision made does represent what would have been decided. There is some evidence that prediction can be very flawed, even where the proxy knows the person well, let alone where the decision-maker is a stranger such as a health carer or a judge (see, for example, Cohen-Mansfield *et al.*, 1991, pp 289–94). Using this test has been unpopular with the UK courts in respect of incompetent adults.[82] Indeed, even in recent legislation governing adults with incapacity, although their wishes are expected to carry considerable weight, this is not the standard that governs here either. Instead, interventions are judged either by the test of the adult's best interests or by what will be of benefit to them.[83]

Nevertheless, this sort of argument has found some favour with courts making decisions about the treatment of babies and young children, such as in *Re J* (1990). Although the court applied the best interests test, as it was required to do, Taylor J gave an interesting interpretation of it:

> I consider the correct approach is for the court to judge the quality of life the child would have to endure if given the treatment and decide whether in all the circumstances such a life would be so afflicted as to be intolerable to that child. I say 'to that child' because the test should not be whether the life would be tolerable to the decider. The test must be whether the child in question, if capable of exercising sound judgment, would consider the life tolerable.[84]

This appears to be a substituted judgment type approach and its use here is doubly surprising, since it is in this context that it is most logically difficult to sustain. Where the patient is a young child, it is unlikely that there will be any evidence of past preferences or values to go on and the child has never known any existence other than the one it now has, nor has any concept of a future. Despite this, it was said by Lord Donaldson in *Re J* (1990) that:

> . . . where a ward of court suffered from physical disabilities so grave that his life would *from his point of view* be so intolerable if he were to continue living that he would choose to die if he were in a position to make a

82 *F v West Berkshire Health Authority and Another* [1989] All ER 545; *Airedale NHS Trust v Bland* [1993] 1 All ER 821, Fam D, CA and HL; *W Healthcare NHS Trust v KH* [2004] EWCA Civ 1324.
83 Mental Capacity Act 2005, Adults with Incapacity (Scotland) Act 2000.
84 *Re J (a minor) (wardship: medical treatment)* [1990] 3 All ER 930, CA, per Taylor J at 945.

sound judgement, the court could direct that treatment without which death would ensue from natural causes need not be given to the ward to prolong his life, even though he was neither on the point of death nor dying.[85]

(Emphasis added)

It will be remembered that a number of variations on the hypothetical choice approach have been proposed. These would be that the courts should choose first, what the adult that the child will become would choose; second, what any adult would choose in that situation, or finally what an adult version of that child would choose (Archard, 2000). As far as the first approach goes, this is difficult to apply when what is at issue is itself whether the child should be given treatment to enable it to survive. It may well be that there is no prospect of a severely ill child reaching adulthood in any event. Lowy has suggested that trying to justify decision-making in terms of future interests fails adequately to take account of this possibility. She advocates that in all cases children's interests in being children and in the satisfaction of interests relevant at that point in time are important. For a terminally ill child, short-term interests may indeed be the only criteria that can be applied (Lowy, 1992). There are further logical difficulties. Even if a child could be treated to enable him or her to become an adult, in many cases of the kind we have discussed the child might not attain a level of competence to be able to make a quality of life choice and this decision would still fall to be decided by others. In any event, for a child that hypothetically could achieve competence, there is the problem of retrospective approval. He or she would only be in a position to give approval because the choice was made to give the treatment and it is by no means certain that such approval would be given. Trying to decide what it is thought that the adult that the child might become would choose seems doomed to failure.

The second approach also has potential problems in asking what an adult would choose in that situation, since it may not always be clear what conclusion an adult would reach. Some have suggested that maximising the potential for the child's development is the strategy that adults would be expected to adopt (Eekelaar, 1986, pp 170–1; Freeman, 1983). This presupposes that the child has developmental potential, which again may not be the case for a seriously ill child. In addition, it presumes that survival and development are necessarily beneficial. Not everyone would wish to live in a certain condition or as a result of particular treatments and there may be scope for a considerable difference of opinion. This can be illustrated by the following two passages, the first by Williams who famously wrote:

---

85 *Re J (a minor) (wardship: medical treatment)* [1990] 3 All ER 930, CA, per Lord Donaldson MR at 938.

> If a wicked fairy told me that she was about to transform me into a Down's baby (or a Down's adult) and asked me whether in these circumstances I should prefer to die immediately, I should certainly answer yes.
>
> (Williams, 1981)

Conversely, as the RCPCH say, 'many people with severe handicap describe a life of high quality and say they are happy to be living it'. They continue:

> Disabled children and adults may not view residual disability as negatively as some able-bodied people do, provided adequate support is available. It is important that society does not devalue disabled people or those living with severe impairments.
>
> (Royal College of Paediatrics and Child Health, 2004, para 2.7.1)

One thing that may be said, then, is that there are clearly dangers in applying an able-bodied adult's perspective in this kind of evaluation and this has been recognised by the courts:

> It is not appropriate for an external decision maker to apply his standards of what constitutes a liveable life and exercise the right to impose death if that standard is not met in his estimation. The decision can only be made in the context of the disabled person viewing the worthwhileness or otherwise of his life in its own context as a disabled person – and in that context he would not compare his life with that of a person enjoying normal advantages. He would know nothing of a normal person's life having never experienced it.[86]

Even so, reaching a judgment on the worthwhileness of the child's life with treatment that would command universal support may prove hard to do. This is a situation where reasonable people could come to opposing conclusions.

The third approach would be to consider what an adult version of that child would choose, without the attributes of childhood such as immaturity. This appears to be the closest to the view of the judges in *Re J* (1990), since they seemed to be attempting to decide what the child would choose if he or she had capacity now. However, it is not easy to see how this is an improvement on either of the previous suggestions. It is simply not possible to say what this child would want any more than it would be to say what an adult version of the child, or adults, would.

---

86 *Re Superintendent of Family and Child Service and Dawson* (1983) 145 DLR (3d) 610, per McKenzie J at 620–1, quoted with approval in *Re J (a minor) (wardship: medical treatment)* [1990] 3 All ER 930, CA, per Lord Donaldson MR at 936.

The courts have expressed some doubts about the legitimacy of using a substituted judgment test in this way. For example, in *Re A conjoined twins* (2000), it was said in discussing *Re J* (1990) that 'Since a "substituted judgment" approach has been rejected by Bland, I doubt whether that view is still good law'.[87] Nevertheless, although it may not be viewed as an independent test, it still seems to be accepted as part of the test that the courts do endorse: the best interests of the child, as may be seen in the case of *Wyatt* (2005). Here the court held that in making his decision 'the judge must look at the question from the assumed point of view of the patient'.[88] Reiterating the concerns raised earlier about the extent to which it is possible to make a substituted judgment for a baby or young child, it has been suggested that in taking this line '. . . the nascent personality of the child often acts like a blank page on which the court will write its own version of the child's interests in his life' (Mason and Laurie, 2006, para 16.13).

Despite the practical and, indeed, logical difficulties of the substituted judgement test in this type of situation it does have some merits in that it emphasises the dangers in basing decisions on an able-bodied adult perspective of benefit. Nevertheless, a more realistic stance may be to apply an objectivist approach; that is to make a welfare decision that does not make any attempt to decide what it is that a child in this situation would want, since this is unknown and unknowable. Of course, this is what the best interests test claims to do and to the extent that it tries to determine the benefits and possible burdens to the child of providing or withholding treatment, this is in line with my own approach. However, I would suggest that where there is no evidence about the child's own preferences, as will usually be the case, trying to subsume a substituted judgment within a welfare assessment is unhelpful. Accordingly I would not advocate importing a substituted judgement into a harm and reasonableness test.

In evaluating the reasonableness of the parents' decision, it is of course the standard of significant risk of serious harm that I believe should be applied. This will require medical evidence on what the practical effects of providing or withholding treatment are thought to be and this will be an important matter for the courts to consider. However, in many cases, the accuracy of this information may be rather less compelling than the courts currently allow for. It has already been suggested that although the courts may feel more comfortable relying on evidence that appears to be objective and to have scientific credibility, there may be doubts about whether it is necessarily either (Maclean, 2001; Herring, 2005, p 162). In many cases, such as the ones that

---

87 *Re A (children)(conjoined twins: surgical separation)* [2000] 4 All ER 961, CA, per Ward LJ at 999.
88 *Wyatt v Portsmouth Hospital NHS and Charlotte Wyatt* [2005] EWCA Civ 1181, CA at para 87.

have been discussed, it may be difficult to make accurate judgments on prognosis. Although, as has been said before, reviewing judgments with hindsight must be undertaken with caution, it is at least worth noting in this context the continued survival of Charlotte Wyatt, long after medical opinion had expected her to succumb to her conditions, and the orders made by the court were subsequently lifted.[89] A greater willingness by the courts to subject medical evidence to scrutiny might be thought appropriate.

However, even with the strongest possible medical evidence, the question remains as what weight should be given to it in the assessment of what course of action should be taken. To some, the usual preference given to medical opinion represents no more than a recognition that parents will be less knowledgeable about the effects of the condition of the child for his or her quality of life than practitioners. This may be especially so in the case of neonates, where most parents will have little experience of what the prognosis for the child will really mean. So it has been said that:

> in the vast majority of cases parents have no yardstick by which to judge the child's quality of life . . . It is only the neonatologist who can base his or her prognosis on experience, and only the neonatologists know their limitations.
>
> (Mason, 1999, p 282)

To others, it provides yet another example of the courts being too ready to agree with professional opinion. It is undoubtedly true that most parents are likely to have little or no experience of caring for a premature baby or child born with disabilities, unlike those who do so as professionals. However, it can be forcefully argued that there is nothing particular in the training or experience of healthcare professionals that makes them better judges of the balance of benefits and burdens for a child of being given certain treatments or of the desirability of living life in a particular condition or for a certain length of time. Why the medical profession, or indeed a court, is in a better position to make a judgment on what is best for the child is debatable, especially when it is remembered that benefits and burdens of treatment are not simply matters of predicted medical outcome, but the effects on the child of those outcomes. It must also be said that the experience of caring for a child on a professional basis may be a world away from caring for a child as a member of a family.

Fortin suggests that a difference may be drawn between a newborn and one who has survived for some longer time, maybe against the odds. In the latter situation parents may feel they have established a warm and loving

---

89 *Re Wyatt (a child) (medical treatment: continuation of order)* [2005] EWHC 693, Fam D.

relationship with their child, which is itself a benefit worth setting against even a poor prospect of the child's long-term survival (Fortin, 2005, p 315). This stance may be seen, for example, in the *Wyatt* case where, despite the child's profound disabilities, as the judge hearing the parents' evidence put it:

> They believe that they have some experience of Charlotte reacting to them and, although they recognise that there has been a recent serious deterioration in her condition, they believe that she still does so. They believe it is their duty to maintain life as they do not believe that she is yet ready to die.[90]

Fortin suggests that more weight should be given to parent's views of the worthwhileness of life to be obtained by treatment where the child is older and shows more cognitive ability and that the courts should be more sceptical of medical opinion on such matters. This is a view I share.

I have also agreed with Ross that in making decisions for their children, parents should be entitled to consider the effects of decisions not only upon the individual child but also upon the family (see Ross, 1998). This is not a matter that so far the courts have been willing to take into account as part of the best interests test when considering withholding or withdrawing treatment from a child, although interestingly there have been some statements showing more sympathy for this view, for example in the case of *Simms v Simms* (2003).[91] This will be considered further in the next chapter, but for the moment it is worth noting that Butler-Sloss J, in deciding whether innovative treatment should be provided to an incapacitated minor, held that the effect on the family of failing to provide treatment should be taken into account in finely balanced cases. This does not appear to square with a traditional interpretation of the best interests test, and it is uncertain how far the courts will in future be prepared to take this line. It could of course be argued that if this approach is taken it runs the risk that parents will not place sufficient weight on the welfare of the child and that they may be tempted either to seek treatment that may cause serious harm or suffering to the child, or that they will wish to have treatment withdrawn when the child could receive benefit from it. It may be seen as placing the child at the mercy of parents who put their own concerns above those of their child. However, that is not the position I take. Where parents do not appear to be giving sufficient priority to the child's welfare then their decisions need not and should not be relied upon (Ross, 1998, ch1; Rhodes and Holzman, 2004, p 375). Nevertheless, while acknowledging the importance of medical views on benefits and burdens of treatment, the social context of the child must not be forgotten nor

---

90 *Wyatt v Portsmouth Hospital NHS Trust* [2005] EWCA 1181, CA, at para 28.
91 *Simms v Simms, A v Another* [2003] 1 All ER 669, Fam D.

underestimated. In common with Fortin, I consider that some account must be taken of the social perspective of the child including his or her capacity for meaningful interactions with others. This is a judgement that in most cases, caring parents should be able to make. If they feel that such interaction is possible and is providing some benefit to the child and the family, then it should take compelling evidence of a serious risk of significant harm before their decisions should be overridden. If parents do not believe there is a benefit to the child and family, then again, unless the court has compelling evidence that their decisions are unreasonable, their views should take precedence.

However, even if a harm and reasonableness test were adopted there may remain a fundamental problem with the courts' current approach. This is that the courts have so far refused to dictate to individual doctors how they should treat their patients, seeing this as being a matter for professional judgement. The terms in which orders are granted are usually permissive in nature, in that they authorise doctors to exercise their clinical judgement in providing or withholding certain forms of treatment.[92] Even in the earliest cases it was said that the courts would not make an order to require a health carer to 'adopt a course of treatment which in the bona fide clinical judgement of the practitioner concerned is contraindicated as not being in the best interests of the patient'.[93] This has been upheld in subsequent cases.[94]

Pedain suggests that the reason for this can be found in the approach that the courts have adopted in cases we have considered in previous chapters: that the courts see parental consent as being a 'key' or a 'flak-jacket' to enable medically recommended treatment to proceed.[95] In cases where parents are unwilling to provide it, the court may do so. By contrast, where parents are seeking to have treatment provided against medical recommendations, the stance is taken that doctors are not under a duty to provide treatment. She maintains that it is in fact a means of disguising the courts unwillingness to enter into resource allocation issues:

> Awareness of the finite nature of the National Health Service's resources is part of the framework in which doctors make their choices, internalised to a degree that certain treatments will seem 'useless' to a doctor precisely because they secure a minimal extension of a miserable life at great cost and use of finite resources. The rationing dimension is implicit in the

92 See, for example, *Wyatt v Portsmouth Hospital NHS Trust* [2005] EWCA Civ 1181, CA affg *Wyatt v Portsmouth Hospital NHS Trust* [2004] EWHC 2247 Fam D.

93 *Re J (a minor) (medical treatment)* [1992] 2 FCR 753, CA, per Lord Donaldson at 764.

94 See for example *Wyatt v Portsmouth Hospital NHS Trust* [2005] EWCA Civ 1181, CA; *R v GMC ex parte Burke* [2005] 3 FCR 169, CA.

95 *Re R (a minor) (wardship: medical treatment)* [1991] 4 All ER 177, CA. *Re W (a minor medical treatment)* [1992] 4 All ER 627, CA.

doctor's clinical judgment that this degree of effort is not worth it in terms of the limited benefits that can be secured.

(Pedain, 2005)

However, the idea that courts will never compel doctors to provide treatment has not gone completely unchallenged. Dame Butler-Sloss P suggested when dealing with a competent patient 'If . . . the doctors are for any reason unable to carry out the wishes of the patient, their duty is to find other doctors who will do so.'[96] Munby J endorsed this at first instance in *R v GMC ex p Burke*. Indeed he went further by suggesting that where doctors find themselves unable in professional conscience to provide a particular form of care for an incompetent patient, the court could make an order that a refusal either to provide such treatment or to transfer the patient to the care of those willing to provide it, was unlawful. A hospital could be required to arrange for the treatment to be commenced or continued by other doctors willing to do so to prevent a breach of the patient's Convention rights.[97] In *R v Portsmouth HA ex p. Glass*, Lord Woolf MR had seemed to go even further when he stated that:

The refusal of the courts to dictate appropriate treatment to a medical practitioner . . . is subject to the power which courts always have to take decisions in relation to the child's best interests.[98]

This could be read as allowing courts to order that doctors must provide treatment. If other doctors are willing to provide care, transferring a patient may pose practical problems, but may be considered a way of resolving the impasse. However, more recently, the Court of Appeal in *Burke* was reluctant to see this as a legal requirement or to propose that more need be done than to arrange a second opinion.[99] Ordering an unwilling doctor to perform a treatment himself or herself might pose additional problems by being potentially in breach of the doctor's own human rights, for example, to freedom of conscience. However, some doubt this. Maclean suggests that:

As public agents the Convention provides no protection to the individual values of the treating physicians and thus the only factor that should be considered is whether the medical treatment can achieve the desired medically accepted goal without being unduly distressing to the individual . . . the preservation of life is an acceptable medical goal and

96 *Re B (adult: refusal of medical treatment)* [2002] 2 All ER 449, Fam D.
97 *R v GMC ex parte Burke* [2004] 3 FCR 579, QB D.
98 *R v Portsmouth Hospital NHS Trust ex parte Glass* [1999] 3 FCR 145, CA at 148.
99 *R v GMC ex parte Burke* [2005] 3 FCR 169, CA at para 50.

thus a request for that goal to be the aim of medical treatment should be respected.

(Maclean, 2001)

Even if the courts were able to insist that doctors give treatment, irrespective of the doctors' views on the matter, there is no evidence so far that they would be willing to do so if the question directly arose. Furthermore, this would not address the point made by Pedain that the subtext in such situations involves considerations of resource allocation that the courts prefer not to engage in. If the courts were to maintain their current reluctance to order doctors to provide treatment, then in practice it seems that the only difference my proposal to dispense with the best interests test would make is to potentially enlarge the type of situation where the courts would not authorise treatment to proceed. In cases where the courts decided that the parents' refusal of treatment was reasonable and should be upheld, then no matter the views of the doctors, it would not be lawful for them to provide it. This would be no different to the position where doctors may have deep professional and personal convictions against a competent patient refusing life-sustaining treatment, but to impose treatment would be unlawful. A greater reliance on parental wishes where the decision is to withhold or withdraw treatment is clearly likely to pose less difficulty in terms of the allocation of scarce resources.

Neonaticide

As a final issue, it might be suggested that if a decision has been made that further treatment is not in the interests of the child and that the child should be enabled to die with dignity, this might be better achieved by providing some positive means of accelerating death, rather than by withdrawal or withholding of treatment. We have seen already that this is prohibited by the criminal law, but it can be argued that there may be nothing inherently more dignified about dying as a result of untreated opportunistic infection than due to a lethal dose of sedative. Some commentators have attempted to draft legislation that would permit positive acts to end the lives of newborns (neonaticide) in specific circumstances (Kuhse and Singer, 1985, p 195). There has been little professional or political enthusiasm for introducing such measures and at present they remain largely a matter of academic consideration. However, it should be recognised that there is some evidence that neonaticide is occurring in an unregulated way already. The study into neonatal medicine focusing on the double-effect doctrine, quoted earlier, also found that 4 per cent of surveyed physicians working in UK neonatal intensive care units reported having administered drugs to a newborn baby with the purpose of ending life (Cuttini et al., 2000). Though the numbers in this survey are small, it seems clear that some practitioners are willing to take positive steps to end a severely ill baby's life, despite the fact that this is unlawful, and more might feel it professionally appropriate to do so were the legal position to change. While competent adults are not permitted to consent to positive steps being taken to end their lives, there can be no logical justification for permitting this decision to be made on behalf of those who cannot make a decision on such matters. Only if the law were to be reformed to allow competent people to seek assistance in dying would it be necessary to consider in more detail whether such conduct could extend to incompetent patients, including children, but in principle such an argument could legitimately be made. Nonetheless, with the acceptance of the court in *Re A* (2000) that surgical separation that would kill one conjoined twin to save the life of another resting to a large extent on considerations of the poor quality of the sick child's life, it might be argued that the case for maintaining a distinction between acts and omissions in this area may be wearing thinner.[100]

Conclusion

Although doctors have no legal dispensation to kill a child in their care and they are normally under a duty to provide treatment, where it is believed that treatment will not benefit the patient or its burdens will outweigh any benefits, they need not provide it. The courts are anxious to stress that that human life is valuable and ought to be protected, but there is no commitment here to upholding an absolute sanctity of life doctrine, which would require all medical means possible to be used to save or prolong life. Instead, an evaluation of the quality of life of the child may be undertaken. While acknowledging the difficulties inherent in doing so, I consider that this is justifiable. However, it seems to me that the courts place too much emphasis on medical evidence when decisions about withholding or withdrawing care are not solely medical matters. In some situations this has led them to fail to set proper boundaries for medical practice and in others, they claim the right to override the wishes of reasonable parents. I have recommended a reassessment of the courts' proper function to meet these criticisms. The uncertainties surrounding prognosis and proper care for premature infants suggest that this is a key area for further research. In spite of this, the legal position on medical research involving children is far from clear and it is to this situation I will now turn.

---

100 *Re A (children) (conjoined twins: surgical separation)* [2000] 4 All ER 961, CA.

Chapter 5

Medical research and innovative treatment

Properly conducted research is of course essential to modern medicine. Today there are higher expectations than ever that safe and effective treatments will be available for children's illnesses. Improving the quality of care depends upon alterations to existing treatments and the search for new ones. It is also important to remember that treating children is not simply a question of adjusting the dosage of medicines. As the Medical Research Council point out, '[c]hildren are not small adults', so that the process of diseases and their reaction to treatment can often only be understood in the context of the child's growth and development. In addition, some conditions are specific to children, so research can only be undertaken with them (Medical Research Council, 2004, para 1.3). These factors are also noted in the European Directive on Clinical Trials 2001:

> Children represent a vulnerable population with developmental, physiological and psychological differences from adults, which make age and developmental related research important for their benefit. Medicinal products, including vaccines, for children need to be tested scientifically before widespread use. This can only be achieved by ensuring that medicinal products which are likely to be of significant clinical value for children are fully studied.[1]

Similar concerns would apply to other types of medical interventions, such as the use of medical devices or innovative techniques in surgery, although most attention is focused on pharmaceuticals (Miller and Kenny, 2002). Failing to conduct research with children to meet their specific needs would clearly represent a huge obstacle to improving their care. Indeed, it could cause significant harm if, for example, untested drugs are prescribed for them that prove to be inappropriate or manufacturers are unwilling to undertake development of drugs for children because they cannot be properly tested before

---

1 EU Directive 2001/20/EC, 4 April 2001, Preamble, para 3.

release. Recent research has indicated that over 50 per cent of all medicines given to children in Europe (and some 90 per cent of those given to the newly born) have never been tested or authorised for use on them (European Commission, 2004). The strong will to change this situation has led to the implementation of new regulations in Europe, which require all drugs to be tested on, and developed for, children, as part of a paediatric investigation plan, unless the manufacturer has been granted a product-specific waiver or deferral.[2] Paediatric investigation plans should also deal with subsets of the child population: the pre-term and term neonate from 0 to 27 days, the infant from 1 month to 23 months, the child from 2 years to 11 years and the adolescent from 12 up to 18 years (European Commission, 2007, para 1.1).[3] As an incentive, additional patent protection will be provided to manufacturers, giving extensions to market exclusivity on products where such studies have been performed. Indeed, some have expressed concern that the way that the new regulations have been framed owes rather too much to the influence of commercial organisations (Liddell *et al.*, 2006). The imperative to conduct clinical trials with children has never been stronger and the need to consider the legal framework in which they will operate is of commensurate practical importance.

Medical research involving children appears to be a fundamental requirement for further advances in improving children's health and, accordingly, it might be argued to be in their best interests. However, here lies another problem when considering the best interests test. It is intrinsic to medical research that the outcome is uncertain (Giesen, 1995, p 35). Since that is the case, how can it be said that involving a particular child in medical research is in his or her best interests when it is possible that existing treatments may be of more benefit or the research might create additional risk? It may well benefit future child patients, but that is not the way that the concept of a child's best interests is traditionally construed by the courts. They have generally insisted that this requires them to select what they see as the single best option for the child from the available options.[4] While this is difficult to establish in many situations, such difficulties are enhanced here and this test may be particularly hard to meet where the research has no direct therapeutic intent for the child. Further problems arise in relation to consent to participate in research. First, if there are doubts over research being in the child's best interests, is this something that parents can consent to on behalf of their children? In fact it is the concept of risk of harm, rather than best interests

---

2   EC Regulation No 1901/2006 of the European Parliament and of the Council on medicinal products for paediatric use.

3   These subsets are derived from the European Medicines Agency (2001) *ICH Topic E 11 Clinical Investigation of Medicinal Products in the Paediatric Population* CPMP/ICH/2711/99, para 2.5.

4   *Re E (a minor) (wardship: medical treatment)* [1992] 2 FCR 219, Fam D.

that appears to be widely used in medical practice. Its extension to judicial intervention, as I advocate, seems justifiable and to provide a more coherent and consistent response. Second, there is the position where children wish to make a decision about participation themselves. In line with my proposals, I suggest that they should be at liberty to do so if they have sufficient competence. It is therefore a matter of concern that recent legal developments seem to be according less, rather than more, autonomy to children in this area. Before turning to these specific issues, a few broad points about the terminology and key concepts used must be made.

Medical research and innovative treatment – definitions

Broadly speaking, to be regarded as properly conducted medical *research*:

> . . . an intervention must form part of a programme of enquiry based on a scientifically plausible hypothesis, must follow a scientifically valid methodology and be intended to produce data of a generalisable nature.
> (Kennedy and Grubb, 2004, para 13.01)

It is thus to be distinguished from *experimentation* which has been explained as involving:

> . . . a more speculative, ad hoc, approach to an individual subject. The distinction is significant in that an experiment may be modified to take into account the individual's response; a research programme is more likely to tie the researcher to a particular course of action until such time as its general ineffectiveness is satisfactorily demonstrated.
> (Mason and Laurie, 2006, para 18.5)

Research also differs from *innovative treatment*, where the intention is to provide care rather than forming part of a scientific enquiry, although it may lead on to this. It has been said that it is:

> . . . the performance of new or non-standard intervention as all or part of a therapeutic activity and not as part of a formal research project . . . innovative therapy may therefore be quite haphazard, starting just when a doctor has a bright idea that he wants to try out . . . [However], [i]f the bright idea seems to be any good, then innovative therapy can become research as soon as the bright idea is examined in a systematic manner.
> (Nicholson, 1986, p 25)

This chapter will concentrate on innovative treatment and formally conducted research projects rather than experimentation, although many of the same principles would be equally applicable to it. Two further widely used classifi-cations of research are those of *therapeutic* and *non-therapeutic research*. Generally speaking, research that may provide some benefit to the group of patients involved is often described as being 'therapeutic'. By contrast, research intended to provide scientific information with no intention of immediate benefit to the subject will be deemed 'non-therapeutic'. 'Thera-peutic research' may be thought of as differing from standard treatment in an important respect, since the primary goal is not simply the treatment of an individual patient, though improvement in their condition may be hoped for, but the testing of a theory about the treatment and the obtaining of data for future patients' care.

Some doubts have been expressed about the use of these terms, however. Given that the purpose of undertaking so-called therapeutic research in patients is to test a hypothesis, there must be the possibility that the hypoth-esis is wrong, otherwise performing the research would be 'scientifically pointless, and hence unethical' (Jackson, 2006, p 477). There is obviously the prospect that the outcome will not prove beneficial for the patient. While this may be true, even for routine treatment for an individual patient, defining research at the outset as being therapeutic when its benefits are unproven may be somewhat misleading (Alderson, 1999). In addition, it has been said that:

> ... the maintenance of the distinction between therapeutic and non-therapeutic research promotes the idea that research designed to make people better is intrinsically less problematic than research designed to improve basic knowledge. In reality, it may often be the case, though obviously open to argument, that fundamental scientific and medical research is of more value in the long term than therapeutic research; and that children are sometimes less protected in therapeutic research than in non-therapeutic research.
>
> (Nicholson, 1986, pp 30–1)

The reason for there potentially being less protection for children participat-ing in therapeutic research is that there is hoped to be some direct benefit to him or her. While, as I will argue, this may still not be easy to reconcile with the notion of best interests, it is more straightforward to do so than where they are subjected to procedures with no expectation of medical benefit to them personally. This may lead to a temptation to minimise risks and to deem a research protocol to be therapeutic in order to make it easier to recruit subjects. To try to avoid this, it has been argued that the claim that research is therapeutic must meet a high standard, so that benefit must be 'likely', 'prob-able' or 'reasonably foreseeable', and that it is the effect on the research subject, rather than the objective of the research that must be considered in this light (Verdun-Jones and Weisstub, 1998). However, it is very likely to be the case that even research which meets this description will include non-therapeutic interventions, for example, blood sampling or other medically unnecessary procedures. Additional problems arise where placebos are used in randomised double-blind trials. This type of trial has been described as the gold standard in medical research (International Conference on Harmonisation, 2000; Miller and Brody, 2002). Here, patients are randomly allocated to receive either the new treatment or a placebo, with neither the patients nor the investigators knowing who has been given which until the end of the trial. The purpose of this is to eliminate any psychological bias caused by the placebo response, where subjects can experience changes in their symptoms, despite being given substances that have no known active properties to achieve such an effect. Although one arm of the trial will be receiving the active drug, and hence could be regarded as taking part in therapeutic research, the other will not. Apart from the possible placebo effect, children in the placebo arm are taking part in non-therapeutic research. As a result, the trial overall may be difficult to categorise.

The British Medical Association have recommended dropping the distinction between therapeutic and non-therapeutic research 'in favour of assessing all research according to the same criteria of risks and benefits' (British Medical Association, 2001, ch 9). This step has already been taken by the World Medical Association (WMA) in the sixth revision of their influential guidelines on medical research – the Declaration of Helsinki – following substantial debate on the subject. The terms have been here replaced by advocating additional safeguards where medical research is combined with medical care.[5] The courts have also shown little interest in drawing a distinction between therapeutic and non-therapeutic procedures or treatments.[6] Nevertheless, the terminology remains widely used. An alternative is to divide medical procedures into (1) routine treatment; (2) innovative treatment; (3) research with therapeutic components; and (4) non-therapeutic research. This distinction recognises that in the first two categories, the intent of doctors is to provide medical benefit to the patient, whereas in the second there is the additional or the sole intent to provide generalisable knowledge for the benefit of future patients or for society in general. It also recognises that even where research may be hoped to have some benefit to the individual patient, additional procedures may be performed for their scientific value alone (see, for example, Peart, 2000, p 429; Weijer, 2000; Weijer and Miller, 2004). The reason for making such a distinction has been explained thus:

5   World Medical Association (1964) Declaration of Helsinki: Ethical Principles for Medical Research involving Human Subjects, Helsinki: WMA. (6th version adopted at the 52nd WMA General Assembly, Edinburgh, Scotland, October 2000). Part C Additional Principles for Medical Research Combined with Medical Care.

6   See, for example, *F v West Berkshire Health Authority and Another* [1989] All ER 545. See, also, *Re B (a minor) (wardship: sterilisation)* [1987] 2 All ER 206, HL; *Re SG* [1991] FCR 329, Fam D and *Re E (a minor)* [1991] FCR 771, Fam D.

... it enables the activities a researcher carries out with therapeutic warrant (i.e. with a reasonable belief that his actions may benefit the individual patient) to be analysed separately from the things the researcher does that are solely intended to serve the public.

(Liddell *et al.*, 2006)

This chapter adopts Weijer's terminology and refers to innovative treatment, research with therapeutic components and non-therapeutic research.

A few final points follow on from what has been said about these categories. Where doctors undertake research with therapeutic components there may be the potential for a conflict of interest, since research has additional goals in mind than providing patient care. A separation of the role of investigator and personal physician is often expected. Where both roles are combined, the doctor's primary duty remains the care of his or her patient.[7] A further issue is that of clinical equipoise. There are a number of different meanings attached to this term:

At its simplest, it can be described as a state of honest doubt as to which of two clinical interventions is more beneficial for the patient. In more formal terms, it concerns the ethics of withholding particular treatment from a patient to gather statistically reliable information.

(Liddell *et al.*, 2006)

In its broadest sense, it may therefore be applicable to innovative treatment, but its use most commonly arises in connection with randomised controlled trials. In essence, the idea behind clinical equipoise in this situation is to seek to ensure that patients are not deprived of treatment that it is believed could be beneficial to them. Although some use the expression to denote the idea that the investigator should be uncertain about the best form of treatment, a better approach may be that described by Freedman, who suggests that there should be honest, professional disagreement in the community of expert practitioners as to the preferred treatment (Freedman, 1987). There remains controversy over how clinical equipoise is to be judged and its consequences, for example, when the trial should be stopped and participants all given what appears to be producing the best outcomes. It also raises the question whether placebos can be used as a control where there is an existing treatment that could be given. According to the WMA, placebos should not ordinarily be used where there are proven therapies. However, it says that this may be ethically acceptable if there are compelling and scientifically sound reasons for its use to determine the efficacy or safety of a medical

---

7   Declaration of Helsinki, Part C Additional Principles for Medical Research Combined with Medical Care.

intervention, or if it relates to a minor condition and the patients who receive a placebo will not be subject to any additional risk of serious or irreversible harm.[8]

The importance of using a components approach to medical research in this context is that in respect of therapeutic elements, clinical equipoise ensures 'a rough parity in terms of benefit, harm and uncertainty between the procedures that patients would receive as a part of clinical practice and therapeutic procedures in a clinical trial' (Weijer, 2004, p 86). The risks arising as part of the non-therapeutic components can and must be judged separately. Imposing these kinds of risks will need to be justified in terms of the scientific benefit to be obtained and the same will be the case for research where there are no therapeutic elements at all. The extent to which they are warranted will in part be determined before parents and children can consent to them, by the need for research to comply with professional standards and during the course of seeking ethical approval. As far as this is concerned, usually the courts would only be involved after the event, where it is alleged that the design or conduct of the research was negligent. However, there are circumstances where they may be asked to consider this in advance, as part of an assessment whether parents' or children's consent to participation should be overridden in the name of the best interests of the child. Until recently, however, there has been little legal authority in this area, so an outline of the way in which professional regulation has developed provides the necessary background for further discussion (for discussion on research generally, see Jackson, 2006, ch 8; Mason and Laurie, 2006, chs 18 and 19).

The development of guidance and regulation of medical research with children

Concern about involving children is not evident in early examples of medical research. It has been said that this history of 'experimentation on humans is as old as that of medicine itself', although a more scientific approach to medical research in the Western world can perhaps be traced back only to the Renaissance (Brieger, 1978, p 684). However, probably the most widely known historical medical experiment on a child was that performed by Edward Jenner in 1796. Although his accreditation as the discoverer of the relationship between cowpox and small pox is disputed, it was in that year that he sought to test his hypothesis that contracting cowpox would lead to immunity from smallpox. He took pus from the cowpox blisters of a milk-maid and injected them into the arm of a 14-year-old boy, James Phipps. The boy suffered a fever and some minor signs of illness, but recovered well. Jenner then injected the boy with a small quantity of smallpox, but the boy

8   Ibid.

developed no symptoms of the disease. This injection of variolus material was repeated and again failed to lead to illness. The report of this and other similar experiments performed by Jenner eventually led to the development of a programme of vaccination against smallpox (Jenner 1798–1800). While to a modern reader, the deliberate injection of smallpox may seem extraordinarily dangerous, it must be remembered that at the time an attempt to introduce smallpox in a controlled manner, known as variolation, was considered the best way to try to induce immunity to a more serious infection.

The use of a child as a test subject was not questioned then, nor were the issues of consent or the best interests of the child raised. Until comparatively recently, the law had little to say about medical treatment in general, let alone medical research. The development of the courts' intervention in parental decision-making, through the concept of the best interests of the child, has also been developed in more modern times. Even with the establishment of medicine as a distinct profession in the nineteenth century, since the law was largely silent on the matter, medical research operated solely under the discretion of practitioners. It was assumed they would act in accordance with good medical practice and professional ethics and, where children were concerned, with the parents' permission. The trust in practitioners to regulate their own practice was shaken by the revelations of the atrocities committed by doctors under the Nazi Regime in the Second World War (for discussion, see McNeill, 1993). For the first time an attempt was made to set out internationally accepted standards for medical research, in the Nuremberg Code (1949).[9] This Code laid down ethical principles to govern the conduct of research in humans, chief among them being the overriding requirement for the consent of the research subject. 'Research was seen as a potential harm from which vulnerable people should be protected' (Medical Research Council, 2004, para 3.1). Given the context in which they were developed, this is perhaps unsurprising. However, the effect of this was to lead to the Code forbidding research upon incompetents, such as young children, since, according to it, the 'voluntary consent of the human subject is absolutely essential'.

The Nuremburg Code (1949) had no legal effect and there are doubts as to the extent this prohibition was ever observed in practice. In one of the first statements on the issue reported in the UK, the Medical Research Council (MRC) distinguished between therapeutic and non-therapeutic research. Basing their guidance on legal opinion given to them at the time, they advised that:

---

9   The Nuremburg Code (1949) contained in 'Trials of War Criminals before the Nuremburg Military Tribunals under Control Council Law No.10' 2:181–2. Washington, DC: US Government Printing Office.

... in the strict view of the law parents and guardians of minors cannot give consent on their behalf to any procedures which are of no particular benefit to them and which may carry some risk of harm.

(Medical Research Council, 1964)

This was widely interpreted as 'placing a complete embargo on non-therapeutic research on children' (Nicholson, 1986, p 6). However, it allowed the possibility of research with therapeutic components, even where children could not consent. Provided that the research was intended to be of direct benefit to the child, parents were regarded as being permitted to consent on the child's behalf.

Increasingly, research was becoming seen as not necessarily a harm from which people should be protected, but as offering potential benefits from which they should not be excluded (British Medical Association, 2001, pp 186–7). At the same time as the MRC guidelines were produced, the stance taken by the WMA was rather different and they suggested that research with children could take place where:

The research is necessary to promote the health of the population represented and this research cannot instead be performed on legally competent persons.[10]

The Declaration of Helsinki remains one of the central statements on the ethical conduct of medical research, although it is not the only one. Other influential statements in the international sphere have been produced by, for example, the Council for International Organizations of Medical Sciences (CIOMS)[11]. In addition to these, a number of professional and governmental organisations in the United Kingdom have produced guidelines on medical research in general and with children in particular. Current national guidance includes the following: Royal College of Paediatric and Child Health, 2000; General Medical Council, 2002; Medical Research Council, 2004; and Department of Health, 2005. These guidelines do not have the force of law and there is little recourse for aggrieved parents or children where there has been a failure to observe them, other than through any sanctions operated by professional bodies or, more dubiously, as will be seen below, where there has been an allegation of negligence and it is sought to demonstrate a failure to comply with professional standards of practice. International guidance on medical research has now also taken on a legal dimension in Europe, with

10 World Medical Association (1964) *Declaration of Helsinki: Ethical Principles for Medical Research involving Human Subjects*, Helsinki: WMA.
11 Council for International Organizations of Medical Sciences (2002) *International Ethical Guidelines for Biomedical Research Involving Human Subjects*, 3rd Revision, Geneva: CIOMS.

the promulgation of the European Convention on Human Rights and Bio-medicine (ECB) and its additional Protocol on Biomedical Research.[12] It is important to remember that the UK has not ratified this Convention, but these provisions provide a further baseline for standards of governance of medical research.

In the absence of clear legal authority in the UK on the approach that should be taken to medical research, international and national professional guidance have assumed considerable importance. Although the recommenda-tions made are not identical, broadly speaking a number of criteria are stated as being necessary for the proper conduct of medical research. These include: that the research must follow good scientific practice, both in terms of prior research before moving on to human trials and in the design and performance of the protocol; that risks must be evaluated and weighed against the pre-dicted benefits; that ideally those involved should be competent and give informed consent; that there should be no disproportionate incentives to people to take part and they should be free to withdraw from a trial at any time without prejudice and that the interests of the research subject are paramount. Additional considerations are called into play where research with incompetent subjects, including children, is concerned. In respect of children, again broadly, it is recommended that such research only take place if it is intended to benefit children and cannot be conducted on adults; there is parental consent and lack of dissent from the child and, in the case of non-therapeutic research, that there is no or minimal risk involved. Safeguards for all participants in research are expected to be provided by having the prior approval of an ethics committee for the project.

In the UK, ethics committees for medical research conducted within the NHS were initially set up by hospitals on an ad hoc basis, largely as a result of recommendations by the Ministry of Health in 1968. There was no legal requirement to do so and there was little practical guidance as to the com-position and function of these committees. However, guidelines issued by the Department of Health (DoH) in 1991 required every health district to establish a local research ethics committee (LREC) and further required all NHS bodies to submit any research proposal falling within their sphere of responsibility to the appropriate LREC for its approval (Department of Health, 1991; in Scotland, the equivalent document was Scottish Office Management Executive, 1992). LRECs were joined by Multi-centre Research Ethics Committees in 1997, where a research project was being undertaken on several sites. Some guidance was issued on the composition of these bodies, which has been revised over the years, so that it now covers a wide range of

---

12 ECB Arts 15–18 and the Additional Protocol to the Convention on Human Rights and Biomedicine, concerning Biomedical Research, 25 January 2005 (not in force at the time of writing).

issues relating to the proper conduct and monitoring of research and the principles to be considered to safeguard participants and maintain the confidence of the wider public.[13] A Central Office for Research Ethics Committees to coordinate research applications and provide guidance and training for ethics committees was set up in 2000. In 2007, it was renamed the National Research Ethics Service and operates as part of the National Patient Safety Agency, but its guidance covers both England and Wales and Scotland (COREC, 2007). The work of ethics committees has been subject to much criticism over the years, including: concerns over their composition; the training of members; the lack of clarity and consistency in their decision-making; the potential conflict between their role to promote research while at the same time safeguarding participants; and the lack of monitoring of research beyond approving applications (see, for example, McHale, 1993). Additional concerns have centred over the lack of remedies for those who claim that research has been inadequately reviewed by ethics committees (Brazier, 1990).

However, recent changes, introduced by the European Directive on Clinical Trials 2001, make the approval of an ethics committee a legal requirement for clinical research in the UK, wherever it is conducted.[14] The Directive was implemented by The Medicines for Human Use (Clinical Trials) Regulations 2004 (CTR 2004), which came into force on 1 May 2004. A new body, known as the United Kingdom Ethics Committee Authority (UKECA), was also established. UKECA has the responsibility to recognise ethics committees for clinical trials throughout the UK. It must be satisfied that the arrangements for the committee enable it to perform the functions of an ethics committee adequately, and to comply with the Regulations.[15] It is now a criminal offence to undertake clinical trials without the requisite approval.[16] The Directive and Regulations are solely aimed at trials involving medicines but, in respect of the NHS, the intention of the DoH is to apply the same structures and procedures to all types of medical research, although there is no legal requirement to do so (for further discussion, see Kerrison and Pollock, 2005; Liddell et al., 2006). There are specific requirements laid down for clinical trials that will be considered later. For the moment, having set out the broad framework of professional guidance and regulation, the approach of the law to other types of medical research and innovative treatment will now be considered.

---

13 Department of Health (2005). There is separate documentation for Scotland: Scottish Executive Health Department (2006).
14 European Directive 2001/20/EC 4 April 2001.
15 The Medicines for Human Use (Clinical Trials) Regulations 2004, SI 2004/1031 (CTR 2004) reg. 7.
16 CTR 2004, reg. 49.

The legal standard of care in medical research and innovative treatment

The law's position on medical research in the UK remained uncharted waters until relatively recently and even now, some areas continue to be untested. Common-law principles have been put forward to support involving children in medical research in professional guidelines, but firm conclusions on their application in the absence of direct legal authority have been difficult to draw. In the absence of case law and statute, guidance could be sought only by inference from general legal principles. The most important of these concern consent and information disclosure. However, something must first be said about the broader issue of standards of care in medical research. To date, no case has been brought in the UK dealing with injuries sustained by taking part in medical research. This may be set to change following the serious injuries and deaths occurring in the first clinical trial of a product known as TGN412 in humans, in March 2006 (Medicines and Healthcare Products Regulatory Agency, 2006). However, at present, the likely approach of the courts remains speculative. An early Scottish case, which may shed some light on the matter, is *Hunter v Hanley* (1955).[17] While it concerned negligent treatment, it shows the approach of the law to departure from standard practice and, accordingly, it is regarded as being of some relevance to the standard of care in medical research.

In this case a doctor used a different gauge needle than was usually used to perform a procedure. The needle broke causing the patient injury. It was held by Lord President Clyde that:

> To establish liability by a doctor where departure from normal practice is alleged, three facts require to be established. First of all it must be proved that there is a usual and normal practice; secondly it must be proved that the defender has not adopted that practice; and thirdly (and this is of crucial importance) it must be established that the course the doctor adopted is one which no professional man of ordinary skill would have taken if he had been acting with ordinary care.[18]

The procedure undertaken could not be described as research, experimentation, or even innovative treatment, in the senses described earlier. Nevertheless, the approach taken indicates that what is regarded as legally acceptable practice primarily depends on the prevailing custom in the profession. This is the standard approach to professional negligence, the leading English case on

---

17 *Hunter v Hanley* 1955 SC 200, CS.
18 Ibid at 206.

medical negligence being that of *Bolam v Friern Hospital Management Committee* (1957).[19]

The perception has been that the judiciary have been too deferential to the medical profession, by contrast to other professions, in allowing them to effectively set their own standards of care, rather than being willing to exercise a judgment on the reasonableness of such standards. Some optimism has been expressed that this approach is changing and that as a result of the case of *Bolitho v Hackney Health Authority* (1997)[20] the judiciary may be more willing to scrutinise expert evidence and form their own conclusions on its acceptability (Teff, 1998; Brazier and Miola, 2000). In *Bolitho* it was said that:

> ... the court has to be satisfied that the exponents of the body of opinion relied on can demonstrate that such opinion has a logical basis. In particular, in cases involving, as they so often do, the weighing of risks against benefits, the judge before accepting a body of opinion as being responsible, reasonable or respectable, will need to be satisfied that, in forming their views, the experts have directed their minds to the question of comparative risks and benefits and have reached a defensible conclusion on the matter.[21]

However, it was equally said that 'in the vast majority of cases the fact that distinguished experts in the field are of a particular opinion will demonstrate the reasonableness of that opinion'. It would only be in 'a rare case, [where] it can be demonstrated that the professional opinion is not capable of withstanding logical analysis, the judge is entitled to hold that the body of opinion is not reasonable or responsible'.[22] Optimism that this case represents a sea change in the way in which courts will approach cases in the future has therefore not been universally shared (Maclean, 2002).

In the case of research, this reluctance to form an independent judgement on medical practice may be compounded by several things. First, it appears from *obiter* statements in a number of cases that the judiciary are concerned not to stifle innovation. Indeed in *Hunter v Hanley* (1955) itself, it was stated that:

> a deviation from standard medical practice is not necessarily evidence of negligence. Indeed it would be disastrous if this were so, for all inducement to progess in medical science would then be destroyed.[23]

19 *Bolam v Friern Hospital Management Committee* [1957] 2 All ER 118, QB D.
20 *Bolitho v Hackney Health Authority* [1997] 4 All ER 771, HL.
21 Ibid per Browne-Wilkinson, LJ at 778.
22 Ibid.
23 *Hunter v Hanley* 1955 SC 200, CS, per Lord President Clyde at 206.

The application of the *Bolam* test to innovative treatment was considered in the case of *Simms v Simms and Another, A v A (A Child) and Another* (2002).[24] It involved a rather different situation from those cited, since it concerned an application to proceed with treatment rather than an allegation that treatment had been negligently performed. It concerned two separate patients, an 18-year-old man (JS) and a 16-year-old girl (JA), both of whom were suffering from probable variant Creutzfeldt-Jakob disease (vCJD). vCJD is a rare disorder in which abnormal prion proteins become deposited in the brain, causing neurological damage. Both patients were conscious but bed-ridden, unable to care for themselves or communicate anything other than their emotional state. There was no recognised effective treatment for the condition. However, research had been carried out abroad using a drug, Pen-tosan Polysulphate (PPS), which inhibited the formation of abnormal protein prion in mice. Although PPS is used to treat thrombosis and other conditions, its effectiveness as a possible treatment for vCJD had not been tested on humans. Nevertheless, having heard about this research, both patients' parents wished them to receive it. They sought declarations that each patient lacked capacity to consent to treatment and that it was lawful as being in their best interests for them to receive the proposed treatment.

These declarations were granted in each case. It will be remembered that where incompetent patients are concerned, it has been said that a two-stage test operates. First, the treatment proposed must meet the *Bolam* test, so that it is in accordance with responsible medical practice. Second, it must still be considered as a separate issue whether treatment is in the patient's best inter-ests.[25] The difficulty with attempting to apply *Bolam* to this procedure was put thus:

> To the question: 'Is there a responsible body of medical opinion which would support the PPS treatment within the United Kingdom?' the answer in one sense is unclear. This is untried treatment and there is so far no validation of the experimental work done in Japan.[26]

However, despite the lack of scientific preparatory work, similar sentiments were expressed to those in *Hunter v Hanley* (1955) and it was concluded that:

> The *Bolam* test ought not to be allowed to inhibit medical progress since it is clear that if one waited for that test to be complied with to its fullest no innovative work in medicine would ever be attempted.[27]

---

24 *Simms v Simms, A v Another* [2003] 1 All ER 669, Fam D.
25 *Re SL (adult patient) (medical treatment)* [2000] 2 FCR 452, sub nom *Re S (adult patient: sterilisation)*, CA, at 464, per Dame Butler-Sloss P.
26 *Simms v Simms, A v Another* [2003] 1 All ER 669, Fam D, at para 48.
27 Ibid.

Harrington suggests that 'what is applied in *Simms*, therefore, is a fairly weak version of the *Bolam* test: one that permits treatment in the absence of negative opinion, rather than on foot of positive endorsements' (sic) (Harrington, 2003). In this situation, there was no evidence to conclude that it would be successful and could be recommended on that basis. However, equally there was no standard practice to depart from, as no other treatment was available as an alternative. In these circumstances the court's approach may be justified. It will still require a careful consideration of the risks and benefits, which will be discussed further, below. In other circumstances, where there are existing treatments and innovative treatment is proposed, then the tests laid out in *Hunter v Hanley* (1955) and *Bolam* (1957) would be expected to apply.

Simms (2002) concerned innovative treatment rather than inclusion in a medical research project. However, research may be regarded as having standard practices too and, accordingly, it has been said that:

> The response of the law is that any innovation that departs from standard practice(s) will be regarded as research if it can be shown that the ordinary principles defining research apply. In such a case, the researcher will be expected to have observed the regulatory procedures.
> (Kennedy and Grubb, 2004, para 13.02)

While there is no case law to support this assertion, it seems probable that failing to observe professionally accepted standards for research would be taken into account by the courts in determining negligence and that departure from such standards would be unlikely to be endorsed without clear and convincing justification.

The second problem, however, is that the testing of new medicinal products and techniques may be deemed to be inherently risky. As Giesen notes '[B]y definition experimental procedures are accompanied by a greater level of risk than procedures which have already established themselves' (Giesen, 1995, p 35). Furthermore, unless and until testing has been undertaken with humans in a properly conducted trial, side-effects may be difficult to predict (McLean, 1992, pp 183–5). It appears that the extent to which it is acceptable to conduct a trial will largely rest on a risk/benefit analysis. While this brings into play questions of consent, which will be discussed subsequently, in what circumstances it would be negligent to expose a patient to the known and unknown risks of a trial remains an issue (Guest, 1997). For cases where a legal dispute arises, here again, the role of the judiciary will be crucial in considering whether professional opinion on the safety of the study and its value should be determinative.

Third, there is an argument that research subjects should be entitled to expect a higher standard of care than those who are receiving normal treatment. This is based on the idea that research is being undertaken not primarily, or at least not solely, to benefit the patient, but to benefit future patients. As such, it is contended that to encourage people to participate and to recognise their altruism, they should be given additional protection (Giesen, 1995). Distinguishing the circumstances in which treatment is given to require a higher standard of care has not so far commended itself to the courts. This has been most apparent in relation to alleged negligence in information disclosure for non-therapeutic procedures, which will be discussed further below. It seems unlikely therefore that the courts would be prepared to require a higher standard of care in the conduct of research than for routine treatment. The level at which these standards are set need not of course be minimal. Nevertheless, while it is possible that the courts could take it upon themselves to adopt a policy of requiring higher standards of care to be provided in a research situation than for routine treatment, for the reasons discussed above, this may be an unrealistic expectation. Though evidence is sparse, the general conclusion is that the professional negligence standard applies to the conduct of research, which is largely controlled by professional practice. This, therefore, sets the parameters in which the conduct of medical research with children will be judged.

Consent, best interests and the harm and reasonableness principle in medical research and innovative treatment

The incompetent child–innovative treatment and research with therapeutic components

The general principles governing consent to treatment of children have been covered in Chapter 2. The application of these principles to medical research is, however, by no means certain. As we have seen from the outset, when considering the requirements for ethically acceptable medical research, consent from the individual subjects has been regarded as a fundamental requirement if they are competent. Such has been the perceived importance of consent that it has even been suggested that a lack of capacity should lead to exclusion from research (The Nuremburg Code, 1949). If this were accepted, then parents should have no power to consent on behalf of their incompetent children to anything other than medical treatment. There is no case law that explicitly considers parental discretion to include their children in medical trials. However, as a general principle, we are familiar with the proposition that parents are permitted to make decisions on their behalf, provided this does not cross a harm threshold, whereby significant interests of the child are thought likely to be compromised. Routine medical treatment is clearly covered, but this principle can be extended to medical research. This is most easily justified in research that can properly be described as having therapeutic components, although as outlined earlier, it is important to remember that any non-therapeutic components will also need to be considered. However, the Department of Health (DoH) advises that:

> Where children lack capacity to consent for themselves, parents may give consent for their child to be entered into a trial where the evidence is that the trial therapy may be at least as beneficial to the patient as the standard therapy.
>
> (Department of Health, 2001a, para 9.1)

It is worth noting that although this formulation does not suggest that the trial therapy must be better than existing treatment, it does propose that it must be regarded as being at least as good. This is consistent with what has been said already about the standard of care, where there is a departure from usual practice in treatment, and with the principle of clinical equipoise. It seems that what is expected, as with any other medical decision, is that parents will be permitted to weigh up the risks and benefits to the child. They are not bound to make their assessment based on a test of the best interests of the child, but must not compromise the child's welfare beyond reasonable societal standards. This is a view I endorse.

If the courts become involved, then it would be anticipated that the best interests test would come into play. The first area to consider is innovative treatment and the case discussed earlier: *Simms* (2002).[28] Since the court decided that the procedure was not in principle impermissible, the question then became whether it would be in the best interests of the patients. Animal studies of the drug's possible application to vCJD were at a very preliminary stage and the results could not necessarily be translated to humans. There were risks associated with the need to administer the drug directly into the brain, with the possibility of general and anaesthetic complications put at 2 per cent. There was also the possibility of brain haemorrhage. Dame Butler-Sloss P, considered this as follows:

> The 5% risk of a haemorrhage encompasses a range of possible outcomes, from a minimal and transient effect, to a maximum effect from a seizure causing death, or an intermediate effect of significant impairment of the present ability of the patient to enjoy life. A 5% risk would not seem to me to fall outside the bounds of responsible surgical and medical treatment so as to be an unacceptable risk.[29]

The potential benefits to the patients in this case were said to be 'less tangible and more difficult to assess. There may not be any obvious benefit or any

---

28 *Simms v Simms, A v Another* (2002) [2003] 1 All ER 669, Fam D.
29 Ibid at para 56.

benefit at all'. However, even though there was thought to be no prospect that the patients would recover, a broad view was taken of what might count as a benefit and be achievable here. This included the possibility of an improvement from the present state of illness, a continuation of the existing state of illness without deterioration, and the prolongation of life.[30] Harrington points out that the opinion of the doctors on whether to proceed was somewhat equivocal. Some suggested that the risks might outweigh the medical benefits and even those most supportive of it were doubtful of the prospects of success. Indeed, there was guidance at the time from the DoH that in the absence of properly conducted human trials, there was 'no rational basis for prescribing PPS' in cases of vCJD. However, the doctors felt here that it would not be 'irresponsible or unethical' to provide it.[31] Harrington concludes that the reason for this was the distinction between the role of doctors as scientists and as clinicians.

> From the generalized perspective of medical research and clinical governance, there were insufficient aggregate data to support the administration of PPS in these cases. As scientists, the experts were, therefore, unwilling to recommend its use. From the individualized perspective of clinical care, by contrast, there remained a chance that therapy might benefit the particular patients. As clinicians, the experts would be willing to try it out.
>
> (Harrington, 2003)

In common with cases considered in the previous chapter, the judge took into account the broader welfare issues of the patients, including their current abilities and their future with or without these procedures. In deciding what would be in their best interests, she undertook an assessment of whether the quality of life of the patients merited its prolongation in the circumstances and held that:

> There is undoubtedly evidence that there is some value to their lives. A reduced enjoyment of life even at quite a low level is to be respected and protected. Each patient is at present within a devoted and wonderfully caring family and is being provided with the best life possible in these tragic circumstances. I consider that even the prospect of a slightly longer life is a benefit worth having for each of these two patients.[32]

Interestingly, it is clear that the judge paid great attention to both the families'

---

30 Ibid at para 57.
31 Ibid at para 33.
32 Ibid at para 61.

wishes and their commitment to their children in this regard, which has some echoes of the way that these kinds of issues were approached in *Re T* (1996).[33] Some concern has been expressed about this:

> But what of the patient's interests where the family is indifferent or downright abusive? Is such a patient worth less, because they are valued less by their relatives? What of the patient who is more or less alone in the world, or who is enmeshed in a web of 'non-standard' relationships? Will the courts in such cases resurrect a set of immutable interests to be respected independently of the patient's social and familial context?
>
> (Harrington, 2003)

My position, however, following from the discussion in the previous chapter, is that taking this line does not suggest that, even if parents were to reject a child, this means that his or her life should be seen as having no, or a dimished, value. Where parents do not appear to be sufficiently concerned with the welfare of their child, then clearly their views need not and should not be accorded determinative weight (Rhodes and Holzman, 2004, p 375; Ross, 1998, ch 1). On the other hand, when assessing the quality of the patient's life to be obtained by treatment, I consider that some account must be taken of the capacity of the child for meaningful interactions with others. This is a judgement that, in most cases, caring parents should be able to make. If they feel that such interaction is possible and is providing some benefit to the child, then it should take compelling evidence of a serious risk of significant harm before their decisions should be overridden. If parents do not believe there is a benefit to the child, then again, unless the court has compelling evidence that their decisions are unreasonable, their views should take precedence. This should apply equally to innovative treatment and to medical research. In most cases, this should not require court involvement, but in some circumstances, independent scrutiny will be justified and this point will be returned to shortly.

It is also significant that Dame Elizabeth Butler-Sloss P in *Simms* (2003) took into account as a separate issue the effect that refusal of the applications might have on the families.

> The impact of refusal by this court of granting the declarations on each set of parents and, in one case, five siblings, and in the other case, one sibling, would in my view be enormous and palpable. In a finely balanced case I should give the views of the parents and the effect upon them of

33 *Re T (a minor) (wardship: medical treatment)* (1996) [1997] 1 All ER 906, CA.

refusal great weight in the wider considerations of the best interests test which the court has to apply to each patient.[34]

This is clearly a departure from the way that the courts usually approach these matters, where it is the child's best interests that are the focus and the views of the family are relevant only to the extent that they impact upon the child, not as freestanding considerations. I have argued that it is appropriate to rely on the views of parents, provided that they are reasonable, and that they may take into account their own and their families' needs and interests (see, also, Ross, 1998, p 8). A widening of the best interests test by the court in this way is therefore an approach I would support, although it does not seem to be permissible, given the meaning usually attributed to a best interests assessment. Again, I consider that parental views on what is necessary and appropriate treatment for the child in the wider context of the family should not be absolute, but the recognition that there are other interests at stake than those of the child is welcome.

One further justification was put forward for permitting the procedure to be performed. The Declaration of Helsinki states at para 32 that:

> In the treatment of a patient, where proven . . . therapeutic methods do not exist or have been ineffective, the physician, with informed consent from the patient, must be free to use unproven or new . . . therapeutic measures, if in the physician's judgement it offers hope of saving life, re-establishing health or alleviating suffering.

The court in *Simms* sought to rely on the idea that potential benefits of new treatments should not be denied to patients because of a lack of capacity:

> A patient who is not able to consent to pioneering treatment ought not to be deprived of the chance in circumstances where he would have been likely to consent if he had been competent.[35]

Of course the difficulty of making judgements about what an incapacitated person would want remains, though it may be more possible to reach a conclusion with adults and older children, where some evidence of past values and beliefs may be available. Here, it was held that there were potential benefits to the patients from this novel procedure and accordingly, it was in the best interests of each patient that it be performed. My preferred approach remains whether the proposed treatment fell within the scope of reasonable parental discretion. Applying this test to the evidence that was given, I would

---

34 *Simms v Simms, A v Another* [2003] 1 All ER 669, Fam D, at para 64.
35 Ibid at para 57.

suggest that a court could still reach the conclusion to allow parents to give consent.

It is finally worth considering why an application to the court was felt necessary, as the reasons for doing so are unclear from the judgment in relation to the child patient. For the adult patient, reluctance to approve the procedure by the hospital may have been a factor. However, judicial scrutiny seems likely to have been prompted by the combination of the fact that this treatment had not been performed before in humans and that both patients were incompetent to weigh up the risks and burdens for themselves. Had they been competent, receiving innovative treatment would usually be regarded as a matter for them to decide in conjunction with medical advice. As noted previously, there may be limits on whether innovative treatment meets professional standards of care and consent, by itself, is not the sole criterion for lawfulness. Nevertheless, provided these boundaries are not overstepped, it is for the competent patient to weigh up the risks and benefits of treatment, whether it is innovative or not. Equally, the involvement of incompetent patients in clinical trials is not usually felt to require a court to determine their best interests. Where children are concerned, treatment decisions usually fall to the parents alone. In spite of this, taking together the highly unusual nature of the treatment and lack of capacity of the patients does suggest the need for an objective assessment of the proposed procedure and it seems wholly appropriate to have done so in this situation. McNeill has discussed the extent to which incompetent patients may be particularly in need of protection from overoptimistic attempts to use untested techniques, at the behest of doctors and their families (McNeill, 1993). The desire to further knowledge to help future patients or as a last attempt to use any means possible to save the life of a patient or loved one may be powerful motivations in which the perspective of the patient may become lost. External scrutiny of innovative treatment may be necessary in such circumstances to ensure it is not.[36] As a postscript to this case, a number of similar applications followed, including one in Scotland (Robertson, 2004). However, although the small number of patients given the treatment appear to have survived for longer than expected, evidence so far seems to suggest that PPS does not halt progression of vCJD, although further research has been recommended (Medical Research Council, 2006).

Despite what has been said about *Simms*, however, there is some evidence of a lack of consistency in the way that the courts may deal with these matters. A more recent case dealing with an incompetent adult took a rather different approach. The case of *A NHS Trust v J* (2006) concerned a woman

---

36 Declaration of Helsinki, Part C Additional Principles for Medical Research Combined with Medical Care.

who had been in a permanent vegetative state (PVS) for three years.[37] Proceedings had been commenced on the application of the Trust caring for her and with the support of her family that life-sustaining medical care and treatment should be withheld. Ordinarily it would have been expected that the application would be approved, in line with the principles set out in *Airedale NHS Trust v Bland*.[38] However, published research had come to the attention of the Official Solicitor representing the interests of the patient, which described the possible effects of treating PVS patients with a drug called Zolpidem. Although usually prescribed for insomnia, it had been reported that giving it to patients in PVS had resulted in the patient temporarily regaining consciousness and being able to communicate (Clauss and Nel, 2006). In this study, the drug had been administered to three patients for a number of years and all of them had been said to have been 'aroused transiently every morning'. The Official Solicitor sought to have Zolpidem administered to the patient in an attempt to revive her before withdrawal of treatment could be authorised.

The patient's family vigorously opposed this on the basis that, even if successful, reviving her might cause her distress at realising the condition she was in. In addition, it would not result in any meaningful quality of life and was contrary to views about what she would have wanted that she had expressed to her family when she was well. Despite reservations expressed by the patient's doctor over the likely effectiveness of the treatment, he considered it would be in her best interests, since 'it was important that any patient in this state should be given a chance to recover if there was any such chance'.[39] He did not believe she would be likely to suffer discomfort or distress. The Court authorised the administration of the drug but, during the agreed trial period of three days, the patient did not regain consciousness. The application to withhold further medical treatment was renewed, the declarations sought were granted and the patient died shortly thereafter.

This case caused considerable controversy, not least because of the evaluation taken of the best interests of the patient, which was flatly contrary to evidence led by her family over what she would have wanted and their own views on the matter (Dyer, 2007a). Of course, when dealing with a young child, evidence of what s/he would want may be entirely lacking or held to be of reduced weight, due to the child's lack of competence, and these issues have been discussed already. However, the point to note here is that it may be suggested that the risk/benefit analysis undertaken yet again seems to give overwhelming priority to the views of medical witnesses. It must be remembered that the doctor's view, which was accepted by the court, was that no

---

37   *A NHS Trust v J* [2006] All ER (D) 73 (Dec), Fam D.
38   *Airedale NHS Trust v Bland* [1993] 1 All ER 821, Fam D, CA and HL.
39   *A NHS Trust v J* [2006] All ER (D) 73 (Dec), Fam D, at para 11.

distress would be caused to the patient, but confidence in this assertion may be doubtful in the light of the opposing evidence put forward by the family. The drug Zolpidem was not being given as part of a recognised trial and so can at best be described as an attempt at innovative treatment where there was no alternative. In the case of children, I have advocated that parental views should take precedence in cases where there is reasonable doubt over the benefits to be obtained by medical intervention. Prioritising a medical view of best interests instead allows their wishes to be overridden and this I believe to be unjustified. The Court in *A NHS Trust v J* (2006) took a very different view of the role of family wishes to that in *Simms* (2003), and I suggest that it is the *Simms* approach that is preferable.

So far, therefore, the discussion has centred on innovative treatment, but the principles discussed here may also be applicable to the therapeutic components of research. As I have outlined, the reason for distinguishing between research with therapeutic components and non-therapeutic research is that a different risk analysis can operate in respect of the individual elements of the research procedures. Accordingly it has been said that:

> The risks associated with activities of [a therapeutic] kind are not special; they occur every time a patient receives treatment from a doctor. Aside from issues of consent, the physician-researcher must simply demonstrate two things: that the risks are compatible with normal clinical standards of care and that he has observed the principle of clinical equipoise. The risks associated with activities of the second kind are special. Here the researcher uses the patient in order to serve a wider population and, hence, special mechanisms of oversight are warranted to ensure that the patient is not exploited inappropriately.
>
> (Liddell, 2006)

In other words, like innovative treatment, the research treatment must meet reasonable standards of care and be considered to be at least as good as any alternative available, before it can be offered as an option for parents to consider. It must be said that choosing whether to allow innovative treatment or research to proceed may involve more difficult questions of risk assessment for the parents, since the nature and likelihood of risk may be less easy to determine than where routine treatment is concerned. This will be returned to later, along with the requirements for information disclosure. However, keeping to the issue of the parental role in decision-making, there will be the same implications for research involving therapeutic elements as in other situations if the courts consider that they have the right to determine the best interests of an incompetent patient, no matter the views of the parents. Naturally, I would suggest that this is not the course that should be adopted. However, the important difference between research and treatment is, of course, the extent to which additional burdens may be placed on the child by any non-therapeutic components of the trial. Of course, in order to establish the relative efficacy of the new treatment, additional procedures may be required to monitor the patients' condition and, in respect of new treatment, this may also be necessary for the patient's safety, since possible side-effects may not be known in advance. It has been suggested that:

> Currently there seems to be no coherent conceptual framework or criteria for judging whether the risks of research are reasonable in relation to what might be gained by the (child) research participant or society.
>
> (Caldwell *et al.*, 2004, p 805)

It is to the assessment of risks related to non-therapeutic research, whether as individual elements or as an entire research project, then, that I will turn.

The incompetent child – non-therapeutic medical research

When the subject of parents giving consent to their child's participation in non-therapeutic research first came into focus, some argued that they could not do so, since it would not directly benefit the child (Ramsey, 1970, reprinted 2002). This rests squarely on the idea that decisions can only be made on behalf of a child which are in his or her best interests and that these are to be judged in terms of medical benefit. Subjecting a child to any degree of risk with no countervailing medical benefit would run counter to this principle. While taken from an American case, the following statement explains the difficulty for the courts if a best interests test is used here:

> It is not in the best interests of a specific child, in a non-therapeutic research project, to be placed in a research environment, which might possibly be, or which proves to be hazardous to the health of the child. We have long stressed that the 'best interests of the child' is the overriding concern of the Court in matters relating to children. Whatever the interests of a parent, and whatever the interests of the general public in fostering research that might, according to a researcher's hypothesis, be for the good of all children, this Court's concern for the particular child and particular case, over-arches all other interests.[40]

There have been similar suggestions by professional organisations in the UK that non-therapeutic research cannot meet a best interests standard (Law Commission, 1995b; British Medical Association and the Law Society, 2004).

---

40 *Grimes v Kennedy-Krieger Institute* (2001) 782 A2d 807.

For those who support the courts using this test, but who see the merits in allowing non-therapeutic research procedures to be performed, one way of attempting to get round this issue would be to look for more intangible benefits to the child. We have seen that the notion of best interests in medical treatment is not confined to a beneficial medical outcome, although in truth this has been given the greatest emphasis by the courts. It could be argued that parents involving children in medical research encourages children to perform altruistic actions and to feel a sense of self-worth and importance. It is thus a chance not only to provide a benefit to society, but to the child him/herself. Provided the level of risk is low, it might be felt that this provides a sufficient level of benefit to allow participation to be regarded as in the child's best interests (McCall Smith, 1989, p 469; see, also, Jackson, 2006, pp 497–8). Nevertheless, as Mason and Laurie explain, this would depend upon the child having a level of understanding to enable them to properly appreciate the nature of altruism and their involvement. Any idea of retrospective approval by the child of involvement in this research, once s/he had come to that level of understanding, faces the problems common to all suggestions for retrospective approval as discussed in Chapter 1. The child may not in fact approve it and presuming that s/he will, is open to question (see, also, Feenan, 1997). However, Mason and Laurie also consider that:

> The Courts have been unsparing in fleshing out the [best interests] test in recent years, and the concept of *overall interests* has been employed time and again. We suggest that it would not be too much a stretch of our imaginations to adopt a similar approach to child research – an approach that reflects the child's interests in his broader relationships with the community; this would be subject always, and of course, to a minimal, negligible or non-existent risk to the child in question.
>
> (Mason and Laurie, 2006, para 19.12)

It is not beyond the bounds of possibility that the courts could employ this kind of concept, though it would require considerable stretching of the best interests test to make it fit (Mumford, 1998). In other situations where this kind of argument has been attempted, such as the donation of organs to siblings, commentators have noted how difficult it is to assess psychological benefit, both present and future, when considering medical interventions on one person that are designed to help others. In addition, in these cases, the courts have been particularly concerned with the relationship between donors and recipients, and the consequential effects on the family's ability to care for the donor if the donation did not take place. This will be discussed further in Chapter 6, but these kinds of criteria seem unlikely to be able to be met where the research is designed to help future patients and society in general. Here, there is no direct relationship between the child taking part in research and possible beneficiaries, and it would amount to only what has been described as 'altruism in an abstract, theoretical sense'.[41] It is equally difficult to see how failing to permit the child's participation in research would affect the care that parents would be able to give him or her.

A slightly different justification for bringing incompetent children's participation in non-therapeutic research procedures within the best interests principle has been put forward by Harris and Holm. They suggest that:

> ... it may be in the best interest of the child to participate in research that does not directly benefit it. Children are moral agents, or moral agents *in spe* and parents are justified in assuming that the child would want to do that which is right.
>
> (Harris and Holm, 2003, p 122)

This view is based on the idea that there is a moral obligation to participate in medical research in certain contexts, since there is both a moral obligation to help others and/or to be just and do one's share. Where people are incompetent, it is contended that the presumption should be that they would want to discharge their moral obligations where their actual preferences are unknown. Accordingly, 'Parents making decisions for their children are therefore fully justified in assuming that their child will wish to do that which is right, and not do that which is wrong' (Harris and Holm, 2003, p 127). The difficulty with this approach is that it depends upon the proposition that moral agents should choose what is in their best interests by identifying their moral obligations to others and acting on them. Although people may in practice act according to their own values, motives and beliefs, that may not include fulfilling their moral obligations. Harris and Holm deny the relevance of this, since their position rests on the idea of what moral agents ought to do rather than what they in fact do.

Although this would allow parents to justify involving children in non-therapeutic procedures, it does not fit easily into the traditional interpretation of the best interests test by the courts. It has never been suggested that this test requires the court to reach a judgment according to what they believe a moral agent should choose to do. So, for example, where the question arose whether an incompetent woman could act as a bone marrow donor for her sister, the fact that this would benefit a family member was said to be irrelevant, unless by doing so it would serve the donor's best interests.[42] It was not proposed that it would be in her best interests because she had a moral obligation to help her sister. This kind of interpretation of the best interests test has been described as being essentially 'self-regarding', rather than allowing the interests of others to be taken into account (Jansen, 2004; see, also, Buchanan and Brock, 1973).

---

41 *Curran v Bosze* (1990) 566 NE 2d 1319.
42 *Re Y (adult patient) (bone marrow: transplant)* (1997) 35 BMLR 111.

An alternative would be, as I propose, to depart from the view that courts must judge interventions according to the best interests of the child standard and to move to the position that the intervention must meet a harm and reasonableness threshold. The international and national guidelines discussed earlier suggest that enabling research to take place where it is not against the interests of the child is ethically acceptable and it appears to be common practice worldwide (Plomer, 2000). Indeed, there is already some support for the UK courts using this kind of approach, for example, in the guidance produced by the DoH:

> Although research has not been specifically considered, the courts have considered whether it would be legal to carry out a medical intervention with no therapeutic purpose on children lacking capacity. It was held that a person with parental responsibility can consent to an intervention which, although not in the best interests of that child, is not against the interests of such a child (the case in question concerned a blood test for non-therapeutic reasons).[43] From this the idea has developed that research which is not of direct benefit to such children may be lawful (with consent from a person with parental responsibility) if it is *not against* the interests of the child and imposes no greater than minimal burden. (Original emphasis)
>
> (Department of Health, 2001a, para 9.3)

This opinion originates of course from the cases involving blood tests to establish paternity. It was said that a reasonable parent would have some regard to the general public interest and would consent to the procedures unless it was clearly against the child's interests.[44] In other words, no positive benefit to the child needed to be established. This could be applied equally well to non-therapeutic medical research. However, an even broader justification can be made as follows:

> Many activities in a typical child's life, in fact, will present greater risks and harms, including such routine activities as participating in contact sports and travelling as a passenger in the family car . . . Parents are morally and legally authorised to decide what risks their child can take and in what settings. Parental authorization or prohibition of a child's participation in [non-therapeutic research] . . . then, is not abusive or neglectful . . .
>
> (Ross, 1997, p 159)

---

43 The kinds of cases referred to here are those where blood testing for paternity purposes has been authorised, such as *S v S, W v Official Solicitor* [1970] 3 All ER 107, HL.

44 Ibid per Lord Reid at 112.

This view had been endorsed earlier by Skegg, who suggested that a parent could legitimately consent to any procedure which a 'reasonable parent' would agree to, although this left open of course whether a court would accept the parents' opinions as being reasonable (Skegg, 1984, p 66). For Ross, though, this would be based on her concept of 'constrained parental autonomy' that allows parents, within reason, to choose to guide the development of their children and shape what kind of people they will become. It thus has a certain resonance with the position described earlier of Harris and Holm, but Ross sees this as having the additional purpose of allowing parents to retain their proper decision-making authority over their children. This assumes particular importance when considering what account should be taken of the child's views, if s/he is capable of expressing them, and will be returned to later.

Notwithstanding these arguments, there remains no direct legal authority on this point in regard to medical research. Although some have suggested that the best interests test can be widened to take account of these kinds of contention, as Mason and Laurie caution:

> The extension of the [best interests test to a not against the interests of the child test] in the contexts of research ... would be a matter for judicial discretion; there is no ruling to date on whether the test would admit of such a generous reading.
>
> (Mason and Laurie, 2006, para 19.12)

It must be remembered that in the paternity testing cases, the courts were not bound to have the child's welfare as their paramount consideration. They would be in the case of an application involving the child's participation in research, since this would take place under either the Children Acts or the courts' inherent jurisdiction. If the courts were to take a strict view of this duty, as seems likely given the stance they have taken in other medical contexts, then they may not be prepared to take a different approach here either. For example, in an *obiter* statement in a case concerning the lawfulness of embryo screening to conceive a child to act as a donor for a sibling, it was said by Lord Hoffman that 'I have no doubt that medical practitioners take very seriously the law that any operation upon a child for which there is no clinical reason relating to the child itself must be justified *as being for other reasons in the child's best interests*' (Emphasis added).[45] That it would be a different approach is also implicit in the following statement by the DoH:

> The courts have held that people with parental responsibility can consent to a non-therapeutic intervention on a child as long as that intervention

---

45 *Quintavalle v Human Fertilisation and Embryology Authority* [2005] UKHL 28, HL, at 38.

is *not against* the interests of the child and imposes only a minimal burden. (This contrasts with interventions that would impose more than
'minimal burden' on a child, such as bone marrow donation . . . where to
be lawful the intervention must be in the child's best interests.)

(Department of Health, 2001b, p 25)

Here again, of course, the non-therapeutic interventions being referred to as
permitting a 'not against the interests of the child' test do not provide authority for the courts taking this view where the best interests of the child are
paramount.

Of course, I consider that the best interests standard ought to be replaced
by one that considers whether the risks that the parent is willing to consent to
are reasonable in exposing the child to a level of risk. This would provide
a level of consistency of approach and solve the difficulties inherent in trying
to argue that research is in the child's best interests. It would hold that participation in non-therapeutic research, or the non-therapeutic elements of a
research project, falls within the sphere of acceptable decision-making by
parents for their children, provided that it does not overstep a harm and
reasonableness threshold.

However, there remain objections to meet if there is to be a departure
from the best interests test, which are explained by Edwards and McNamee
(2005). While discussing the possible discrepancies between the principles
contained in the Declaration of Helsinki, compared with other international
and national guidance on research with incompetent children, the points
raised are equally relevant to a discussion of the best interests or harm principle debate. Clause 5 of the Declaration of Helsinki provides that:

> In medical research on human subjects, considerations related to the
> well-being of the human subject should take precedence over the interests
> of science and society.

Edwards and McNamee suggest that this may be based on a version of Kant's
categorical imperative, which states that you must:

> Act in such a way that you always treat humanity, whether in your own
> person, or in the person of any other, never simply as a means, but always
> at the same time as an end.

(Kant 1785, reprinted 1994, p 279)

Relying on this, they suggest that '. . . it could reasonably be claimed that any
morally defensible involvement of a child in clinical research must be in the
child's best interests, not merely *not contrary* to the child's interests'. (Original
emphasis) This is because of the Kantian injunction not to use a person
merely as a means:

The child has not consented (let us agree), and the research is not being performed for the benefit of the child. Surely such a child *is* being used simply as a means. It may be true that the use serves a morally good end, but . . . being beneficial to third parties may be a necessary condition of defensible research, but it is not a sufficient one.

(Edwards and McNamee, 2005)

This point about being used as a means may be made in relation to all non-therapeutic research, whatever the competence of the research participant and whatever the level of risk. However, the essential difference is that a competent person must give consent to such use being made of him or her. In effect, voluntary participation and assumption of potential risks makes inclusion in research part of the subject's own ends and serves to prevent violation of the Kantian principle (Jonas, 1969). This justification for allowing non-therapeutic research is absent for children who are unable to consent.

As Jackson points out, however, medical research is one area in which 'medical law has to weigh the interests of society against the welfare of individuals'. While noting that a deontological approach, such as that typified by Kant's categorical imperative, might prohibit research on non-volunteers, she contrasts this with a utilitarian perspective, which might justify conducting research involving considerable risk, even without consent, on a small group of people to benefit the rest of society. She concludes that:

Both extreme utilitarianism and its opposite are unattractive and carica-tured moral positions. In practice, most people adopt some sort of mixed approach, which takes into account both individual rights and the common good. . . . All attempts to regulate research therefore try to effect . . . [a] compromise between the need to promote medical progress by conducting research on humans, and the need to promote the well-being and integrity of individual research subjects.

(Jackson, 2006, p 449)

Just this sort of compromise can be seen where justifications for involving children in non-therapeutic research are concerned. Ross, of course, has also defended 'constrained parental autonomy' on the basis of Kantian principles. Here, the compromise is between the protection of children from harmful behaviour of parents and allowing parents to bring up their children as they feel is appropriate. She mandates external intervention only where parents' decisions fail to protect children's basic interests (Ross, 1998, ch 1). Unless we are to deprive children of the benefits of developing new methods of treating illness and injury specific to their needs, then, subject to appropriate safeguards, entering them into research trials is a practical necessity. The justification for doing so is unlikely to be found by an application of the best interests test, but rather in deeming this to be a reasonable exercise of parental discretion. The question remains however, what level of risk it is reasonable for parents to expose their children to as part of a research project.

Risk assessment

It has been said that:

> It is evident that an analysis of the risks and benefits of a proposed research project is a necessary part both of the scientific and ethical assessment of the project.
>
> (Nicholson, 1986, p 232)

However, how the level of acceptable risk should be established is far from clear. Obviously it may not be possible to quantify all possible risks of the research in advance. Some may become apparent only as a result of a trial, and indeed this is one of the reasons for undertaking research before new treatments are incorporated into routine care. Nevertheless, to the extent that it is possible, risks and benefits in the form of health indicators, will need to be clearly and fairly identified and parents given this information. A procedure that may be regarded as a small risk to an adult, such as taking a blood sample, may be a higher risk when considering young children and infants. Along with this is the possibility that interventions, while not in themselves likely to produce physical harm to a child, may be distressing or inconvenient for them. A procedure may therefore be low risk, but burdensome to a child. Lewis has suggested that the concentration in guidelines on risks, rather than burdens of research, is unfortunate, although some advice does address this issue (Lewis, 2002; but see, for example, Department of Health, 2001a and 2001b). The evaluation of risks, burdens and benefits in research has been considered most closely in the context of non-therapeutic research projects, since here the possible dangers associated with interventions are not being evaluated against any direct medical benefit to the child, but against its benefit to society. However, the same principles would apply to non-therapeutic components of research.

There are many ways in which risks of non-therapeutic research may be categorised (see, for example, the discussion in Nicholson, 1986, ch 5). Generally, a conservative approach is taken to the permissible level of risk that incompetent patients can be exposed to. The CIOMS guidelines, for example, state that in general, where the research subject is incapable of giving informed consent and there is no prospect of direct benefit to the individual, the risk from research should be 'no more likely and not greater than the risk attached to routine medical or psychological examination of such persons'. Although they go on to say:

> Slight or minor increases above such risk may be permitted when there is

an overriding scientific or medical rationale for such increases and when an ethical committee has approved them.[46]

The difficulty, particularly with this formulation, is that when dealing with sick children, they may routinely be subjected to painful and distressing examinations. Following these guidelines would seem to give them less protection from involvement in medical research than their healthy counterparts, which is arguably the contrary approach that one would expect if seeking to safeguard their wellbeing. At a European level, the ECB's additional protocol on biomedical research provides that research that has no benefit to the participant must entail only minimal risk and minimal burden for the individual concerned.[47] Additional potential benefits of the research shall not be used to justify an increased level of risk or burden.[48] Minimal risks and burdens are defined as follows:

> ... research bears a minimal risk if, having regard to the nature and scale of the intervention, it is to be expected that it will result, at the most, in a very slight and temporary negative impact on the health of the person concerned.

> It is deemed that it bears a minimal burden if it is to be expected that the discomfort will be, at the most, temporary and very slight for the person concerned. In assessing the burden for an individual, a person enjoying the special confidence of the person concerned shall assess the burden where appropriate.[49]

It is interesting to note the weight being given here to a person close to the patient in assessing the burdens to the research subject, which could be taken to place a high priority on the views of parents. The most popular current approach in UK guidance takes a different approach again and divides risks into *minimal risk, low-risk* and *high-risk* procedures. The Medical Research Council (MRC) has endorsed this approach, which had been proposed by the Royal College of Paediatrics and Child Health (RCPCH). It describes these categories as follows:

> *Minimal* (the least possible) risk describes procedures such as questioning, observing and measuring children, provided that procedures are carried

---

46 Council for International Organizations of Medical Sciences (2002) *International Ethical Guidelines for Biomedical Research Involving Human Subjects*, 3rd Revision, Geneva: CIOMS, Guideline 9.
47 Additional Protocol to the Convention on Human Rights and Biomedicine, concerning Biomedical Research, 25 January 2005 (not in force at the time of writing).
48 Ibid Article 15(2)(ii).
49 Ibid Article 17.

out in a sensitive way, respecting the child's autonomy and that consent has been given. Procedures with minimal risk include obtaining bodily fluids without invasive intervention, e.g. taking saliva or urine samples. It is expected that research of minimal risk would not result in more than a very slight and temporary negative impact on the health of the person concerned.

Low risk describes procedures that might cause no more than brief pain or tenderness, and small bruises or scars, or very slight temporary distress; e.g. a blood test

High risk procedures such as lung or liver biopsy, arterial or lumbar puncture and cardiac catheterisation are not justified for research purposes alone with children. They should be carried out only when research is combined with diagnosis or treatment intended to benefit the child concerned.

(Medical Research Council, 2004, p 15; Royal College of Paediatrics and Child Health: Ethics Advisory Committee, 2000, p 179)

It is further stated that research 'in which children are submitted to more than minimal risk with only slight, uncertain or no benefit to themselves deserves serious ethical consideration'. Blood sampling is cited as an example where low, rather than minimal, risk could be incurred by injections and venepuncture. While the MRC is silent on the point, it was concluded by the RCPCH that parents may consent to this for non-therapeutic purposes if they have a full understanding of the reasons for it and have balanced the risk to the child (Royal College of Paediatrics and Child Health: Ethics Advisory Committee, 2000, p 179). It appears likely that the categories of minimal and low risk put forward here would equate with the ECB criteria for minimal risk and burdens. However, much still depends on the interpretation of these terms in respect of particular interventions on a particular child and whether a court would reach the same conclusions on acceptable risks and burdens as researchers, ethics committees and parents. It must be remembered in this context that children's reactions to, and perceptions of, procedures may differ markedly from adults. The RCPCH, for example, note that:

Researchers sometimes underestimate high risk of pain if the effects are brief, whereas the child or parents may consider the severe transient pain is not justified by the hoped for benefit. There is evidence that tolerance of pain increases with age and maturity when the child no longer perceives medical interventions as punitive.

(Royal College of Paediatrics and Child Health: Ethics Advisory Committee, 2000, pp 178–9)

The threshold for harm that I have proposed is the serious risk of significant harm to the child. Applying this to the scheme put forward by the MRC, it would justify parents being enabled to allow non-therapeutic procedures described as minimal and low risk, but would not permit those described as high risk. While the terminology adopted differs, the same principle that parents should not be allowed to subject their children to risks that are deemed to be unreasonable applies. Of course, a court could intervene if it believed this were the case and a careful evaluation of the risks and burdens on the individual child will need to be made. However, in line with the ECB's approach, I suggest that in most cases, parents are in the best position to make these judgements and should be free to do so.

So far, no judicial authority exists on whether research comes within the category of procedures that requires both parents to consent.[50] Research with non-therapeutic elements involves placing the child at some level of risk for the benefit of society. It therefore has some grounds in common with the public health interest in permitting immunisations. However, immunisation is also being undertaken to provide benefits for the child him/herself. As we have seen, it is much more debatable whether any benefits can be said to accrue to the child undergoing non-therapeutic research procedures, subject to the qualification that they are necessary for the safety of a child involved in therapeutic research procedures. However, research projects will have been subjected to external scrutiny of the risks and burdens involved through the operation of prior ethical review. Although questions remain about the adequacy of ethics committees and their approval does not avoid the need for an individual assessment of the risks in relation to the particular child, it is submitted that this additional safeguard provides some basis for allowing the decision of a single parent to be acted on. Accordingly, I believe that it should be for an objecting parent to bring the case before the courts in the event of disagreement over the involvement of a child in medical research, although in practice, researchers may be unwilling to proceed without both parents' consent, where there is joint parental responsibility. This is in accordance with the advice given by the MRC (Medical Research Council, 2004, para 5.1.4.a)

Information disclosure

Where parents are asked to act as proxy decision-makers for their children, research has suggested that they can be:

> ... uncomfortable with this referred responsibility because of concerns about unknown or unexpected future side-effects and the possibility that

---

50 *Re J (child's religious upbringing and circumcision)* [2000] 1 FCR 307, CA; *Re B (a child) (immunisation)* [2003] 3 FCR 156, CA.

the treatment their child receives might later be discovered to be ineffective or even harmful.

(Caldwell *et al.*, 2003, pp 555–60)

The same study indicated that they may be more reluctant to consent on
behalf of their children than if they were asked to participate themselves. For
parents faced with such a decision, clearly information about the child's condition, prognosis, available treatments and the nature and implications of the
trial will be necessary. The issue of adequate information disclosure has been
outlined in Chapter 2. The DoH advises that 'The same legal principles apply
when seeking consent from patients for research purposes as when seeking
consent for investigations or treatment.' Nevertheless, it recognises the additional feature of research, that it may not have direct benefits for the patient,
and quotes the GMC's position that ' "particular care" should be taken to
ensure that possible research subjects have the fullest possible information
about the proposed study and sufficient time to absorb it' (Department
of Health, 2001a, ch 1, para 15; General Medical Council, 1998 and 2002).
This raises an interesting point, since some have suggested that involvement
of people in medical research ought to require a higher standard of information disclosure (Giesen, 1995, p 35; Beauchamp and Childress, 2001, p 443;
Kennedy and Grubb, 2004, para 13.87). This would apply equally to disclosure to research subjects or those entrusted with making decisions on their
behalf. Kennedy explains this as follows:

> The researcher's duty . . . is not confined to what was set out by the
> House of Lords in *Sidaway*. Rather, it is a much more extensive duty,
> namely, to bring to the attention of the volunteer all that information
> which, from what the volunteer has said and the researcher knows and
> reasonably ought to know, the volunteer would wish to know. What is
> known to the researcher about such matters as risks, inconvenience, or
> side-effects of the proposed procedure must be passed on to the volunteer
> in a manner and form which is comprehensible.
>
> (Kennedy, 1998, p 735)

In addition, it has been suggested that it would be expected that 'the
patient must be informed, not only of the risks known to accompany the
procedure, but also of the fact that there may be unknown risks, or at least
that the doctor has reason to believe that unknown risks could materialise' (Giesen, 1995, p 35). In the Canadian case of *Halushka v University
of Saskatchewan* (1965), this kind of idea was accepted. The judge held
that:

> In my opinion, the duty imposed upon those engaged in medical research
> . . . to those who offer themselves as subjects for experimentation . . . is at

least as great as, if not greater than, the duty owed by the ordinary physician or surgeon to his patient. . . .

. . . The subject of medical experimentation is entitled to full and frank disclosure of all the facts, probabilities and opinions which a reasonable man might be expected to consider before giving his consent.[51]

Imposing this standard of disclosure was at the time a departure from the usual standard applied to routine treatment, which was judged by reference to the information that would have been disclosed by a reasonable doctor, rather than that which would be needed by a reasonable patient. In Canada, the reasonable patient standard was subsequently endorsed for all types of medical interventions.[52] By contrast, so far as there is any relevant case law in the UK, it appears to take the view that no difference should pertain between information disclosure about routine treatment and that which is being undertaken for reasons other than illness or injury. So, for example, the courts have refused to demand a higher level of disclosure for so-called non-therapeutic treatment in the case of an elective sterilisation.[53] However, as discussed in Chapter 2, there are some signs of a move away from the professional standard of information disclosure towards a reasonable patient standard, even for established treatment. If this is the case, then, even if the courts were not prepared to adopt a higher standard of disclosure in respect of research procedures, a higher standard may be achieved by default. This remains speculative in the absence of clear judicial authority. It is also interesting to note that the CTR 2004 refers to the concept of 'informed consent', which is generally taken as a legal doctrine to refer to the reasonable patient standard of disclosure, although whether it will be interpreted in this way is perhaps doubtful in the absence of any express definition on this point in the Regulations.

Involving incompetent children in research without parental consent

The importance of including children in research has already been discussed and to many, failure to conduct it is itself unethical, since it would be to deprive children of the benefits that can be obtained from research. However, there are concerns that children are underrepresented as a population within trials (Caldwell *et al.*, 2004; European Commission, 2004). Particular worries have surfaced where very sick children are concerned, as to the understanding and willingness of parents to involve their young children. On the one hand,

---

51 *Halushka v University of Saskatchewan*, 53 Dominion Law Rpts. (2d) 436 (1965), at 443–4.
52 *Reibl v Hughes* (1980) 114 DLR (3d) 1.
53 *Gold v Haringey Health Authority* [1987] 2 All ER 888, CA.

there are concerns that parents may be willing to agree to any research, no matter how risky, if it seems to offer some otherwise unattainable benefit (Royal College of Psychiatrists, 2001). Naturally, caring parents wish to have the best available treatment for their children and may feel torn between wanting them to have proven treatments and allowing them to take part in research of unproven treatments that may be better, but may also involve additional risks. The need for parents to have full information and the time to consider this properly is therefore evident, but it also underlines the importance of the risks of the research being properly evaluated before parents are asked to make a choice on the matter. On the other hand, there are equally worries whether parents are able, at what may be an extremely stressful and distressing time, to give a valid consent. This may be compounded where the situation has arisen in an emergency.

An example of this was provided by the controversy surrounding research carried out into the use of ventilators in a neonatal intensive care unit, which prompted a report into it. The Griffiths Inquiry reported that 'In some instances no matter how often and how carefully a project was explained to a parent . . . it was not possible to be sure that any consent given was valid consent' (NHS Executive: West Midlands, 2000). As a result of the controversy surrounding this research, the RCPCH issued specific guidance on the involvement of babies in research, noting the difficulties in obtaining adequately informed consent where a newborn was seriously ill. As a way of dealing with this problem, they suggested that a form of provisional consent should be available. Essentially, in an emergency situation, a parent could agree in principle that a child could be allocated to a method of treatment, including a research treatment, provided that this approach had the specific prior approval of a research ethics committee. The parents might lack the time to assess the trial fully before giving this agreement, but would be given full information and the time to consider it, subsequently to decide whether or not to allow the type of treatment given to be continued (Royal College of Paediatrics and Child Health: Ethics Advisory Committee, 1999). This suggestion, while having practical utility, is subject to the objection that it acknowledges that a valid consent has not been obtained at the time of entering the child into the trial. It relies on the problematic concept of deferred consent.

Despite this, in some cases it may be necessary for improving future care to allow research to take place under this kind of framework and it has been justified in international guidance too. For example, the Declaration of Helsinki states at para 26 that:

> Research on individuals from whom it is not possible to obtain consent, including proxy or advance consent, should be done only if the physical/mental condition that prevents obtaining informed consent is a necessary characteristic of the research population. The specific reasons

for involving research subjects with a condition that renders them unable to give informed consent should be stated in the experimental protocol for consideration and approval of the review committee. The protocol should state that consent to remain in the research should be obtained as soon as possible from the individual or a legally authorized surrogate.[54]

It is also permitted under the Additional Protocol to the ECB.[55] Even so, the limits on the circumstances in which this type of deferred consent will be applicable in the UK are unclear and the implementation of the CTR 2004 in fact raises more problems than it solves in this regard.

Assent or dissent by incompetent children

There remains the question whether children may or should be placed in trials if they refuse or appear to object. If a child is not judged competent, their unwillingness to take part is unlikely to be determinative of the legality of the intervention, any more than where routine treatment is considered. Nevertheless, many guidelines stress that children's views on participation should be given substantial weight and even be conclusive. The MRC states that:

> If the child is able to give assent to decisions about participation in research, the investigator must obtain that assent in addition to the consent of the legally authorised representative. If the child does not assent, this should be respected.
>
> (Medical Research Council, 2004, para 5.1.4.a)

Similarly, it goes on to advise that 'If a child becomes upset by a procedure, researchers must accept this as a valid refusal' (see, also, the Royal College of Paediatrics and Child Health: Ethics Advisory Committee, 2000, p 180). This position does not appear to be limited to where the child is judged to be competent and is consistent with that taken by the WMA and the ECB.[56] The same stance is taken by commentators such as Bartholome, who regards this as necessary to show respect to the child (Bartholome, 1996, pp 356–61). Rossi, Reynolds and Nelson take the view that when children are very young, developmentally delayed or seriously ill, it may not be possible to gain assent. If there are possible therapeutic benefits only in a research setting, waiver of

---

54 See, also, ICH-GCP and the Additional Protocol to the Convention on Human Rights and Biomedicine, concerning Biomedical Research, 25 January 2005.

55 Additional Protocol to the Convention on Human Rights and Biomedicine, concerning Biomedical Research, 25 January 2005 (not in force at the time of writing).

56 WMA Declaration on the Rights of the Child to Health Care. Adopted by the 50th World Medical Assembly Ottawa, Canada, October 1998.

assent may be appropriate (Rossi *et al.*, 2003). By contrast, for non-therapeutic research, if children are capable of giving assent, it must be obtained. However, they note that many discussions on children's assent describe it in terms equating to that required to give a legally valid consent. This being so, they suggest this leaves younger children vulnerable to their views either not being sought or being too readily dismissed. They suggest a developmental approach, viewing assent as a continuum ranging from mere affirmation in the youngest children to the equivalent of the informed consent process in the mature adolescent. Assent should be obtained:

> ... when a child would be able to tell if a procedure is or is not for his or her own personal benefit. This approach would support the view that a younger child may be capable of assent to research procedures even in the absence of understanding a limited set of elements of informed consent.
>
> (Rossi *et al.*, 2003, p 135)

Their research also suggests that there are many factors that may influence the decision to give assent, including potential parent–child conflict and parental undue influence on research participation. These are undoubtedly important in assessing the extent of children's voluntariness, but there are those that would challenge the need to seek assent at all because of a different view taken of what it means to be respectful to children (Ross, 1998 and 2006). Part of Ross's general thesis is that children are unable to sufficiently consider their long-term interests and so cannot be held competent to make decisions, even in respect of routine treatment, much less so for research. It follows that she does not believe that a child's assent should be relied on by itself in any situation.

> A parent may choose to restrain a child's short-term autonomy (current choices) to promote her lifetime autonomy. As such, it may be respectful of parents to prohibit their child's participation in non-therapeutic research despite the child's desire to do so.
>
> (Ross, 2004, p 352)

Furthermore, notwithstanding professional guidance to the contrary, she believes the child's agreement need not even be sought, except in limited circumstances. This stems from her views about the importance of the parental role, discussed earlier, in guiding their children's development and the need for latitude in order to enable parents to properly fulfil their responsibilities without unnecessary interference.

Accordingly, while Bartholome views with considerable dissatisfaction an example of a father insisting that his child should participate in minimal risk research as, to him, this only teaches a child that he has no control over his environment and is subject to forced interventions, Ross disagrees (Bartholome, 1996, pp 352–3). Instead she considers that:

> Although empowering a child to be able to veto minimal risk research may teach the child that he has some control over his environment, it also teaches the child that strangers can restrain his parents' authority, even when they are not abusive or neglectful. It ignores how important it is for children to view their parents as fully autonomous agents.
>
> (Ross, 2004, p 354)

Nonetheless, in the case of non-therapeutic research that entails more than minimal risk, Ross does suggest that a child's dissent should be determinative. This exception is justified by relying on the contention that 'an intractable objection by the child particularly if it is based upon anxiety or fear which cannot be allayed regarding an experimental procedure' should be decisive, because respect for the child requires us 'to decide whether his well-being is served or not violated by participation' (Ackerman, 1979, p 348). Parental insistence on participation here is judged sufficiently against the welfare of the child to merit not relying on their wishes. I share some of Bartholome's concerns and believe that children's views must be ascertained, where they are capable of giving them. This is consistent with the recognition of this aspect of children's rights, for example, in the UN Convention on the Rights of the Child. However, unless a child is deemed to be competent, their views should not necessarily be determinative. Parents generally should be able to make choices for their children, based on what they see as being in their welfare and on this point I agree with Ross, though my formulation differs slightly. Welfare considerations may allow parents to enter their children into research, despite their children's unwillingness, provided that non-therapeutic components are not likely to impose significant risks of serious harm on the child. In assessing risks, the distress that may be caused to an individual child who is reluctant to participate may outweigh the benefits of allowing parents to exercise their authority and would take the decision out of the bounds of reasonable parental decision-making.

The competent child – medical research and innovative treatment

Given what has already been said about consent being the primary justification for involving people in medical research, it might be expected that where a child is held to be competent, his or her consent would be both necessary and sufficient. All of the current international and national guidelines referred to earlier expect that children's consent would be obtained where this is possible. However, matters are not so simple from a legal perspective. It will be recalled that in England and Wales, consent to medical treatment by those of or over the age of 16 is governed by the Family Law Reform Act 1969. The DoH has stated that:

> Section 8 of the Family Law Reform Act applies only to the young person's own treatment. It does not apply to an intervention which is not potentially of direct health benefit to the young person, such as blood donation or non-therapeutic research on the causes of a disorder. However, a young person may be able to consent to such an intervention under the standard of Gillick competence. . . .
>
> (Department of Health, 2001a, Ch 3, para 2.1)

The powers accorded to the young person by this statute are deemed to be limited solely to medical treatment and to diagnostic procedures, but this would seem to cover innovative treatment as well as that which is routine. While it could potentially also allow children to consent to the therapeutic components of a research project on their own behalf, of course there will be no value to this if they cannot agree to any non-therapeutic elements as well. The source of this opinion appears to be Lord Donaldson MR's judgment in *Re W* (1992).[57] In it, he suggested that Parliament, in enacting this section, had endorsed the approach of the Latey Committee that statute should not authorise people under 18 to give blood. If this is accepted, it seems to mean that, in England and Wales, consent to participation in research by anyone under the age of 18 is governed solely by the common law, unless the research comes within the CTR 2004.

The problems associated with *Gillick* in relation to medical treatment have already been discussed at length and many of the same issues arise here too. For example, there is the issue of the level of understanding that a child must demonstrate in order to be judged competent. It has already been said that deciding whether to take part in research may be more difficult than deciding whether to accept standard treatment, because the benefits and harms may be less predictable and involve more complex assessments. This provides another example of why simply equating the level of competence required with the gravity of the procedure or seriousness of outcome may be a flawed approach. Nevertheless, Lord Donaldson MR seemed to be proceeding on just this basis when he went on to say that he believed it would be possible for a child of any age to be *Gillick* competent to consent to blood donation. However, he contended that finding a child *Gillick* competent to consent to a serious non-therapeutic procedure such as organ donation would be 'a highly improbable conclusion'.[58] Although there remains debate on the matter, I have argued that there is evidence to suggest that children may be

---

57 *Re W (a minor) (medical treatment)* [1992] 4 All ER 627, CA.
58 Ibid at 634.

capable of understanding issues at a young age if they are explained properly (Alderson and Montgomery, 1996b, ch 5). This is no less likely to be the case for medical research than for treatment. Provided that they have developed the skills to make a sufficiently reasoned and autonomous decision, there should in principle be no reason for a child's consent to be invalid here either.

However, at present, as well as issues of competence, there remains the problem with the application of *Gillick* to medical research that the subsequent interpretation of this case requires the child's decision to be in his or her best interests. It will be remembered that the court in *Re W* (1992) declined to draw a distinction between ordinary treatment and extraordinary treatment situations: all are governed by the same principle.[59] This being the case, it seems that even if children are judged competent, their wish to participate in research could still be overridden by the courts. As discussed earlier in relation to parental consent, permitting consent to any non-therapeutic intervention is hard to square with the courts' usual interpretation of the best interests test. For a child's consent to stand, even to a non-therapeutic procedure as minor as blood sampling, it must rest either on the notion that by doing so the child is gaining some intangible benefit that outweighs the risks involved, such as the knowledge and satisfaction of acting altruistically, or that in fact the best interests test can be stretched to accommodate the child making some medical decisions that only meet a 'not against the child's interests' threshold. Lord Donaldson's opinions are *obiter* and neither approach has been directly considered by the courts in the context of medical research.

Some, such as Ross, contend that as a matter of principle, even competent children should not be able to give a legally valid consent. She suggests that:

> To empower adolescents to consent for themselves in research may not adequately protect their long-term interests even if it respects their current interests. Additionally, extrapolation of the mature minor doctrine to research decisions denies that parents have a legitimate interest in what types of non-therapeutic research their children participate in, despite the fact that the parents will bear the consequences if anything were to go wrong. [Sic]
>
> (Ross, 2004, p 351)

I acknowledge that parents may be affected by a child's choice to take part in non-therapeutic procedures, but this is not sufficient in my view to outweigh the importance of respect for an autonomous child's wishes about whether to undertake medical interventions. Whether they involve therapeutic and non-therapeutic components or are wholly non-therapeutic is of no consequence,

---

59 Ibid at 646.

save in respect of the level of risk it is acceptable to expose any participant to, whatever their age. Furthermore, their consent should be determinative. Allowing children to consent to research on this basis avoids strained interpretations of the best interests test to arrive at the same outcome.

If a child is able to give a legally valid consent to participation in medical research, then even according to *Gillick*, the consent of a parent or guardian would not be necessary, and this would of course be the case under my preferred approach.[60] Nevertheless, it is common practice to ask for parental consent as well as that of the child, whatever the lack of legal foundation for this (Medical Research Council, 2004, paras 5.1.2, 5.1.4). This raises the question of whether parents or courts can authorise entering competent children into trials against their wishes. Judicial statements suggest that UK courts can override a competent child's consent and that they and parents can override a competent child's refusal of consent to medical treatment, if it is in the child's best interests.[61] In theory, it seems that this could extend to medical research, although again, doing so would seem to require some considerable manipulation of the best interests test and in my view taking such steps is unwarranted in any event. It is potentially of great concern, therefore, that matters seem to be taken a stage further than even the common law may allow by the CTR 2004. According to these regulations, parental consent appears to be mandatory and the wishes of competent children, whether to consent or refuse, are of no legal weight at all. This will be discussed in further detail, below.

In Scotland, the Age of Legal Capacity Scotland Act 1990 gives legal capacity to 16-year-olds to give legally valid consent on most matters, including medical treatment. There is no reason to suppose that this would not also cover consent to participation in medical research. Indeed, it seems to be the case that those under this age also have a statutory right to decide for themselves whether to take part. The wording in s 2(4) refers to those under 16 being deemed to have legal capacity to consent 'to any surgical, medical or dental *procedure or treatment*' (emphasis added). The use of these words is likely to be wide enough, not only to cover diagnosis and treatment, as in the FLRA 1969, but also to extend to medical research (Thomson, 2006). The level of understanding that a child must demonstrate and whether his or her views are determinative are unsettled in Scots law in general and there is no judicial authority on these matters with regard to medical research. However, my contention is that, to the extent that it seems more likely to recognise the autonomy of competent children, the Scottish approach is preferable.

The legal principles so far discussed have largely concerned domestic law,

---

60 *Gillick v West Norfolk and Wisbech Area Health Authority* 3 All ER 402, HL at 423–4.
61 *Re R (a minor) (wardship: medical treatment)* [1991] 4 All ER 177, CA. *Re W (a minor)-(medical treatment)* [1992] 4 All ER 627, CA.

but it is important to take into account the potential impact of international law, particularly as a result of the European Clinical Trials Directive 2001 and the consequent enactment of the Medicines for Human Use (Clinical Trial Regulations) 2004 (CTR 2004). Some points have already been referred to, but it is necessary to examine this in closer detail.

The Medicines for Human Use (Clinical Trials) Regulations 2004 (CTR 2004)

These regulations represent the first UK-wide attempt to legislate for the conduct of medical research with human subjects.[62] They were introduced as a result of a European Directive that set out requirements for trials involving medicinal products in Member States.[63] They include provisions on the conduct of such trials and their governance, including the establishment of ethics committees to oversee them. The Directive starts from the position that:

> The accepted basis for the conduct of clinical trials in humans is founded in the protection of human rights and the dignity of the human being with regard to the application of biology and medicine, as for instance reflected in the 1996 version of the Declaration of Helsinki.[64]

Nevertheless, the potential benefits of research are assumed, provided that there is appropriate protection for participants. Emphasis is placed on the need to give special protection to persons who are incapable of giving legal consent to participate and it is stated as a general principle that '[s]uch persons may not be included in clinical trials if the same results can be obtained using persons capable of giving consent'.[65] Additional considerations are to be taken into account where children may be involved, due to their developmental, physiological and psychological differences from adults, and their being seen as a vulnerable population.[66]

The Directive prescribes the circumstances where the involvement of children in clinical trials can be justified and these provisions have been incorporated into UK law by the CTR 2004. In this legislation a minor is defined as 'a person under the age of 16' which, while it is unexceptional for Scotland, is worth noting as being inconsistent with the usual definition of children in England and Wales, and also conflicts with the definitional subsets of

---

62 The Human Fertilisation and Embryology Act 1990 concerns regulation of research on in-vitro human embryos, but they are not regarded as having legal personality.
63 European Directive 2001/20/EC 4 April 2001. Medicinal products are defined in EU Directive 65/65/EEC, January 1965, Art 1.
64 EU Directive 2001/20/EC, 4 April 2001, Preamble, para 2.
65 Ibid para 3.
66 Ibid.

children set out in the paediatric investigation plans guideline.[67] A minor may be included in research only if:

- the clinical trial relates directly to a clinical condition from which the minor suffers or is of such a nature that it can only be carried out on minors;[68]
- some direct benefit for the group of patients involved in the clinical trial is to be obtained from that trial[69] *and*
- the clinical trial is necessary to validate data obtained in other clinical trials involving persons able to give informed consent, or by other research methods.[70]

This may be contrasted with the position for adults with incapacity under these regulations. Although for them it is also stated that the trial must be necessary to validate existing data, it is here required that the research 'relates directly to a life threatening or debilitating clinical condition from which the incapacitated adult concerned suffers'.[71] Furthermore, for incapacitated adults there must be 'grounds for expecting that administering the medicinal product . . . will produce a benefit to the subject outweighing the risks or produce no risk at all'.[72] The approach taken to including children in clinical trials is arguably less protective of them than incapacitated adults. No restriction is placed on the seriousness of condition that the child is suffering from and direct benefit to the research group, rather than the individual child, is sufficient. Interestingly, there is no attempt to proscribe research in the CTR 2004 by reference to the levels of risk that children may be exposed to. This remains likely to be governed by the existing guidance on this subject already discussed.

There are also additional points to note about the CTR 2004 in connection with its approach to consent. It is stated that a person can give informed consent only if his decision is given freely after being informed of the nature, significance, implications and risks of the trial, and the same definition applies where consent is given on behalf of the trial subject.[73] In line with the Directive's stipulation, the regulations require that either a person with parental responsibility or a child's legal representative must give his informed

---

67 CTR 2004 r 2(1). See, also, European Medicines Agency (2001) *ICH Topic E 11 Clinical Investigation of Medicinal Products in the Paediatric Population* CPMP/ICH/2711/99, para 2.5.
68 CTR 2004, Schedule 1, Part 4, para 9.
69 Ibid para 10.
70 Ibid para 11.
71 CTR 2004, Schedule 1, Part 5, para 11.
72 Ibid para 9.
73 CTR 2004, Schedule 1, Part 1, para 3(1).

consent to the child's participation.[74] A legal representative's consent can only be given if 'by reason of the emergency nature of the treatment provided as part of the trial, a person with parental responsibility cannot be contacted'.[75] In so far as parents are enabled to consent to their young children's participation in research, this may at first glance be regarded as no more than a statutory enactment of the common-law position. There are, however, a number of issues arising from this provision. The first is who the legal representative, if a parent is unavailable, might be. This is defined as:

(i)   a person, other than a person involved in the conduct of the trial, who –

  (aa) by virtue of their relationship with . . . that minor, is suitable to act as their legal representative for the purposes of that trial, and

  (bb) is available and willing to so act for those purposes, or

(ii)   if there is no such person, a person, other than a person connected with the conduct of the clinical trial, who is –

  (aa) the doctor primarily responsible for the medical treatment provided to that adult, or

  (bb) a person nominated by the relevant health care provider.[76]

The first alternative appears to envisage some connection with the child, but the nature of that relationship is not further explained. Certainly it does not appear to require a familial connection and it is questionable how broadly it may be construed. One would presume that it would not stretch to all professional relationships, such as that of a child's teacher, but could it include, for example, those involved with a child in care, like social workers? This question remains unresolved.

The second alternative is even more problematic since, in relation to adults, it allows for the medical practitioner caring for the child to act as the child's legal representative, provided s/he is not involved in the conduct of the trial. This in itself raises some questions about the proper role of clinicians, but aside from this, the section is silent as to whether a *child's* doctor can act in this way. This omission may be an oversight, but as it stands, it appears such involvement is not a possibility. Circumstances in which this situation may arise may be thought to be limited, but concerns were expressed over the potential difficulties in involving adults with incapacity in trials in emergency medicine because of the requirement to have the prior consent of the adult's

74 CTR 2004, Schedule 1, Part 4, para 4.
75 Ibid para 4.
76 CTR 2004, Schedule 1, Part 1, para 2.

legal representative (Beyleveld and Pattinson, 2006; Liddell, 2006). An amend-ment to the CTR 2004 was passed to enable incapacitated adults to be entered into clinical trials without satisfying the need for consent by a legal representative if the urgency of the situation did not make it reasonably prac-ticable to do so, and provided the trials have appropriate ethical approval.[77] However, this amendment concerns only adults and if the child's medical practitioner is not permitted to act as the child's legal representative, this does give less scope for the involvement of children in clinical research in emer-gency medicine. Whether there will be similar calls for amendments in this situation, taken together with other concerns about parents' capacity to give appropriately informed consent raised earlier, remains to be seen. Somewhat puzzlingly, draft guidance produced at European level, while recognising that the European Clinical Trials Directive 2001 does not permit deferred consent, notes how important emergency research may be and suggests that:

> In these situations, consent should be obtained according to national law. It has been suggested to obtain consent from one or several designated individuals, aware of the research purpose, but fully independent of the research team when the national law allows it. Ethics committee should assess the protection provided in such trials. Retrospective informed con-sent from the parent(s)/legal representative should be obtained as soon as possible.
>
> (European Commission, 2006, para 6.5)

While this approach would be in accordance with that taken by the ECB's additional protocol, described earlier, the call to circumvent the clear provi-sions of the Directive is remarkable. It is uncertain how Member States will respond to this, especially since, in the UK, the national law in respect of deferred parental consent is itself unclear. It seems that further amendments to the CTR 2004 to permit this, as with emergency research with incapacitated adults, would be at the least a helpful clarification, if not a legal requirement.

A further important issue is the position of the competent child. As we have seen, the common law has not given clear guidance on the extent to which competent children may be able to consent validly on their own behalf to take part in research. Nevertheless, it has been regarded as within the scope of their decision-making to do so, although the question of whether it can or must be considered to be in their best interests is unresolved. However, the CTR 2004 makes no mention at all of a requirement to obtain their consent and their refusal does not appear to be considered binding either. It is stated as a principle that:

---

77 The Medicines for Human Use (Clinical Trials) Amendment (No.2) Regulations 2006/2984, s 2.

> Informed consent given by a person with parental responsibility or a legal representative to a minor taking part in a clinical trial shall represent the minor's presumed will.[78]

The involvement of the child in decision-making is limited to the following conditions, that:

- The minor has received information according to his capacity of understanding, from staff with experience with minors, regarding the trial, its risks and its benefits.[79]
- The explicit wish of a minor who is capable of forming an opinion and assessing the information referred to in the previous paragraph to refuse participation in, or to be withdrawn from, the clinical trial at any time is considered by the investigator.[80]

Children under 16 therefore, whatever their competence, appear entitled to information disclosure about a proposed trial, but their consent is not of itself valid without the consent of a parent or legal representative, and their refusal of consent is only a matter to be considered. In relation to refusal of consent, the basis on which the final decision is to be made by the investigator is not further defined, but if it is read to mean that it depends upon a best interests evaluation, then it may reflect the position at common law in England and Wales. However, in respect of consent, the CTR 2004 appears to go much further in undermining the competent child's decision-making than even *Gillick* would allow. It also appears to be a complete departure from the legal position in Scotland on both counts and it contrasts sharply with the national and international guidance on this issue discussed earlier. Perhaps surprisingly, it also appears to be in conflict with the existing European legal approach on this matter, as set out in the ECB and its additional protocol on research, which provides that research may only be carried out on people who lack capacity if they do not object.[81] This being the case, allowing a competent child's refusal of consent to participate to be overridden must be prohibited also. The approach taken by the CTR 2004 is not one I can support, in light of my view that the wishes of competent children should take precedence, even for routine treatment. Acting against a competent child's wishes is even less justifiable where the benefits to be obtained are not contended to be for the child, but for others. These provisions must also be read in the light of further specific requirements in the CTR 2004.

---

78 CTR 2004, Schedule 1, Part 4, para 13.
79 Ibid para 6.
80 Ibid para 7.
81 ECB, Art 17 (1)(v), Additional Protocol to the Convention on Human Rights and Biomedicine, concerning Biomedical Research Strasbourg, Article 15(1)(v), 25 January 2005.

In terms of the protection of the interests of the child, aside from the considerations already mentioned, the Regulations state as principles that:

- The clinical trial has been designed to minimise pain, discomfort, fear and any other foreseeable risk in relation to the disease and the minor's stage of development.[82]
- The risk threshold and the degree of distress have to be specially defined and constantly monitored.[83]
- The interests of the patient always prevail over those of science and society.[84]

If the interests of the patient must be given precedence over the benefits to society it would seem difficult to argue that a competent child's refusal of consent can be disregarded.

Concerns about the stance taken on consent have already been raised by the House of Lords EU Sub-Committee on Social Policy and Consumer Affairs (2006, paras 65–73). It was noted that guidance on the ethics of studying children for the Clinical Trials Directive 2001 was being drawn up at European level. The Sub-Committee was, however, 'very troubled by this issue and not convinced from the evidence we have had that it has so far been given the necessary serious consideration' (House of Lords EU Sub-Committee on Social Policy and Consumer Affairs, 2006, para 72). It is hard not to share their unease when evidence given by the Minister of State for Health included the statement that she 'hoped that the guidelines would . . . avoid the possibility that deference to children's rights might undermine the randomness essential for successful trials' (House of Lords EU Sub-Committee on Social Policy and Consumer Affairs, 2006, para 71). There seems little concern here for the right to respect for autonomy or even priority being given to the interests of the research subject, compared with those of society. It appears that no help can be expected from the drafting of guidelines at European level either. At the time of writing, a draft has been produced which reiterates the position that even competent children's wishes to consent or refuse should not be determinative (European Commission, 2006). Indeed, it takes the view that children are only capable of giving assent and that consent must come from parents in all circumstances. It does say that:

> Objections raised by a child at any time during a trial should be considered. The child's will should be respected provided it is not considered

---

82 CTR 2004, Schedule 1, Part 4, para 14.
83 Ibid para 15.
84 Ibid para 16.

detrimental to his/her health. The child should not be forced to provide reasons.

(European Commission, 2006, para 7)

Applying a criterion of harm to a child's health to permit overriding their refusal of consent to non-therapeutic procedures seems hard to maintain, though it might perhaps be argued that they are necessary to monitor the safety of therapeutic components. Nevertheless, where there are alternative therapies available, even this weak justification may not be applicable. This might give some grounds for optimism that children's refusal of consent might in fact be required to carry more weight than the CTR 2004 implies. Nevertheless, this is far from a ringing endorsement of children's rights to self-determination. The House of Lords Sub-Committee recommended that 'in drawing up the guidelines underpinning the Clinical Trials Directive, the Government should ensure that particular attention is paid to the rights and capacity of children to give informed consent to trials' (para 75), but whether it will prove any more likely to make this the governing factor seems doubtful. Of course, it must be remembered that ethical and professional guidance does place a very high premium on the child's views, so it may be that, while legally permissible, in practice, researchers would not be prepared to act on the basis of parental consent where a child is clearly unwilling to take part. However, this does not seem to me to provide a sufficiently robust or principled safe-guard for the protection of children's rights and that ensuring the random-ness of clinical trials is not an adequate justification for riding roughshod over them. The approach adopted by the CTR 2004 shows a trend away from protecting even the slender rights of children provided by the previous position of the law, and as such is deeply worrying.

Conclusion

Innovative treatment may be required to deal with individual treatment situ-ations, especially where no alternatives exist. The benefits to be obtained from medical research with children have also been strongly advocated to the extent that failing to conduct such research may be seen to be unethical. Difficulties remain, however, in the justification for involving individual chil-dren in medical research projects, particularly where they involve no realistic prospect of benefit to them and where there may be a risk of harm or burdens imposed upon them. In this context, reliance on the welfare of the child or his or her best interests as being the paramount consideration would prevent much needed research from taking place and suggestions have been made to avoid this conclusion. The lack of legal clarity in this area is disappointing and despite the introduction of new legislation dealing with some aspects of medical research, many areas of doubt remain. It is particularly regret-table that, with increasing attention being paid to children's rights to act as decision-makers, recent developments may be seen as being disempowering in this respect. The best interests test is ill-suited to deal with innovative treatment and the therapeutic components of research, and even less so for non-therapeutic procedures. Instead, where incompetent children are concerned, parents should be permitted to enter children into trials, unless the level of risk of harm to them is believed to be unreasonable. Equally, where children are competent, their consent should be necessary and sufficient to enable them to choose whether to participate. The final area for consideration, where again the best interests test fails to meet the needs of the situation, is that where the interests of more than one child are before the court and the last chapter will address this issue.

Chapter 6

Best interests between children: donation of tissues and organs and conjoined twins

So far the cases considered have concerned making decisions for individual children. When parents make decisions for their incompetent children, I have suggested that it may be possible for reasonable parents to take into account a range of factors, which potentially could include the needs of other family members (see, also, Ross, 1998). The extent to which this should be permissible is controversial, but the issue comes into sharp focus where treatment for one child involves a medical procedure being performed upon another. This is most likely to occur where bone marrow or organ donations between siblings are proposed. The need to consider intrafamilial donations has become more pressing with the development of methods of assisted reproductive technology and pre-implantation genetic diagnosis. These make it possible for a couple to conceive a child that could then act as a tissue-matched donor for a sick brother or sister.[1] In the absence of effective alternatives, it can be expected that sibling donations, particularly involving very young infants, will be sought in increasing numbers. With older and competent children, the question of whether they should be able to make the decision to donate will also need to be asked. A more rare situation where medical interventions might be undertaken to benefit another child is that of conjoined twins. The most dramatic example of this in the UK has been the case of Jodie and Mary, where surgical separation was necessary to save the life of one, but would inevitably kill the other.[2] What these situations have in common is that medical procedures are being proposed to meet the needs of one child, but that have no medical benefit and in some cases considerable risk, even extending to the certainty of death, to another. If the proper test for the courts is the best interests of the child, how can this be applied when two children are involved and their best interests appear to be incompatible? These issues will be considered here.

---

1 This situation arose was considered in *Quintavalle v Human Fertilisation and Embryology Authority* [2005] UKHL 28, HL.
2 *Re A (children) (conjoined twins: surgical separation)* [2000] 4 All ER 961, CA.

Living donation of blood, tissues and organs

Blood and bone marrow donation

Blood transfusions are of course vital in many medical situations, ranging from the treatment of accident victims, people with blood disorders and as part of surgery. Blood contains several components that can be used for specific purposes, but although there are a number of blood types, these can usually be sourced from the general population and there is no need to seek donations specifically from children. The National Blood Service will only accept blood donations from those over the age of 17. Another important form of treatment involves bone marrow transplants. Hematopoietic stem cell transplantation (HSCT) involves taking stem cells from a donor and giving them to the recipient by an intravenous transfusion. Hematopoietic stem cells are immature blood cells that can develop into all of the different types. They can be taken from umbilical cord blood after the birth of a child or from peripheral blood, but most usually, when a transplant to another person is concerned, they are taken from bone marrow, where the greatest source of these cells can be found. Bone marrow donation may be the only hope for children with a number of disorders. Sometimes it is needed as a result of intensive radiotherapy or chemotherapy to treat types of cancer, such as leukaemia, where the bone marrow of the patient is destroyed and needs to be replaced by healthy new bone marrow. In other cases, the transplant is required to treat the condition itself, such as aplastic anaemias, immune deficiency and hereditary disorders. Many of these conditions are more common in, and may even be exclusive to, children. For the transplant to be most successful, there must be a compatibility of tissue types between donor and recipient, known as human leukocyte antigen (HLA) types. The best hope of an HLA match is within the family, specifically with a sibling, as 'there is a one-in-four chance that two children from the same family have the same tissue type'. As families in the UK are generally small, there is estimated to be around a 30 per cent chance of finding a suitable family donor (Scottish National Blood Transfusion Service, 1998, pp 3–4).

Apart from siblings, other members of a child's family have only a small chance of being HLA-compatible. There have been recent advances in techniques to use related donors who are not an exact tissue match, but this is only advised where the condition is life-threatening, because of lower success rates and higher risks of significant complications (Human Fertilisation and Embryology Authority, 2004, para 22). Outside the family, the development of national registries has increased the number of donors available to provide bone marrow, but the numbers needed to provide a suitable match from a general population would be around 150,000 donors to give a 50 per cent chance of a match (Scottish National Blood Transfusion Service, 1998, pp 3–4). It remains likely therefore that the first course of action for parents where a child has a condition requiring a bone marrow donation will be to request testing the child's brothers and sisters, or if there are none that are a suitable match, to even consider attempting to conceive one. There are a number of Bone Marrow Registries in the UK maintaining registers of potential donors. Although they will not accept people under the age of 18 as donors, they do not deal with donations taking place within the family.[3]

Risks associated with bone marrow donation

The procedure usually involves a general anaesthetic, with bone marrow being taken by aspirations from the hip and an overnight stay in hospital. There are risks associated with anaesthesia and any surgical procedure, such as bleeding and infection of the wound. Occasionally a blood transfusion to combat anaemia may be needed if the donor and recipient differ greatly in size, although the need for this can be minimised by processing the bone marrow in the operating theatre to return red blood cells to the donor (Browett and Palmer, 1996; see, also, British Medical Association, 2001, para 8.2.2). Other complications have been said to include the possible need for many needle insertions as part of the aspiration procedure, nerve damage and a higher risk of infection while bone marrow stocks replenish (Ross, 1998, p 113). Opinions differ as the degree of pain and discomfort experienced by donors and also about the level of risk involved. For example, Browett and Palmer suggest that:

> Discomfort after the procedure is usually mild and may be relieved with simple oral analgesics. . . . The overall risk of the procedure is low and for all ages of donors is comparable to that seen with other minor operative procedures.
>
> (Browett and Palmer, 1996, citing Bortin and Bucker, 1993)

Discomfort has however been described as 'moderate' in other research (Rowley *et al.*, 2001). The Department of Health (DoH) in guidance on consent to medical treatment in 2001 considered that '[d]onation of bone marrow can be painful and carries some significant risks. It is not a minimal intervention' (Department of Health, 2001a, ch 3, para 16).

In addition to physical risks of donation, there may be concerns about the donor child's emotional reaction. Macleod, Whitsett, Mash and Pelletier have reviewed some of the research into the psychological factors surrounding

---

3   The British and the Welsh Bone Marrow Registries are both part of the National Blood Service and the Registry. Scottish donations are sourced through the Scottish National Blood Transfusion Service, but are registered on the British Bone Marrow Registry. There is also the independent charity, the Anthony Nolan Trust.

bone marrow donation by children to siblings in their own study on the psychosocial experiences of children. They cite previous studies indicating a variety of responses to the illness in siblings and their role in treatment for them (Macleod *et al.*, 2003, p 224). It is noted that children are already in a stressful situation where a member of the family is chronically sick, which may result in negative feelings towards the sick brother or sister and lead to behavioural problems. Both donor and non-donor siblings have indicated feelings of loneliness, lack of understanding of the transplant procedures and lack of attention to them by their parents. Furthermore, donor children report feeling there had been a lack of choice about the decision to donate and an absence of support groups to help them. However, some psychological effects of donation deemed to be positive have also been cited: donor children seemed to show a greater sensitivity to other peoples' needs, greater levels of self-sufficiency and were more independent.

The research by Macleod, Whitsett, Mash and Pelletier looked at sibling donors in Canada where HSCT had been both successful and unsuccessful to try to establish if there were common and differing factors in the children's experiences. A number of themes emerged. Chief among them was the perception by children that they had no choice but to donate. Nearly all children said this but it is worth noting that two-thirds believed that this was due to their own moral beliefs rather than due to external pressure. Still, a third felt they were under pressure from families or doctors. Reluctance to donate was said to stem from fear of the procedures and pain associated with them, rather than a lack of desire to help. Interestingly, several of those who felt that they had not given a willing agreement at the time said that they probably would do so now, believing that their unwillingness had been due to their young age. Older donors were more able to take into account the effects of a failure to donate on their brother or sister, and unlike younger donors, were less focused on the immediate prospect of pain and fear in connection with the procedures.

Once the procedures had been performed, even younger children reported that, despite their fears, the degree of pain and discomfort was less than they had anticipated. Where transplants were successful, most donors described the process as having a mainly positive effect on them, including their feelings about themselves and others, their contribution to treatment and their understanding of their sibling's illness. Some positive feelings were also expressed by those where the donation had been unsuccessful, but much more common were negative responses such as anger, depression and, most frequently, guilt. While the researchers themselves advise caution in interpreting the study findings due, among other things, to small sample size, narrow demographics and imperfect recall by participants, nevertheless they do suggest that parents and doctors need to be much more aware of the differing approaches of older and younger children in order to provide them with age appropriate information and support. This needs to be considered, especially when it comes to assessing the child's competence and whether they are acting willingly, when agreeing to be a donor.

The studies therefore indicate a range of potential negative and positive experiences for child donors, much seeming to depend upon the outcome of the transplant. However, the British Medical Association (BMA) regards the available research as being conflicting and has stated that 'we are not aware of any clear evidence that bone marrow donation benefits the donor' (British Medical Association, 2005). Against this, it is important to remember that the kinds of experiences related by children in these studies would need to be weighed against those of children where donation was not undertaken, either because the child refused or consent was not given by parents to allow this to take place. If feelings of guilt may be experienced by children where donation had gone ahead, but had proved unsuccessful, it can be imagined that there would also be such feelings if death had resulted where transplantation was an option that was not pursued. The consequences to the family of the death of a child are inevitably serious and potentially extremely damaging and where it may be felt that this could have been avoided, they may be even greater. Research into this area is difficult to conduct and views on this remain speculative.

Despite bone marrow donation from children being regarded as an established procedure, its legality has not been tested by the UK courts (Human Fertilisation and Embryology Authority, 2004, para 15). The position of young children who are not considered competent to consent will be considered first.

Incompetent children

Information provided by one of the organisations registering bone marrow donors states that 'even young children have successfully donated bone marrow', though a minimum age for a donor is not given (Scottish National Blood Transfusion Service 1998: 6). However, it has been reported that:

> ... obtaining bone marrow for the treatment of siblings from children from the age of one year was a relatively routine treatment strategy where no other matched donor was available.
> (Human Fertilisation and Embryology Authority, 2004, para 26)

The difficulty in using the best interests test to authorise medical interventions of no medical benefit to the child has already been considered in the context of non-therapeutic medical research. It was suggested that the courts might expand the best interests test to allow medical interventions that are not against the interests of the child, provided that they involved no more than a minimal risk. However, it seems unlikely that the courts would be prepared to take this kind of approach (Mason and Laurie, 2006, para 19.12).

More probable is that in such situations, the procedures would have to be justified 'as being for other reasons in the child's best interests'.[4] The case in which Lord Hoffman made this statement – *Quintavalle* (2005) – involved judicial review of the refusal of the Human Fertilisation and Embryology Authority (HFEA) to permit pre-implantation genetic screening of an embryo to take place. The purpose behind the embryo screening was to conceive a child that would be free from an inherited disorder, but that could also, when born, act as a tissue-matched bone marrow donor for a sick sibling with the disorder. Accordingly, a determination of the lawfulness of a proposed donation was not directly in issue and a consideration of the issues raised by this case is outwith the scope of this discussion (see Gavaghan, 2007). Nonetheless, the *obiter* remark by Lord Hoffman on this point is consistent with guidance given by the Department of Health (DoH), which has advised that for interventions 'that would impose more than "minimal burden" on a child, such as bone marrow donation . . . to be lawful the intervention must be in the child's best interests' (Department of Health, 2001b, p 25).

It must therefore be considered whether bone marrow donation could meet the best interests test. The case of *R v Cambridge Health Authority, ex parte B* (1995) prompted some discussion of the issue in the UK. In this case, judicial review was sought of a Health Authority's decision to refuse 10-year-old Jaymee Bowen further treatment for acute myeloid leukaemia, based in part on resource allocation issues.[5] Its relevance here is that it was clear from the evidence that bone marrow had been taken from her younger sister and given to her as part of previous treatment. This was not thought worthy of any comment by the judge, although of course it was Jaymee Bowen that was the subject of the legal action, not her sister (Delaney, 1996; see, also, Mumford, 1998; Bridge, 1999b). Delaney reached the conclusion that a 'not against the interests of the child' standard would be insufficient to protect the child and that the best interest test must be applied. She went on to argue that while there are health risks to the child donor, as well as the pain and discomfort associated with the removal of bone marrow, 'the only positive aspects of the intervention are likely to be psychological'. If the child is too young to have established an emotional bond with the proposed recipient of the bone marrow, donation may be positively against the child's interests. She proposed that legislation should prohibit unauthorised donations and allow them only in the child donor's best interests. These would be determined by referring to a statutory checklist of factors, including the ascertainable wishes of the child. In addition, a forum independent of both the parents and the medical team, should consider each case. However, this forum could

---

4   *Quintavalle v Human Fertilisation and Embryology Authority* [2005] UKHL28, Per Lord Hoffman *obiter*, 38.
5   *R v Cambridge Health Authority, ex parte B* [1995] 2 All ER 129, CA.

either be an informal tribunal or an independent social worker, rather than necessarily being a court.

This article was responded to by a number of commentators, most of whom believed that this approach was too restrictive, in failing to give proper weight to the interests of the donor child in having a whole family, over-estimating the potential risks and burdens associated with the retrieval of bone marrow and not taking into account the view that parents are best placed to evaluate the needs of the child and the family, rather than an independent forum (Month, 1996; Savelescu, 1996; Browett and Palmer, 1996). However, as we shall see, there are echoes of Delaney's views in the way these issues have been dealt with in the case of an adult donor[6] and by the subsequent requirements set for bone marrow donations from incompetent children under the Human Tissue Act 2004 (HTA 2004) and the Human Tissue (Scotland) Act 2006 (HT(S)A 2006). These provide for a statutory regulator, the Human Tissue Authority (HTA), to review and approve such procedures; its role will be discussed later.

As far as the courts are concerned, the only reported UK case to consider the proposed donation of regenerative tissue involved an incompetent adult donor, *Re Y* (1997).[7] In respect of children, the statements made are therefore *obiter*, but it remains the most relevant guidance we have from the courts as to the factors likely to be taken into account in this area. A 36-year-old woman with non-Hodgkins lymphoma brought the case. Her condition was rapidly deteriorating and it was believed that a bone marrow transplant represented the best hope of saving her life, improving prospects of survival from, at best, 30 per cent to 40 per cent. Her sister, aged 25, was regarded as likely to be the best match for her, but she was severely mentally and physically disabled and incapable of giving consent. The older sister sought a declaration from the court to permit testing her younger sister and, if the results showed a match, to permit taking bone marrow from her for a transplant. The declaration for testing was granted.

It was clear to the judge that the correct test to apply was that of the best interests of the incompetent adult. If the procedures were not in her best interests, they would be unlawful and amount to assaults.[8] It was equally clear that the judge was not prepared to enter into a balancing test; weighing the risks and benefits to both sisters by holding that:

> The test to be applied in a case such as this is to ask whether the evidence shows that it is in the best interests of the defendant for such procedures to take place. The fact that such a process would obviously benefit the

---

6   *Re Y (adult patient) (bone marrow: transplant)* (1997) 35 BMLR 111, Fam D.
7   Ibid.
8   *F v West Berkshire Health Authority and Another* [1989] All ER 545, HL.

plaintiff is not relevant unless, as a result of the defendant helping the plaintiff in that way, the best interests of the defendant are served.[9]

Instead, the judge had to decide if there were benefits to the mentally incapacitated woman from donation and if so, whether these outweighed any possible detriment to her. It was not contended that Y had a close relationship with her sister, due in part to the fact that she was being cared for in a residential home and her sister's illness had prevented them from having much contact. However, she did appear to have a close relationship with her mother, and it was believed that the death of Y's sister would further affect the poor health of their mother. Along with the need to provide care for a grandchild that would be left behind in the event of her older daughter's death, this would mean the mother was less able to visit Y. These visits were regarded as valuable, providing Y with a link to her family and the outside world. Against this were the risks of the anaesthesia, which in this case were described by the judge as being 'extremely low: less than one per 10,000 and are no greater than those faced by the average patient in hospital'.[10] He also held that her pain could be controlled adequately and that she could be accompanied by a relative to reduce her anxiety. Accordingly it was held that:

> It was to the emotional, psychological and social benefit of the defendant to act as donor to her sister because in this way her positive relationship with her mother was most likely to be prolonged. The disadvantages to the defendant of the harvesting procedure were very small. The bone marrow donated by the defendant would cause her no loss and she would suffer no real long-term risk.[11]

The authorisation was limited to testing Y for tissue compatibility, and only if she did not appear to object. If she was a suitable match, the matter would have to return to the courts for a separate ruling on the actual retrieval of bone marrow, but no further application was reported.

Of course, this case concerned two adults rather than two children, and the best interests test applied only to the incompetent adult. It might be contended that the matter would need to be dealt with differently where two children are concerned, both of whose best interests should be considered. This does not in fact appear to be the position. The DoH has issued guidance on bone marrow donation from children lacking capacity as part of its general advice on consent to medical treatment. It stated that receiving a bone marrow donation may clearly be in the interests of the recipient child. However:

---

9 *Re Y (adult patient) (bone marrow: transplant)* (1997) 35 BMLR 111, Fam D, at 114.
10 Ibid at 116.
11 Ibid.

In relation to medical interventions it is not acceptable for the needs of one sibling to be balanced against the needs of another. The legal test is whether donating bone marrow is in the best interests of the healthy child.

(Department of Health, 2001a, Ch 3, Para 16)

While no authority is cited, as a matter of law this may simply be because only one child would be the subject of the proceedings – the potential donor. What is at issue is the lawfulness of a medical intervention upon a child that is not for his or her medical benefit. It is therefore only the donor child's best interests that the court is required to consider as being paramount. The situation may be different if more than one child is the subject of proceedings, as we shall see later in the context of conjoined twins. However, there are good reasons why a purely utilitarian calculation balancing the risks and benefits to both children should not be adopted. If it were, then this could permit high risks of pain and distress, and even long-term prejudice to the health of the donor, if the prospect of saving the life of the recipient were at stake. This might turn on the prospects of success and the quality of life to be achieved by the recipient, but it illustrates the dangers in ignoring the donor child's own rights to health and wellbeing.

Recent draft guidance by the Human Tissue Authority (HTA) for clinical teams and assessors concerning bone marrow donation from children states that:

It is a non-therapeutic procedure for the donor and the need for the person with parental responsibility and the clinical team to balance the interest of one child against others in the family may lead to a conflict of interest and the dangers of wrong decision.

(Human Tissue Authority, 2006e)

For the reasons given, this perceived need to balance interests does not appear to accord with the legal position. As we have seen, though, it is fair to say that the fact that there may be a temptation to take whatever steps are possible to save the life of a child is a valid concern. In this regard, the DoH notes that:

It may be extremely difficult for a person with parental responsibility who has one dying child to take a dispassionate view of the best interests of that child's healthy sibling. . . . Health professionals may also find it difficult to assess the needs of the children independently. However, without such dispassionate assessment the treatment may not be lawful.

(Department of Health, 2001a, para 16.1)

At present, then, it is only the best interests of the incompetent donor child that the courts must consider. It is therefore important to look at the way that the court approached this test in *Re Y* (1997). Feenan saw the case as being a step in the right direction in recognising that an incompetent adult's best interests might include non-medical factors.[12] The courts, of course, subsequently endorsed the relevance of a broader conception of best interests.[13] However, it was the emphasis on relationships that Feenan believed was of most interest. He suggests that this is important to 'redress the privileging of concepts of self-determination and autonomy in modern legal and ethical discourse in matters of healthcare' (Feenan, 1997, citing Campbell, 1994). This is particularly relevant where the individual has never shown capacity and no meaningful attempt to take autonomy-based principles into account can be made, as discussed in Chapter 4. A relationship approach has been taken by some American cases, most notably *Curran v Bosze* (1990), which was referred to at some length in *Re Y* (1997).[14] In this case, the Supreme Court of Illinois refused to authorise testing of twin 3-year-old children for bone marrow donation to their half-brother. It applied the best interests test and, basing its judgment on earlier American cases, focused particularly on the need for a close relationship between donor and recipient. Passages from the judgment quoted in *Re Y* include the following:

> ... there must be an existing, close relationship between the donor and recipient. The evidence clearly shows that there is no physical benefit to a donor child. If there is any benefit to a child who donates bone marrow to a sibling it will be a psychological benefit. According to the evidence, the psychological benefit is not simply one of personal, individual altruism in an abstract theoretical sense, although that may be a factor.

> The psychological benefit is grounded firmly in the fact that the donor and recipient are known to each other as family. Only where there is an existing relationship between a healthy child and his or her ill sister or brother may a psychological benefit to the child from donating bone marrow to a sibling realistically be found to exist. The evidence establishes that it is the existing sibling relationship, as well as the potential for a continuing sibling relationship, which forms the context in which it may be determined that it will be in the best interests of the child to undergo a bone marrow harvesting procedure for a sibling.[15]

In the *Curran* case, the parents were separated and the sick child lived with his father, who had requested the testing. The twins lived with their mother who

---

12 Compared with *F v West Berkshire Health Authority and Another* [1989] All ER 545, HL.
13 *Re SL (adult patient) (medical treatment)* [2000] 2 FCR 452, CA.
14 *Curran v Bosze* (1990) 566 NE 2d 1319.
15 Ibid per Calvo J at 1331.

refused her consent. In the circumstances, the court found that there was insufficient evidence of a close personal relationship between the children and hence testing and bone marrow donation was not in their best interests.

It seems that, as in *Curran*, the sisters in *Re Y* did not have a close sibling relationship, for the reasons described. If this was the critical factor in *Curran*, it suggests that testing ought not to have been allowed in *Re Y* either. However, it is arguable that the judge in *Re Y* took a much broader approach to best interests, allowing it to encompass 'emotional, psychological and social' benefits in terms of maintaining family relationships, not simply an emotional bond between the donor and recipient.[16] This focus on the effect of decisions on the wellbeing of the individual, rather than on the need to establish a particular relationship, appears to be the current thinking of both the UK courts and the legislation in respect of incompetent adults.[17] Some of the statements made in *Curran* might also be thought to pose difficulties in application to very young children (Delaney, 1996, p 240). Affection might well flow from an older child to a younger one but to say that, for example, an infant has developed the kind of close emotional bond that appears to be envisaged in the first paragraph, quoted from *Curran*, may be thought unrealistic. Against this, though, it must be remembered that the children there were not living in the same family unit and that in the second paragraph, what is required is simply an existing sibling relationship and the prospect of this continuing. That does seem likely to be satisfied where children are living together, whatever their ages. Although his position must be considered with some caution, given the earlier discussion on the difficulty in establishing psychological benefits and harms, Savelescu suggests that for young children:

> . . . even if the attachment or bond is only potential, donors in future enjoy a sense of achievement and the love and gratitude of a sibling who might otherwise have died. There are also benefits to the family. The relationship is affected by the health of other siblings. No child has an interest in living in a family under the shadow of avoidable, premature death.
>
> (Savelescu, 1996, p 241)

Nevertheless, if children are separated, for example living in different families or one is being cared for in hospital and there is little contact between them, the *Curran* approach appears more restricted than *Re Y*. *Re Y* would presumably allow testing and potentially donation to be authorised if, for example,

---

16 *Re Y (adult patient) (bone marrow: transplant)* (1997) 35 BMLR 111, Fam D.
17 *Re MB (an adult: medical treatment)* [1997] 2 FCR 541, CA; *Re A (medical treatment: male sterilisation)* [2000] 1 FCR 193, CA; Official Solicitor's Practice Note, July 2006; Mental Capacity Act 2005, Adults with Incapacity (Scotland) Act 2000.

the death of the sick child would affect the care of the proposed donor because of its likely impact on a parent.

Other issues also arise in the potential application of *Re Y* to children. It must be remembered that the risks and burdens of procedures, including anaesthesia and hospitalisation, may be greater on children, especially young ones, than on an adult. To extrapolate from *Re Y* and say that the risks of donation for a child are comparable with the average child undergoing similar operations is not necessarily an answer, since in the case of donation, the risks cannot be set off against any medical benefit for the donor child. Commensurately higher levels of more intangible benefit to counterbalance the risks would seem to be required, although the problems in predicting and evaluating such benefits have already been described. Serious doubts about the strength and quality of the evidence provided to reach the conclusions made even in *Re Y* have been expressed (Feenan, 1997; Kennedy and Grubb, 2000, pp 788–789). Quite how such evidence is to be measured and how broadly emotional, psychological and social benefits would be construed before donation can be said to be in a child's best interests is difficult to predict. Factors such as the likelihood of success of the transplant may need to be scrutinised particularly carefully and UK case law has not yet had the opportunity to factor this into the equation.

From the perspective of the intended recipient's best interests, health considerations are likely to be clearly in favour of permitting the donation to take place, although this should not be taken for granted. However, despite the possibility that a failure to obtain a suitably matched transplant would lead to the death of the intended recipient, it is highly improbable that s/he would have any enforceable right to insist on a sibling being a donor. It has already been said that a utilitarian calculation is impermissible where it may prejudice significant interests of a prospective donor. Even where the risks are low, although it may be a virtuous act to risk one's own health to save the life of another, and some go further to argue that there is a moral obligation to help others (Harris and Holm, 2003), translating this into a legal obligation would go far beyond what is presently countenanced. In the American case of *McFall v Shimp* (1978), a court refused to order that a man donate bone marrow to his cousin, even though it found the decision 'morally indefensible'.[18] Although it could be contended that obligations between siblings were more significant, this is contested (Jansen, 2004; Ladd, 2004). In any event, an incompetent child may not be capable of being regarded as a moral agent. As an alternative, Harris and Holm have argued that parents should treat children as if they were moral agents and be permitted to make decisions on that basis (Harris and Holm, 2003). Even if this were accepted, such an approach is still far from justifying the existence of a legal obligation on the proposed

18 *McFall v Shimp* (1978) 10 Pa. D. & C.3d 90.

donor or parents, or a right that can be claimed by the intended recipient, to proceed with removal of tissue from another person.

While there is no reported case law involving bone marrow donation by children, extrajudicial guidance has adopted a conservative stance. The DoH has referred to the provisions of the European Convention on Bio-medicine (ECB), Arts 20 and 6. These set out a general prohibition on removing organs and tissue for transplantation from a person who does not have the capacity to consent. Exceptionally, removal of regenerative tissue for transplant may be permitted under national law, provided that: there is no alternative means of treatment or source of material, such as from a deceased person or a compatible donor who can consent; the donation has the potential to be life-saving for the recipient who must be a brother or sister of the donor; authorisation has been given specifically by the indi-vidual's representative or a person or body authorised by law. The opinion of a minor must be taken into consideration as an increasingly determina-tive factor in proportion to his or her age and degree of maturity in all medical situations, but in the case of donation, a child must not object to the procedure. The World Health Organisation (WHO, 1991) also gives simi-lar guidance.

Of course, the UK is not a signatory to the ECB, so its provisions are not binding here. However, the DoH recommended as best practice that there should be some form of independent scrutiny of the donor child's best inter-ests. It was suggested, for example, that this could be by:

> ... an assessor who is independent of the team responsible for the sick child, or consideration of the case by a hospital clinical ethics committee or other multidisciplinary board convened for the purpose. If there is any doubt about the healthy child's best interests, a ruling from the court should be sought before undertaking the intervention.
>
> (Department of Health, 2001a, ch 3, para 16.2)

The courts' involvement was not seen as being a requirement for the lawful undertaking of bone marrow donation – the assumption appearing to be that a combination of the parents' consent, the willingness of the medical team to proceed and oversight by local scrutiny would suffice to protect the best interests of the child. It was only in cases where there was doubt (and presumably also disagreement) about this that resort to a legal forum was recommended. While independent review of the proposed donation was cited as best practice, it too was not mandatory (see, also, DoH, 2001b, p 20).

However, recent reforms have introduced new regulation in this area. Live tissue donation is now governed in England and Wales by the Human Tissue Act 2004 (HTA 2004) and in Scotland by the Human Tissue (Scot-land) Act 2006 (HT(S)A 2006). Both Acts are supplemented by additional regulations.[19] The scope of the legislation differs in the two jurisdictions. The HTA 2004 is a wide-ranging piece of legislation, which covers the storage and use of material from humans in a variety of circumstances and the removal of material from the deceased. It also creates a regulatory body – the Human Tissue Authority (HTA) – to oversee activities covered by the Act.[20] The guiding principle of the HTA 2004 is to obtain the consent of the person from whom the bodily material is obtained, if this is possible, although other people may be able to give consent if the person is unable to do so. Where material is being taken from a living person, the actual consent to removal is governed by common law with the storage and use of such material being governed by the Act (see also Human Tissue Authority, 2006c). However, an offence is created of removing or using transplantable material from a living donor unless conditions specified in the regulations are met.[21] Where material is removed from a living person, transplantable material is generally defined as being organs or parts of organs, bone marrow and peripheral blood stem cells: Human Tissue Act 2004 (Persons Lacking Capacity to Consent to Transplant) Regulations 2006 (the PLCCT Regs 2006). The conditions concerning competent children will be considered below, but if a child lacks capacity, additional scrutiny is required. This will be undertaken by the HTA.

In Scotland, the HT(S)A 2006 is primarily concerned with the removal and use of material from the deceased, but does have provisions concerning restrictions on transplants from live donors. Again, there are offences for removing or using organs, parts of organs or tissues from a living person for transplant, unless certain conditions are met.[22] In this statute, tissue is defined as including skin, corneas and bone marrow.[23] Where children who lack capacity are concerned, additional regulations set out the circumstances in which such tissues may be lawfully removed for transplant: The Human Organ and Tissue Live Transplants (Scotland) Regulations 2006 (the HOTLT Regs 2006). Although in Scotland the legislation is drafted to state that approval must be given by the Scottish Ministers, to ensure consistency across the UK, these decisions will in fact be made by the HTA (Scottish Executive Note, May 2006; HOTLT Regs, 2006; see, also, Human Tissue Authority, 2006f).

As a result, in Scotland and in England and Wales, donation of bone

---

19 These include the Human Tissue Act 2004 (Persons who Lack Capacity to Consent and Transplants) Regulations 2006, SI 2006/1659 and the Human Organ and Tissue Live Transplants (Scotland) Regulations 2006, SSI 2006/390.

20 HTA 2004, ss 13–15 and Sch 2. At the time of writing the draft Human Tissues and Embryos Bill (Cm 7087) is in progress which will combine the statutory functions of the HTA and the HFEA with the establishment of the new Regulatory Authority for Tissues and Embryos (RATE).

21 HTA 2004, s 33.

22 HT(S)A 2006, s 17.

23 HT(S)A 2006, s 60(1).

marrow and peripheral blood stem cells [PBSC] by children who lack competence to consent must be approved by the HTA. Such procedures must comply with statutory regulations[24] and Codes of Practice drafted by the HTA (Human Tissue Authority, 2006a and 2006d). An Accredited Assessor must first assess all cases where it is proposed to remove bone marrow for transplant from an incompetent child. The Assessor will act both as representative of the HTA and an advocate for the donor and must conduct an interview with a parent and the child, to the extent that the child is capable of being involved. The Assessor must be satisfied on a number of matters: that the person giving consent has been given and understood information; that there is no evidence of reward, coercion or pressure to consent; that there is no other suitable donor capable of giving consent; that the best interests of the child donor have been properly considered and that the family understand the nature of the procedure and any risks and side-effects. It is said that in some cases court authorisation may be needed to determine the issue of best interests, but this is not mandatory as a matter of routine practice. It has also been said in draft guidance to clinical teams and Assessors that the possible need to refer cases to court does not apply to Scotland, although no authority is provided for this and it seems doubtful (Human Tissue Authority, 2006e, p 5). The final decision whether to allow the child to provide bone marrow or PBSC rests with the HTA. The report submitted to the HTA remains valid for six months, but a new report is required if for some reason the approved transplant has not taken place within that time, in case circumstances have changed.

Despite concerns over the appropriateness of performing medical interventions that are of no medical benefit to an incompetent child, a broad construction of the best interests test might allow such decisions to be made. This seems to be assumed in current professional guidance and in the new regulatory frameworks that permit donation of regenerative material from children, subject to conditions. Nevertheless, no court ruling has made this explicit and it is of course my contention that this is not the correct test to be applied in any event. In line with the position I have taken throughout, it is whether the parents' decision poses a significant risk of serious harm to the child and whether it is unreasonable.

Many of the justifications I would put forward for applying this approach to bone marrow donation have already been considered in Chapter 5, when discussing non-therapeutic medical interventions on incompetent children, and they need not be repeated at length here. Suffice it to say that there are similar concerns about whether a child is being used solely as a means to an end: in this case, to save the life of a sibling (Holm, 2004, p 158). Applying the judge's reasoning in *Re Y* (1997) seems to suggest that there are stronger

---

24 PLCCT Regs. 2006 in England and Wales or the HOTLT Regs. 2006 in Scotland.

welfare arguments to support permitting donation than there are to permit non-therapeutic research, since the approach was taken that there are possible benefits to incompetent donors from helping a member of their family. If this is so, then these benefits would derive not just from abstract notions of altruisim and self-worth that may be generated, but due to the impact that the death of a brother or sister might have on the family, and hence to the care able to be given to the child. This is important to this line of reasoning because, as discussed previously, it is difficult to attribute ideas such as altruism to a child who is incapable of understanding them and in such cases, they would face the problems of retrospective approval.

The ability of parents to make decisions that will benefit the family has of course been strongly endorsed by Ross (Ross, 1998). She justifies parental decision-making in this context on a rather wider view of the benefits to be achieved. According to her view the idea is that in intimate families, 'the well-being of families is intertwined with the well-being of other family members . . . as such [a child's] participation benefits her indirectly' (Ross, 1998, p 114). Ross would allow parents to make decisions that would benefit some members more than others, provided that they do not harm the 'basic interests' of any of their children (Ross, 1998). So even if the care of the child would not be directly affected by the death of a brother or sister, as was argued would be the case for Y if her sister died, the damage to the family that would result could be taken into account in assessing the child's welfare. Nonetheless, the fact remains that in any donation scenario the primary motivation is to provide benefit to the recipient and any benefits to the donor child are incidental and uncertain. This has led writers like Jansen to conclude that it is a mistake to focus upon the interests of the family as if it were simply a freestanding entity since:

> This obscures a true and important fact about family members – namely, that, although they share interests and concerns, they also have interests and concerns of their own that can and often do come into conflict with the interests and concerns of other family members.
>
> (Jansen, 2004, p 135)

Given the doubts about the benefits to be obtained by donor children, I would suggest that allowing parents to consent to bone marrow donations by their incompetent children is more realistically justified on the basis that it is reasonable for parents to make decisions that take account of the needs of all their children, rather than because they are in the donor child's best interests. However, a parental power to consent to donation cannot be unlimited and this would rest on an assessment of the level of risks involved (see, also, Bridge, 1999b; a comparable point is made in respect of organ donation by Steinberg, 2004). It is legitimate for parents to decide how they bring up their children, and what the welfare of individual members and common goals for the family require. In doing so, they may choose to accept medical interventions on a child, which may expose him or her to some risks to achieve those objectives. This has been used as the justification for involving children in non-therapeutic research and the same must surely apply to donation of regenerative tissue. Crouch and Elliot have taken a similar line in denying the applicability of the best interests test to transplantation in general. They contend that:

> .... justification must rest on other grounds that take account of the fact that such transplantations are done not to advance the interests of the child donor as an individual, but for the sake of another family member, and for the sake of the family as a whole. Justification must reckon honestly with the risks to the donor, the likelihood that the procedure will succeed, the possible benefits to the recipient, and the potential alternatives. It must take account of the fact that parents have obligations not only to the child who is to donate the kidney, but to the sick child who is to receive it, whose life and welfare may be in mortal danger. And most crucially, any justification for sibling kidney transplantation must cast a critical eye on the question whether parents can legitimately expect their children to bear some burdens for the sake of family interests, even interests that the children might not yet explicitly endorse.
>
> (Crouch and Elliot, 1999, p 285)

These points are of course equally relevant here. The question remains: what level of burdens could a child legitimately be expected to bear on his or her family's behalf? Ross distinguishes between situations where there is a minimal-to-minor increase over a minimal risk, such as bone marrow donation, and those where there is a more than minor increase over minimal risk, such as kidney transplantation. She contends that it is legitimate for parents to consent to the former for incompetent children, but not the latter. This would increase the level of risk that parents could consent to, compared with non-therapeutic research, which is justified on the basis that a benefit to the family is envisaged. This adds an element that can be set off against the additional degree of risk.

Some are suspicious of this notion of intrafamilial trade-offs. Jansen's objections are based first on the idea already mentioned: that there is no such collective entity as 'the family' that has goals to be pursued and second, that this principle restricts child organ donation to family members of the organ donor, but that it is not possible to define adequately what the family is or how far its boundaries extend (Jansen, 2004, p 137; see, also, Ladd, 2004). Instead, Jansen prefers to consider the question in terms of 'intimate attachments', so that child organ donations are ethically permissible if there exists an attachment between the child donor and the recipient such that the wellbeing of the former depends, in part at least, on the wellbeing of the latter

(Jansen, 2004, p 140). In many cases, she recognises that this would still lead to parents being enabled to make consent to intrafamilial donations. However, it denies that simply being a member of a family is enough to justify imposing such burdens on a child, while at the same time expanding the potential number of people that parents or a court could decide warranted the child acting as a donor for, because this would advance his or her own interests. The idea here is attractive in that mere biological or genetic relationship is not necessarily sufficient and this has been recognised in cases such as *Curran*. It also focuses on the welfare of the child, which may be served by interests wider than those promoted by family membership. International guidance precludes organ donation except between siblings, but it may be that if the idea behind this is to safeguard a child's welfare then this might, in some cases, need to be reassessed.

Others may be unconvinced that parents should have the authority to make any decisions of this kind, since they breach the right to bodily integrity of the child and subject him or her to risks with no clear benefit that can be demonstrated. As Jansen notes, in the main this would rest on an interpretation of the child's best interests that denies the relevance of the social context in which the child is being cared for. Jansen cites Buchanan and Brock as an example of this kind of approach to best interests (Jansen, 2004, p 138 citing Buchanan and Brock 1973, p 226. She goes on to say that:

> This has made their principle vulnerable to the objection that it is based on an atomistic conception of the well-being of children, one that fails to give due weight to the interests they have in forming and maintaining intimate relations with others.
>
> (Jansen, 2004, p 138, quoting Schoeman, 1980)

My own view is that while there are doubts about the extent to which an individual child obtains benefit from acting as a donor, permitting parents to consent to this may be justifiable. I also consider that, where parents are believed to be properly concerned with the welfare of all their children, this would justify exposing a child to a slightly higher level of risk than would be justified for participating in therapeutic research. Thus far I broadly share the view suggested by Ross, although, as noted, I consider that welfare considerations might not restrict this to donations to siblings. However, given the uncertainty about potential risks and benefits, and the possibility for parents and those concerned with the care of the sick child to underestimate harm to the proposed donor, this is a situation where I consider that some independent scrutiny is justified.

The position taken by the legislation on court authorisation was set out earlier (Human Tissue Authority, 2006a and 2006d; Human Tissue Authority, 2006e, p 5). I have some reservations about this, particularly the approach suggested for Scotland. In some cases, the protection of the interests of the child may require judicial scrutiny and I can see no reason why this should not apply in both jurisdictions. However, my view would be that in most cases review by a body such as the HTA would provide an appropriate level of oversight, given the kinds of criteria for approval set out in the Codes of Practice. Resort to the courts would be required only where there were concerns over whether the proposed course of action would compromise significant interests of the prospective donor. A careful assessment of the possible risks and benefits to the individual child will still be necessary, but generally I would suggest that parents consenting to bone marrow donation would not be deemed to be unreasonable. Taking this line accepts that a child's welfare includes taking account of his or her social context and recognises parents' responsibility to safeguard the welfare of all their children. This does not allow parents to sacrifice the needs of the donor child to this end and this leads on to the question of the extent to which a child who is incapable of giving a legally valid consent must nevertheless not object to donation.

As we have seen, this is the position taken by *Re Y* (1990) and in the ECB and in the WHO draft guidelines (WHO, 1991). Ross, however, disagrees with this type of approach (Ross, 1998, ch 6). Unlike non-therapeutic research of a comparable level of risk, Ross suggests that parents should be enabled to override a child's dissent where there is a minor increase in risk over minimal risks involved in donation. This seems essentially to be because here, the parents are taking into account the needs of the family rather than the more general needs of society. As with non-therapeutic research, my contention is that the degree of distress that may be caused to a child who is reluctant to be a donor may take the decision out of the bounds of reasonable parental decision-making, since it increases the level of risk of harm to the child beyond acceptable limits. On this point, therefore, I do not share Ross's view. The assessment of risk is undoubtedly difficult, but it is not simply a utilitarian one based on the benefits to the recipient against the harms to the proposed donor. Similarly, the interests of the family cannot be permitted to harm significant interests of the child, which I would suggest would be the case if s/he were forced to donate. It could even be argued that forced donation would be contrary to the child's human rights, such as Art 3 of the European Convention on Human Rights (ECHR). Although procedures that are medically necessary do not amount to torture, inhuman or degrading treatment, that is where they are medically necessary for the person undergoing them.[25] Where a child has sustained objection to undergoing procedures for tissue removal, it is possible that this would be in breach of this Article. There are those perhaps who would say that any removal of material from an incompetent child for donation breaches this provision in itself, but I believe this position could only be maintained if donation was being undertaken using

---

25 *Herczegfalvy v Austria* (1992) 18 BMLR 48, (1992) 15 EHRR 437, ECtHR.

the child simply as a means to an end, not where considerations of the welfare of the child, as discussed, are being properly considered.

Competent children

In England and Wales, the common law has been said to govern the position on donations for everyone under the age of 18. Lord Donaldson stated that:

> A minor of any age who is '*Gillick* competent' in the context of particular treatment has a right to consent to that treatment which again cannot be overridden by those with parental responsibility, but can be overridden by the court . . . this common law right extends to the donation of blood or organs.[26]

As Mason and Laurie note there is some difficulty in interpreting this statement, since *Gillick* competence is logically irrelevant to those between the ages of 16 and 18 (Mason and Laurie, 2006, para 14.22). It seems to be a consequence of Lord Donaldson's view that the right to give consent under s 8 of the FLRA 1969 does not include non-therapeutic procedures, so some way of approaching the competence of people under 18 in such situations had to be found. It is important to remember that his statement was *obiter*, but this position has been taken in a number of guidelines (British Medical Association, 2001, para 8.24; Department of Health, 2001b, p 20; Human Tissue Authority, 2006d). An ability to give a legally valid consent is not determinative as it is still subject to being overruled by a court, if not a parent, if donation is deemed not to be in the best interests of the young person.

In England and Wales, the HTA, which now oversees organ and tissue donations, does not have responsibility for approving them where individuals are competent to give consent to bone marrow or PBSC donation. Whether they are adults or children, this falls outside the regulations and 'will continue to be approved locally' (Human Tissue Authority, 2006d, para 45) The medical team's leader must be satisfied that the requirements of the relevant HTA Code of Practice have been met and sign a declaration to that effect. He or she must also complete a consent form that includes a statement by the donor confirming the receipt and understanding of sufficient information to give informed consent. Neither the declaration nor the consent form need to be submitted to the HTA, but must be available to it on request (Human Tissue Authority, 2006d, pp 45–6).

The degree of understanding required to be shown by a child to consent to donation has been briefly stated in previous DoH guidance using the

---

26 *Re W (a minor) (medical treatment)* [1992] 4 All ER 627, CA.

formulation from Lord Scarman in *Gillick*: that the child shows 'sufficient understanding and intelligence to enable him or her to understand fully what is proposed' (Department of Health, 2001b, p 20). This prompts the question how young a child may be before s/he can be deemed to be *Gillick* competent to donate regenerative tissue. Evidence has been given to support the notion that quite young children may be able to make such a decision. Alderson and Montgomery, for example, argue that:

> Assumptions about the age at which children are able to make wise decisions tend to be based on ill-founded historical prejudices about children's supposed abilities and psychological research about their responses to hypothetical questions. Children who have experience of severe illnesses and treatments tend to give far more informed responses than inexperienced ones. Young siblings of children in need of bone marrow transplants are likely to know a great deal about the implications of offering or withholding this treatment and to have clear views of their own.
>
> (Alderson and Montgomery, 1996a)

All guidance emphasises the need to provide information in a way that the child will understand. Looking at the HTA's guidance, the information that should be given to children mirrors nearly exactly what is said to be necessary for an adult donor (Human Tissue Authority, 2006d, para 36 for adults, para 37 for children). There are minor differences, such as not giving details of the exact names of viruses that will be screened for. More surprisingly however, while adults must be informed that they have a right to be free of any coercion or threat against them or anyone else and that this would invalidate their consent, the comparable paragraph for children states only that:

> . . . they should feel free to discuss any worries with others members of the bone marrow transplant team (including nurses, play therapists, psychologists) and other family members, teachers or friends.
>
> (Human Tissue Authority, 2006d, para 37)

Given the serious concerns there may be about familial pressure to donate and that research suggests that children do not feel they have a choice whether to donate or not, the lack of a requirement to tell children as well as adults that their consent must be voluntary is puzzling to say the least. Despite this, where the child is competent, although it is regarded as best practice to seek the views of parents and to try to involve them in decision-making with the child, it is also clearly stated that 'the decision to consent must be that of the child' (Human Tissue Authority, 2006d, paras 45–7 and 28). This seems to rule out the possibility of parents overriding an unwilling competent child and insisting that a donation take place. While the role of the courts is not mentioned, the same would surely be true for them also. If it is controversial for the courts to override children's refusal of their own medical treatment, it must be even more doubtful that it could ever be said to be in a child's best interests to have tissue compulsorily removed to treat another. There is also the possibility that this would be a breach of the child's human rights under Arts 3 and 8 of the ECHR. The consent of a competent child, then, would seem to be necessary and sufficient for donation to proceed, although, notwithstanding my reservations on this matter, it might still be possible to refer the matter to a court if there were doubts about the donation being in his or her interests.

Paradoxically, however, despite the widely taken view that children in Scotland have greater powers to make decisions about medical matters than those south of the border, in respect of bone marrow donation, this appears to no longer be the case. The wording of s 2(4) of the Age of Legal Capacity Scotland Act 1991 (ALC(S)A 1991), which governs consent by those under the age of 16, does not refer to treatment, but to medical procedures. Accordingly, it had been argued that the effect of this was that competent children could consent to non-therapeutic measures including tissue and even organ donation (Sutherland, 1999, para 3.69; Thomson, 2006). This was the position taken by the Scottish Law Commission in its report, which paved the way for the ALC(S)A Act 1991 (Scottish Law Commission, 1987, paras 3.76–8). Of course, it would be dependent on children being deemed to have legal capacity as a result of the medical practitioner's assessment of their 'understanding of the nature and possible consequences' of what was proposed and, in addition, there remained the thorny issue of whether such consent could be trumped by an application of the best interests test. Nevertheless, it seemed that in principle there was no difficulty in competent children being able to consent to donation of regenerative tissue and their consent was sufficient.

As a result of the HT(S)A 2006 and the HOTLT Regs 2006, even where children are deemed competent to consent to such procedures, their consent is not now regarded as being sufficient. The decision whether to allow the donation to proceed must be made by the HTA, acting on behalf of the Scottish Ministers. In considering an application, the HTA can take into account the views of those with parental responsibility, although a local authority has no standing in this regard.[27] As with incompetent children, the HTA will need to be satisfied that the requirements of the regulations and its Codes of Practice have been satisfied. There are a number of matters that must specifically be considered by the HTA. These are set out in the HOTLT Reg 2006 and are the same as are required for an incompetent child. They include the need to interview the parents and child, and to be sure there is proper understanding

27 HOTLT Regs 2006, Part 4, para 5. See, also, Human Tissue Authority (2006) *Scottish Annex: requirements relating to live donations*, London: Human Tissue Authority, 3.

of the procedures and that there has been no duress or coercion.[28] Obviously the interview with the child assumes more legal significance where it is the child that is providing consent to the procedures but, while it would be expected that the views of a competent child would carry more weight than one who is not competent, in Scotland, relying on a competent child's consent alone is no longer lawful.

My views on this can be stated briefly and are that once a child is deemed to be competent and provided that the choice is sufficiently voluntary, the child should be able to give his or her own consent. There is no place for a best interests test in this situation. While Ross also agrees that best interests is not the correct test to be applied, in line with the position that she takes to competent children as discussed in Chapter 1, she contends that they should only be able to give assent. Agreement to act as a donor would require the parents' consent. Furthermore, she believes that parents should be able to override a competent child's dissent because:

> . . . the risks and likelihood that a bone marrow donation will threaten [a child's] short-term and life-time autonomy is small and the risk must be balanced against the potential harm that his refusal can cause his family.
>
> (Ross, 1998, p 118)

This is not a view I can endorse here any more than I have done previously. However, since there are legitimate concerns over the voluntary participation of children in this scenario, I believe that there is something to be said for requiring independent scrutiny of the process of obtaining consent, by, for example, a body such as the HTA. The HTA's role here would not be to give approval but simply to ensure that appropriate, impartial advice has been given and that the child has been made fully aware of the need for the decision to be his or her own. The HTA could make recommendations as a result of its enquiries, but would not have the responsibility for authorising the procedures to take place. My position is therefore that both parents of incompetent children and competent children should be permitted to give consent to donation of regenerative tissues. Even more contentious than this situation is, however, whether non-regenerative tissues or organs can be removed from children to treat a sibling.

Organ donation

By far the majority of organs used in transplants are from deceased donors. However, the number of living donations in general is increasing with the most common organ donated by a living person being a kidney. This is

28 HOTLT Regs 2006, Part 4.

because, from the perspective of the donor, a healthy person can usually be expected to lead a normal life with only one functioning kidney. For the recipient there are also advantages. Kidneys transplanted from living donors have a better chance of long-term survival than those transplanted from people who have died. There are a number of reasons for this, chiefly that the donor is alive and healthy so that the organ that is taken will be in optimum condition.[29] The operation can also be performed electively, allowing thorough testing and preparation of both donor and recipient to perform the procedures at the most appropriate time. In 2005–2006 nearly one in three of all kidney transplants were from a living donor (NHS Blood and Transplant, 2006). These figures do not give any information about the number of child donors or if indeed there were any in the time frame covered, although as we shall see, this seems unlikely.

NHS Transplant UK is responsible for providing support for transplant services and since 2005 has operated as a division of UK Blood and Transplant. It reported that in 2006, the average waiting time for a kidney transplant for children was between six to 12 months and for some children the wait could take up to five years.[30] Where a child is involved, donors are normally close relatives with parents being the most usual donors. However, the British Transplantation Society and The Renal Association point out that, in common with bone marrow donation, HLA typing is highly significant to the success of the transplant. Again, siblings provide the best chance of a match, put at one in four. Another point they note is that:

> ... when a poorly matched kidney transplant fails because of rejection the recipient is at high risk of becoming highly sensitised, restricting options for repeat transplantation. This is relevant for paediatric recipients who are likely to require re-transplantation within their lifetime and for whom avoiding sensitisation, particularly to common antigens, is important.
>
> (British Transplantation Society and The Renal Association, 2005, para 8.2)

The implications of this are that using the best matched tissue possible may be even more crucial for a child than an adult, given the increased likelihood of the need for further transplants.

The procedures and risks involved in kidney donation are outlined by UK Transplant. Removing a kidney in the UK takes place under general anaesethetic and has usually involved open surgery, making an incision in the side or abdomen. Increasingly, keyhole surgery may be used instead. The average

29 See the website of UK Blood and Transplant. Http//:www/uktransplant.org.uk.
30 Ibid.

stay in hospital after surgery is between four to 10 days. Strong pain relief is needed afterwards and antibiotics may also be required. It is stated that:

> All operations carry some risk and this is no different for living donation. Donors are at risk of infections (eg chest, wound or urine) and, more rarely, bleeding or blood clots. There is a very small risk of death for the donor: this is estimated at 1 in 3,000 for this operation.[31]

These risks may be expected to concern adult rather than child donors and specific or additional risks to them are not given.[32] Ross also notes that there may be major perioperative complications and that even without them the recovery period may last several weeks (Ross, 1998, p 111). Although the discussion here will concentrate on kidney transplants, other organs from living adult donors that are currently used for transplants include part of a liver or lung and in a very small number of cases, part of the small bowel. The same legal and ethical principles would apply to any proposed non-regenerative organ donations from children.

The removal of non-regenerative organs from children may be viewed with particular unease. Indeed, there is international guidance that specifically prohibits this practice. For example, the WHO Draft Guiding Principles on Human Organ Transplantation specifically forbids organ donations from living children.[33] Article 20 of the ECB also bans the donation of non-regenerative organs by an incompetent person. The BMA shares this view and has stated that 'minors should not donate whole organs and only competent adults should be considered as live donors' (British Medical Association, 2001, p 161). It is also the position of the British Transplantation Society and Renal Association in their joint guidelines on the matter where they state that:

> The moral arguments for not subjecting young people, under the age of 18 years, to the rigours of living kidney donation are compelling and minors should rarely be considered as potential living donors unless sanctioned by the court. There are genuine concerns about autonomy and the validity of consent from minors in this situation.
>
> (British Transplantation Society and The Renal Association, 2005, para 3.5)

There has been limited legislation covering organ donation. It banned commercial dealing in organs and donation of organs from living donors except

---

31 Ibid.
32 Ibid.
33 WHO Guiding Principles on Human Organ Transplantation 1991, Principle 4.

to genetic relatives and to people with close personal relationships, although the latter had to be approved by The Unrelated Live Transplants Regulatory Authority.[34] Independent review was thought necessary to ensure that donations by unrelated people were not subject to coercion or pressure and, in particular, were not prompted by any prospect of financial reward. Donation of organs or parts of organs between relatives was not dealt with by statute, despite the possibility that pressure to donate may be at least as significant within families as where payment is involved. This framework has now been replaced by the Human Tissue Acts but, since they deal with a broader range of issues, before turning to them it is worth setting out how the law stood before their enactment.

Although there have not been any cases directly concerning organ donation by children in the UK, some *obiter* remarks have been made about the common-law position in England and Wales, so far as it concerns a competent child, in *Re W* (1992).[35] Lord Donaldson took the view that a child could be *Gillick* competent to consent to some donations, such as blood, but he considered that:

> Organ transplants are quite different and, as a matter of law, doctors would have to secure the consent of someone with the right to consent on behalf of a donor under the age of 18 or, if they relied upon the consent of the minor himself or herself, be satisfied that the minor was '*Gillick* competent' in the context of so serious a procedure which could not benefit the minor. This would be a highly improbable conclusion.[36]

As has been said, applying the notion of *Gillick* competence to 16–18-year-olds is dubious, but given Lord Donaldson's construction of the FLRA 1969, it was clearly difficult to suggest how else to proceed. Whatever the justification for this, it suggests great reluctance to permit a child or young person to consent to donation, by setting the standard of competence at such a high level that it is 'highly improbable' a minor could attain it. The degree of misgiving shown by Lord Donaldson over the donation of organs by children was further illustrated by what he next went on to say:

> But this is only to look at the question as a matter of law. Medical ethics also enter into the question. The doctor has a professional duty to act in the best interests of his patient and to advise accordingly. It is inconceivable that he should proceed in reliance solely upon the consent

---

34 The Human Organs Transplants Act 1989 and the Human Organ Transplants (Unrelated Persons) Regulations 1989, SI 1989/2480.
35 *Re W (A Minor) (Medical Treatment)* [1992] 4 All ER 627, CA, per Lord Donaldson at 634.
36 Ibid.

of an under-age patient, however '*Gillick* competent', in the absence of supporting parental consent and equally inconceivable that he should proceed in the absence of the patient's consent. In any event he will need to seek the opinions of other doctors and may be well advised to apply to the court for guidance . . .[37]

No case has directly addressed this issue but the strong inference is that the courts should be asked to consider whether donation is in the best interests of competent children. If this is the case, then it must surely be at least as applicable to children who are incompetent and I will look at their position first.

The need for court approval for serious, irreversible or controversial operations on incompetent children has been considered in Chapter 2. Proposing that the courts should play a role in protecting the interests of the proposed donor child, where s/he is incompetent, would therefore seem to follow. According to *Re Y* (1997), the fact that the donation would be in the recipient child's best interests cannot be weighed in the balance against the best interests of the proposed donor. Indeed, such is the comparative seriousness of the removal of a non-regenerative organ, such as a kidney, that even a broad version of the best interests test, encompassing 'emotional, psychological and social' factors might not be sufficient to allow donations to be made. In *Re Y* (1997), for example, the perceived low risks of testing for bone marrow donation were a highly significant factor and the judge was careful to say that his judgment should not be taken as a precedent where more intrusive non-regenerative donations were at issue.[38] The position in Scotland has not been addressed by the courts, but it might be expected to follow that in England and Wales.

Some American case law has permitted parents to consent to the removal of a kidney from one of their children to be given to another using the best interests test. In *Little v Little* (1979), removal of a kidney from a mentally incompetent 14-year-old girl for transplant to her younger brother was authorised by the court and approved on appeal.[39] The close relationship between the children was emphasised along with the girl's apparent awareness of her brother's condition and that she could help him. The risks to her, both physical and psychological, were held to be minimal, but the psychological benefit to her predicted to be substantial. Authorisation was not to be regarded as automatic, however, and was refused in *Richardson* (1973). Here, the court was asked to consider a proposed donation from a 17-year-old with the mental age of a young child. It held that a court was empowered to

---

37 *Re W (A Minor) (Medical Treatment: Court's Jurisdiction)* [1993] Fam. 64, 78–9.
38 *Re Y (adult patient) (bone marrow: transplant)* (1997) 35 BMLR 111, Fam D, at 116.
39 *Little v Little* (1979) 576 SW 2d, Tex.

authorise the transplant, provided it was in the minor's best interests, but before ruling on best interests:

> It must be clearly established that the surgical intrusion is urgent, that there are no reasonable alternatives, and that the contingencies are minimal. These requirements of prerequisites are not met in this case.[40]

Accordingly, the court did not need to consider the donation further. Nevertheless, to say that a court could *never* be persuaded that donation from an incompetent was in his or best interests would clearly be too sweeping a statement.

In England and Wales, where older children with no mental incapacity are concerned, it seems it may be very difficult to convince a court that a child is *Gillick* competent to make a decision of this kind for himself or herself. It is likely that cases would deal with the child on the basis that s/he is incompetent. Even if a court was prepared to hold that the child's decision was sufficiently informed and voluntary, there remains the question whether it would use the best interests test to override it. There would be greater scope to take into account a competent child's views than those of an incompetent child, which might make it easier to meet a best interests standard, but it is by no means certain that court approval would be given. By contrast, in Scotland, as noted earlier, it has been thought that under s 2(4) of the ALC(S)A 1991, competent children could give a valid consent to organ donation and that this is not subject to a best interests test, although this position has not been tested by the courts.

The position of the law has now changed with the enactment of the Human Tissue Acts. Previous legislation on organ transplants has now been replaced and expanded by the HTA 2004, the HT(S)A 2006 and the creation of the HTA. The HTA now has responsibility for approving all living donor organ transplants. As with the position on donation of regenerative tissue, there are however some differences between the Scottish and the English and Welsh position. In Scotland, a child (a person under the age of 16) can only be a donor of regenerative tissue (including bone marrow and peripheral blood stem cells), not organs or parts of organs unless the donation is taking place as part of a domino transplant operation.[41] A domino transplant operation involves removing additional organs to impaired ones for ease of surgery. This may happen where, for example, heart and lungs are removed in a block, but the heart is healthy and may be given to someone else. Additional regulations are also in place in Scotland, specifying more details about the proper conduct of live transplants, to the limited extent they are permitted

---

40 *In Re Richardson* (1973) 284 SO 2d 185, La.
41 HT(S)A 2006, ss 17 (1), (2), (4) and (6).

(HOTLT Regs 2006). A Scottish annex to the HTA's Code of Practice on transplantation sets out the main features of the Scottish legislation (Human Tissue Authority, 2006f). For incompetent children, given some of the observations made earlier about the effect of a sibling's death on the family and the possibility that in exceptional cases broader welfare issues might even satisfy a best interests test, it may be asked whether a complete ban on non-regenerative organ donations, apart from domino transplants, is an appropriate response. The gravity of donating an organ or part of one and its irreversibility, seems to have persuaded the Scottish Parliament that no psychological or social welfare considerations can ever outweigh the physical and emotional risks of such procedures. This is in line with the view taken by international statements already discussed (WHO 1991, ECB). What is rather more surprising though is that this approach reverses what has generally been regarded as being the greater respect shown towards competent children in Scotland, since it bans most organ donations irrespective of the child's competence. The only reason for this must be importing welfare considerations into an area where they were not previously thought to be relevant.

In England and Wales the legislation does permit the donation of organs by children, with certain conditions. The provisions of the relevant regulations and HTA Code of Practice must be complied with (PLCCLT Regs 2006; Human Tissue Authority, 2006b). The Code of Practice states that the removal of solid organs remains governed by the common law and that as a matter of good practice such cases should be referred to the courts, regardless of the child's competence. This reflects the concerns addressed earlier that such serious procedures should be subject to oversight by the judiciary. In addition, having obtained court approval, they must also be approved by the HTA (Human Tissue Authority, 2006b, para 28). Whether the courts would be keen to be asked to authorise a donation in the knowledge that it may not be approved by the HTA is open to question. It might be thought that they would wish to take into account the views of the HTA before making a ruling.[42] Nonetheless, in this instance, it is unusually the English and Welsh approach that is more permissive than that in Scotland.

My view is of course that parents should only be able to consent to donation of organs from incompetent children under the principles I have set out previously. Accordingly, although it would be likely to be an exceptional case that would satisfy the reasonableness test, in the light of the serious and irreversible nature of organ donation, it would not be impossible and a total prohibition is not appropriate. All such cases should be referred to the courts and I would suggest that review by the HTA should be a preliminary to this. Where competent children are concerned, again the criteria that I would apply are competence and voluntariness. As for the donation of regenerative

42 See, for example, the statement in *Simms* by Butler-Sloss.

tissue, I consider that an independent review of the consent process would be appropriate although, again, the HTA would not be responsible for approving the decision. Since the criteria under my scheme rely on respect for autonomy, not the best interests of the child, it is debatable whether the courts should be asked to consider such cases. It might be suggested that particular care need be taken in assessing the competence of the child because of the gravity of the procedures. As I have argued, I do not believe that this is a relevant factor. It is the complexity of the decision that requires higher decision-making skills. Nonetheless, given the short- and possible long-term consequences for donors, such decisions do raise potentially complex issues. Furthermore, there are reservations about the voluntariness of the child's decision, which might be said to warrant a higher level of scrutiny. On balance, I believe that these issues could be adequately safeguarded by independent oversight by the HTA although, in appropriate cases, judicial review might be thought appropriate. Any dissent from the child should be decisive (see, also, Ross, 1998, p 118).

In concluding this discussion, whatever the legal framework might be, it has been said that in fact 'transplant surgeons have developed their own code of practice, in respect of live donation by minors' (Mason and Laurie, 2006, para 14.25). Mason and Laurie report that their inquiries indicated that no currently practising British transplant surgeon would accept an organ donation from a living child and only one case, involving 17-year-old identical twins, has arisen in the UK in the last 20 years. This once more raises the matter of the control of doctors over what procedures they are prepared to perform and it is hard not to share Mason and Laurie's feeling in consequence that 'discussion of the matter lies at the academic rather than the practical level' (Mason and Laurie, 2006, para 14.25). Whether the reluctance of surgeons to proceed is justifiable would depend on the reasons for it. If it is based, for example, on a denial that a child could be competent to give a legally valid consent or because it is believed it can never satisfy welfare considerations, then for the explanations I have given under my proposals, this becomes more open to question. Having considered the position on donation, one last situation where the best interests test may fail to provide a suitable means of determining the issues is that of conjoined twins.

Conjoined twins

In the case of transplants, only the prospective donor is likely to be the subject of the best interests test. However, the case of the conjoined twins, Jodie and Mary, in 2001, presented substantial difficulties for the courts, since each child's best interests was required to be the court's paramount consideration.[43] The case is well known, so only a brief outline of it will be given here.

---

43 *Re A (Conjoined Twins)* [2000] 4 All ER 961, CA.

The parents of the twins were Maltese, but had chosen to have the babies delivered at a Manchester hospital for specialist care after discovering during the pregnancy that the twins were ischiophagus conjoined twins. The babies were joined at the hip through their lower spines and spinal cords and they shared some organs, including a bladder and an aorta. Although Mary had a heart and lungs, these did not work and she was dependent upon Jodie for the circulation of blood. Mary also had additional severe problems, including very compromised brain functioning to the extent that she was described as having only 'a primitive brain', but Jodie appeared to have normal brain function and responses.[44]

Mary's condition meant that if matters were left as they were, Jodie's heart and lungs could not continue to support them both indefinitely as they grew. It was estimated that within six months to two years, Jodie's heart would cease to function and the twins would die. Alternatively, it was thought possible that Mary would die sooner, through an event such as blood vessel thrombosis. If this happened, the twins would have to be separated in an emergency procedure to try to preserve Jodie's life. The prospects of saving Jodie in this situation were estimated to be about 40 per cent. If, however, the twins were separated now under controlled conditions, then the chances of saving Jodie were estimated as being nearly certain, at 94 per cent. The only way to achieve this would be to shut off the blood supply from Jodie to Mary first, which would of course result in Mary's death. If, as expected, Jodie survived, she would still have physical abnormalities that would need operations, but it was thought that she could still lead a relatively normal life. The parents refused their consent to this surgery, based on their religious beliefs. They were Roman Catholics and felt it was against their faith to kill one of their daughters to save the life of the other. Faced with this situation, the hospital's trust sought a declaration from the courts that separation would be lawful. A declaration was granted but the parents and the Official Solicitor appealed the judgment. The Court of Appeal also granted the declaration and the surgery was performed. As a result, Mary's death was inevitable, but Jodie survived and has been subsequently reported as being a normal baby and likely to have an excellent quality of life (Reid, 2001).

The case provoked great controversy in the media and has produced reams of academic commentary because of the legal and ethical minefields through which the court had to walk (for a range of useful discussions see, for example, Clucas and O'Donnell, 2002; Freeman, 2001; Harris, 2001; Huxtable, 2001; Michalowski, 2001 and 2002). While to some, the decision was morally and legally defensible, to others it set a dangerous precedent reached by highly dubious reasoning. There are many areas of significance

---

44 Ibid per Ward LJ at 975.

covered by the lengthy judgment, but the main focus of interest here is the way in which the court approached the best interests test in this complex situation.

The legal personality of Mary

The first issue that needs to be considered is whether in fact there was a conflict of interests. If it was judged that because of Mary's compromised condition she was not a person, then only Jodie's interests would fall to be considered. Both Mason and Harris have discussed this in some detail (Mason, 2001; Harris, 2001). Both conclude that Mary should not have been regarded as a living person, though for very different reasons. Mason contends that on the medical evidence Mary should have been termed to be heart-lung dead at birth. He suggests that, if it had wished to, the court could have concluded that 'Jodie was born attached to her still-born sister' (Mason, 2001). There are significant problems with the definition of when a child is born alive and what criteria are appropriate, as noted in Chapter 4. In addition, as Mason acknowledges, the medical evidence on Mary's condition at birth was not conclusive.

Harris, in line with his well-known account of personhood, argues that neither Mary nor Jodie were persons at the time of the surgery (Harris, 2001, p 234; for further discussion of his views on personhood, see Harris, 1985 and 1996). He states that:

> Persons, whom I believe are characterised by possessing the capacity to value existence, can be harmed by being killed or allowed to die because they may thereby lose something they value. Non-persons, which lack such a capacity cannot, by hypothesis, be deprived by death of something they could coherently be said to value.
>
> (Harris, 2001, p 234)

Accordingly, neither Mary nor Jodie were persons in this sense and, to him, this explains why it was not unethical to operate in the knowledge that Mary would die. On the other hand, he argues, that had the wishes of the parents been followed, this would not have involved the premature death of any persons either. Like Mason's proposition, Harris has the benefits of avoiding the potential for conflict between children's interests, though in this case he does so by denying that failing to intervene can harm either of them. Clearly though, his views do not represent the current approach of UK law. Despite the possibility for more detailed scrutiny of Mary's legal status, the court concluded with very little discussion that Mary was a legal person and hence deserving all the protection that the law accords to children – the same as her sister Jodie.

The problem of best interests

Unlike the situations discussed earlier, then, both children had to be considered to be the subjects of the legal action before the court. Medical intervention would be upon shared parts of the body and would affect both, so it could not be treated as being an application on behalf of one or other of the children. An attempt to suggest that the operation would be performed on Jodie and not on Mary was dismissed by Ward LJ:

> If it is theoretically possible to cut precisely down the mid-line separating two individual bodies, that is not surgically feasible. Then the doctors have to ascertain which of the organs belong to each child. That is impossible to do without invading Mary's body in the course of that exploration.[45]

The welfare of both children, then, according to the Children Act 1989 (CA 1989), had to be the paramount consideration of the court. How this was to be achieved proved difficult, given that seeking the best chance of saving the life of one would inevitably kill the other. While much of the judgment concentrates on the issue of whether separation would be lawful in the context of the criminal law, it was stated that this was only the second stage of the court's enquiry, the first being to determine whether the separation would be in each child's best interests.

This first stage of enquiry was dealt with by Ward LJ and his position on this was adopted by Brooke LJ; so on this the majority in the Court of Appeal were in agreement. At first instance, Mr Justice Johnson had stated that it was not appropriate to enter into a balancing test of the interests of the twins:

> If, which I do not, I were to balance the interests of Jodie against those of Mary, then Jodie's chance of a virtually normal life would be lost in order to prolong the life of Mary for those few months.[46]

This is exactly the kind of utilitarian calculation that was discussed and rejected earlier in respect or tissue and organ donation. Ward LJ concluded, however, that it was in Mary's best interests as well as in Jodie's for the operation to proceed. Both he and Brooke LJ had no difficulty in agreeing with the court of first instance that elective separation would be in Jodie's best interests. There was expected to be low risk to her of further injury by the surgery and with corrective operations she was expected to be able to lead a fairly normal life with no reduction in life expectancy. Her intellectual functioning was also thought to allow her the capacity to enjoy her life. The effect

---

45 *Re A (Conjoined Twins)* [2000] 4 All ER 961, CA, at 1003.
46 Ibid quoted at 998.

of performing the operation against her parents' wishes on her welfare was treated as a separate issue.

The question of Mary's best interests was to prove much more difficult. For Ward LJ, the starting point was to consider the judgment in *F* (1990) on the meaning of best interests where treatment of an incompetent was proposed:

> The operation or other treatment will be in their best interests if, but only if, it is carried out in order either to save their lives, or to ensure improvement or prevent deterioration in their physical or mental health.[47]

In these terms, no benefit to Mary could be found from immediate separation. In addition, 'no other needs social, emotional, psychological or whatever' could be established either. The only benefit which Ward LJ could suggest was a rather puzzling one, in that 'the operation would, if successful, give Mary the bodily integrity and dignity which is the natural order for all of us'. However, he recognised that:

> . . . .this is a wholly illusory goal because she will be dead before she can enjoy her independence and she will die because, when she is independent, she has no capacity for life.[48]

The idea of bodily integrity was regarded as rather more significant by Brooke LJ, who stated as part of his reasoning that:

> . . . the doctrine of the sanctity of life respects the integrity of the human body. The proposed operation would give these children's bodies the integrity which nature denied them.[49]

Despite lengthy discussion of the way in which Mary's interests would be affected by the operation, it appears that creating bodily integrity was given the greatest weight and was the determining factor for the remaining judge, Walker LJ, who held that:

> Every human being's right to life carries with it, as an intrinsic part of it, rights of bodily integrity and autonomy – the right to have one's own body whole and intact and (on reaching an age of understanding) to take decisions about one's own body.

> By a rare and tragic mischance, Mary and Jodie have both been deprived of the bodily integrity and autonomy which is their natural right. There

47 Ibid quoted at 997.
48 Ibid at 998.
49 Ibid at 1052.

is a strong presumption that an operation to separate them would be in the best interests of each of them.

While the doctrine is applied equally to Jodie, it is its application to Mary that is of most significance, since Jodie's interests in having the operation seemed not to require additional support.

The judges' views on the indignity of sharing a body have been challenged by a number of commentators. Clucas and O'Donnell, for example, suggest that:

> What all the judges fail to accept is that Mary and Jodie already have bodily integrity: they have a conjoined body. . . . The judges identify conjoined bodies as lacking in both integrity and dignity, clearly only able to conceive of integrity and dignity as belonging to separated bodies.
>
> (Clucas and O'Donnell, 2002, para 3.3b)

The court's interpretation is also criticised by Harris, who argues that the idea of bodily integrity used in statutes and common law is to prevent people from violations of their bodies, not to separate them from life-preserving contact with other bodies or things (Harris, 2001, pp 226–7). Indeed, one can go further and suggest that both the doctrine of sanctity of life and the concept of respect for bodily integrity provide support for non-intervention rather than the reverse.

The view that Ward and Brooke LJJ took on the sanctity of life principle has been discussed in Chapter 4, but, briefly, was to adopt the reasoning of Keown, which regards all human lives as equally valuable, but does not require all steps possible be taken to preserve them. It allows treatment to be withheld or withdrawn but 'the question is always whether the treatment would be worthwhile, not whether the patient's life would be worthwhile' (Keown, 1997). Despite this, the judges were unable to apply this analysis to the conjoined twins. It will be remembered that part of the law's approach to life-ending decisions is to differentiate between acts and omissions.[50] While this has its own problems, as we have already seen, in the conjoined twins case the doctors were not seeking to withhold or withdraw medical treatment or care from Mary; instead they were seeking authority to perform an operation upon her. All three judges held that this could not be categorised, as the judge at first instance had done, as an omission by withdrawing her blood supply. As a result, for Ward LJ this much was clear:

---

50 *Airedale NHS Trust v Bland* [1993] 1 All ER 821, Fam D, CA and HL, *Law Hospital NHS Trust v Lord Advocate* 1996 SCLR49, IHCS, *Re J (a minor) (wardship: medical treatment)* [1990] 3 All ER 930, CA.

The question is whether this proposed operation is in Mary's best interests. It cannot be. It will bring her life to an end before it has run its
natural span. It denies her inherent right to life. There is no countervailing advantage for her at all. It is contrary to her best interests. Looking at
her position in isolation and ignoring, therefore, the benefit to Jodie, the
court should not sanction the operation on her.[51]

If it was accepted that there was a conflict between the best interests of Jodie
and Mary, how was the court to proceed?

Conflicting best interests

Ward LJ noted that there had been previous cases in other areas of child law
where the question had arisen of two or more children being parties in an
action concerning their welfare. In particular he referred to a case involving a
baby's upbringing, where the mother was a child herself, *H* (1994).[52] At first
instance, the court had attempted to avoid the issue of conflict by holding that
since the question involved the baby's upbringing, it was the baby's interests
that must be considered paramount. However, this position was rejected on
appeal where it was said that the upbringing of both mother and daughter was
involved and therefore both children's welfare must be the paramount consideration under s 1(1) of the CA 1989.[53] Despite this, the Court of Appeal
found that this was impossible if either the ordinary or the dictionary meaning of 'paramount' was considered, since as discussed in Chapter 1, this
means one set of interests must rank above all others. The welfare, or best
interests, principle is simply not designed for decisions involving more than
one child. The appeal judges noted that the difficulty that would arise where
two or more children came before the court had been foreseen by the Law
Commission,[54] but that the CA 1989 had not been drafted to take this into
account. Accordingly, the court would have to 'resolve the dilemma itself' and
'try and give the statutory provision such meaning as it can sensibly bear'.[55]
Lord Justice Balcombe considered that the way to do this was by starting from
the position that while a child's interests would be paramount over those of an
adult, where two children are concerned:

> You start with an evenly balanced pair of scales. Of course, when you
> start to put into the scales the matters relevant to each child – and in

51 *Re A (children) (conjoined twins: surgical separation)* [2000] 4 All ER 961, CA.
52 *Birmingham City Council v H (a minor)* [1994] 1 All ER 12, HL.
53 *Birmingham City Council v H (a minor)* [1993] 1 FLR 883, CA.
54 Law Commission Working Paper No. 96, para 6.16 and Report No. 172, paras 3.13 and 3.14
    and s 1(2) of the Draft Bill appended to the Report.
55 *Birmingham City Council v H (a minor)* [1993] 1 FLR 883, CA, at 890–2.

particular those listed in s 1(3) – the result may come down in favour of one rather than the other, but that is a balancing exercise which the court is well used to conducting in cases concerning children.[56]

This approach was agreed by the other two judges with Lord Evans concluding that:

> . . . the [paramountcy] requirement must be regarded as qualified, in the cases where the welfare of more than one child is involved, by the need to have regard to potential detriment for one in the light of potential benefit for the other. Only in this way, it seems to me, can the section be applied and the manifest objects of the Act achieved.[57]

The House of Lords did not discuss this aspect of the case on a further appeal, choosing to return to the view that it was the child whose upbringing was in question, the baby, who was the subject of the proceedings and so her interests were paramount.[58] However, the Court of Appeal took the same approach it had adopted in *H* (1994) in a case concerning the residence of children in *Re T and E (proceedings: conflicting interests)* (1995).[59] This left Ward LJ to treat the Court of Appeal's approach as persuasive, if not binding, upon him in how he should consider the welfare of Mary and Jodie. As he put it:

> Given the conflict of duty, I can see no other way of dealing with it than by choosing the lesser of the two evils and so finding the least detrimental alternative. A balance has to be struck somehow and I cannot flinch from undertaking that evaluation, horrendously difficult though it is.[60]

Harris argues that this approach is inconsistent with moral and legal principles (Harris, 2001). If, as the judges have said, the value of Mary's and Jodie's lives are equal, then the value to be given to each child's welfare must surely also be equal. He suggests that if two lives could be saved by sacrificing one, then in a value-of-life sense, the principle of life having 'ineliminable value' can operate. If all the lives are equal then there is nothing to balance, and conversely if they can be balanced then they are not equal. However, where, as here, it is the saving of one life at the expense of another that is at issue, the principle cannot be relied upon. This also appears to have been the view taken in the case by Walker LJ. He was plainly uncomfortable with

56 Ibid.
57 Ibid at 896.
58 *Birmingham City Council v H (a minor)* [1994] 1 All ER, 12, HL.
59 *Re T and E (children's proceedings: conflicting interests)* [1995] 3 FCR 260, CA.
60 *Re A (Conjoined Twins)* [2000] 4 All ER 961, CA, at 1006.

the idea that the interests of the children should be balanced against each other. While noting that this had been the approach advocated in other areas of child law, though admittedly the case law was sparse, he considered that this situation was very different.

> . . . the decisions in which those conflicts of interests arose were decisions as to matters such as residence and contact which, however anxious and difficult, are routinely made by family judges. They were not decisions on a matter of life or death. The notion that the court should ever undertake the evaluation of the lives of two innocent human beings, with a view to deciding which should live and which should die, could not be reconciled with the law's respect for the sanctity (or inviolability) of human life, either before or after the incorporation of the European Convention on Human Rights.[61]

Nevertheless, according to Ward and Brooke LJJ, a balancing exercise of the interests of the children was permitted and even apparently required of the court. Having decided this, the relative values of performing the operation fell to be considered.

Ward LJ was adamant that following the sanctity of life principle, he could not compare the value of each child's life because each were of equal value, regardless of the difference in physical and mental capacities. What he could do, however, was to consider the worthwhileness of the treatment for each twin and compare this. In doing so, it was possible 'to have regard to the actual condition of each twin and hence the actual balance sheet of advantage and disadvantage which flows from the performance or the non-performance of the proposed treatment'.[62] As noted in Chapter 4, the effect of this is in fact to allow a quality of life judgment to be made as part of the best interests test. As Clucas and O'Donnell explain:

> The Court of Appeal concluded that Jodie's (potential) long term con-tinued life was worth more than Mary's inevitably short life. However . . . this valuation was not simply a quantitative one based on their relative life expectancies: the judgments repeatedly refer to the near normal qual-ity of life which Jodie is expected to enjoy, as contrasted with the poor quality of life which Mary enjoys and would continue to enjoy. The balancing exercise which has been carried out depends upon value judg-ments about the quality of life, which detract from the absolute nature of the right which is at stake: the right to life.
>
> (Clucas and O'Donnell, 2002)

61 Ibid per Walker LJ at 1054–5.
62 Ibid at 1010.

Given that Mary's death was certain, with or without the operation, but that Jodie had a very good prospect of a normal life only if the surgery took place, Ward LJ concluded that the balance was heavily in Jodie's favour. He considered that this was bolstered by the fact that Mary would not now be alive if it were not for the support of her sister and that it was this strain that would kill Jodie. Jodie could be helped, but Mary could not, and the interests of fairness and justice between the children also leant in favour of separation.[63] Brooke J agreed that the balancing of the children's interests was in favour of elective separation.

By contrast, since Walker LJ did not consider it was appropriate to attempt to balance the interests of the children, if the operation was to be permitted it could only be done on the basis that the operation was in both their interests. This he found to be the case by holding that:

> . . . to prolong Mary's life for a few months would confer no benefit on her but would be to her disadvantage. If Mary had been born separated from Jodie but with the defective brain and heart and lungs which she has, and if her life were being supported, not by Jodie but by mechanical means, it would be right to withdraw that artificial life-support system and allow Mary to die.[64]

He regarded it as significant that separation would give each of the twins' bodily integrity, though the justification for this, as has been said, is highly questionable.

The role of parents

The extent to which the parents' views about the separation should be taken into consideration by the courts was dealt with separately. There were two main ways in which they could be relevant, first in respect of whether they, rather than the courts, were in the best position to judge their children's best interests and second, in establishing what the best interests of the children required. The answer to the first question is clear: despite the strong presumption that parents will be permitted to make decisions about what their young children's interests require, the court can override them if it disagrees with the parents' assessment. However, interestingly, Ward LJ stated that:

> It would . . . have been a perfectly acceptable response for the hospital to bow to the weight of the parental wish however fundamentally the medical team disagreed with it. Other medical teams may well have accepted

---

63 Ibid at 1010.
64 Ibid at Walker J at 1057.

the parents' decision. Had St. Mary's done so, there could not have been the slightest criticism of them for letting nature take its course in accordance with the parents' wishes. Nor should there be any criticism of the hospital for not bowing to the parents' choice.

Failure to intervene and allowing both babies to die in accordance with parental wishes was thus seen as perfectly acceptable. The reason for doing so would presumably have to rest on classing this as a lawful omission to treat under the kinds of principles already discussed. This may be understandable in relation to Mary, who could be described as being in a position similar to a terminally ill child being maintained on a ventilator. If the burdens outweighed the benefits in such a case, support could be withdrawn. Statements by the judges stressed the poor quality of Mary's life, although not all commentators have been convinced by the rhetoric employed. However, such an analysis is much more difficult to maintain in relation to Jodie. Here we are faced with a child who could have a life of a normal length and good quality. For parents to authorise doctors to fail to save the life of such a child would not usually be accepted, unless we are to return to the position taken in *R v Arthur* (1981) that doctors acting in accordance with professional standards of practice and parental wishes acquire legal immunity.[65] Indeed, the use of the phrase 'allowing nature to take its course' in the quote above has uncomfortable echoes of the *Arthur* case.

It is also unclear whether medical and parental unanimity would enable the opposite conclusion to hold true: that if both the medical team and the parents had favoured separation of the twins, that there would have been no requirement to refer the case to the courts. Cases where doctors and parents have been in agreement over proposed treatment of children and have been overruled by the courts are rare indeed.[66] However, the problem here is rather different, since it concerns whether the proposed procedure would be lawful, given that it would result in the premature death of an infant through an intentional act, traditionally frowned upon by the law. This point is made by Huxtable, who suggests that while parents may be able to consent to treatment of a child that incidentally involves a risk of death, the situation must surely be different where the risk of death is high or as here, 100 per cent, with no corresponding medical benefit (Huxtable, 2002). If there is a requirement to seek the permission of a court before a sterilisation or other controversial, irreversible medical procedures can be undertaken, it may be hard to understand why this kind of situation should not be covered by the same principle (see discussion in Chapter 2).

Since *Re A* (2000), other cases involving the separation of conjoined twins

---

65 *R v Arthur* (1981) 12 BMLR 1.
66 *Re D (a minor) (wardship: sterilisation)* [1976] 1 All ER 326, Fam D.

have been reported in the UK media, but none have reached the courts (BBC News, 12 December 2001; BBC News, 18 May 2002).

The second aspect – the impact of the parent's views on the welfare of the child – raised a number of issues. The parents' objections were to a large part based on their religious beliefs and their firm opposition to taking any action that would kill one of their daughters, even to save the other. As they put it:

> We cannot possibly agree to any surgery being undertaken that will kill one of our daughters. We have faith in God and are quite happy for God's will to decide what happens to our two young daughters.

However, in addition to this, they raised serious concerns over what would happen, even if surgery resulted in saving Jodie. They were extremely anxious about the prospect of future surgery needed for Jodie to correct remaining abnormalities and the difficulties for them in providing it, since specialist facilities were not available in their homeland. They envisaged considerable financial expense for treatment and travelling or staying in the UK, which they did not think they would be able to afford. The alternative would be to leave their daughter in the UK for her to be cared for by others, which would 'break their hearts', but they saw it might be the only feasible option to provide her with appropriate medical care, assuming that she were in fact able to remain in the UK.

The judges expressed considerable sympathy with the parents' dilemma and found that they were devoted and responsible parents. Indeed, Walker J said of their religious views that they might be described as controversial, but that they 'were not contrary to any view generally accepted by our society', nor did anyone 'suggest that it was selfish or unreasonable that they should have concerns about their ability, either financially or personally to care for [the surviving twin] at home'.[67] As Freeman points out, though it is unclear why more respect should have been due to their religious views than any other sincerely held but controversial views a parent might have (Freeman, 2001). However, the court remained of the view that in this case the interests of Jodie would not be so adversely affected by her parents' dissent or the potential consequences to outweigh the benefits to her of the treatment.

Lawfulness

Once the decision was found to be either in the best interests of both twins, as per Walker LJ, or was not, but represented the least detrimental alternative, as per the majority, the court still had to consider whether the operation

---

67 *Re A (children) (conjoined twins: surgical separation)* [2000] 4 All ER 961, CA.

would be lawful. The judgments on the criminal law aspect of the case are at least as complex and contentious as those on the subject of the children's best interests, but it is not necessary for the purposes of this discussion to do more than outline them here. In fact there was even less agreement over the way in which the surgical separation could be deemed to be unlawful, once it was accepted that this would amount to an act rather than an omission. Ward LJ held that Mary's death would be intended and would normally amount to murder, but that it should be regarded as a situation analogous to self-defence. Brooke LJ also concluded that Mary's death would be an intentional act, but for him it could be justified on the basis of the defence of necessity. Finally, Walker LJ is rather less clear, but seemed to be seeking to apply the principle of double effect, so that Mary's death was foreseeable, but was not intended.[68]

It is the assumption by many commentators that this was an example of the courts taking a utilitarian view of the situation. Two lives could not be saved; therefore, it was better to attempt to save one. Although this offends against the perspective that all lives are equal and hence should be allowed to continue their natural course, with no interventions being performed that will deliberately shorten one person's life, the court regarded the alternative as being even more unpalatable.

Harm and reasonableness as a solution

My own tentative solution relies on the concept that where both children meet the conditions for legal personhood, they must be regarded as having the same legal rights and the welfare of both children must be considered. However, it is not sufficient to simply make a utilitarian calculation of the relative interests of each child, for the reasons already given. Instead, in the circumstances of *Re A* (2000), Jodie had clear interests in being separated to save her life. The approach taken to Mary should have depended upon whether, if she were being maintained on a ventilator, this support could have been withdrawn. Given her condition, there seems no doubt treatment withdrawal would be permitted. In such situations, it should be lawful to allow parents to consent to surgical separation, even though this will result in a child's premature death. Although it amounts to a positive act, I have expressed my reservations about the rationale for this distinction and would see this as an example where it creates more difficulties than it resolves. I suggest that, provided that steps to minimise any pain and distress are undertaken, no greater harm to the welfare of the child would result from surgical separation than from treatment withdrawal. At the same time, the welfare of the healthy twin is safeguarded. In consequence, I believe that courts would be justified in overriding a parental refusal of consent, as I do not consider

68 Ibid.

that a refusal in these circumstances would be reasonable. Put in this way, the case of Mary and Jodie is in fact at the easier end of the scale for decision-making (for a similar view, see Freeman, 2001).

A more difficult situation would be where neither child would be considered as candidates for treatment withdrawal, but there is a prospect of saving one life at the expense of the other. This might occur where, for example, twins shared a vital organ that could not support both of them indefinitely. Some, taking a utilitarian approach would consider that it is appropriate to try to save one life rather than lose two; others, that one child should not be sacrificed for the benefit of the other. My own view is that the separation should not proceed. Doing so would deny the right of each child to respect for his or her life. We do not usually permit the significant interests of one child to be sacrificed for another and this situation, desperate though it is, does not provide a reason to depart from it. This is not a situation where I consider it would be reasonable to proceed and parents should not be able to give a lawful consent (see also, Sheldon and Wilkinson, 1997).

In the light of the significant differences of opinion there have been over the correct approach to this situation, it could be argued that this provides a basis for parents to be permitted to reach what decision seems best to them. I have contended that the role of the courts should be simply to set the parameters for parental decision-making rather than substitute the decisions of reasonable parents. Accordingly, courts adopting this approach could disagree with my analysis of the reasonableness of surgical separation, but that is not, to me, a reason to abandon the underlying framework I have proposed. The fundamental difficulty for the present approach of the law is put by in this way:

> . . . conjoined twins can be seen as inhabiting an intermediate category of embodiment between one and two, yet exist in a society which seems unable to contemplate with equanimity the degree of blendedness and interrelatedness which conjoined twins exhibit, or the idea that such intermediate categories may exist or need to be constructed. The current rules by which society is regulated, being focussed on individualised rights, have difficulty in accommodating these categories of interrelatedness and interdependence.
>
> (Clucas and O'Donnell, 2002)

I would see the best interests test as a prime example of the kind of principle that is most clearly inadequate in such cases as this.

Conclusion

The application of the best interest test to the situation where treating one child requires medical procedures to be undertaken on another highlights some of the difficulties in its application. In the case of donation of bodily materials, it requires a broad construction of best interests to be able to include psychological benefit and allows this to be privileged over medical and psychological harms, even on potentially slim evidence. It can be applied, however, since only the prospective donor is the subject of the court proceedings. In the case of conjoined twins, this route does not appear to be open, placing the court in a difficult position if the interests of the children appear to conflict. The solution to this dilemma is currently uncertain, since while the majority of the Court of Appeal have considered that the only way it can be resolved is by balancing the interests of the children, the extent to which this is legally permissible or an acceptable solution is in doubt. Although my solution will not satisfy all readers either, it is least free of the logical difficulties that beset a best interests test here.

Concluding remarks

I set out to challenge the assumption that the best interests of the child test does and should govern medical interventions. On starting out I was conscious of the scale of the task and it has not lessened as the work progressed. I have somewhat ruefully found myself agreeing with Eekelaar when he says that 'The "welfare" or "best interests" principle has, from time to time, been subjected to critical scrutiny. But it is easier to criticise the principle than come up with an alternative' (Eekelaar, 2002, p 237).

I recognise that the solutions I have advocated will be unsatisfactory to many for a variety of reasons. I have suggested that decisions concerning incompetent children should be based on the threshold of a serious risk of significant harm to the child and that the decision by parents must be reasonable. These can be criticised for the kinds of indeterminacy that bedevil the best interests test and take us no further forward than we were before. However, I return to the point made by Diekema:

> ... there will always be an interpretive element in judging whether a parental decision crosses the threshold for state intervention. The biggest problem with a best interest standard is not its subjectivity, but that it represents the wrong standard. State intervention is not justified because a decision is contrary to the child's best interest, but because it places the child at significant risk of serious harm.
>
> (Diekema, 2004)

There will also be those who will be unhappy with the idea of replacing a best interests standard, since they may feel this risks losing hard won ground in shifting the proper focus of attention from adults' concerns to those of children. To base a test on the reasonableness of the parents' decision might then be seen as a step backward, rather than forward. This, though, would be to imply two things: first, that a child's welfare can be judged in isolation from the family in which s/he lives. Although unhappily it does not always prove to be borne out in practice, it is still the case that families are felt to be the best way in which to provide support and care for children. This inevitably means there are limitations on the extent to which outside intervention is necessary or appropriate in order for parents to fulfil their role. Second, children are not the only ones who have interests. As Herring says:

> We do children no favours by regarding their interests as the only relevant ones. We must treat children with respect by bringing them up as members of families, of communities and of a society which values and upholds the rights and obligations of everyone, with the interests of children held in the highest esteem.
>
> (Herring, 1999)

My proposals do not suggest anything other than that the welfare of children should be a central concern for parents, doctors and the courts. Nonetheless, since it is my belief that in most cases what is *best* for the child is indeterminate, parents should be able to judge what they consider this is, unless the harm threshold is likely to be breached. This is in fact the way that the overwhelming majority of decisions are reached about the healthcare of children and I believe that there is no good reason why courts should not adopt the same approach.

Where competent children are concerned, again there seems to me to be no clear justification for failing to accord them the right to make decisions, even if they are ones that others do not believe are best for them. This is, after all, exactly the situation where upholding the right to respect for autonomy is of most importance. Some would say this is an argument to allow children to make as foolish and misguided decisions as adults, and that this is not a conclusion that ought to be striven for. I believe that this does an injustice to children and young people, and in any event I would return to my point that once a person has gained autonomy then they are judged to be capable of taking responsibility for themselves, whether they choose to exercise it in a way we would approve, or not.

I am conscious that I have only scratched the surface in seeking to set out the way that my approach would apply in practice. There are whole books on many of the individual issues I have covered, and what seems like whole libraries on some of them. It is inevitable that many points have not been able to be dealt with in the depth that they deserve, but I hope I have been able to give enough of an indication of my thoughts on particular points to make mention of them worthwhile.

I am also conscious that I am not blazing a trail, but in the vanguard of those who have already decided that the best interests test has served its purpose and should be retired gracefully. However, I suspect that day is still rather distant. In the meantime, I hope I may have made enough of a challenge to the best interests test to justify at least some more caution in the assumptions that it contains in its application to healthcare.

Bibliography

Ackerman, TF (1979), 'Fooling ourselves with child autonomy and assent in non-therapeutic clinical research', 27 *Clinical Research*, 345.

Adler, R (1985), *Taking Juvenile Justice Seriously*, Edinburgh: Scottish Academic Press.

Alderson, P (1999), 'Did children change or the guidelines?', 150 *Bulletin of Medical Ethics*, 44.

Alderson, P (2006), in E Parens (ed) (2006), *Surgically Shaping Children Technology, Ethics, and the Pursuit of Normality*, Baltimore: Johns Hopkins University Press.

Alderson, P and Montgomery, J (1996a), 'Children may be able to make their own decisions', *British Medical Journal* 50.

Alderson, P and Montgomery J (1996b), *Health Care Choices: making decisions with children*, London: Institute for Public Policy Research.

Alston, P, Parker, S and Seymour, J (eds) (1992, reprint 1995), *Children, Rights and the Law*, Oxford: Clarendon Press.

Archard, DW (2002), 'Children's Rights' in EN Zalta (ed), *The Stanford Encyclopedia of Philosophy* (Winter 2002), http://plato.stanford.edu/archives/win2002/entries/rights-children/ (accessed 1 May 2007).

'Ashley blog' – The Ashley Treatment http://ashleytreatment.spaces.live.com/blog/cns!E25811FD0AF7C45C!1837.entry?_c=BlogPart (accessed 1 May 2007).

Bainham, A (1992), 'The judge and the competent minor', 108 *Law Quarterly Review*, 194.

Bainham, A (2005), *Children: the Modern Law*, 3rd edn, Bristol: Jordan Publishing.

Baroness David (1989), House of Lords, Official Report, 19 January 1989, col 405.

Bartholome, WG (1996), 'Ethical issues in pediatric research' in HY Vanderpool (ed), *The Ethics of Research Involving Human Subjects: Facing the 21st Century*, Frederick, MD: University Publishing Group 339.

Battin, M (1994), *The Least Worst Death: Essays in Bioethics on the End of Life*, New York, Oxford: Oxford University Press.

BBC News (12 December 2001), '*Pioneering Siamese Twin Op*', http://news.bbc.co.uk/1/hi/health/1705771.stm (accessed 1 May 2007).

BBC News (18 May 2002), '*Siamese Twins Die*', http://news.bbc.co.uk/1/hi/health/1994607.stm (accessed 1 May 2007).

BBC News (18 April 2007) '*Euthanasia Woman Drops Case*', http://news.bbc.co.uk/1/hi/england/bristol/6568217.stmcase (accessed 1 May 2007).

Beyleveld, D and Pattinson, SD (2006), 'Medical research into emergency treatment: regulatory tensions in England and Wales', 5 *Web JCLI*.

Bevan, HK (1989), *Child Law*, London: Butterworths.

Beauchamp, TL and Childress, JF (2001), *Principles of Biomedical Ethics*, 5th edn, Oxford: Oxford University Press.

Blackie, J and Patrick, H (2001), in A Cleland and E Sutherland (eds), *Children's Rights in Scotland*, 2nd edn, Edinburgh: W.Green/Sweet and Maxwell.

Bortin, MM and Bucker, CD (1993), 'Major complications of marrow harvesting for transplantation', 11 *British Journal of Haematology* 916.

Boyd, K (1995), 'Euthanasia: back to the future', in J Keown (ed), *Euthanasia Examined*, Cambridge: Cambridge University Press.

Brazier, M (1990), 'Liability of ethics committees and their members', *Professional Negligence* 186.

Brazier, M (2005), 'Case Commentary: an intractable dispute: when parents and professionals disagree', 13(3) *Medical Law Review* 412.

Brazier, M and Bridge, C (1996), 'Coercion or caring: analysing adolescent autonomy', 16 *Legal Studies* 84.

Brazier, M and Miola, J (2000), 'Bye-Bye *Bolam*: a medical litigation revolution?', 8 *Medical Law Review* 85.

Breen, C (2002), *The Standard of the Best Interests of the Child: A Western Tradition in International and Comparative Law, International Studies in Human Rights Vol.72*, The Hague: Martinus Nijhoff.

Bridge, C (1999a), 'Religious beliefs and teenage refusal of medical treatment', 62 *Modern Law Review* 585.

Bridge, C (1999b), 'Religion, culture and conviction – the medical treatment of young children', 11(1) *Child and Family Law Quarterly* 1.

Brieger, GH (1978), 'History: Human Experimentation', in WT Reich (ed), Vol. 2, *Encyclopedia of Bioethics*, New York: The Free Press.

Bristol Royal Infirmary Inquiry (2001), *The Report of the Public Inquiry into children's heart surgery at the Bristol Royal Infirmary 1984–1995: Learning from Bristol* (Cm 5207), London: The Stationery Office.

British Medical Association (1995), *Assessment of Mental Capacity*, London: BMJ Books.

British Medical Association (1999), *The Law and Ethics of Abortion*, London: British Medical Association.

British Medical Association (2000), *The Impact of the Human Rights Act 1998 on Medical Decision Making*, http://www.bma.org.uk/ap.nsf/Content/HumanRights Act?OpenDocument&Highlight=2,human,rights (accessed 1 May 2007).

British Medical Association (2001), *Consent, Rights and Choices in Health Care for Children and Young People*, London: BMJ Books.

British Medical Association (2005) *Human Tissue (Scotland) Bill: Stage 1, Written submission to the Scottish Parliament Health Committee*.

British Medical Association (2006a), *Parental Responsibility*, http://www.bma.org.uk/ ap.nsf/Content/Parental?OpenDocument&Highlight=2,parental,responsibility (accessed 1 May 2007).

British Medical Association (2006b), *The Law and Ethics of Male Circumcision*, http://www.bma.org.uk/ap.nsf/Content/malecircumcision2006?OpenDocument &Highlight=2,circumcision, (accessed 1 May 2007).

British Medical Association (2007), *Withholding and Withdrawing Life Prolonging Medical Treatment*, London: BMA.

British Medical Association and The Law Society (2004), *Assessment of mental capacity: guidance for doctors and lawyers*, 2nd edn, London: BMJ Books.

British Transplantation Society and the Renal Association (2005), *United Kingdom Guidelines for Living Donor Kidney Transplantation*, 2nd edn, London: BTS/RTS.

Brosco, JF (2006), 'Growth attenuation: a diminutive solution to a daunting problem', 160 *Arch Pediatr Adolesc Med* 1077.

Browett, P and Palmer, S (1996), 'Legal barriers might have catastrophic effects', 312 *British Medical Journal* 242.

Buchanan, AE and Brock, DW (1973), *Deciding for Others: The Ethics of Surrogate Decision Making*. New York: Cambridge University Press.

Caldwell, PHY, Butow, PN and Craig, JC (2003), 'Parents attitudes to randomised controlled trials', 142(5) *Journal of Paediatrics* 554.

Caldwell, PHY *et al.* (2004), 'Clinical trials in children', 364 *The Lancet* 803.

Campbell, AV (1994), 'Dependency: the foundational value in medical ethics', in KWM Fulford, G Gillet and JM Soskice (eds), *Medicine and Moral Reasoning*, Cambridge: Cambridge University Press.

Campbell, TD (1992), 'The rights of the minor: as person, as child, as juvenile, as future adult', in P Alston, S Parker, and J Seymour (eds) (1992, reprint 1995), *Children, Rights and the Law*, Oxford: Clarendon Press.

Cauffman, E and Steinberg, L (1995), 'The cognitive and affective influences on adolescent decision-making', 68 *Temple Law Review* 1763.

Clauss, R and Nel, W (2006), 'Drug induced arousal from the permanent vegetative state', 21(1) *NeuroRehabilitation* 23.

Clucas, B and O'Donnell, K (2002), 'Conjoined twins: the cutting edge', 5 *Web JCLI*.

Cohen-Mansfield, J, Rabinovich, B A, Lipson, S *et al.* (1991), 'The decision to execute a durable power of attorney for health care and preferences regarding the utilization of life-sustaining treatments in nursing home residents', 151 *Arch Int Med* 289.

Coleman, J and Hendry, L (1999), *The Nature of Adolescence*, London: Routledge.

COREC (2007), *Press Release: Launch of National Research Ethics Service*, 29 March 2007.

Council for International Organizations of Medical Sciences (2002), *International Ethical Guidelines for Biomedical Research Involving Human Subjects*, 3rd Revision, Geneva: CIOMS.

Crouch, RA and Elliot, C (1999), 'Moral agency and the family: the case of living related organ transplants', 8(3) *Cambridge Quarterly of Healthcare Ethics* 275.

Cuttini M, Nadai M, Kaminski, M *et al.* (2000), 'End-of-life decisions in neonatal intensive care: physicians' self-reported practices in seven European countries', 355 *Lancet* 2112.

Davies, M (1996), *Textbook on Medical Law*, London: Blackstone Press.

Davis, A (1994), 'All babies should be kept alive as far as possible', in R Gillon (ed), *Principles of Health Care Ethics*, London: John Wiley & Sons.

Delaney, L (1996), 'Protecting children from forced altruism: the legal approach', 312 *British Medical Journal* 240.

Department of Health (1991), *Local Research Ethics Committees*, HSG (91)5, London: DoH.

Department of Health (2001a), *Reference Guide to Consent for Examination and Treatment*, London: DoH.

Department of Health (2001b), *Seeking Consent: Working with Young People*, London: DoH.

Department of Health (2004), *Children's National Service Framework for Children, Young People and Maternity Services*, http://www.dh.gov.uk/PolicyAndGuidance/HealthAndSocialCareTopics/ChildrenServices/ChildrenServicesInformation/ChildrenServicesInformationArticle/fs/en?CONTENT_ID=4089111&chk=U8Ecln (accessed 1 May 2007).

Department of Health (2005), *Research Governance Framework for Health and Social Care*, 2nd edn, London: DoH.

Department of Health (2007), *Immunisation*, http://www.dh.gov.uk/en/Policyand guidance/Healthandsocialcaretopics/Immunisation/index.htm (accessed 1 May 2007).

Dickens, B (1981), 'The modern function and limits of parental rights', 97 *Law Quarterly Review* 462.

Diekema, DS (2004), 'Parental refusals of medical treatment: the harm principle as threshold for state intervention', 25(4) *Theoretical Medicine and Bioethics* 243.

Disability Rights Commission (2007), *Ashley X statement: Medical steps not the answer to dealing with social care crisis says DRC*, http://www.drc-gb.org/news room/news_releases/2007/ashley_x_statement.aspx (accessed 1 May 2007).

Douglas, G (2004), *An Introduction to Family Law*, Oxford: Oxford University Press.

Down's Syndrome Association (1999), 'He'll never join the army: people with Down's Syndrome denied medical care', London: Down's Syndrome Association available at http://www.downs-syndrome.org.uk/pdfs/Hewillneverjointhearmy.doc (accessed 1 May 2007).

Down's Syndrome Scotland (1998), *Cosmetic Surgery for Children with Down's Syndrome*, http://www.dsscotland.org.uk/news-and-events/press-releases/cosmetic-surgery (accessed 1 May 2007).

Dvorsky, G (2006), 'Helping families care for the helpless', 1 November 2006, http://ieet.org/index.php/IEET/more/809/ (accessed 1 May 2007).

Dworkin, G (1982), 'Consent, representation and proxy consent', in W Gaylin and R Macklin (eds), *Who Speaks for the Child: the Problems of Proxy Consent*, New York: Plenum Press.

Dworkin, R (1977), *Taking Rights Seriously*, London: Duckworth.

Dworkin, R (1993), *Life's Dominion*, London: Harper Collins.

Dyer, C (January 2007a), 'Husband says judge's ruling on wife's treatment was "inhumane" ', 334 *British Medical Journal* 176.

Dyer, C (February 2007), 'Dying woman seeks backing to hasten death', 334 *British Medical Journal* 329.

Eddy, MB (1875) (2000 reprint), *Science and Health with Key to the Scriptures*, Florida: The Writings of Mary Baker Eddy.

Edwards, L and Griffiths, A (2006), *Family Law*, 2nd edn, Edinburgh: Thomson, W. Green.

Edwards, SD and McNamee, MJ (2005), 'Ethical concerns regarding guidelines for the conduct of clinical research on children', 31 *J Medical Ethics* 351.

Eekelaar, J (1986), 'The emergence of children's rights', 6(2) *Oxford Journal of Legal Studies* 161.

Eekelaar, J (1991), Regulating Divorce, Oxford: Clarendon Press.

Eekelaar, J (1994), 'The interests of the child and the child's wishes: the role of dynamic self-determinism', 8 *International Journal of Law and the Family* 42 (also published in P. Alston (ed) (1994), *The Best Interests of the Child*, Oxford: Clarendon Press).

Eekelaar, J (2002), 'Beyond the Welfare Principle', 14 *Child and Family Law Quarterly* 237.

Eekelaar, J and Dingwall, R (1990), *The Reform of Child Care Law. A Practical Guide to the Children Act 1989*, London: Routledge.

Elliston, S (1996), 'If you know what's good for you: refusal of consent to medical treatment by children', in SAM McLean (ed), *Contemporary Issues in Law, Medicine and Ethics*, Aldershot: Dartmouth Publishing.

Elliston, S (2004), 'Treating the Preterm Infant: managing risk in clinical practice', in J Norman and I Greer (eds), *Preterm Labour*, Cambridge: Cambridge University Press.

Elster, J (1987), 'Solomonic Judgements: Against the Best Interest of the Child', 54 *University Chicago Law Review* 1.

European Commission (2004), *Staff Working Paper*, 13880/04 ADD 1 SEC 2004 1144, dated 25 October 2004.

European Commission (2006), Ad Hoc Group for the development of implementing guidelines for Directive 2001/20/EC relating to good clinical practice in the conduct of clinical trials on medicinal products for human use, *Ethical Considerations for Clinical Trials Performed in Children*, Draft version 4 October 2006.

European Commission (2007), *Commission Guideline on the Format and Content of Applications for Agreement or Modification of a Paediatric Investigation Plan and Requests for Waivers or Deferrals and Concerning the Operation of the Compliance Check and on Criteria for Assessing Significant Studies*, Draft Version January 2007.

Farson, R (1974), *Birthrights*, London: Collier Macmillan.

Feenan, D (1997), 'A good harvest?', 9(3) *Child and Family Law Quarterly* 305.

Feinberg, J (1984), *Harm to Others: The Moral Limits of the Criminal Law*, New York: Oxford University Press.

Feldman, D (2002), *Civil Liberties and Human Rights in England and Wales*, 2nd edn, Oxford: Oxford University Press.

Flamm, A and Forster, H (2000), 'Legal limits: when does autonomy in health care prevail?', in M Freeman and ADE Lewis (eds), *Law and Medicine: Current Legal Issues 2000: Volume 3*, Oxford: Oxford University Press.

Fortin, J (1999b), 'Rights brought home for children', 62(3) *Modern Law Review* 350.

Fortin, J (1999b), 'The HRA's impact on litigation involving children and their families', 11(3) *Child and Family Law Quarterly* 237.

Fortin, J (2003), *Children's Rights and the Developing Law*, 1st edn, London: Butterworths.

Fortin, J (2005), *Children's Rights and the Developing Law*, 2nd edn, London: Butterworths.

Fortin, J (2006), 'Accommodating children's rights in a post Human Rights Act era', 69(3) *Modern Law Review* 299.

Foster, H and Freed, D (1972), 'A bill of rights for children', *Family Law Quarterly* 343.

Fox, M and McHale, J (1997), 'In Whose Best Interests?', 60(5) *Modern Law Review* 700.

Fox, M and Thomson, M (2005), 'A covenant with the status quo? Male circumcision and the new BMA guidance to doctors', 31 *Journal of Medical Ethics* 463.

Freedman, B (1987), 'Equipoise and the Ethics of Clinical Research', 317 *New England Journal of Medicine* 141.

Freeman, M (1983), *The Rights and Wrongs of Children*, London: Frances Pinter.

Freeman, M (2001), 'Whose life is it anyway?', 9(3) *Medical Law Review* 259.

Garwood-Gowers, A (2001), 'Time for competent minors to have the same right of self-determination as competent adults with respect to medical intervention?', in A Garwood-Gowers, J Tingle and T Lewis (eds), *Healthcare Law: The Impact of the Human Rights Act 1998*, London: Cavendish.

Gavaghan, C (2007), *Defending the Genetic Supermarket: law and ethics of selecting the next generation*, Oxford: Routledge-Cavendish.

General Medical Council (1997), *Guidance for Doctors who are Asked to Circumcise Male Children*, London: GMC.

General Medical Council (1998), *Seeking Patient's Consent: the Ethical Consider- ations*, London: GMC.

General Medical Council (2002), *Research: the Role and Responsibilities of Doctors*, London: GMC.

General Medical Council (2002b), *Withholding and Withdrawing Life Prolonging Medical Treatment*, London: GMC.

General Medical Council (2006), *Good Medical Practice*, London: GMC.

Gibbs, N (9 Jan 2007) Pillow Angel Ethics, Part 2, *Time*, http://www.time/printout/ 0,8816,1575325,00.html (accessed 1 May 2007).

Giesen, D (1995), 'Civil liability of physicians for new methods of treatment and experimentation: a comparative examination', 3 *Medical Law Review* 22.

Goeke, J, Kassow, D, May, D and Kundert, D (2003), 'Parental opinions about facial plastic surgery for individuals with Down Syndrome', 41(1) *Mental Retardation* 29–34.

Goldstein, J, Freud, A and Solnit, AJ (1980), *Beyond the Best Interests of the Child*, London: Burnett Books.

Grisso, T and Vierling, L (1978), 'Minors' consent to treatment: a developmental perspective', 9 *Professional Psychology* 412.

Grubb, A (1997), 'Commentary on *Houston*, applicant', 5(2) *Medical Law Review* 237.

Guest, S (1997), 'Compensation for subjects of medical research: the moral rights of patients and the power of research ethics committees', 23 *J Medical Ethics* 181.

Gunn, MJ and Smith, JC (1985), 'Arthur's case and the right to life of a Down's Syndrome child', *Criminal LR* 705.

Gunther, DF and Diekema, DS (2006), 'Attenuating growth in children with pro- found developmental disability: a new approach to an old dilemma', 160 *Arch Pediatr Adolesc Med* 1013.

Harrington, J (2003), 'Deciding best interests: medical progress, clinical judgment and the "good family"', 3 *Web Journal of Current Legal Issues*.

Harris, J (1982), 'The political status of children', in K Graham (ed), *Contemporary Political Philosophy*, Cambridge: Cambridge University Press.

Harris, J (1985), *The Value of Life*, London: Routledge Keegan and Paul.

Harris, J (1994), 'Not all babies should be kept alive as far as possible', in R Gillon (ed), *Principles of Health Care Ethics*, London: John Wiley & Sons.

Harris, J (1996), 'What is the good of health care?', 10(4) *Bioethics* 269.

Harris, J (2001), 'Human beings, persons and conjoined twins: an ethical analysis of the judgment in *Re A*', 9 *Medical Law Review* 221.

Harris, J and Holm, S (2003), 'Should we presume moral turpitude in our Children?: small children and consent to medical research', 24 *Theoretical Medicine* 121.

Hart, HLA (1973), 'Bentham on Legal Rights', in AW Simpson (ed), *Oxford Essays in Jurisprudence*, 2nd series, Oxford: Clarendon Press.

Herring, J (1999a), 'The Human Rights Act and the welfare principle in family law-conflicting or complementary?', 11(3) *Child and Family Law Quarterly* 223.

Herring, J (1999b), 'The welfare principle and parents' rights', in A Bainham, S Day Sclater and M Richards (eds), *What is A Parent? A Socio-Legal Analysis*, Oxford: Hart Publishing.

Herring, J (2005), 'Farewell welfare?', 27(2) *J Social Welfare and Family Law* 159.

Hodges, FM, Svoboda, JS and van Howe, RS (2002), 'Prophylactic interventions on children: balancing human rights with public health', 28 *J Medical Ethics* 10.

Holm, S (2004), 'The child as organ and tissue donor: discussion in the Danish Council of Ethics', 13 *Cambridge Quarterly of Healthcare Ethics* 156.

Holt, J (1974), *Escape from Childhood: The Needs and Rights of Children*, New York: EP Dutton and Co.

Hope, T, Savulescu, J and Hendrick, J (2003), *Medical Ethics and Law, the core curriculum*, London: Churchill Livingstone.

House of Lords EU Sub-Committee on Social Policy and Consumer Affairs (2006), *Paediatric Medicines: Proposed EU Regulation*, 20th report of session 2005/06, HL paper 101.

House of Lords Select Committee on Medical Ethics (1994), *Select Committee on Medical Ethics Report, Vol II Oral Evidence*, 1993–94, London: HMSO (HL Paper 21–1).

Human Fertilisation and Embryology Authority (2004), *Report: Preimplantation Tissue Typing*, London: HFEA.

Human Tissue Authority (2006a), *Code of Practice 1 – Consent*, London: HTA.

Human Tissue Authority (2006b), *Code of Practice 2 – Donation of Solid Organs*, London: HTA.

Human Tissue Authority (2006c), *Code of Practice 5 – The removal, storage and disposal of human organs and tissue and cells for transplantation*, London: HTA.

Human Tissue Authority (2006d), *Code of Practice 6 – Donation of allogeneic bone marrow and peripheral blood stem cells for transplantation*, London: HTA.

Human Tissue Authority (2006e), *Donation of Allogeneic Bone Marrow and Peripheral Blood Stem Cells for Transplantation: draft guidance for transplant teams and Accredited Assessors*, London: HTA.

Human Tissue Authority (2006f), *Scottish Annex: requirements relating to live donations*, London: HTA.

Huxtable, R (2000), 'Case commentary: time to remove the "flak jacket"? *Re M (Medical Treatment: Consent)*', 12(1) *Child and Family Law Quarterly* 83.

Huxatable, R (2001), 'Logical separation? Conjoined twins, slippery slopes and resource allocation', 23(4) *Journal of Social Welfare and Family Law* 459.

Huxtable, R (2002) 'Separation of conjoined twins: where next for the law?', *Criminal Law Review* 459.

Huxtable, R (2004), '*Glass v UK*: maternal instinct v medical opinion', 16(3) *Child and Family Law Quarterly* 339.

International Conference on Harmonisation (2000), *Choice of Control Group and Related Issues in Clinical Trials* (E10) 20 July.

Jackson, E (2006), *Medical Law: Text, Cases and Materials*, Oxford: Oxford University Press.

Jacob, JM (1988), *Doctors and Rules: A Sociology of Professional Values*, London: Routledge.

Jansen, LA (2004), 'Child organ donation, family autonomy and intimate attachments', 13 Cambridge Quarterly of Healthcare Ethics 133.

Jehovah's Witness Society (1990), *How Can Blood Save Your Life*, Watch Tower Bible and Tract Society of Pennsylvania.

Jenner, E (1798–1800) (reprinted 2001), 'The three original publications on vaccination against smallpox', Vol. XXXVIII Part 4 *The Harvard Classics*, New York: P.F. Collier & Son, 1909–14, http://www.bartleby.com/38/4/1001.html.

Jonas, H (1969), 'Philosophical reflections on experimenting with human subjects', 98 *Daedalus* 219.

Jones, RB (2000), 'Parental Consent to Cosmetic Facial Surgery in Down's Syndrome', 26 *J Medical Ethics* 101.

Kant, I (1785) (Reprinted 1994), 'Foundations of the Metaphysics of Morals', in P Singer (ed), *Ethics*, Oxford: Oxford University Press, p 274.

Kennedy, I (1991, reprinted 1994), 'The doctor, the pill and the fifteen year old girl', in I Kennedy, *Treat Me Right*, Oxford: Clarendon Press.

Kennedy, I (1992), 'Consent to treatment and the capable person', in C Dyer (ed), *Doctors, Patients and the Law*, Oxford: Oxford Blackwell Scientific Publications.

Kennedy, I and Grubb, A (2000), *Medical Law: Text with Materials*, 3rd edn, London: Butterworths.

Kennedy, I and Grubb, A (eds) (2004), *Principles of Medical Law*, 2nd rev edn, Oxford: Oxford University Press.

Keown, J (1997), 'Restoring Moral and Intellectual Shape to the Law after Bland', 113 *Law Quarterly Review* 481.

Kerrison, S and Pollock, AM (2005), 'The reform of UK research ethics committees: throwing the baby out with the bath water?', 31 *J Medical Ethics* 487.

Keywood, K (2001), ' "I'd Rather Keep Him Chaste", Retelling the Story of Sterilisation, Learning Disability and (Non)Sexed Embodiment', *Feminist Legal Studies* 185.

Kramer, MH (1998), 'Rights without trimmings', in MH Kramer, NE Simmonds and H Steiner, *A Debate Over Rights, Philosophical Enquiries*, Oxford: Clarendon Press.

Ladd, RE (2004), 'The Child as Living Donor: Parental Consent and Child Assent', 13(2) *Cambridge Quarterly Healthcare Ethics* 143.

Latey Report (1967), Lord Chancellor, Great Britain Committee on the Age of Majority, *Report of the Committee on the Age of Majority*, Cmnd. 3342, London: HMSO.

Laurie, G (1999), 'Parens Patriae jurisdiction in the medico-legal context: the vagaries of judicial activism', 3(1) *Edinburgh Law Review* 95.

Laurie, G (2003), 'Better to hesitate at the threshold of compulsion: PKU testing and the concept of family autonomy in Eire', 28 *Journal of Medical Ethics* 136.

Laurie, G (2006), 'The autonomy of others', in SAM McLean (ed), *First Do No Harm: law and ethics in healthcare*, Aldershot: Ashgate.

Law Commission (1995a), *Consent in the Criminal Law*, Consultation Paper No. 139, London: HMSO.

Law Commission (1995b), *Mental Incapacity*, London: HMSO.

Lee, JM and Howell, JD (2006), 'Tall girls: the social shaping of a medical therapy', 160 *Arch Pediatr Adolesc Med* 1035.

Lee, S (1987), 'Towards a jurisprudence of consent', in J Eekelaar and J Bell (eds), *Oxford Essays in Jurisprudence: 3rd series*, Oxford: Oxford University Press.

Leshin, L (2000), 'Plastic surgery in children with Down Syndrome', http://www.ds-health.com/psurg.htm (accessed 1 May 2007).

Lewis, P (1999), 'Feeding anorexic patients who refuse food', 7(1) *Medical Law Review* 21.

Lewis, P (2002), 'Procedures that are Against the Medical Interests of Incompetent Adults', 22 *Oxford Journal of Legal Studies* 575.

Liddell, K *et al.* (2006), 'Medical Research Involving Incapacitated Adults: Implications Of The EU Clinical Trials Directive 2001/20/EC', 14 *Medical Law Review* 367.

Linacre Centre London (1994), *Submission to the House of Lords Select Committee on Medical Ethics*, HL Paper 21–1, London: HMSO.

Loewy, EH (1991), 'Involving patients in do not resuscitate (DNR) decisions: an old issue raising its ugly head', 17 *J Med Ethics* 156–60.

Lord Chancellor's Department (1997), *Who Decides? Making decisions on behalf of mentally incapacitated adults*, Consultation paper, London: Lord Chancellor's Department.

Lord Fawsley (Wednesday 31 January 2007), House of Lords Debates, Hansard.

Lowe, N and Juss, S (1993), 'Medical Treatment – Pragmatism and the Search for Principle', *Modern Law Review* 865.

Lowy, C (1992), 'Autonomy and the appropriate projects of children: a comment on Freeman', in P Alston, S Parker and J Seymour (eds) (1992, reprint 1995), *Children, Rights and the Law*, Oxford: Clarendon Press.

MacCormick, D (1976), 'Children's rights: a test case for theories of right', LXII *Archiv fur Rechts und Sozialphilosophie* 305, reprinted in D MacCormick (1982), *Legal Right and Social Democracy*, Oxford: Clarendon Press.

Maclean, AR (2001), 'A crossing of the Rubicon on the human rights ferry', *Modern Law Review* 775.

Maclean, AR (2002), 'Beyond *Bolam* and *Bolitho*', 5 *Medical Law International* 205.

MacLeod, KD, Whitsett, SF, Mash, EJ and Pelletier, W (2003), 'Pediatric sibling Donors of successful and unsuccessful hematopoietic stem cell transplants (HSCT): a qualitative study of their psychosocial experience', 28(4) *J Pediatric Psychology*, 223.

Mason, JK (1999), *Medico-Legal Aspects of Parenthood and Reproduction*, 2nd edn, Ashgate: Dartmouth Publications.

Mason, JK (2001), 'Conjoined twins: a diagnostic conundrum', 5(1) *Edinburgh Law Review* 226.

Mason, JK and Laurie, GT (2006), *Mason and McCall Smith's Law and Medical Ethics*, 7th edn, Oxford: Oxford University Press.

McCall Smith, A (1989), 'Research and experimentation involving children', in JK Mason (ed), *Paediatric Forensic Medicine and Pathology*, London: Chapman and Hall.

McHaffie, HE (2001), Withdrawing treatment from infants: key elements in the support of families, 7(3) *Journal of Neonatal Nursing* 85–89.

McHaffie, HE in association with Fowlie, PW *et al.* (2001), *Crucial Decisions at the Beginning of Life: parents' experiences of treatment withdrawal from infants*, Oxford: Radcliffe Medical Press.

McHale, J (1993), 'Guidelines for medical research – some ethical and legal problems', 1 *Medical Law Review* 160.

McLean, SAM (1989), *A Patient's Right to Know: Information Disclosure, the Doctor and the Law*, Aldershot, Dartmouth Publications.

McLean, SAM (1992), 'Medical experimentation with children', 6 *International Journal of Law and the Family* 173.

McLean, SAM (1997), *Consent and the Law: Review of the Provisions in the Human Fertilisation and Embryology Act 1990 for the UK Health Ministers*, Consultation Document and Questionnaire.

McLean, SAM and Elliston, S (2004), 'Death, decision-making and the law', 3 *Juridical Review* 265.

McNeill, PM (1993), *The Ethics and Politics of Human Experimentation*, Cambridge: Cambridge University Press.

Medical Research Council (1964), 'Responsibility in investigations on human subjects', *Report of the Medical Research Council 1962–3*, London: HMSO.

Medical Research Council (2004), *Medical Research Involving Children, MRC Ethics Guide*, London: MRC.

Medical Research Council (2006), *Findings of MRC monitoring study of Pentosan Polysulphate treatment in CJD patients*, Press release 11 July 2006 (see also Bone, I (2006) *Intraventricular Pentosan Polysulphate in Human prion disease – A study of experience in the United Kingdom*, London: MRC).

Medicines and Healthcare Products Regulatory Agency (2006), *TGN1412: MHRA response to final report by independent expert working group on phase 1 clinical trials*, London: MHRA.

Michalowski, S (2001), 'Reversal of fortune – *Re A (Conjoined Twins)* and beyond: Who should make treatment decisions on behalf of young children?', 9 *Health Law Journal*, 149–169.

Michalowski, S (2002), 'Sanctity of life – are some lives more sacred than others?', 22 *Legal Studies*, 377–397.

Mill, JS (1859), *On Liberty*, London: Parker.

Miller, F and Brody, H (2002) 'What makes placebo-controlled trials unethical?' 2(2) *The American Journal of Bioethics* 3.

Miller, PB and Kenny, NP (2002), 'Walking the moral tightrope: respecting and protecting children in health related research', 11(3) *Cambridge Quarterly of Healthcare Ethics* 217.

Mnookin, RH and Szwed, E (1983), 'The Best Interests Syndrome as the Allocation of Power in Child Care', in H Geach and E Szwed (eds), *Providing Civil Justice for the Child*, London: Edward Arnold.

Month, S (1996), 'Preventing children from donating may not be in their interests', 312 *British Medical Journal* 240.

Mouradian, WE *et al*. (2006), 'Are we helping children: outcome assessments in craniofacial care', in E Parens (ed), *Surgically Shaping Children Technology, Ethics, and the Pursuit of Normality*, Baltimore: Johns Hopkins University Press.

Mumford, SE (1998), 'Bone marrow donation: the law in context', 10(2) *Child and Family Law Quarterly* 135.

Murphy, J (1992), 'Whither adolescent autonomy?', *Journal of Social Welfare and Family Law* 539.

National Down Syndrome Society, *NDSS Position Statement on Cosmetic Surgery for Children with Down Syndrome*, http://www.ndss.org/index.php?option=com_content&task=view&id=34&Itemid=194 (accessed 1 May 2007).

New South Wales Law Reform Commission (2004), *Minors' consent to medical treatment, Issues Paper 24*, http://www.lawlink.nsw.gov.au/lrc.nsf/pages/ip24toc (accessed 1 May 2007).

NHS Blood and Transplant (2006), *Transplant Activity 2005–2006*, London: Statistics and Audit Directorate, UK Transplant.

NHS Executive: West Midlands (2000), *Report of a Review of the Research Framework in North Staffordshire Hospital NHS Trust* (Griffiths Inquiry), Birmingham: NHS Executive.

NHS Management Executive in Scotland (1992, October), *A Guide to Consent to Examination, Investigation, Treatment or Operation*.

Nicholson, R (ed) (1986), *Medical Research with Children: Ethics, Law, and Practice* (The Report of an Institute of Medical Ethics Working party), Oxford: Oxford University Press.

Norrie, KMcK (1991), 'The age of legal capacity (Scotland) Act 1991', 36 *Journal of the Law Society of Scotland* 111.

Norrie, KMcK (1994), 'Medical treatment of children and young persons', in D Morgan and G Douglas (eds), *Archiv fur Rechts und Sozialphilosophie* – Beihefte, 57, *Constituting Families: a Study in Governance*, Stuttgart: Steiner Franz Verlag.

Norrie, KMcK (2001), 'The child's right to care and protection', in A Cleland and E Sutherland (eds), *Children's Rights in Scotland*, 2nd edn, Edinburgh: W Green/ Sweet and Maxwell.

Nuffield Council on Bioethics (2006), *Critical Care Decisions in Fetal and Neonatal Medicine*, London: Nuffield Council on Bioethics.

Parens, E (ed) (2006), *Surgically Shaping Children Technology, Ethics, and the Pursuit of Normality*, Baltimore: Johns Hopkins University Press.

Parkinson, PN (1986), 'The Gillick case – just what has it decided?', 16 *Family Law* 11.

Patrick, H (2006), *Mental Health, Incapacity and the Law in Scotland*, Edinburgh: Tottel Publishing.

Peart, N (2000), 'New Zealand health research with children', in M Freeman and A Lewis (eds), *Law and Medicine: Current Legal Issues 3*, Oxford: Oxford University Press.

Pedain, A (2005), 'Doctors, parents, and the courts: legitimising restrictions on the continued provision of lifespan maximising treatments for severely handicapped, non-dying babies', 17(4) *Child and Family Law Quarterly* 535.

Piaget, J and Inhelder, B (1969), *The psychology of the child*, Basic Books, New York.

Piper, C (2000), 'Assumptions about children's best interests', 22(3) *Journal of Social Welfare and Family Law* 261.

Plomer, A (2000), 'Participation of children in clinical trials: UK, European and international perspectives on consent', 5 *Medical Law International* 1.

Purdy, L (1992), *In Their Best Interest? The case against equal rights for children*, Cornell: Cornell University Press.

Ramsey, P (1970, reprinted 2002), *The Patient as Person: Explorations in Medical Ethics*, 2nd edn, New Haven, CT: Yale University Press.

Rawls, J (1971), *A Theory of Justice*, Harvard: Harvard University Press.

Raymont, V, Bingley, B, Buchanan, A, David, AS, Hayward, P, Wessley, P and Hotopf, M (2004), 'Prevalence of mental incapacity in medical inpatients and associated risk factors:cross-sectional study', 364 *The Lancet* 1421.

Raz, J (1986), *The Morality of Freedom*, Oxford: Clarendon Press.

Reece, H (1996), 'The Paramountcy Principle: Consensus or Construct?', 49 *Current Legal Problems* 267.

Reid, T (2001), 'Separated twin goes home to row over £1m media deal', *The Times*, 18 June.

Retained Organs Commission (2002), *Organ Retention at Central Manchester and Manchester Children's University Hospitals Trust: Report of an Independent Investigation*, London: DoH.

Rhodes, R and Holzman, IR (2004), 'The not unreasonable standard for assessment of surrogates and surrogate decisions', 25 *Theoretical Medicine* 367.

Robertson, J (1981), 'Substantive criteria and procedures in withholding care from defective newborns', in SF Spicker, JM Healey Jr and H Tristram Engelhardt Jr (eds), *The Law-Medicine Relation: a philosophical exploration*, Dordrecht, Holland: D Reidel Publishing.

Robertson, J (2004), 'vCJD sufferer is granted the right to receive new treatment', *The Scotsman* (24 January).

Ross, LF (1997), 'Children as research subjects: a proposal to review the current federal regulations using a moral framework', 8 *Stanford Law and Policy Review* 159.

Ross, LF (1998, reprinted 2004), *Children, Families and Health Care Decision-Making*, New York: Oxford University Press.

Ross, LF (2004) 'Informed consent in pediatric research', 13 *Cambridge Quarterly of Healthcare Ethics* 346.

Ross, LF (2006), *Children in Medical Research: Access versus Protection*, Oxford: Oxford University Press.

Rossi, WC, Reynolds, W and Nelson, RM (2003), 'Child assent and parental permission in pediatric research', 24 *Theoretical Medicine* 131.

Roth, LH, Meisel, A and Lidz, CW (1977), 'Tests of competency to consent to treatment', 184 *American J Psychiatry* 279.

Rowley, SD, Donaldson, G, Lilleby, K, Bensinger, WI and Appelbaum, FR (2001), 'Experiences of donors enrolled in a randomized study of allogenic bone marrow or peripheral blood stem cell transplantation', 97 *Blood* 2541.

Royal College of Paediatrics and Child Health (2004), *Withholding or Withdrawing Life Sustaining Treatment in Children: A Framework for Practice*, 2nd edn, London: RCPCH.

Royal College of Paediatrics and Child Health: Ethics Advisory Committee (1999),

Safeguarding Informed Parental Involvement in Clinical Research Involving Newborn Babies and Infants, London: RCPCH (also in (2000) 154 *Bulletin Medical Ethics* 8).

Royal College of Paediatrics and Child Health: Ethics Advisory Committee (2000), 'Guidelines for the ethical conduct of medical research involving children', in 82(2) *Archives of Disease in Childhood* 177.

Royal College of Psychiatrists (2001), *CR82. Guidance for researchers and for research ethics committees on psychiatric research involving human participants*, London: RCP.

Royal College of Surgeons of England (2002), *Code of Practice to the Surgical Management of Jehovah's Witnesses*, London: RCSEng.

Rutter M and Rutter, M (1993), *Developing Minds: Challenge and Continuity across the Life Span*, London: Penguin.

Savelescu, J (1996), 'Substantial harm but substantial benefit', 312 *British Medical Journal* 241.

Scanlon, TM (1998), *What We Owe to Each Other*, Cambridge, MA: Belknap Press, Harvard University Press.

Schoeman, F (1980), 'Rights of families: rights of parents, and the moral basis of the family', 91 *Ethics* 6.

SCOPE (2007), *The Ashley X treatment – Join us to defend disabled children's rights* http://www.scope.org.uk/childrensrights/ (accessed 1 May 2007).

Scottish Executive (2005), *Health for All Children 4: guidance on implementation in Scotland*, Edinburgh: SE.

Scottish Law Commission (1987), *Report on the Legal Capacity and Responsibility of Minors and Pupils*, Scot. Law Com No 110, Edinburgh: HMSO (HC Paper [Session 1987–88]).

Scottish Law Commission (1992), *Report on Family Law*, Scot. Law Com No 135, Edinburgh: HMSO (HC Paper [Session 1992–93]).

Scottish National Blood Transfusion Service (1998) *Bone Marrow Transplants and Bone Marrow Donation: a Guide for Volunteers*, Edinburg: SNBTS.

Scottish Office Management Executive (1992), *NHS Circular 1992 (GEN) 3*.

Seymour, J (1994), 'Parens Patriae and wardship powers: their nature and origins', 14(2) *Oxford Journal of Legal Studies* 159.

Sheldon, S and Thomson, M (eds) (1998), *Feminist Perspectives on Healthcare Law*, London: Cavendish Publications.

Sheldon, S and Wilkinson, S (1997), 'Separating conjoined twins: the legality and ethics of sacrifice' 5 *Medical Law Review* 149.

Simons, J (2000), 'Giving Information to Parents with an Unwell Child', in Bristol Royal Infirmary Inquiry (2001), *The Report of the Public Inquiry into children's heart surgery at the Bristol Royal Infirmary 1984–1995: Learning from Bristol* (Cm 5207), Appendix B, Paper 10k, London: The Stationery Office.

Skegg, PDG (1984), *Law Ethics and Medicine*, Oxford: Clarendon Press.

Steinberg, D (2004), 'Kidney transplants from young children and the mentally retarded', 25 *Theoretical Medicine* 229.

Sumner, LW (1987), *The Moral Foundation of Rights*, Oxford: Clarendon Press

Sutherland, E (1999), *Child and Family Law*, Edinburgh: T&T Cark Ltd.

Suziedelis, AK (2006), 'Adding burden to burden: cosmetic surgery for children with Down syndrome', 8 *Virtual Mentor* 538, http://www.ama-assn.org/ama/pub/category/16570.html (accessed 1 May 2007).

Teff, H (1998), 'The standard of care in medical negligence – moving on from *Bolam*?', 18 *Oxford Journal of Legal Studies* 473.

Thomson, J (2006), *Family Law in Scotland,* 5th edn, Glasgow: Tottel Publishing.

Thornton, R (1992), 'Multiple keyholders – wardship and consent to treatment', *Cambridge Law Journal*, 34.

Van Beuren, G (1995), *The International Law on the Rights of the Child*, Netherlands: Martinus Nijhoff.

Veatch, RM and Spicer, CM (1996), 'Futile care: physicians should not be allowed to refuse to treat', in TL Beauchamp and RM Veatch (eds), *Ethical Issues in Death and Dying*, 2nd edn, London: Prentice Hall.

Verdun-Jones, SN and Weisstub, DN (1998), 'Drawing the distinction between therapeutic research and non-therapeutic experimentation: clearing a way through the definitional thicket', in DN Weisstub (ed), *Research on Human Subjects: Ethics, law and Social Policy*, Oxford: Elsevier Oxford.

Verhovek, SH (2007), 'Parents defend decision to keep disabled girl small', *Los Angeles Times* 3 January.

Viens, AM (2004), 'Value judgment, harm, and religious liberty', 30 *Journal of Medical Ethics* 241.

Ward, A (2003), *Adult Incapacity*, Edinburgh: W Green.

Weijer, C (2000), 'Ethical analysis of risk', 28 Journal of Law, Medicine and Ethics 344.

Weijer, C (2004), 'The ethical analysis of risk in intensive care unit research', 8 *Critical Care* 85.

Weijer, C and Miller, P (2004), 'When are Research Risks Reasonable in Relation to Anticipated Benefits?', 10(6) *Nature Medicine* 570.

Weithorn, LA and Campbell, SB (1983), 'The competency of children and adolescents to make informed treatment decisions', 9 *Child Development* 285.

Wilkinson, AB and Norrie, KMcK (1999), *The Law Relating to Parent and Child in Scotland*, 2nd edn, Edinburgh: W Green.

Williams, G (1981), 'Down's Syndrome and the duty to preserve life', 131 *New Law Journal* 1020.

Worsfold, V (1974), 'A philosophical justification for children's rights', 44 *Harvard Educational Review* 142.

Index